Let Us C

Third Edition

Yashavant Kanetkar

BPB PUBLICATIONS
B-14, CONNAUGHT PLACE, NEW DELHI-110001

Distributors:

MICRO BOOK CENTRE
2, City Centre, CG Road,
AHMEDABAD-380009 Phone: 6421611

COMPUTER BOOK CENTRE
12, Shrungar Complex, M. G. Road,
BANGALORE-560001 Phone: 5587923, 5584641

MICRO BOOKS
Shanti Niketan Building, 8, Camac Street,
CALCUTTA-700017
Phone: 2426518, 2426519

BUSINESS PROMOTION BUREAU
8/1, Ritchie Street, Mount Road,
CHENNAI-600002 Phone: 834796, 8550491

BPB BOOK CENTRE
376, Old Lajpat Rai Market,
DELHI-110006 Phone: 2961747

DECCAN AGENCIES
4-3-329, Bank Street,
HYDERABAD-500195 Phone: 512280, 593826

MICRO MEDIA
Shop No. 5, Mahendra Chambers,
150 D.N. Road, Next To Capital Cinema, V.T. (C.S.T.)
MUMBAI-400001 Phone: 2078296, 2078297, 2002732

INFO TECH
G-2, Sidhartha Building, 96 Nehru Place,
NEW DELHI-110019 Phone: 6438245, 6415092, 6234208

INFO TECH
Shop No. 2, F-38, South Extension-1,
NEW DELHI-110049 Phone: 4691288, 4641941

INFO TECH
B-11, Vardhman Plaza, Sector-16, Electronics Nagar,
NOIDA-201301 Phone: 91-531346

COMPUTER BOOK CENTRE
SCF No.-65, Sector-6, PANCHKULA-134109,
CHANDIGARH Phone: 561613, 567538

ISBN 81-7656-040-5

Published by Manish Jain for BPB Publications, B-14, Connaught Place,
New Delhi-110001 and Printed by him at Taj Press, New Delhi.

Dedicated to baba
Who couldn't be here to see this day...

About the Author

Yashavant Prabhakar Kanetkar obtained his B.E. from VJTI Bombay and his M. Tech. from IIT Kanpur. A Mechanical Engineer by education, he switched to computers a decade ago and hasn't looked back since. Mr. Kanetkar is an author of several books including *Exploring C, Working With C, C Projects, Undocumented DOS Through C, Writing TSRs Through C, Unix Shell Programming, Test Your C Skills, C Pearls, Understanding Pointers In C* and *Visual C++ Programming* published by BPB Publications and Tech Publications, Singapore. Today Yashavant divides his working hours among writing articles for Express Computer, writing books, teaching classes and conducting seminars in C/C++/Unix/VC++/Internet Programming. Since 1987 he has been Director of ICIT, a Training and Software Development firm which he set up at Nagpur.

Acknowledgments

Before we get into thick of the things I would like to add a few heartfelt words for the people who were part of this book in numerous ways... people who gave unending support right from the stage the book idea was conceived. In particular, I wish to thank Manish Jain for having faith in this book idea.

I thank Seema for reviewing the entire manuscript with painstaking attention for detail. And more so for her uncanny ability to spot the spelling mistakes in paragraphs which I had reviewed many times over.

Ajay joshi ran all the programs in this book and to my horror found several that did not run correctly in certain situations. I trust all these bugs have been fixed. If not, you know whom to blame in addition to me. Chandrahas and Ashish keyed in major portions of this manuscript. Many thanks to them for their efficiency, cheerful readiness and most of all to their ability to decipher my handwriting.

There are times in such projects when the clock beats you time and again and you run out of energy and you just want to finish it once and for ever. Ammi and dada made me endure such times with their unfailing humour and warm wishes.

To Shailesh I owe more than what I can mention... mostly for teaching me to see the silver lining in every dark cloud.

And finally heartfelt appreciation to those countless students who made me to delve deeper and deeper in C... to an extent that now I firmly believe that C is an attitude, a philosophy of life.

Preface to the Second Edition

As I write this preface, I feel like a man who planned to fix the porch steps of his house, then decided to work on the porch door, then the porch ceiling, and finally ended up rebuilding his whole house. I had intended to do just a "quick-and-dirty" rewrite, but somehow the 512-page first edition ended up swelling to over 650 pages, and I still feel like I'm just skimming the surface. That's the way C is - a bottomless pit.

The second edition of this book has three main objectives - first, a general updation and revision of text, secondly an improvement of the presentation of the material, and thirdly and more importantly to make the book complete by incorporating complicated topics like array of pointers, variable number of arguments etc. I am hopeful that the readers would find improvement in presentation of several topics. This is largely due to the suggestions received from both, the students and the teachers who have been using this book since last three years.

Preface to the Third Edition

When I wrote the second edition of this book I had heaved a sigh of relief thinking that I won't ever be required to make any changes in the book in future. I never imagined that the second edition would be as successful as it has been. From the feedback that I get from the readers the most common reason attributed to its popularity is its 'simplicity'. But then this is how I found C language - Simple, no laces, no frills - only raw power. And this is the power that I have tried to harness further in this edition. In addition to a chapter on Graphics, a chapter on Mouse programming and a completely re-vamped chapter on VDU Basics, I have also provided additional exercises for practise. I trust that readers would find these additions useful and *simple*.

Contents

xv

Introduction

I have two inter-connected goals in writing this book: to teach the C programming language, and to show how C can be used to write serious programs on the IBM compatible microcomputers. Thus, this book is about innards of C and about the knowledge and concepts that are needed to exploit the capabilties of the microcomputer through C.

The Turbo C Compiler and the Quick C Compiler are the most widely used professional software development tools on microcomputers. Turbo C offers an easy-to-use integrated development environment, ideally suitable for those learning C. This book primarily written for Turbo C works even with Quick C Compiler by making a few changes in the standard library functions.

Who This Book Is For

This book expects no formal education in computers. Of course those who have already used a computer are likely to derive more benifits from this book. If you are a student interested in learning C, with a microcomputer at your disposal, this book will provide an easy-to-follow but thorough introduction to the language. If you have an idea for a new program or an idea for improvement to an existing program, and want to transform your ideas into a professional, marketable program, this book will show you how. If you feel cramped while using languages like Basic, Cobol, dBASE etc. because of their inherent limitations, this book would show you how to get around these limitations. This book is also for those who want to interact with the hardware in a more powerful way than what conventional languages can offer.

What's Different About This Book

Many introductory books on C present the language either in a Unix based environment or in a theoretical context, ignoring the machine the language is running on. This book uses a different approach: it teaches C in the context of IBM compatibles and MS-DOS operating system. This method offers several advantages:

First, concentrating on a specific machine makes learning the language easier and more interesting.

Also, as we move on to the complex aspects of C language, C constructs that might otherwise seem theoretical and mysterious can be explained by relating them to actual applications on the IBM compatibles.

Finally, if your goal is to write programs specifically for the IBM compatibles, then learning C in the IBM environment, with examples using specific aspects of the IBM compatible hardware, will give you a head start in the creation of practical programs.

Learn by Doing

I have used a hands-on approach in this book. I believe that trying things yourself is the best way to learn, so examples are presented as complete working programs, which can be typed in and executed. In general, I have shown what the output from the examples look like, so you can be sure your program is functioning correctly. Very short examples are given at the beginning of the book, working up to longer and more sophisticated programs at the end.

I have also given exercises at the end of each Chapter. These exercises are to test your general understanding of the material covered. You would be best-advised to answer all these questions so that you understand how to put the concepts to work in real-life programs.

What Equipment You Need to Use This Book

You can use this book with a variety of hardware and software configurations. Here's what you will need.

Hardware:

You should have an access to an IBM compatible PC, PC/XT, PC/ AT, PC/AT386 or PC/AT486 machine, with either a monochrome or a colour monitor.

You will need either dual floppy drives or a hard disk with a single floppy drive. Most modern C compilers are so large that juggling disks in a dual floppy drive system becomes a problem, and even otherwise floppies work much slower compared to a hard disk. So you will save so much time with a hard disk that it is almost an essential investment.

Finally, while it's not absolutely essential, you will probably want a printer to generate program listings and record program output.

Software:

You should use MS-DOS operating system, version 2.0 or greater. You will need either Turbo C or Quick C Compiler. All examples in this book would work on Turbo C. Actually, most of the material in this book is applicable no matter which compiler you are using. Of course some of the library functions have minor variations between compilers.

Chapter Organisation

The serialising of the various topics has been done with easier ones first (from my perspective), and more difficult ones last. You could if you feel skip some topics but I'd rather you didn't.

The first 7 Chapters focus on elementary C language features. In the first Chapter you will learn to write your first C program and understand its rudiments like constants, variables, keywords and how these interact with each other to form C instructions. This will give you an idea of how the language looks like and how it is used.

Chapter 2, 3 and 4 cover the basic control structures of C: decision, loop and case. Chapter 5 describes functions, Chapter 6 covers various data types and their storage classes, Chapter 7 covers C preprocessor directives. Several programming examples are used to demonstrate the various topics. Chapter 8 describes arrays and Chapter 9 covers strings: a special type of array. Chapter 8 and 9 introduces pointers, a data type very widely used in C but unknown or little used in most other languages. In fact pointers are so widely used in C that after Chapter 8 it keeps coming up time again in rest of the Chapters.

At this point the focus shifts to advanced features of C language. In Chapter 10 we look closely at structures, whereas Chapter 11 shows I/O in action. Standard as well as system I/O is covered in this

Chapter.

Now we digress a bit from mainstream C and delve into the IBM compatible: objective being, if we want to interact with the hardware, we first need to know it in and out. With this aim in mind Chapter 12 is dedicated to the mother board, its components and their functions. Similarly, Chapter 13 describes OS fundamentals, Chapter 14 contains Disk Basics, Chapter 15 the VDU basics and Chapter 16 the keyboard basics. Chapter 17 contains details of CPU registers, interrupts, and the IVT and also gives you the first feel of how to interact with hardware with several real-world examples. The exercise in this Chapter opens new horizons for interaction with hardware.

Chapter 18 teaches you how to take a byte, bit by bit, using bitwise operators. Chapter 19 concludes the book with a discussion on some of the finer points of C language.

Eight power packed appendices are also provided to help you learn C and to make the book easier to use as a reference. The first Appendix gives the precedence table of all the operators available in the C language. Appendix B gives a list of popularly used standard library functions in Turbo C. In case you have tried a program, retried it and tried again and still you are unable to locate the bug, Appendix C might just provide a clue to chase the bug out. At many places in this book we talk in hex. To help you know what we are talking about hexadecimal numbering system is disscussed in Appendix D. Appendix E contains the Ascii table and various box drawing characters used to generate boxes in text mode. The peculiar addressing scheme of 8086 family is discussed in Appendix F. Appendix G and H are the real treasure, held back till the last. You would go treasure hunting into these in search of ROM-BIOS and selected DOS services.

Lastly, I hope you get as much pleasure reading this book, as I had writing it. In short, after reading this book if you are able to combine the left brain lobe's desire to write powerful programs and the right lobe's functionality, then I think the purpose of writing this book is served.

1 *Getting Started*

Before we can begin to write serious programs in C, it would be interesting to find out what really is C, how it came into existence and how does it compare with other computer languages. In this chapter we would briefly outline these issues.

Three important aspects of any language are the way it stores data, how it accomplishes input and output, and the operators it uses to transform and combine data. These are the three kinds of building blocks we will discuss in this chapter. Of course, in a single chapter we can't present every aspect of each of these topics; much will remain to be said in the later chapters. However, what we cover here will be enough to get you off the ground.

In the following chapters we will put these building blocks to use exploring the control statements of the language: decision, loop and case.

What is C

C is a programming language developed at AT & T's Bell Laboratories of USA in 1972. It was designed and written by a man named Dennis Ritchie. In the late seventies C began to replace the more familiar languages of that time like PL/I, ALGOL etc. No one pushed C. It wasn't made the 'official' Bell Labs language. Thus, without any advertisement C's reputation spread and its pool of users grew. Ritchie seems to have been rather surprised that so many programmers preferred C to older languages like FORTRAN or PL/I, or the newer ones like Pascal and APL. But, that's what happened.

Possibly why C seems so popular is because it is reliable, simple and easy to use. Out of the dozens of languages available, the prize of purity is often given to PASCAL, C's pretty sister. C wasn't meant to win prizes; it was meant to be friendly, capable and reliable. Therefore, quite a few programmers who begin by falling in love with Pascal, end up happily married to C.

Historical Development of C

By 1960 a hoarde of computer languages had come into existence,
almost each for a specific purpose. For example, COBOL was being
used for Commercial Applications, FORTRAN for Engineering and
Scientific Applications and so on. At this stage people started thinking that instead of learning and using so many languages, each for a
different purpose, why not use only one language which can program
all possible applications. Therefore, an international committee was
set up to develop such a language. This committee came out with a
language called ALGOL 60. However, ALGOL 60 never really
beacame popular because it seemed too abstract, too general. To
reduce this abstractness and generality, a new language called Combined Programming Language (CPL) was developed at Cambridge
University. CPL was an attempt to bring ALGOL 60 down to earth.
However, CPL turned out to be so big, having so many features, that
it was hard to learn and difficult to implement.

Basic Combined Programming Language (BCPL), developed by
Martin Richards at Cambridge University aimed to solve this problem by bringing CPL down to its basic good features. But unfortunately it turned out to be too less powerful and too specific. Around
same time a language called B was written by Ken Thompson at AT
& T's Bell Labs, as a further simplification of CPL. But like BCPL,
B too turned out to be very specific. Ritchie inherited the features of
B and BCPL, added some of his own and developed C. Ritchie's main
achievement is the restoration of the lost generality in BCPL and B,
and still keeping it powerful.

C's compactness and coherence is mainly due to the fact that it's a
one man language. Other examples of one man languages are LISP,
PASCAL and APL. Counter examples include many headed
monsters like PL/I, ALGOL 60 and ADA. Figure 1.1 shows the
various stages in evolution of C language.

Year	Language	Developed by	Remarks
1960	ALGOL	International Committee	Too general, too abstract
1963	CPL	Cambridge University	Hard to learn, difficult to implement.
1967	BCPL	Martin Richards at Cambridge University	Could deal with only specific problems
1970	B	Ken Thompson at AT & T	Could deal with only specific problems
1972	C	Dennis Ritchie at AT & T	Lost generality of BCPL and B restored

Figure 1.1

Where C Stands

Let us now see how does C compare with other programming languages. All the programming languages can be divided into two categories:

(a)   Problem oriented languages or High level languages:
      These languages have been designed to give a better programming efficiency, i.e. faster program development. Examples of languages falling in this category are FORTRAN, BASIC, PASCAL etc.

(b)   Machine oriented languages or Low level languages:
      These languages have been designed to give a better machine efficiency, i.e. faster program execution. Examples of languages falling in this category are Assembly language and Machine language.

C stands in between these two categories. That's why it is often called a Middle level language, since it was designed to have both: a relatively good progamming efficiency (as compared to Machine oriented languages) and a relatively good machine efficiency (as compared to Problem oriented languages).

Getting Started with C

Communicating with a computer involves speaking the language the computer understands, which immediately rules out English as the language of communication with computer. However, there is a close analogy between learning English language and learning C language. The classical method of learning English is to first learn the alphabets or characters used in the language, then learn to combine these alphabets to form words, which in turn are combined to form sentences and sentences are combined to form paragraphs. Learning C is similar and much more easy.

Therefore, instead of straight-away learning how to write programs, we must first know what alphabets, numbers and special symbols are used in C, then how using these constants, variables and keywords are constructed, and finally how are these combined to form an instruction. A group of instructions would be combined later on to form a program. This is illustrated in the Figure 1.2.

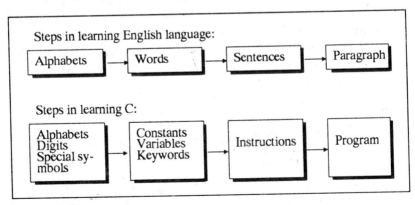

Figure 1.2

The C Character Set

A character denotes any alphabet, digit or special symbol used to represent information. Following table shows the valid alphabets, numbers and special symbols allowed in C:

Alphabets	A, B, ... , Y, Z a, b, ... , y, z
Digits	0, 1, 2, 3, 4, 5, 6, 7, 8, 9
Special symbols	~ ' ! @ # % ^ & * ( ) _ - + = | \ { } [ ] : ; " ' < > , . ? /

Figure 1.3

Constants, Variables and Keywords

The alphabets, numbers and special symbols when properly combined form constants, variables and keywords. Let us see what are 'constants' and 'variables' in C. A constant is a quantity that doesn't change. This quantity can be stored at a locations in the memory of the computer. A variable can be considered as a name given to the location in memory where this constant is stored. Naturally the contents of the variable can change. For example in the equation

$$3X + Y = 20$$

since 3 and 20 cannot change, they are called constants, whereas the quantities X & Y can vary or change hence are called variables.

To be able to write error free programs, we will now take up a detailed discussion about the different fundamental elements of C language, viz., constants, variables and keywords. Possibly, an absolutely clear understanding about the constants, variables and keywords and their interaction with each other is the single most important factor contributing towards writing error free programs.

Types of C Constants

C constants can be divided into two major categories:

(a)   Primary Constants
(b)   Secondary Constants

These constants are further categorised as shown in Figure 1.4.

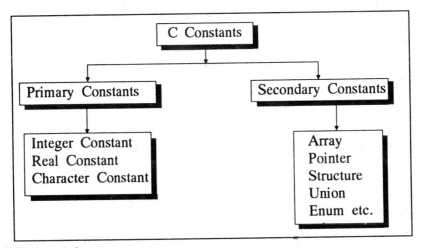

Figure 1.4

At this stage we would restrict our discussion to only Primary Constants, namely, Integer, Real and Character constants. Let us see the details of each of these constants. For constructing these different types of constants certain rules have been laid down. These rules are as under:

Rules for Constructing Integer Constants

(a) An integer constant must have at least one digit.
(b) It must not have a decimal point.
(c) It could be either positive or negative.
(d) If no sign precedes an integer constant it is assumed to be positive.
(e) No commas or blanks are allowed within an integer constant.
(f) The allowable range for integer constants is -32768 to +32767.

Integer constants must fall within this range because the IBM compatible microcomputers are usually 16 bit computers which cannot support a number falling outside the above mentioned range. For a 32 bit computer of course the range would be much larger.

Ex.: 426
+782
-8000
-7605

Rules for Constructing Real Constants

Real constants are often called Floating Point constants. The real constants could be written in two forms, Fractional form and Exponential form.

Following rules must be observed while constructing real constants expressed in fractional form:

(a) A real constant must have atleast one digit.
(b) It must have a decimal point.
(c) It could be either positive or negative.
(d) Default sign is positive.
(e) No commas or blanks are allowed within a real constant.

Ex.: +325.34

```
426.0
-32.76
-48.5792
```

The exponential form of representation of real constants is usually used if the value of the constant is either too small or too large. It however dosen't restrict us in any way from using exponential form of representation for other real constants.

In exponential form of representation, the real constant is represented in two parts. The part appearing before 'e' is called mantissa, whereas the part following 'e' is called exponent.

Following rules must be observed while construction of real constants expressed in exponential form:

(a)   The mantissa part and the exponential part should be separated by a letter e.
(b)   The mantissa part may have a positive or negative sign.
(c)   Default sign of mantissa part is positive.
(d)   The exponent must have at least one digit which must be a positive or negative integer. Default sign is positive.
(e)   Range of real constants expressed in exponential form is -3.4e38 to 3.4e38

```
Ex.:   +3.2e-5
       4.1e8
       -0.2e+3
       -3.2e-5
```

Rules for Constructing Character Constants

(a)   A character constant is either a single alphabet, a single digit or a single special symbol enclosed within single inverted commas Both the inverted commas should point to the left. For example, 'A' is a valid character constant whereas 'A' is not.

(b)   The maximum length of a character constant can be 1 charac-
        ter.

Ex.:   'A'
       'I'
       '5'
       '='

Types of C Variables

In C, a quantity which may vary during program execution is called
a variable. Variable names are names given to locations in the
memory of computer where different constants are stored. These
locations can contain integer, real or character constants. In any
language, the types of variables that it can support depends on the
types of constants that it can handle. This is because a constant stored
in a location with a particular type of variable name can hold only
that type of constant. For example, a constant stored in a memory
location with an integer variable name must be an integer constant,
one stored in location with a real variable name must be a real
constant and the one stored in location with a character variable name
must be a character constant.

The rules for constructing different types of constants are different.
However, for constructing variable names of all types the same set
of rules apply. These rules are given below.

Rules for Constructing Variable Names

(a)   A variable name is any combination of 1 to 8 alphabets, digits
        or underscores. Some compilers allow variable names whose
        length could be upto 40 characters. Still, it would be safer to
        stick to the rule of 8 characters.
(b)   The first character in the variable name must be an alphabet.
(c)   No commas or blanks are allowed within a variable name.

(d)   No special symbol other than an underscore (as in **gross_sal**) can be used in a variable name.

Ex.:   si_int
        m_hra
        pop_e_89

These rules remain same for all the types of primary and secondary variables. Naturally, the question follows... how is C able to differentiate between these variables? This is a rather simple matter. C compiler is able to distinguish between the variable names, by making it compulsory for you to declare the type of any variable name which you wish to use in a program. This type declaration is done at the beginning of the program. Following are the examples of type declaration statements:

Ex.:   int si, m_hra;
        float bassal;
        char code;

Since the maximum length of a variable name is 8 characters, an enormous number of variable names can be constructed using the afore-mentioned rules. It is a good practice to exploit this enormous choice in naming variables by using meaningful variable names.

Thus, if we want to calculate simple interest, it is always advisable to construct meaningful variable names like **prin, roi, noy** to represent Principle, Rate of interest and Number of years rather than using the variables **a, b, c**.

C Keywords

Keywords are the words whose meaning has already been explained to the C compiler (or in a broad sense to the computer). The keywords **cannot** be used as variable names because if we do so we are trying to assign a new meaning to the keyword, which is not allowed by the computer. Some C compilers allow you to construct variable names which exactly resemble the keywords. However, it would be safer not to mix up the variable names and the keywords. The keywords are also called 'Reserved words'.

There are only 32 keywords available in C. Following is the list of keywords in C, given here for your ready reference. A detailed discussion of each of these keywords would be taken up in later chapters wherever their use is relevant.

auto	double	if	static
break	else	int	struct
case	enum	long	switch
char	extern	near	typedef
const	float	register	union
continue	far	return	unsigned
default	for	short	void
do	goto	signed	while

Figure 1.5

C Instructions

Now that we have seen the different types of constants, variables and keywords the next logical step is to learn how they are combined to form instructions. There are basically four types of instructions in C:

(a) Type Declaration Instruction
(b) Input/Output Instruction
(c) Arithmetic Instruction
(d) Control Instruction

The purpose of each of these instructions is given below:

(a)   Type declaration instruction   -   to declare the type of variables used in a C program.

(b)   Input/Output instruction   -   to perform the function of supplying input data to a program and obtaining the output results from it.

(c)   Arithmetic instruction   -   to perform arithmetic operations between constants and variables.

(d)   Control instruction   -   to control the sequence of execution of various statements in a C program.

Since, the elementary C programs would usually contain only the type declaration and the arithmetic instructions, we would discuss only these two instructions at this stage. The other types of instructions would be discussed in detail in the subsequent chapters.

Type Declaration Instruction

This instruction is used to declare the type of variables being used in the program. Any variable used in the program must be declared before using it in any statement. The type declaration statement is usually written at the beginning of the C program.

Ex.:   int bas ;
        float rs, grosssal ;
        char name, code ;

Arithmetic Instruction

A C arithmetic instruction consists of a variable name on the left hand side of = and variable names & constants on the right hand side of =. The variables and constants appearing on the right hand side of = are connected by arithmetic operators like +, -, *, and /.

Ex.: int ad ;
      float kot, deta, alpha, beta, gamma ;
      ad = 3200 ;
      kot = 0.0056 ;
      deta = alpha * beta / gamma + 3.2 * 2/5 ;

Here,

>   *, /, -, + are the arithmetic operators.
>   = is the assignment operator.
>   2, 5 and 3200 are integer constants.
>   3.2 and 0.0056 are real constants.
>   **ad** is an integer variable.
>   **kot, deta, alpha, beta, gamma** are real variables.

The variables and constants together are called 'operands' which are operated upon by the 'arithmetic operators' and the result is assigned, using the assignment operator, to the variable on left hand side.

A C arithmetic statement could be of three types. These are as follows:

(a)   Integer mode arithmetic statement - is an arithmetic statement in which all operands are either integer variables or integer constants.

>   Ex.:   int i, king, issac, noteit ;
>   i = i + 1 ;
>   king = issac * 234 + noteit - 7689 ;

(b)   Real mode arithmetic statement - is an arithmetic statement in which all operands are either real constants or real variables.

    Ex.:   float qbee, antink, si, prin, anoy, roi ;
           qbee = antink + 23.123 / 4.5 * 0.3442 ;
           si = prin * anoy * roi / 100.0 ;

(c)   Mixed mode arithmetic statement - is an arithmetic statement in which some of the operands are integers and some of the operands are real.

    Ex.:   float si, prin, anoy, roi, avg ;
           int a, b, c, num ;
           si = prin * anoy * roi / 100.0 ;
           avg = (a + b + c + num) / 4 ;

It is very important to understand how the execution of an arithmetic statement takes place. Firstly, the right hand side is evaluated using constants and the numerical values stored in the variable names. This value is then assigned to the variable on the left hand side.

Though, Arithmetic instructions look simple to use, many a times one commits mistakes in writing them. Let us take a closer look at these statements. Note the following points carefully.

(a)   C allows only one variable on left hand side of =. That is, $z = k * l$ is legal, whereas $k * l = z$ is illegal.

(b)   A statement similar to arithmetic instruction is many a times used for storing character constants in character variables.

    char a, b, d ;
    a = 'F' ;
    b = 'G' ;
    d = '+' ;

(c)   Arithmetic operations can be performed on **ints, floats** and **chars.**

Thus the statements,

```
char x, y ;
int z ;
x = 'a' ;
y = 'b' ;
z = x + y ;
```

are perfectly valid,

since the addition is performed on the ASCII values of the characters and not on characters themselves. The ASCII values of 'a' and 'b' are 97 and 98 (refer the ASCII Table in Appendix E), and hence can definitely be added.

(d)   No operator is assumed to be present. It must be written explicitly. In the following example, the multiplication operator after **b** must be explicitly written.

```
a = c.d.b(xy)              usual arithmetic statement
b = c * d * b * ( x * y )       C statement
```

(e)   Unlike other high level languages, there is no operator for performing exponentiation operation. Thus following statements are invalid.

```
a = 3 ** 2 ;
b = 3 ^ 2 ;
```

Integer and Float Conversions

In order to effectively develop C programs, it will be necessary for you to understand the rules that are used for the implicit conversion of floating point and integer values in C. These are mentioned below. Note them carefully.

(a)   An arithmetic operation between an integer and integer always yields an integer result.

(b)   Operation between a real and real always yields a real result.

(c)   Operation between an integer and real always yields a real result.

I think a few practical examples shown in the following figure would put the issue beyond doubt.

Operation	Result	Operation	Result
5 / 2	2	2 / 5	0
5.0 / 2	2.5	2.0 / 5	0.4
5 / 2.0	2.5	2 / 5.0	0.4
5.0 / 2.0	2.5	2.0 / 5.0	0.4

Figure 1.6

Type Conversion in Assignments

It may so happen that the type of the expression and the type of the variable on the left hand side of the assignment operator may not be same. In such a case the value of the expression is promoted or demoted depending on the type of the variable on left hand side of =.

For example, consider the following assignment statements.

```
int i ;
```

```
float b ;
i = 3.5 ;
b = 30 ;
```

Here in the first assignment statement though the expression's value is a **float** (3.5) it cannot be stored in **i** since it is an **int**. In such a case the **float** is demoted to an **int** and then its value is stored. Hence what gets stored in **i** is 3. Exactly opposite happens in the next statement. Here, 30 is promoted to 30.000000 and then stored in **b**, since **b** being a **float** variable cannot hold anything except a **float** value.

Thus while storing the value the expression always takes the type of the variable into which its value is being stored.

Instead of the simple expression used in the above examples if a complex expression occurs still the same rules apply. For example, consider the following program fragment.

```
float a, b, c ;
int s ;
s = a * b * c / 100 + 32 / 4 - 3 * 1.1 ;
```

Here, in the assignment statement some operands are **int**s whereas others are **float**s. As we know during evaluation of the expression the **int**s would be promoted to **float**s and the result of the expression would be a **float**. But when this **float** value is assigned to **s** it is again demoted to an **int** and then stored in **s**.

Observe the results of the arithmetic statements shown in Figure 1.7. It has been assumed that **k** is an integer variable and **a** is a real variable.

Arithmetic Instruction	Result	Arithmetic Instruction	Result
k = 2 / 9	0	a = 2 / 9	0.0
k = 2.0 / 9	0.0	a = 2.0 / 9	0.2222
k = 2 / 9.0	0.0	a = 2 / 9.0	0.2222
k = 2.0 / 9.0	0.0	a = 2.0 / 9.0	0.2222
k = 9 / 2	4	a = 9 / 2	4.0
k = 9.0 / 2	4	a = 9.0 / 2	4.5
k = 9 / 2.0	4	a = 9 / 2.0	4.5
k = 9.0 / 2.0	4	a = 9.0 / 2.0	4.5

Figure 1.7

Hierarchy of Operations

While executing an arithmetic statement which has two or more operators, we may have some problems as to how exactly does it get executed. For example, does the expression 2 * x - 3 * y correspond to (2x)-(3y) or to 2(x-3y)? Similarly, does A / B * C correspond to A / (B * C) or to (A / B) * C? To answer these questions satisfactorily one has to understand the 'hierarchy' of operations. The priority or precedence in which the operations in an arithmetic statement are performed is called the hierarchy of operations. The hierarchy of commonly used operators is shown in Figure 1.8.

Priority	Operators	Description
1st	* / %	multiplication, division, modular division
2nd	+ -	addition, subtraction
3rd	=	assignment

Figure 1.8

Now a few tips about usage of operators in general.

(a)   In case of a tie between operations of same priority preference
        is given to the operator which occurs first. For example,
        consider the statement ,

        z = a * b + c / d ;

        Here, **a * b** will be performed before **c / d** even though * and /
        has same or equal priority. This is because * appears prior to
        the / operator.

(b)   Within a parentheses, the same hierarchy as mentioned in
        Figure 1.11 is operative. Also, if there are more than one set of
        parentheses, the operations within the innermost parentheses
        will be performed first, followed by the operations within the
        second innermost pair and so on.

(c)   We must always remember to use pairs of parentheses. A
        careless imbalance of the right and left parentheses is a com-
        mon error.

A few examples would clarify the issue further.

Example 1.1: Determine the hierarchy of operations and evaluate the
following expression:

        i = 2 * 3 / 4 + 4 / 4 + 8 - 2 + 5 / 8

Stepwise evaluation of this expression is shown below:

        i = 2 * 3 / 4 + 4 / 4 + 8 - 2 + 5 / 8
        i = 6 / 4 + 4 / 4 + 8 - 2 + 5 / 8   operation: *
        i = 1 + 4 / 4 + 8 - 2 + 5 / 8   operation: /
        i = 1 + 1 + 8 - 2 + 5 / 8   operation: /
        i = 1 + 1 + 8 - 2 + 0   operation: /
        i = 2 + 8 - 2 + 0   operation: +

```
i = 10 - 2 + 0                    operation: +
i = 8 + 0                         operation : -
i = 8                             operation: +
```

Note that 6 / 4 gives 1 and not 1.5. This so happens because 6 & 4 both are integers and therefore would evaluate to only an integer constant. Similarly 5/ 8 evaluates to zero, since 5 and 8 are integer constants and hence must return an integer value.

Example 1.2:Determine the hierarchy of operations and evaluate the following expression:

```
kk = 3 / 2 * 4 + 3 / 8 + 3
```

Stepwise evaluation of this expression is shown below:

```
kk = 3 / 2 * 4 + 3 / 8 + 3
kk = 1 * 4 + 3 / 8 + 3            operation: /
kk = 4 + 3 / 8 + 3               operation: *
kk = 4 + 0 + 3                   operation: /
kk = 4 + 3                       operation: +
kk = 7                           operation: +
```

Note that 3/8 gives zero, again for the same reason mentioned in the previous example.

All operators in C are ranked according to their precedence. And mind you there are as many as 45 odd operators in C, and these can affect the evaluation of an expression in subtle and unexpected ways if we aren't careful. Unfortunately, there are no simple rules that one can follow, such as "BODMAS" that tells algebra students in which order does an expression evaluate. We have not encountered many out of these 45 operators, so we won't pursue the subject of precedence further here. However, it can be realised at this stage that it would be almost impossible to remember the precedence of all these operators. So a full-fledged list of all operators and their precedence is given in

Appendix A. This may sound daunting, but when its contents are absorbed in small bites, it becomes more palatable.

So far we have seen how the computer evaluates an arithmetic statement written in C. But our knowledge would be incomplete unless we know how to convert a general arithmetic statement to a C statement.C can handle any complex expression with ease. Some of the examples of C expressions are shown in Figure 1.9.

Algebric Expression	C Expression
$a \times b - c \times d$	a * b - c * d
$(m + n)(a + b)$	(m + n) * (a + b)
$3x^2 + 2x + 5$	3 * x * x + 2 * x + 5
$\dfrac{a + b + c}{d + e}$	(a + b + c) / (d + e)
$\left[\dfrac{2BY}{d+1} - \dfrac{x}{3(z+y)} \right]$	2 * b * y / (d + 1) – x / (3 * (z + y))

Figure 1.9

Whenever we combine variables, constants and operators as per the syntax (grammar) of the language we get an 'expression'. Knowingly or unknowingly we have used several 'expressions' in the previous section.

The First C Program

Armed with the knowledge about the types of variables, constants & keywords, and the hierarchy of operations, we would now try to write down our first C program.

Each instruction in a C program is written as a separate statement. Therefore a complete C program will comprise of a series of statements. These statements must appear in the same order in which we wish them to be executed; unless of course the logic of the problem demands a deliberate 'jump' or transfer of control to a statement which is out of sequence.

However big a program, the following rules are applicable to all C statements:

(a)   Blank spaces may be inserted between two words to improve the readability of the statement. However, no blank spaces are allowed within a variable, constant or keyword.
(b)   Usually all statements are entered in small case letters.
(c)   C has no specific rules for the position at which a statement is to be written. That's why it is often called a free-form language.
(d)   Any C statement always ends with a ;

Let us now write down a simple C program to calculate simple interest.

```c
/* Calculation of simple interest */
/* Author gekay  Date: 25/12/1994 */
main( )
{
    int p, n ;
    float r, si ;

    p = 1000 ;
    n = 3 ;
    r = 8.5 ;
    si = p * n * r / 100 ;

    printf ( "%f" , si ) ;
}
```

Now a few useful tips about the program...

-        Comment about the program should be enclosed within /* */.
         For example the first two statements in our program are com-
         ments.

-        Any number of comments can be given at any place in the
         program.

-        Comments cannot be nested. For example,

         /* Cal of SI /* Author sam date 01/01/90 */ */

         is invalid.

-        A comment can be split over more than one line, as in,

         /* This is
          a jazzy
          comment */

         Although a lot of comments are probably not necessary in this
         program, it is usually the case that programmers tend to use
         too few comments rather than too many. Comments should be
         used at any place where there is a possibility of confusion. We
         will refrain from repeating the standard lecture on how ade-
         quate number of comments can save hours of misery and
         suffering when you later try to figure out what the program
         does.

-        Any C program is nothing but a combination of functions.
         main( ) is one such function. Empty parentheses after **main** ar
         enecessary.

-        The set of statements belonging to a function are enclosed
         within a pair of braces. For example,

```
main( )
{
    statement 1 ;
    statement 2 ;
    statement 3 ;
}
```

Any variable used in the program must be declared before using it. For example,

```
int p, n ;
float r, si ;
```

- Any C statement always ends with a ;

For example,

```
float r, si ;
r = 8.5 ;
```

- In the statement,

```
si = p * n * r / 100 ;
```

* and / are the arithmetic operators. The arithmetic operators available in C are +, -, * and /. C is very rich in operators. There are about 45 operators available in C. Surprisingly, there is no operator for exponentiation... a slip, which can be forgiven considering the fact that C is a one man language.

- **printf( )** is a function which is used to print on the screen the value contained in a variable.

The general form of **printf** statement is ,

```
printf ( "<format string>", <list of variables> ) ;
```

<format string> could be,

%f for printing real values
%d for printing integer values
%c for printing character values

Following are some examples of usage of **printf** statement:

```
printf ( "%f", si ) ;
printf ( "%d %d %f %f", p, n, r, si ) ;
printf ( "Simple interest = Rs. %f", si ) ;
printf ( "Prin = %d \nRate = %f", p, r ) ;
```

The output of the last statement would look like this...

```
Prin = 1000
Rate = 8.5
```

What is '\n' doing in this statement? It is called newline and it takes the cursor to the next line. Therefore, you get the output split over two lines. '\n' is one of the several escape sequences available in C. These are discussed in detail in Chapter 11. Right now, all that we can say is '\n' comes in handy when we want to format the output properly on separate lines.

In the above progam we assumed the values of **p, n** and **r** to be 1000, 3 and 8.5 . If we want to make a provision for supplying the values of **p, n** and **r** through the keyboard, a statement called **scanf** should be used. This is illustrated in the program shown below.

```
/* Calculation of simple interest */
/* Author gekay Date 12/01/90 */
main( )
{
    int p, n ;
    float r, si ;
```

```
        printf ( "Enter values of p, n, r" ) ;
        scanf ( "%d %d %f", &p, &n, &r ) ;

        si = p * n * r / 100 ;
        printf ( "%f" , si ) ;
    }
```

The first **printf( )** statement outputs the message 'Enter values of p, n, r' on the screen. Here we have not used any variables in **printf( )** which means that using variables in **printf( )** is optional. Note that the ampersand (&) before the variables in the **scanf** statement is a must. **&** is a pointer operator. The meaning and working of this pointer operator would be taken up later during the discussion on pointers in Chapter 5. Also note that the values for **p**, **n** and **r** to be supplied through the keyboard, must be seperated by a blank, a tab or a newline.

Ex.:   The three values separated by blank.
       1000 5 15.5

Ex.:   The three values separated by tab.
       1000   5   15.5

Ex.:   The three values separated by newline.
       1000
       5
       15.5

So much for the tips. How about another program to give you a feel of things...

```
        /* Just for fun. Author: Bozo */
        main( )
        {
            int num ;

            printf ( "Enter a number" ) ;
```

```
        scanf ( "%d", &num ) ;
        printf ( "Now I am letting you on a secret..." ) ;
        printf ( "You have just entered the number %d", num ) ;
}
```

Control Instructions in C

As the name suggests the 'Control Instructions' enable us to specify the order in which the various instructions in a program are to be executed by the computer. In other words the control instructions determine the 'flow of control' in a program. There are four types of control instrutions in C. They are:

(a)   Sequence Control Instruction
(b)   Selection or Decision Control Instruction
(c)   Repitition or Loop Control Instruction
(d)   Case Control Instruction

The Sequence control instruction ensures that the instructions are executed in the same order in which they appear in the program. Decision and Case control instructions allow the computer to take a decision as to which instruction is to be executed next. The Loop control instruction helps computer to execute a group of statements repeatedly. In the following chapters we are going to learn these instructions in detail.

Try your hand at the Exercise presented on the following pages before proceeding to the next chapter, which discusses the decision control instruction.

Summary

In this chapter we have introduced some of the most fundamental parts of C: constants, variables, keywords, type declaration instruction, arithmetie instruction and input/output instructions. You have learnt that there are three primary constant and variable types in C: integer, float and character. You have learnt how to declare variables, initialise variables and how to use them in arithmetic statements. You have also learnt how the precedence rules work with arithmetic statements and how the integer and floating point conversions take place.

Among input/output statements you have learnt to use **scanf( )** and **printf( )**, and how to handle input/output of different types of variables using these.

With these fundamentals under your belt you should be ready to wade into the next few chapters, where we discuss different types of control instructions.

Exercise

[A] Which of the following are invalid variable names and why?

InterestPaid
si-int
AVERAGE
percent.
123
dist in km
ot pay
Name
FLOAT

[B] Point out the errors, if any, in the following C statements:

(a) int = 314.562 * 150 ;

(b) name = 'Ajay' ;

(c) 3.14 * r * r = area ;

(d) k = a * b + c (2.5a + b) ;

(e) m_inst = rate of interest * amount in rs ;

(f) si = principal * rateofinterest * numberofyears / 100 ;

(g) area = 3.14 * r ** 2 ;

[C] Evaluate the following expressions and show their hierarchy.

(a) g = big / 2 + big * 4 / big - big + abc / 3 ;
(abc = 1.5, big = 3, assume **g** to be a float)

(b) on = ink * act / 2 + 3 / 2 * act + 2 + tig ;
(ink = 3, act = 2, tig = 3.2, assume **on** to be an int)

(c) s = qui * add / 4 - 6 / 2 + 2 / 3 * 6 / god ;
(qui = 2, add = 4, god = 3, assume **s** to be an int)

[D] Convert the following equations into corresponding C statements.

(a) $$Z = \frac{8.8\,(a+b)\ 2/c - 0.5 + 2a/(q+r)}{(a+b)\ *\ (1/m)}$$

(b) $$X = \frac{-b + (b*b) + 2 - 4ac}{2a}$$

(c) $$R = \frac{2v + 6.22\ (c + d)}{g + v}$$

[E] What would be the output of the following program segment:

```
int i = 2, j = 3, k, l ;
float a, b ;
k = i / j * j ;
```

```
l = j / i * i ;
a = i / j * j ;
b = j / i * i ;
printf( "%d %d %f %f", k, l, a, b ) ;
```

[F]   Pick up the correct alternative for each of the following questions:

(a)   C language has been developed by
      (1) Ken Thompson
      (2) Dennis Ritchie
      (3) Peter Norton
      (4) Martin Richards

(b)   C language has been developed at
      (1) Microsoft Corp., USA
      (2) AT & T Bell Labs, USA
      (3) Borland International, USA
      (4) IBM, USA

(c)   C language came into existence in the year
      (1) 1971
      (2) 1957
      (3) 1972
      (4) 1983

(d)   C is a
      (1) Middle level language
      (2) High level language
      (3) Low level language
      (4) None of the above

(e)   C can be used on
      (1) Only MS-DOS operating system
      (2) Only Unix operating system
      (3) Only Xenix operating system
      (4) All the above

(f)   C programs are converted into machine language with the help of
    (1) An interpreter
    (2) A compiler
    (3) An operating system
    (4) None of the above

(g)   The real constant in C can be expressed in which of the following forms
    (1) Fractional form only
    (2) Exponential form only
    (3) ASCII form only
    (4) Both fractional and exponential forms

(h)   A character variable can at a time store
    (1) 1 character
    (2) 8 characters
    (3) 254 characters
    (4) None of the above

(i)   Which of the following is NOT a character constant
    (1) 'Thank You'
    (2) 'Enter values of P, N, R'
    (3) '23.56E-03'
    (4) All the above

(j)   The maximum value that an integer constant can have is
    (1) -32767
    (2) 32767
    (3) 1.7014e+38
    (4) -1.7014e+38

(k)   The maximum width of a C variable name can be
    (1) 6 characters
    (2) 8 characters
    (3) 10 characters
    (4) 20 characters

(l)   A C variable cannot start with
    (1) An alphabet
    (2) A number
    (3) A special symbol
    (4) Both (B) & (C) above

(m)   Which of the following statement is wrong
    (1) mes = 123.56 ;
    (2) con = 'T' * 'A' ;
    (3) this = 'T' * 20 ;
    (4) 3 + a = b ;

(n)   Which of the following shows the correct hierarchy of arithmetic operations in C
    (1) ( ), **, * or /, + or -
    (2) ( ), **, *, /, +, -
    (3) ( ), **, /, *, +, -
    (4) ( ), / or *, - or +

(o)   In b = 6.6 / a + (2 * a + (3 * c) / a * d) / (2 / n) ; which operation will be peformed first?
    (1) 6.6 / a
    (2) 2 * a
    (3) 3 * c
    (4) 2 / n

(p)   Which of the following is allowed in a C Arithmetic instruction
    (1) [ ]
    (2) { }
    (3) ( )
    (4) None of the above

(q)   Which of the following statements is false
    (1) Each new C instruction has to be written on a separate line
    (2) Usually all C statements are entered in small case letters
    (3) Blank spaces may be inserted between two words in a C statement

(4) Blank spaces cannot be inserted within a integer variable

(r)   If a is an integer variable, a = 5 / 2 ; will return a value
        (1) 2.5
        (2) 3
        (3) 2
        (4) 0

(s)   The expression, a = 7 / 22 * (3.14 + 2) * 3 / 5 ; evaluates to
        (1) 8.28
        (2) 6.28
        (3) 3.14
        (4) 0

(t)   The expression, a = 30 * 1000 + 2768 ; evaluates to
        (1) 32768
        (2) -32768
        (3) 113040
        (4) 0

(u)   The expression x =4 + 2 % -8 evaluates to
        (1) -6
        (2) 6
        (3) 4
        (4) None of the above

(v)   Hierarchy decides which operator
        (1) is most important
        (2) is used first
        (3) is fastest
        (4) operates on largest numbers

[G]   Write C programs for the following:

(a)   Ramesh's basic salary is input through the keyboard. His
        dearness allowance is 40% of basic salary, and house rent

allowance is 20% of basic salary. Write a program to calculate his gross salary.

(b) The distance between two cities (in km.) is input through the keyboard. Write a program to convert and print this distance in meters, feet, inches and centimeters.

(c) If the marks obtained by a student in five different subjects are input through the keyboard, find out the aggregate marks and percentage marks obtained by the student. Assume that the maximum marks that can be obtained by a student in each subject is 100.

(d) Temperature of a city in farenheit degrees is input through the keyboard. Write a program to convert this temperature into centigrade degrees.

(e) The length & breadth of a rectangle and radius of a circle are input through the keyboard. Write a program to calculate the area & perimeter of the rectangle, and the area & circumference of the circle.

(f) Two numbers are input through the keyboard into two locations C and D. Write a program to interchange the contents of C and D.

(g) If a five digit number is input through the keyboard, write a program to calculate the sum of its digits.

(Hint: Use the modulus operator '%')

The division operator /, returns the quotient on dividing one number by another, whereas the modulus operator % gives the remainder on dividing one number by another. For example,

a = 12 % 3 would store 0 in **a**
a = 13 % 5 would store 3 in **a**

(h)   If a five digit number is input through the keyboard, write a program to reverse the number.

(i)   If a four digit number is input through the keyboard, write a program to obtain the sum of the first and last digit of this number.

2 The Decision Control Structure

W e all need to alter our actions in the face of changing circumstances. If the weather is fine, then I will go for a stroll. If the highway is busy I would take a diversion. If the pitch takes spin, we would win the match. If she says no, I would look elsewhere. If you like this book, I would write the next one on viruses. If you notice all these decisions depend on some condition being met.

C language too must be able to perform different sets of actions depending on the circumstances. In fact this is what makes it worth its salt. C has three major decision making instructions: the **if** statement, the **if-else** statement, and the **switch** statement. A fourth, somewhat less important structure is the one which uses conditional operators. In this chapter we will explore all these ways (except **switch**, which has a separate chapter devoted to it, later) in which a C program can react to changing circumstances.

Decisions! Decisions!

In the programs written in chapter 1 we have used sequence control structure in which the various steps are executed sequentially, i.e. in the same order in which they appear in the program. In fact to execute the instructions sequentially, we don't have to do anything at all. By default the instructions in a program are executed sequentially. However, in serious programming situations, seldom do we want the instructions to be executed sequentially. Many a times, we want a set of instructions to be executed in one situation, and an entirely different set of instructions to be executed in another situation. This kind of situation is dealt in C programs using a decision control instruction. As mentioned earlier a decision control instruction can be implemented in C using:

(a)   The **if** statement
(b)   The **if-else** statement
(c)   The conditional operators

Now let us learn each of these and their variations in turn.

The *if* Statement

Like most languages, C uses the keyword **if** to implement the decision control instruction. The general form of **if** statement looks like this:

```
if ( this condition is true )
     execute this statement ;
```

The keyword **if** tells the compiler that what follows, is a decision control instruction. The condition following the keyword **if** is always enclosed within a pair of parentheses. If the condition, whatever it is, is true, then the statement is executed. If the condition is not true then the statement is not executed; instead the program skips past it. But how do we express the condition itself in C? And how do we evaluate its truth or falsity? As a general rule, we express a condition using C's 'relational' operators. The relational operators allow us to compare two values to see whether they are equal to each other, unequal, or whether one is greater than the other. Here's how they look and how they are evaluated in C.

this expression	is true if
x == y	x is equal to y
x != y	x is not equal to y
x < y	x is less than y
x > y	x is greater than y
x <= y	x is less than or equal to y
x >= y	x is greater than or equal to y

Figure 2.1

The relational operators should be familiar to you except for the equality symbol == and the inequality symbol !=. Note that = is used for assignment, whereas == is used for comparison of two quantities. Here is a simple program which demonstrates the use of **if** and the relational operators.

```
/* Demonstration of if statement */
main( )
{
    int num ;

    printf ( "Enter a number less than 10 " ) ;
    scanf ( "%d", &num ) ;

    if ( num <= 10 )
        printf ( "What an obedient servant you are !" ) ;
}
```

On execution of this program, if you type a number less than or equal to 10, you get a message on the screen through **printf( )**. If you type some other number the program doesn't do anything.

To make you comfortable with the decision control instruction one more example has been given below. Study it carefully before reading further. To help you understand it easily, the program is accompanied by an appropriate flowchart.

Example 2.1: While purchasing certain items, a discount of 10% is offered if the quantity purchased is more than 1000. If quantity and price per item are input through the keyboard, write a program to calculate the total expenses.

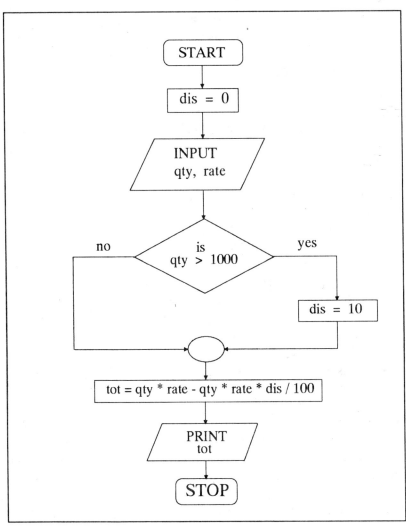

Figure 2.2

```
/* Calculation of total expenses */
main( )
{
    int qty, dis = 0 ;
    float rate, tot ;
```

```
        printf ( "Enter quantity and rate " ) ;
        scanf ( "%d %f", &qty, &rate) ;

        if ( qty > 1000 )
            dis = 10 ;

        tot = ( qty * rate ) - ( qty * rate * dis / 100 ) ;
        printf ( "Total expenses = Rs. %f", tot ) ;
    }
```

Here is some sample interaction with the program.

```
    Enter quantity and rate 1200 15.50
    Total expenses = Rs. 16740.000000

    Enter quantity and rate 200 15.50
    Total expenses = Rs. 3100.000000
```

In the first run of the program, the condition evaluates to true, since 1200 (value of **qty**) is greater than 1000. Therefore, the variable **dis** which was earlier set to 0, now gets a new value 10. And using this new value total expenses are calculated and printed.

In the second run the condition evaluates to false, since 200 (the value of **qty**) isn't greater than 1000. Thus, **dis** which is earlier set to 0, remains 0, and hence the expression after the minus sign evaluates to zero, thereby offering no discount.

Is the statement **dis = 0** necessary? The answer is yes, since in C, a variable if not specifically initialised contains some unpredictable value (garbage value).

Multiple Statements within *if*

It may so happen that in a program we want more than one statement to be executed if the condition following **if** is satisfied. If such multiple statements are to be executed then they must be placed within a pair of braces, as illustrated in the following example.

Example 2.2: The current year and the year in which the employee joined the organisation are entered through the keyboard. If the number of years for which the employee has served the organisation is greater than 3 then a bonus of Rs. 2500/- is given to the employee. If the years of service is not greater than 3, then the program should not do anything.

```
/* Calculation of bonus */
main( )
{
    int bonus, cy, yoj, yr_of_ser ;

    printf ( "Enter current year and year of joining " ) ;
    scanf ( "%d %d", &cy, &yoj ) ;

    yr_of_ser = cy - yoj ;

    if ( yr_of_ser > 3 )
    {
        bonus = 2500 ;
        printf ( "Bonus = Rs. %d", bonus ) ;
    }
}
```

Observe that here the two statements to be executed on satisfaction of the condition have been enclosed within a pair of braces. If a pair of braces is not used then the C compiler assumes that the programmer wants only the immediately next statement after the **if** to be executed on satisfaction of the condition. In other words we can say that the default scope of the **if** statement is the immediately next statement after it.

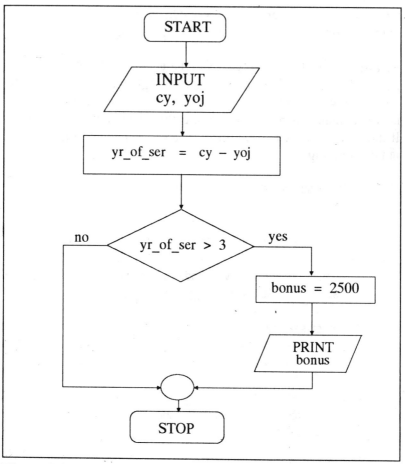

Figure 2.3

The *if-else* Statement

The **if** statement by itself will execute a single statement, or a group of statements, when the condition following **if** is true. It does nothing when the condition is false. Can we execute one group of statements if the condition is true and another group of statements if the condition is false? Of course. This is what is the purpose of the **else** statement, which is demonstrated in the following example:

Example 2.3: In a company an employee is paid as under:

If his basic salary is less than Rs. 1500, then HRA = 10% of basic salary and DA = 90% of basic. If his salary is either equal to or above Rs. 1500, then HRA = Rs. 500 and DA = 98% of basic salary. If the employee's salary is input through the keyboard write a program to find his gross salary.

```
/* Calculation of gross salary */
main( )
{
     float bs, gs, da, hra ;

     printf ( "Enter basic salary " ) ;
     scanf ( "%f", &bs ) ;

     if ( bs < 1500 )
     {
          hra = bs * 10 / 100 ;
          da = bs * 90 / 100 ;
     }
     else
     {
          hra = 500 ;
          da = bs * 98 / 100 ;
     }

     gs = bs + hra + da ;
     printf ( "gross salary = Rs. %f", gs ) ;
}
```

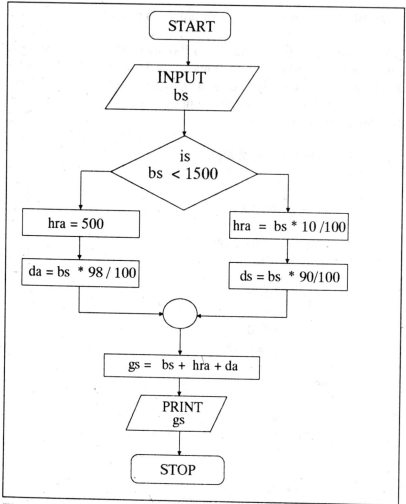

Figure 2.4

A few points worth noting...

(a)   The group of statements after the **if** upto and not including the **else** is called an 'if block'. Similarly, the statements after the else form the 'else block'.

(b) Notice that the **else** is written exactly below the **if**. The statements in the if block and those in the else block have been indented to the right. This formatting convention is followed throughout the book to enable you to understand the working of the program better.

(c) Had there been only one statement to be executed in the if block and only one statement in the else block we could have dropped the pair of braces.

(d) As with the **if** statement, the default scope of **else** is also the statement immediately after the **else**. To override this default scope a pair of braces as shown in the above example must be used.

Nested *if-elses*

It is perfectly alright if we write an entire **if-else** construct within either the body of the **if** statement or the body of an **else** statement. This is called 'nesting' of **ifs**. This is shown in the following program.

```
/* A quick demo of nested if-else */
main( )
{
    int i ;

    printf ( "Enter either 1 or 2 " ) ;
    scanf ( "%d", &i ) ;

    if ( i == 1 )
        printf ( "You would go to heaven !" ) ;
    else
    {
        if ( i == 2 )
            printf ( "Hell was created with you in mind" ) ;
        else
```

```
            printf ( "How about mother earth !" ) ;
    }
}
```

Note that the second **if-else** construct is nested in the first **else** statement. If the condition in the first **if** statement is false, then the condition in the second **if** statement is checked. If it is false as well, the final **else** statement is executed.

You can see in the program how each time a structure is nested within another structure, it is also indented for clarity. Inculcate this habit of indentation, otherwise you would end up writing programs which nobody (you included) can understand easily at a later date.

In the above program an **if-else** occurs within the **else** block of the first **if** statement. Similarly, in some other program an **if-else** may occur in the **if** block as well. There is no limit on how deeply the **ifs** and the **elses** can be nested.

Forms of *if*

The **if** statement can take any of the following forms:

```
(a)    if ( condition )
           do this ;

(b)    if ( condition )
       {
           do this ;
           and this ;
       }

(c)    if ( condition )
           do this ;
       else
           do this ;
```

(d)   if (condition)
```
       {
            do this ;
            and this ;
       }
       else
       {
            do this ;
            and this ;
       }
```

(e)   if (condition)
```
            do this ;
       else
       {
            if ( condition )
                do this ;
            else
            {
                do this ;
                and this ;
            }
       }
```

(f)   if (condition)
```
       {
            if ( condition )
                do this ;
            else
            {
                do this ;
                and this ;
            }
       }
       else
            do this ;
```

Use of Logical Operators

C allows usage of three logical operators:

(a)   && (read as AND)
(b) || (read as OR)
(c)   ! (read as NOT)

There are several things to note about these logical operators. Most obviously, two of them are composed of double symbols: || and &&. Don't use the single symbol | and &. These single symbols also have a meaning. They are bitwise operators, which we will examine in Chapter 18.

The first two operators, && and ||, allow two or more conditions to be combined in an **if** statement. Let us see how they are used in a program. Consider the following problem.

Example 2.4: The marks obtained by a student in 5 different subjects are input through the keyboard. The student gets a division as per the following rules:

>   Percentage above or equal to 60 - First division
>   Percentage between 50 and 59 - Second division
>   Percentage between 40 and 49 - Third division
>   Percentage less than 40 - Fail

Write a program to calculate the division obtained by the student.

Here is the program...

```
main( )
{
    int m1, m2, m3, m4, m5, per ;

    printf ( "Enter marks in five subjects " ) ;
```

```
scanf ( "%d %d %d %d %d", &m1, &m2, &m3, &m4, &m5 ) ;

per = ( m1 + m2 + m3 + m4 + m5 ) / 5 ;

if ( per >= 60 )
    printf ( "First division " ) ;
else
{
    if ( per >= 50 )
        printf ( "Second division" ) ;
    else
    {
        if ( per >= 40 )
            printf ( "Third division" ) ;
        else
            printf ( "Fail" ) ;
    }
}
}
```

Observe that the program uses nested **if-elses**. This leads to three disadvantages:

(a)   As the number of conditions go on increasing the level of indentation also goes on increasing. As a result the whole program creeps to the right.

(b)   Care needs to be exercised to match the corresponding **if**s and **else**s.

(c)   Care needs to be exercised to match the corresponding pair of braces.

All these three problems can be eliminated by usage of 'Logical operators'. The following program illustrates this.

```
main( )
{
    int m1, m2, m3, m4, m5, per ;
```

```
printf ( "Enter marks in five subjects " ) ;
scanf ( "%d %d %d %d %d", &m1, &m2, &m3, &m4, &m5 ) ;

per = ( m1 + m2 + m3 + m4 + m5 ) / 5 ;

if ( per >= 60 )
    printf ( "First division" ) ;

if ( ( per >= 50 ) && ( per < 60 ) )
    printf ( "Second division" ) ;

if ( ( per >= 40 ) && ( per < 50 ) )
    printf ( "Third division" ) ;

if ( per < 40 )
    printf ( "Fail" ) ;
}
```

As can be seen from the second **if** statement, the **&&** operator is used to combine two conditions. 'Second division' gets printed if both the condtitions evaluate to true. If one of the conditions evaluate to false then the whole thing is treated as false.

Two distinct advantages can be cited in favour of this program:

(a)   The matching (or do I say mismatching) of the **if**s with their corresponding **else**s gets avoided, since there are no **else**s in this program.

(b)   In the earlier program the statements went on creeping to the right. This effect becomes more pronounced as the number of conditions go on increasing. This would make the task of matching the **if**s with their corresponding **else**s and matching of opening and closing braces that much more difficult.

Another place where logical operators are useful is when we want to write down programs for complicated logics which ultimately boil down to only two answers. For example, consider the following problem:

Example 2.5: A company insures its drivers in the following cases:

- if the driver is married.
- If the driver is unmarried, male & above 30 years of age.
- If the driver is unmarried, female & above 25 years of age.

In all other cases the driver is not insured. If the marital status, sex and age of the driver are the inputs, write a program to determine whether the driver is to be insured or not.

We can write a program for the above problem in two ways:

(a)   Without using **&&** and **||** operators
(b)   Using **&&** and **||** operators

Method (a)

```
/* Insurance of driver - without using logical operators */
main( )
{
    char sex, ms ;
    int age ;

    printf ( "Enter age, sex, marital status " ) ;
    scanf ( "%d %c %c", &age, &sex, &ms ) ;

    if ( ms == 'M' )
        printf ( "Driver is insured" ) ;
    else
    {
        if ( sex == 'M' )
        {
            if ( age > 30 )
                printf ( "Driver is insured" ) ;
```

```
                else
                    printf ( "Driver is not insured" ) ;
            }
            else
            {
                if ( age > 25 )
                    printf ( "Driver is insured" ) ;
                else
                    printf ( "Driver is not insured" ) ;
            }
        }
    }
```

Method (b)

As mentioned above, in this example we expect the answer to be either 'Driver is insured' or 'Driver is not insured'. If we list down all those cases in which the driver is insured, then they would be:

(a)   Driver is married.
(b)   Driver is an unmarried male above 30 years of age.
(c)   Driver is an unmarried female above 25 years of age.

Since all these cases lead to the driver being insured, they can be combined together using **&&** and **||** as shown in the program below:

```
/* Insurance of driver - using logical operators */
main( )
{
    char sex, ms ;
    int age ;

    printf ( "Enter age, sex, marital status " ) ;
    scanf ( "%d %c %c" &age, &sex, &ms ) ;

    if ( ( ms == 'M' ) || ( ms == 'U' && sex == 'M' && age > 30 ) ||
            ( ms == 'U' && sex == 'F' && age > 25 ) )
```

```
            printf ( "Driver is insured" ) ;
        else
            printf ( "Driver is not insured" ) ;
    }
```

In this program it is important to note that:

- The driver will be insured only if one of the conditions enclosed in parentheses evaluates to true.

- For the second pair of parentheses to evaluate to true, each condition in the parentheses separated by **&&** must evaluate to true.

- Even if one of the conditions in the second parentheses evaluates to false, then the whole of the second parentheses evaluates to false.

- The last two of the above arguments apply to third pair of parentheses as well.

Thus we can conclude that the **&&** and **||** are useful in the following programming situations:

(a)   When it is to be tested whether a value falls within a particular range or not.

(b)   When after testing several conditions the outcome is only one of the two answers.

So far we have used only the logical operators **&&** and **||**. The third logical operator is the NOT operator, written as **!**. This operator reverses the value of the expression it operates on; it makes a true expression false and a false expression true. Here is an example of the NOT operator applied to a relational expression.

```
    ! ( y < 10 )
```

This means "not y less than 10". In other words, if y is less than 10, the expression will be false, since (y < 10) is true. We can express the same condition as (y >= 10).

The NOT operator is often used to reverse the logical value of a single variable, as in the expression

    if (! flag)

this is another way of saying

    if (flag == 0)

Does the NOT operator sound confusing? Avoid it if you find it confusing, since the same thing can be always said without using the NOT operator.

Hierarchy of Logical Operators

Since we have now added the logical operators to the list of operators we know, it is time to review these operators and their priorities.

Operators	Type
!	Logical NOT
* / %	Arithmetic and modulus
+ −	Arithmetic
< > <= >=	Relaional
== !=	Relational
&&	Logical And
‖	Logical OR
=	Assignment

Figure 2.5

Figure 2.5 summarizes the operators we have seen so far. The **higher** an operator is in the table, the higher is its priority. (A full-fledged precedence table of operators is given in Appendix A.)

A Word of Caution

What will be the output of the following program:

```
main( )
{
    int i ;

    printf ( "Enter value of i " ) ;
    scanf ( "%d", &i ) ;

    if ( i = 5 )
        printf ( "You entered 5" ) ;
    else
        printf ( "You entered something other than 5" ) ;
}
```

And here is the output of two runs of this program...

```
Enter value of i 200
You entered 5
Enter value of i 9999
You entered 5
```

Surprising? You have entered 200 and 9999, and still you find in either case the output is 'You entered 5'. This is because we have written the condition wrongly. We have used the assignment operator = instead of the relational operator ==. As a result, the condition gets reduced to **if** (**5**), irrespective of what you supply as the value of **i**. And remember that in C 'truth' is always non-zero, whereas 'falsity' is always zero. Therefore, **if** (**5**) always evaluates to true **and hence** the result.

Another common mistake while using the **if** statement is to write a semicolon (;) after the condition, as shown below:

```
main( )
{
    int i ;

    printf ( "Enter value of i " ) ;
    scanf ( "%d" &i ) ;

    if ( i == 5 ) ;
        printf ( "You entered 5" ) ;
}
```

The ; makes the compiler to interpret the statement as if you have written it in following manner:

```
if ( i == 5 )
    ;
printf ( "You entered 5" ) ;
```

Here, if the condition evaluates to true the ; (null statement, which does nothing on execution) gets executed, following which the **printf( )** gets executed. If the condition fails then straightaway the **printf( )** gets executed. Thus, irrespective of whether the condition evaluates to true or false the **printf( )** is bound to get executed. Remember that the compiler would not point out this as an error, since as far as the syntax is concerned nothing has gone wrong, but the logic has certainly gone awry. Moral is, beware of such pitfalls.

The Conditional Operators

The conditional operators **?** and **:** are sometimes called ternary operators since they take three arguments. In fact, they form a kind of foreshortened if-then-else. Their general form is, expression 1 ? expression 2 : expression 3

What this expression says is: "if **expression 1** is true (that is, if its value is non-zero), then the value returned will be **expression 2** otherwise the value returned will be **expression 3**". Let us understand this with the help of a few examples:

Examples:

(a)   int x, y ;
        scanf ("%d", &x) ;
        y = (x > 5 ? 3 : 4) ;

This statement will store 3 in **y** if **x** is greater than 5, otherwise it will store 4 in **y**.

The equivalent **if** statement will be,

        if (x > 5)
            y = 3 ;
        else
            y = 4 ;

(b)   char a ;
        int y ;
        scanf ("%c", &a) ;
        y = (a >= 65 && a <= 90 ? 1 : 0) ;

The following points may be noted about the conditional operators:

(a)   It's not necessary that the conditional operators should be used only in arithmetic statements. This is illustrated in the following examples:

        Ex.:

        int i ;

```
scanf ( "%d", &i ) ;
( i == 1 ? printf ( "Amit" ) : printf ( "All and sundry" ) ) ;
```

Ex.:

```
char a = 'z' ;
printf ( "%c" , ( a >= 'a' ? a : '!') ) ;
```

(b)   The conditional operators can be nested as shown below.

```
int big, a, b, c ;
big = ( a > b ? ( a > c ? 3: 4 ) : ( b > c ? 6: 8 ) ) ;
```

The limitation of the conditional operators is that after the ? or after the : only one C statement can occur. In practise rarely is this the requirement. Therefore, in serious C programming conditional operators aren't as frequently used as the **if-else**.

Summary

You now know a good deal about the major elements of decision-making in C. You have learnt about the **if**, and the **if-else**. You have also seen how **if** statements can be nested within one another. You have also learnt about the three logical operators AND (&&), OR (||) and NOT (!). Finally you learnt about the conditional operators and the fact that they are sparingly used in C.

Exercise

if, if-else, **Nested** *if-elses*

[A]   What will be the output of the following programs:

(a)   main( )
        {

```
            int a = 300, b, c ;
            if ( a >= 400 )
                b = 300 ;
                c = 200 ;
                printf ( "\n%d %d", b, c ) ;
    }
```

(b)   main( )
```
    {
        int a = 500, b, c ;
        if ( a >= 400 )
            b = 300 ;
            c = 200 ;
            printf ( "\n%d %d", b, c ) ;
    }
```

(c)   main( )
```
    {
        int x = 10, y = 20 ;
        if ( x == y ) ;
            printf ( "\n%d %d", x, y ) ;
    }
```

(d)   main( )
```
    {
        int x = 3, y = 5 ;
        if ( x == 3 )
            printf ( "\n%d", x ) ;
        else ;
            printf ( "\n%d", y ) ;
    }
```

(e)   main( )
```
    {
        int x = 3 ;
        float y = 3.0 ;
```

```
            if ( x == y )
                printf ( "\nx and y are equal" ) ;
            else
                printf ( "\nx and y are not equal" ) ;
        }
```

(f)   main( )
        {
            int x = 3, y, z ;
            y = x = 10 ;
            z = x < 10 ;
            printf ("\nx = %d y = %d z = %d", x, y, z) ;
        }

(g)   main( )
        {
            int k = 35 ;
            printf ("\n%d %d %d", k == 35, k = 50, k > 40) ;
        }

[B]   Point out the errors, if any, in the following programs:

(a)   main( )
        {
            float a = 12.25, b = 12.52 ;
            if (a = b)
                printf ("\na and b are equal") ;
        }

(b)   main( )
        {
            int j = 10, k = 12 ;
            if (k >= j)
            {
                {
                    k = j ;
```
```

```
                        j = k ;
                  }
            }
      }
```

(c)   main( )
       {
            if ('X' < 'x')
                  printf ("\nascii value of X is smaller than that of x") ;
       }

(d)   main( )
       {
            int x = 10 ;
            if(x >= 2) then
                  printf ("\n%d", x) ;
       }

(e)   main( )
       {
            int x = 10 ;
            if x >= 2
                  printf ("\n%d", x) ;
       }

(f)   main( )
       {
            int x = 10, y = 15 ;
            if (x % 2 = y % 3)
                  printf ("\nCarpathians") ;
       }

[C]   Attempt the following:

(a)   If cost price and selling price of an item is input through the keyboard, write a program to determine whether the seller has made profit or incurred loss. Also determine how much profit he made or loss hc incurred.

(b) Any integer is input through the keyboard. Write a program to find out whether it is an odd number or even number.

(c) Any year is input through the keyboard. Write a program to determine whether the year is a leap year or not.

(Hint: Use the % (modulus) operator)

(d) According to the Gregorian calendar, it was monday on the date 01/01/1900. If any year is input through the keyboard write a program to find out what is the day on 1st January of this year.

(e) A five digit number is entered through the keyboard. Write a program to obtain the reversed number and to determine whether the original and reversed numbers are equal or not.

Logical Operators

[D] if x = 11, y = 6, z = 1, find the values of the expressions in the following table:

Expression	Value
x > 9 && y != 3 x == 5 || y != 3 ! (x > 14) ! (x > 9 && y != 23) 5 && y != 8 || 0	1

[E] What will be the output of the following programs:

(a) main( )

```
    {
        int i = 4, z = 12 ;
        if ( i = 5 || z > 50 )
            printf ( "\nDean of students affairs" ) ;
        else
            printf ( "\nDosa" ) ;
    }
```

(b)   main( )
```
    {
        int i = 4, z = 12 ;
        if ( i = 5 && z > 5 )
            printf ( "\nLet us C" ) ;
        else
            printf ( "\nWish C was free !" ) ;
    }
```

(c)   main( )
```
    {
        int i = 4, j = -1, k = 0, w, x, y, z ;
        w = i || j || k ;
        x = i && j && k ;
        y = i || j && k ;
        z = i && j || k ;
        printf ( "\nw = %d x = %d y = %d z = %d", w, x, y, z ) ;
    }
```

(d)   main( )
```
    {
        int i = 4, j = -1, k = 0, y, z ;
        y = i + 5 && j + 1 || k + 2 ;
        z = i + 5 || j + 1 && k + 2 ;
        printf ( "\ny = %d z = %d", y, z ) ;
    }
```

(e)   main( )

```
    {
        int i = -3, j = 3 ;
        if ( !i + !j * 1 )
            printf ( "\nMassaro" ) ;
        else
            printf ( "\nBennarivo" ) ;
    }
```

[F] Point out the errors, if any, in the following programs:

(a)
```
    /* This program
    /* is an example of
    /* using Logical operators */
    main( )
    {
        int i = 2, j = 5 ;
        if ( i == 2 && j == 5 )
            printf ( "\nSatisfied at last" ) ;
    }
```

(b)
```
    main( )
    {
        int code, flag ;
        if ( code == 1 & flag == 0 )
            printf ( "\nThe eagle has landed" ) ;
    }
```

(c)
```
    main( )
    {
        char spy = 'a', password = 'z' ;
        if ( spy == 'a' or password == 'z' )
            printf ( "\nAll the birds are safe in the nest" ) ;
    }
```

(d)
```
    main( )
    {
```

```
        int i = 10, j = 20 ;
        if ( i = 5 ) && if ( j = 10 )
            printf ( "\nHave a nice day" ) ;
}
```

[G]   Attempt the following:

(a)   Any year is entered through the keyboard, write a program to determine whether the year is leap or not. Use the logical operators **&&** and **||**.

(b)   Any character is entered through the keyboard, write a program to determine whether the character entered is a capital letter, a small case letter, a digit or a special symbol.

The following table shows the range of ascii values for various characters.

Characters	Ascii values
A - Z	65 - 90
a - z	97 - 122
0 - 9	48 - 57
special symbols	0 - 47, 58 - 64, 91 - 96, 123 - 127

(c)   An Insurance company follows following rules to calculate premium.

(1) If a person's health is excellent and the person is between 25 and 35 years of age and lives in a city and is a male then the premium is Rs. 4 per thousand and his policy amount cannot exceed Rs. 2 lakhs.

(2) If a person satisfies all the above conditions except that the sex is female then the premium is Rs. 3 per thousand and her policy amount cannot exceed Rs. 1 lakh.

(3) If a person's health is poor and the person is between 25 and 35 years of age and lives in a village and is a male then the premium is Rs. 6 per thousand and his policy cannot exceed Rs. 10,000.
(4) In all other cases the person is not insured.

Write a program to ouput whether the person should be insured or not, his/her premium rate and maximum amount for which he/she can be insured.

(d) A certain grade of steel is graded according to the following conditions:

(1) Hardness must be greater than 50
(2) Carbon content must be less than 0.7
(3) Tensile strength must be greater than 5600

The grades are as follows:

Grade is 10 if all three conditions are met
Grade is 9 if conditions (i) and (ii) are met
Grade is 8 if conditions (ii) and (iii) are met
Grade is 7 if conditions (i) and (iii) are met
Grade is 6 if only one condition is met
Grade is 5 if none of the conditions are met

Write a program which will require the user to give values of hardness, carbon content and tensile strength of the steel under consideration and output the grade of the steel.

Conditional Operators

[H] What will be the output of the following programs:

(a)
```
main( )
{
    int i = -4, j, num ;
```

```
        j = ( num < 0 ? 0 : num * num ) ;
        printf ( "\n%d", j ) ;
}
```

(b)
```
main( )
{
    int k, num = 30 ;
    k = ( num > 5 ? ( num <= 10 ? 100 : 200 ) : 500 ) ;
    printf ( "\n%d", num ) ;
}
```

[I]   Point out the errors, if any, in the following programs:

(a)
```
main( )
{
    int tag = 0, code = 1 ;
    if ( tag == 0 )
        ( code > 1 ? printf ( "\nHello" ) ? printf ( "\nHi" ) ) ;
    else
        printf ( "\nHello Hi !!" ) ;
}
```

(b)
```
main( )
{
    int ji = 65 ;
    printf ( "\nji >= 65 ? %d : %c", ji ) ;
}
```

(c)
```
main( )
{
    int i = 10, j ;
    i >= 5 ? ( j = 10 ) : ( j = 15 ) ;
    printf ( "\n%d %d", i, j ) ;
}
```

[J]   Rewrite the following programs using conditional operators.

(a)   main( )
      {
          int x, min, max ;
          scanf ("\n%d %d", &max, &x) ;
          if (x > max)
              max = x ;
          else
              min = x ;
      }

(b)   main( )
      {
          int code ;
          scanf ("%d", &code) ;
          if (code > 1)
              printf ("\nJerusalem") ;
          else
              if (code < 1)
                  printf ("\nEddie") ;
              else
                  printf ("\nC Brain") ;
      }

[K]   Attempt the following:

(a)   Using conditional operators determine:

      (1) Whether the character entered through the keyboard is a
          lower case alphabet or not.
      (2) Whether a character entered through the keyboard is a
          special symbol or not.

(b)   Write a program using conditonal operators to determine
      whether a year entered through the keyboard is a leap year or
      not.

3 The Loop Control Structure

The programs that we have developed so far used either a sequential or a decision control structure. In the first one, the calculations were carried out in a fixed order, while in the second, an appropriate set of instructions was executed depending upon the outcome of the condition being tested (or a logical decision being taken).

These programs were of limited nature, because when executed, they always performed the same series of actions, in the same way, exactly once. Almost always, if something is worth doing, it's worth doing more than once. You can probably think of several examples of this from real life, such as eating a good dinner or going for a movie. Programming is the same; we frequently need to perform an action over and over, often with variations in the details each time. The mechanism which meets this need is the 'loop', and loops is the subject of this chapter.

Loops

The versatility of the computer lies in its ability to perform a set of instructions repeatedly. This involves repeating some portion of the program either a specified number of times or until a particular condition is being satisfied. This repetitive operation is done through a loop control structure.

There are three methods by way of which we can repeat a part of a program. They are:

(a) Using a **for** statement
(b) Using a **while** statement
(c) Using a **do-while** statement

Each of these methods are discussed in the following pages.

The *while* Loop

It is often the case in programming that you want to do something a fixed number of times. Perhaps you want to calculate gross salaries of ten different persons, or you want to convert temperatures from centigrade to farenheit for 15 different cities. The **while** loop is ideally suited for such cases. Let us look at a simple example which uses a **while** loop. The flowchart shown below would help you to understand the operation of the **while** loop.

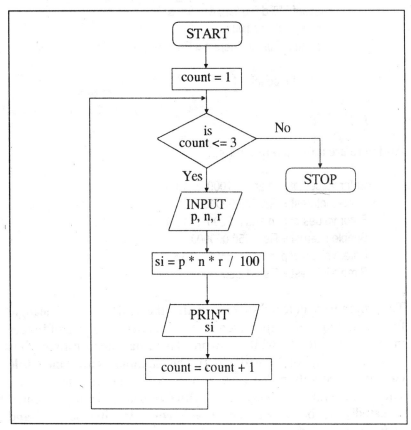

Figure 3.1

```
/* Calculation of simple interest for 3 sets of p, n and r */
main( )
{
    int p, n, count ;
    float r, si ;

    count = 1 ;
    while ( count <= 3 )
    {
        printf ( "\nEnter values of p, n and r " ) ;
        scanf ( "%d %d %f", &p, &n, &r ) ;
        si = p * n * r / 100 ;
        printf ( "Simple interest = Rs. %f", si ) ;

        count = count + 1 ;
    }
}
```

And here are a few sample runs...

```
Enter values of p, n and r  1000  5  13.5
Simple interest = Rs. 675.000000
Enter values of p, n and r  2000  5  13.5
Simple interest = Rs. 1350.000000
Enter values of p, n and r  3500  5  3.5
Simple interest = Rs. 612.500000
```

The program executes all statements after the **while** 3 times. The logic for calculating the simple interest is written within a pair of braces immediately after the **while** keyword. These statements form what is called the 'body' of the **while** loop. The parentheses after the **while** contains a condition. So long as this condition remains true all statements within the body of the **while** loop keep getting executed repeatedly. To begin with the variable **count** is initialised to 1 and everytime the simple interest logic is executed the value of **count** is incremented by one. The variable **count** is many a times called either a 'loop counter' or an 'index variable'.

Finally, what for are we using the '\n' in the **printf ( )**? Just to ensure that every time after printing out the value of simple interest, the cursor should go to the next line, so that the message 'Enter values of p, n and r' appears on a new line. As seen in the first chapter '\n' is called 'newline' and is an escape sequence. More about escape sequences later in Chapter 11. The operation of the **while** loop is illustrated in the following figure.

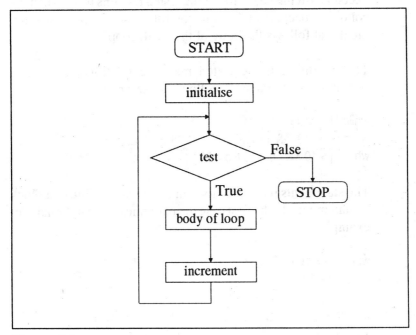

Figure 3.2

Tips and Traps

The general form of **while** is as shown below:

```
initialise loop counter ;
while ( test loop counter using a condition )
{
    do this ;
```

```
        and this ;
        increment loop counter ;
    }
```

Note the following points about **while**...

- The statements within the **while** loop would keep on getting executed till the condition being tested remains true. When the condition becomes false, the control passes to the first statement that follows the body of the **while** loop.

- The condition being tested may use relational or logical operators as shown in the following examples:

```
while ( i <= 10 )
while ( i <= 10 && j <= 15 )
while ( j > 10 && ( b < 15 || c < 20 )
```

- The statements within the loop may be a single line or a block of statements. In the first case the parentheses are optional. For example,

```
while ( i <= 10 )
    i = i + 1 ;
```

is same as

```
while ( i <= 10 )
{
    i = i + 1 ;
}
```

As a rule the **while** must test a condition that will eventually become false, otherwise the loop would be executed forever, indefinitely.

```
main( )
```

```
{
    int i = 1 ;
    while ( i <= 10 )
        printf ( "%d\n", i ) ;
}
```

This is an indefinite loop, since **i** remains equal to 1 forever. The correct form would be as under:

```
main( )
{
    int i = 1 ;
    while ( i <= 10 )
    {
        printf ( "%d\n", i ) ;
        i = i + 1 ;
    }
}
```

Instead of incrementing a loop counter, we can even decrement it and still manage to get the body of the loop executed repeatedly. This is shown below:

```
main( )
{
    int i = 5 ;
    while ( i >= 1 )
    {
        printf ( "\nMake the computer literate!" ) ;
        i = i - 1 ;
    }
}
```

It is not necessary that a loop counter must only be an **int**. It can even be a **float**.

```
main( )
```

```
{
    float a = 10.0 ;
    while ( a <= 10.5 )
    {
        printf ( "\nRaindrops on roses..." ) ;
        printf ( "...and whiskers on kittens" ) ;
        a = a + 0.1 ;
    }
}
```

Even floating point loop counters can be decremented. Once again the increment and decrement could be by any value, not necessarily 1.

What do you think will be the output of the following program?

```
main( )
{
    int i = 1 ;
    while ( i <= 32767 )
    {
        printf ( "%d\n", i ) ;
        i = i + 1 ;
    }
}
```

No, it doesn't print numbers from 1 to 32767. It's an indefinite loop. To begin with, it prints out numbers from 1 to 32767, after that value of **i** is incremented by 1, therefore it tries to become 32768, which falls outside the valid integer range, so it goes to other side and becomes -32767 which would certainly satisfy the condition in the **while**. This process goes on indefinitely.

What will be the output of the following program?

```
main( )
```

```
{
    int i = 1 ;
    while ( i <= 10 ) ;
    {
        printf ( "%d\n", i ) ;
        i = i + 1 ;
    }
}
```

This is another indefinite loop, and it doesn't give any output at all. The reason is, we have carelessly given a ; after the **while**. This would make the loop work like this...

```
while ( i <= 10 )
{
    ;
}
```

Since the value of **i** is not getting incremented the control would keep rotating within the loop, eternally.

More Operators

There are variety of operators which are frequently used with **while**. To illustrate their usage let us consider a problem wherein numbers from 1 to 10 are to be printed on the screen. The program for performing this task can be written using **while** in the following different ways:

```
(a)    main( )
       {
           int i = 1 ;
           while ( i <= 10 )
           {
               printf ( "%d\n", i ) ;
               i = i + 1 ;
```

```
        }
    }
```

(b)   ```
       main( )
       {
           int i = 1 ;
           while (i <= 10)
           {
               printf ("%d\n", i) ;
               i++ ;
           }
       }
       ```

Note that the increment operator **++** increments the value of **i** by 1, everytime the statement **i++** gets executed. Similarly, to reduce the value of a variable by 1 a decrement operator **--** is also available.

However, never use **n+++** to increment the value of **n** by 2, since C doesn't recognise the operator **+++**.

(c)    ```
       main( )
       {
           int i = 1 ;
           while ( i <= 10 )
           {
               printf ( "%d\n", i ) ;
               i += 1 ;
           }
       }
       ```

Note that **+=** is a compound assignment operator. It increments the value of **i** by 1. Similarly, **j = j + 10** can also be written as **j += 10**. Other compound assignment operators are **-=**, ***=**, **/=** and **%=**.

(d)   main( )

```
{
    int i = 0 ;
    while ( i++ < 10 )
        printf ( "%d\n", i ) ;
}
```

In the statement **while (i++ < 10)**, first the comparison of value of **i** with 10 is performed, and then the incrementation of **i** takes place. When the control reaches **printf ( )**, **i** has already been incremented, hence **i** must be initialised to 0.

(e)   main( )

```
{
    int i = 0 ;
    while ( ++i <= 10 )
        printf ( "%d\n", i ) ;
}
```

In the statement **while (++i <= 10)**, first incrementation of **i** takes place, then the comparison of value of **i** with 10 is performed.

The *for* Loop

Perhaps one reason why few programmers use **while** is that they are too busy using the **for**, which is probably the most popular looping control. The **for** allows us to specify three things about a loop in a single line:

(a)   setting a loop counter to an initial value.

(b)   testing the loop counter to determine whether its value has reached the number of repetitions desired.

(c)   increasing the value of loop counter each time the program segment within the loop has been executed.

The general form of **for** statement is as under:

```
for ( initialise counter ; test counter ; increment counter )
{
    do this ;
    and this ;
    and this ;
}
```

Let us write down the simple interest program using **for**. Compare this program with the one which we wrote using **while**. The flowchart is also given below for clarity:

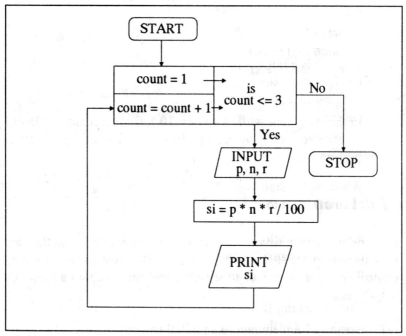

Figure 3.3

```
/* Calculation of simple interest for 3 sets of p, n and r */
main ( )
{
    int p, n, count ;
    float r, si ;

    for ( count = 1 ; count <= 3 ; count = count + 1 )
    {
        printf ( "Enter values of p, n, and r " ) ;
        scanf ( "%d %d %f", &p, &n, &r ) ;

        si = p * n * r / 100 ;
        printf ( "Simple Interest = Rs.%f\n", si ) ;
    }
}
```

If this program is compared with the one written using **while**, it can be seen that the three steps - initialisation, testing and incrementation - required for the loop construct have now been incorporated in the **for** statement.

Let us now examine how the **for** statement gets executed:

-   When the **for** statement is executed for the first time, the value of **count** is set to an initial value 1.

-   Now the condition **count <= 3** is tested. Since **count** is 1 the condition is satisified and the body of the loop is executed for the first time.

-   Upon reaching the closing brace of **for**, computer sends the control back to the **for** statement, where the value of **count** gets incremented by 1.

-   Again the test is performed to check whether the new value of **count** exceeds 3.

-      If the value of **count** is still within the range 1 to 3, the statements within the braces of **for** are executed again.

-      The body of the **for** loop continues to get executed till **count** doesn't exceed the final value 3.

-      When **count** reaches the value 4 the control exits from the loop and is transferred to the statement (if any) immediately after the body of **for**.

The following figure would help in further clarifying the concept of execution of the **for** loop.

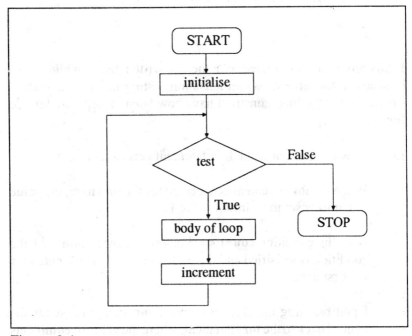

Figure 3.4

Let us now write down the program to print numbers from 1 to 10 in different ways. This time we would use a **for** loop instead of a **while** loop.

(a)
```
main( )
{
    int i ;
    for ( i = 1 ; i <= 10 ; i = i + 1 )
        printf ( "%d\n", i ) ;
}
```

Note that the initialisation, testing and incrementation of loop counter is done in the **for** statement itself. Instead of **i = i + 1**, the statements **i++** or **i += 1** can also be used.

Since there is only one statement in the body of the **for** loop, the pair of braces have been dropped. As with the **while**, the default scope of **for** is the immediately next statement after **for**.

(b)
```
main( )
{
    int i ;
    for ( i = 1 ; i <= 10 ; )
    {
        printf ( "%d\n", i ) ;
        i = i + 1 ;
    }
}
```

Here, the incrementation is done within the body of the **for** loop and not in the **for** statement. Note that inspite of this the semicolon after the condition is necessary.

(c)
```
main( )
{
    int i = 1 ;
    for ( ; i <= 10 ; i = i + 1 )
        printf ( "%d\n", i ) ;
}
```

Here the initialisation is done in the declaration statement itself, but still the semicolon before the condition is necessary.

(d)
```
main( )
{
    int i = 1 ;
    for ( ; i <= 10 ; )
    {
        printf ( "%d\n", i ) ;
        i = i + 1 ;
    }
}
```

Here, neither the initialisation, nor the incrementation is done in the **for** statement, but still the two semicolons are necessary.

(e)
```
main( )
{
    int i ;
    for ( i = 0 ; i++ < 10 ; )
        printf ( "%d\n", i ) ;
}
```

Here, the comparison as well as the incrementation is done through the same statement, **i++ < 10**. Since the **++** operator comes after **i** firstly comparison is done, followed by incrementation. Note that it is necessary to initialise **i** to 0.

(f)
```
main( )
{
    int i ;
    for ( i = 0 ; ++i <= 10 ; )
        printf ( "%d\n", i ) ;
}
```

Here, both, the comparison and the incrementation is done through the same statement, **++i <= 10**. Since **++** precedes **i** firstly incrementation is done, followed by comparison. Note that it is necessary to initialise **i** to 0.

Nesting of Loops

The way **if** statements can be nested, similarly **while**s and **for**s can also be nested. To understand how nested loops work, look at the program given below:

```
/* Demonstration of nested loops */
main( )
{
    int r, c, sum ;
    for ( r = 1 ; r <= 3 ; r++ )   /* outer loop */
    {
        for ( c = 1 ; c <= 2 ; c++ ) /* inner loop */
        {
            sum = r + c ;
            printf ( "r = %d c = %d sum = %d\n", r, c, sum ) ;
        }
    }
}
```

When you run this program you will get the following output:

```
r = 1 c = 1 sum = 2
r = 1 c = 2 sum = 3
r = 2 c = 1 sum = 3
r = 2 c = 2 sum = 4
r = 3 c = 1 sum = 4
r = 3 c = 2 sum = 5
```

Here, for each value of **r** the inner loop is cycled through twice, with the variable **c** taking values from 1 to 2. The inner loop terminates when the value of **c** exceeds 2, and the outer loop terminates when the value of **r** exceeds 3.

As you can see, the body of the outer **for** loop is indented, and the body of the inner **for** loop is further indented. These multiple indentations make the program easier to understand.

Instead of using two statements, one to calculate **sum** and another to print it out, we can compact this into one single statement by saying:

```
printf ( "r = %d c = %d sum = %d\n", r, c, r + c ) ;
```

The way **for** loops have been nested here, similarly, two **while** loops can also be nested. Not only this, a **for** loop can occur within a **while** loop, or a **while** within a **for**.

Multiple Initialisations in the *for* Loop

The initialisation expression of the **for** loop can contain more than one statement separated by a comma. For example,

```
for ( i = 1, j = 2 ; j <= 10 ; j++ )
```

Multiple statements can also be used in the incrementation expression of **for** loop; i.e., you can increment (or decerement) two or more variables at the same time. However only one expression is allowed in the test expression. This expression may contain several conditions linked together using logical operators.

Use of multiple statements in the initialisation expression also demonstrates why semicolons are used to separate the three expressions in the **for** loop. If commas had been used, they could not also have been used to separate multiple statements in the initialisation expression, without confusing the compiler.

The Odd Loop

The loops that we have used so far executed the statements within them a finite number of times. However, in real life programming one comes across a situation when it is not known beforehand how many times the statements in the loop are to be executed. This situation can be programmed as shown below:

```
/* Execution of a loop an unknown number of times */
main( )
{
    char another = 'y' ;
    int num ;

    while ( another == 'y' )
    {
        printf ( "Enter a number " ) ;
        scanf ( "%d", &num ) ;
        printf ( "square of %d is %d", num, num * num ) ;
        printf ( "\nWant to enter another number y/n " ) ;
        scanf ( "%c", &another ) ;
    }
}
```

And here is the sample output...

```
Enter a number 5
square of 5 is 25
Want to enter another number y/n y
Enter a number 7
square of 7 is 49
Want to enter another number y/n n
```

In this program the **while** loop would keep getting executed till the user continues to answer y. The moment he answers n, the loop terminates, since the condition (**another == 'y'**) fails.

The *break* Statement

We often come across situations where we want to jump out of a loop instantly, without waiting to get back to the conditional test. The keyword **break** allows us to do this. When the keyword **break** is encountered inside any C loop, control automatically passes to the first statement after the loop. A **break** is usually associated with an **if**. As an example, let's consider the following problem.

Example: Write a program to determine whether a number is prime or not. A prime number is one which is divisible only by 1 or itself.

All we have to do to test whether a number is prime or not, is to divide it successively by all numbers from 2 to one less than itself. If remainder of any of these divisions is zero, the number is not a prime. Following program implements this logic.

```
main( )
{
    int num, i ;

    printf ( "Enter a number" ) ;
    scanf ( "%d", &num ) ;

    i = 2 ;
    while ( i <= num - 1 )
    {
        if ( num % i == 0 )
        {
            printf ( "Not a prime number" ) ;
            break ;
        }
        i++ ;
    }

    if ( i == num )
```

```
        printf ( "Prime number" ) ;
    }
```

In this program the moment **num** % **i** turns out to be zero, (i.e. **num** is exactly divisible by **i**) the message "Not a prime number" is printed and the control breaks out of the **while** loop. Why does the program require the **if** statement after the **while** loop at all? Well, there are two ways the control could have reached outside the **while** loop:

(a)   It jumped out because the number proved to be not a prime.
(b)   The loop came to an end because the value of **i** became equal to **num**.

In the second case it means that there was no number between 2 and **num - 1** that could exactly divide **num**. That is, **num** is indeed a prime. If this is true, the program should print out the message "Prime number".

The keyword **break**, breaks the control only from the **while** in which it is placed. Consider the following program which illustrates this fact.

```
main( )
{
    int i = 1 , j = 1 ;

    while ( i++ <= 100 )
    {
        while ( j++ <= 200 )
        {
            if ( j == 150 )
                break ;
            else
                printf ( "%d %d\n", i, j ) ;
        }
    }
}
```

In this program when **j** equals 150, **break** takes the control outside the inner **while** only, since it is placed inside the inner **while**.

The *continue* Statement

In some programming situations we want to take the control to the beginning of the loop, bypassing the statements inside the loop which have not yet been executed. The keyword **continue** allows us to do this. When the keyword **continue** is encountered inside any C loop, control automatically passes to the beginning of the loop.

A **continue** is usually associated with an **if**. As an example, let's consider the following program.

```
main( )
{
    int i, j ;

    for ( i = 1 ; i <= 2 ; i++ )
    {
        for ( j = 1 ; j <= 2 ; j++ )
        {
            if ( i == j )
                continue ;

            printf ( "\n%d %d\n", i, j ) ;
        }
    }
}
```

The output of the above program would be...

1 2
2 1

Note that when the value of **i** equals that of **j**, the **continue** statement takes the control to the **for** loop (inner) bypassing rest of the statements pending execution in the **for** loop (inner).

The *do-while* Loop

The **do-while** loop looks like this:

```
do
{
    this ;
    and this ;
    and this ;
    and this ;
} while ( this condition is true ) ;
```

There is a minor difference between the working of **while** and **do-while** loops. This difference is the place where the condition is tested. The **while** tests the condition before executing any of the statements within the **while** loop. As against this, the **do-while** tests the condition after having executed the statements within the loop.

This means that **do-while** would execute its statements at least once, even if the condition fails for the first time itself. The **while**, on the other hand will not execute its statements if the condition fails for the first time. This difference is brought about more clearly by the following program.

```
main( )
{
    while ( 4 < 1 )
        printf ( "Hello there \n") ;
}
```

Here, since the condition fails for the first time itself the **printf( )** will not get executed at all. Let's now write the same program using a **do-while** loop.

```
main( )
{
    do
    {
        printf ( "Hello there \n") ;
    } while ( 4 < 1 ) ;
}
```

In this program the **printf( )** would be executed once, since first the body of the loop is executed and then the condition is tested.

Apart from this peculiarity of the **do-while**, the **while** and **do-while** behave exactly identically. **do-while** loops are rarely used in C programs, since there are comparatively fewer occasions when we want to execute a loop at least once no matter what.

break and **continue** are used with **do-while** just as they would be in a **while** or a **for** loop. A **break** takes you out of the **do- while** bypassing the conditional test. A **continue** sends you straight to the test at the end of the loop. Figure 3.5 would clarify the execution of **do-while** loop still further.

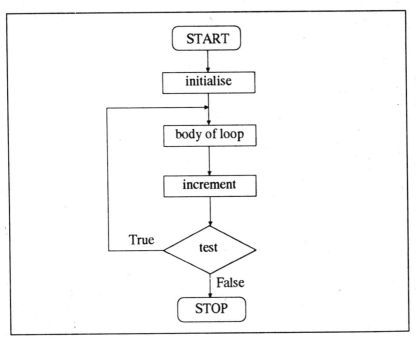

Figure 3.5

Summary

This chapter has focussed on three types of loops available in C: **for**, **while**, and **do-while**. You have learnt how to create and use them in a variety of situations. You have also learnt how to nest one loop inside another, how to write multiple statements inside a loop, how to **break** out of a loop and how to **continue** working within the loop. You have also added to your operators kit-bag a few useful operators which make writing of loops a little more compact. In short you are ready to do things again and again... and yet again.

Exercise

while Loop

[A]   What will be the output of the following programs:

(a)   main( )
       {
           int j ;
           while (j <= 10)
           {
               printf ("\n%d", j) ;
               j = j + 1 ;
           }
       }

(b)   main( )
       {
           int i = 1 ;
           while (i <= 10) ;
           {
               printf ("\n%d", i) ;
               i++ ;
           }
       }

(c)   main( )
       {
           int j ;
           while (j <= 10)
           {
               printf ("\n%d", j) ;
               j = j + 1 ;
           }
       }

(d)   main( )
```
{
    int x = 1 ;
    while ( x == 1 )
    {
        x = x - 1 ;
        printf ( "\n%d", x ) ;
    }
}
```

(e)   main( )
```
{
    int x = 1 ;
    while ( x == 1 )
        x = x - 1 ;
    printf ( "\n%d", x ) ;
}
```

(f)   main( )
```
{
    char x ;
    while ( x = 0 ; x <= 255 ; x++ )
        printf ( "\nAscii value %d Character %c", x, x ) ;
}
```

(g)   main( )
```
{
    int x = 4, y, z ;
    y = --x ;
    z = x-- ;
    printf ( "\n%d %d %d", x, y, z ) ;
}
```

(h)   main( )
```
{
    int x = 4, y = 3, z ;
```

```
        z = x-- -y ;
        printf ( "\n%d %d %d", x, y, z ) ;
    }
```

(i)   main( )
```
    {
        while ( 'a' < 'b' )
            printf ( "\nmalyalam is a palindrome" ) ;
    }
```

(j)   main( )
```
    {
        int i = 10 ;
        while ( i = 20 )
            printf ( "\nA computer buff!" ) ;
    }
```

[B]   Pick the odd one out:

1. a = a + 1 ;
2. a += 1 ;
3. a++ ;
4. a =+ 1 ;

[C]   Attempt the following:

(a)   Write a program to calculate overtime pay of 10 employees. Overtime is paid at the rate of Rs. 12.00 per hour for every hour worked above 40 hours. Assume that employees do not work for fractional part of an hour.

(b)   Write a program to find the factorial value of any number entered through the keyboard.

(c)   Two numbers are entered through the keyboard. Write a program to find the value of one number raised to the power of another.

(d)   Write a program to print all the ascii values and their equivalent characters using a **while** loop. The ascii values vary from 0 to 255.

(e)   Write a program to print out all Armstrong numbers between 1 and 500. If sum of cubes of each digit of the number is equal to the number itself, then the number is called an Armstrong number. For example, $153 = (1 * 1 * 1) + (5 * 5 * 5) + (3 * 3 * 3)$.

(f)   Write a program for a match-stick game between the computer and a user. Your program should ensure that the computer always wins. Rules for the game are as follows:

-   There are 21 match-sticks.
-   The computer asks the player to pick 1, 2, 3, or 4 match-sticks.
-   After the person picks, the computer does its picking.
-   Whoever is forced to pick up the last match-stick loses the game.

for, break, continue, do-while

[D]   What will be the output of the following programs:

(a)   ```
main( )
{
    int i = 0 ;
    for (; i ;)
        printf ("\nHere is some mail for you") ;
}
```

(b)    ```
main( )
{
    int i ;
    for ( i = 1 ; i <= 5 ; printf ( "\n%d", i ) ) ;
        i++ ;
```

```
        }

(c)     main( )
        {
            int i = 1, j = 1 ;
            for ( ;; )
            {
                if ( i > 5 )
                    break ;
                else
                    j += i ;
                printf ( "\n%d", j ) ;
                i += j ;
            }
        }
```

[E]   Answer the following:

(a)   The three parts of the loop expression in the **for** loop are:

       the i_____ expression
       the t_____ expression
       the i_____ expression

(b)   An expression contains relational operators, assignment
       operators, and arithmetic operators. In the absence of paren-
       theses, they will be evaluated in which of the following order:

       1.   assignment, relational, arithmetic
       2.   arithmetic, relational, assignment
       3.   relational, arithmetic, assignment
       4.   assignment, arithmetic, relational

(c)   The **break** statement is used to exit from:

       1.   an **if** statement
       2.   a **for** loop

    3. a program

    4. the **main( )** function

(d)   A **do-while** loop is useful when we want that the statements within the loop must be executed:

    1. Only once

    2. Atleast once

    3. More than once

    4. None of the above

[F]   Attempt the following:

(a)   Write a program to print all prime numbers from 1 to **300**. (Hint: Use nested loops, **break** and **continue**)

(b)   Write a program to fill the entire screen with a smiling face. The smiling face has an ascii value 1.

(c)   Write a program to add first seven terms of the following series using **for** loop:

$$\frac{1}{1!} + \frac{2}{2!} + \frac{3}{3!} + \ ......$$

(d)   Write a program to produce the following output:

```
A  B  C  D  E  F  G  F  E  D  C  B  A
A  B  C  D  E  F     F  E  D  C  B  A
A  B  C  D  E           E  D  C  B  A
A  B  C  D                 D  C  B  A
A  B  C                       C  B  A
A  B                             B  A
A                                   A
```

(e)   Write a program to generate all combinations of 1, 2 and 3 using **for** loop.

(f)   According to a study, the approximate level of intelligence of a person can be calculated using the following formula:

$$i = 2 + (y + 0.5x)$$

Write a program, which will produce a table of values of **i**, **y** and **x**, where **y** varies from 1 to 6, and, for each value of **y**, **x** varies from 5.5 to 12.5 in steps of 0.5.

4 *The Case Control Structure*

I n real life we are often faced with situations where we are required to make a choice between a number of alternatives rather than only one or two. For example, which school to join or which hotel to visit or still harder which girl to marry (you almost always end up making a wrong decision is a different matter altogether!). Serious C programming is same; the choice we are asked to make is more complicated than merely selecting between two alternatives. C provides a special control statement that allows us to handle such cases effectively; rather than using a series of **if** statements. This control instruction is infact the topic of this chapter. Towards the end of the chapter we would also study a keyword called **goto**, and understand why we should avoid its usage in C programming.

Decisions Using *switch*

The control statement which allows us to make a decision from the number of choices is called a **switch**, or more correctly a **switch-case-default**, since these three keywords go together to make up the control statement. They most often appear as follows:

```
switch ( integer expression )
{
    case constant 1 :
        do this ;
    case constant 2 :
        do this ;
    case constant 3 :
        do this ;
    default :
        do this ;
}
```

The integer expression following the keyword **switch** is any C expression that will yield an integer value. It could be an integer constant like 1, 2 or 3, or an expression that evaluates to an integer.

The keyword **case** is followed by an integer or a character constant. Each constant in each **case** must be different from all the others. The "do this" lines in the above form of **switch** represent any valid C statement.

What happens when we run a program containing a **switch**? First, the integer expression following the keyword **switch** is evaluated. The value it gives is then matched, one by one, against the constant values that follow the **case** statements. When a match is found, the program executes the statements following that **case**, and all subsequent **case** and **default** statements as well. If no match is found with any of the **case** statements, only the statements following the **default** are executed. A few examples will show how this control structure works.

Consider the following program:

```
main( )
{
    int i = 2 ;

    switch ( i )
    {
        case 1 :
            printf ( "I am in case 1 \n" ) ;
        case 2 :
            printf ( "I am in case 2 \n" ) ;
        case 3 :
            printf ( "I am in case 3 \n" ) ;
        default :
            printf ( "I am in default \n" ) ;
    }
}
```

The output of this program would be:

```
I am in case 2
I am in case 3
```

I am in default

Definitely not what we expected. We didn't expect the second and third line in the above output. The program prints cases 2 and 3 and the default case. Well, yes. We said the **switch** executes the case where a match is found and all the subsequent **cases** and the **default** as well.

If you want that only case 2 should be executed, it is upto you to get out of the control structure then and there by using a **break** statement. The following example shows how this is done. Note that there is no need for a **break** statement after the **default**, since the control comes to the end anyway.

```
main( )
{
    int i = 2 ;

    switch ( i )
    {
        case 1 :
            printf ( "I am in case 1 \n" ) ;
            break ;
        case 2 :
            printf ( "I am in case 2 \n" ) ;
            break ;
        case 3 :
            printf ( "I am in case 3 \n" ) ;
            break ;
        default :
            printf ( "I am in default \n" ) ;
    }
}
```

The output of this program would be:

I am in case 2

The operation of **switch** is shown below in the form of a flowchart for a better understanding.

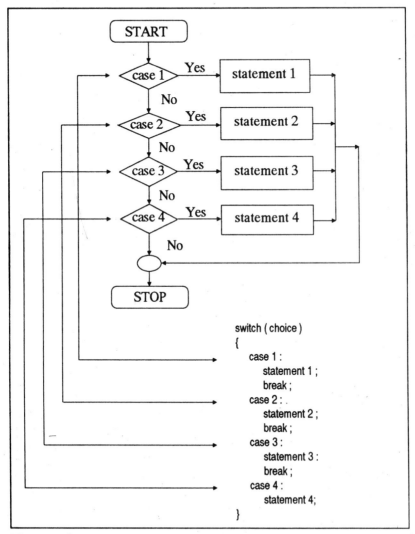

Figure 4.1

The Tips and Traps

A few useful tips about the usage of **switch** and a few pitfalls to be avoided:

(a)   The earlier program which used **switch** may give you the wrong impression that you can use only cases arranged in ascending order, 1, 2, 3 and default. You can in fact put the cases in any order you please. Here is an example of scrambled case order:

```
main( )
{
    int i = 22 ;

    switch ( i )
    {
        case 121 :
            printf ( "I am in case 121 \n" ) ;
            break ;
        case 7 :
            printf ( "I am in case 7 \n" ) ;
            break ;
        case 22 :
            printf ( "I am in case 22 \n" ) ;
            break ;
        default :
            printf ( "I am in default \n" ) ;
    }
}
```

The output of this program would be:

I am in case 22

(b)   You are also allowed to use **char** values in **case** and **switch** as shown in the following program:

```
main( )
{
    char c = 'x' ;

    switch ( c )
    {
        case 'v' :
            printf ( "I am in case v \n" ) ;
            break ;
        case 'a' :
            printf ( "I am in case a \n" ) ;
            break ;
        case 'x' :
            printf ( "I am in case x \n" ) ;
            break ;
        default :
            printf ( "I am in default \n" ) ;
    }
}
```

The output of this program would be:

I am in case x

(c)   We can mix integer and character constants in different **cases**
       of a **switch**.

```
main( )
{
    int c = 3 ;

    switch ( c )
    {
        case 'v' :
            printf ( "I am in case v \n" ) ;
            break ;
        case 3 :
```

```
                printf ( "I am in case 3 \n" ) ;
                break ;
            case 12 :
                printf ( "I am in case 12 \n" ) ;
                break ;
            default :
                printf ( "I am in default \n" ) ;
        }
    }
```

(d) Sometimes there may not be any statement in some of the **cases**
     in **switch**, but still they might turn out to be useful. This is
     shown below with an example.

```
main( )
{
    char ch ;

    printf ( "Enter any of the alphabet a, b, or c" ) ;
    scanf ( "%c", &ch ) ;

    switch ( ch )
    {
        case 'a' :
        case 'A' :
            printf ( "a as in ashar" ) ;
            break ;
        case 'b' :
        case 'B' :
            printf ( "b as in brain" ) ;
            break ;
        case 'c' :
        case 'C' :
            printf ( "c as in cookie" ) ;
            break ;
        default :
            printf ( "wish you knew what are alphabets" ) ;
```

```
        }
    }
```

Here, we are making use of the fact that once a **case** is satisfied the control simply falls through the **case** till it doesn't encounter a **break** statement. That is why if an alphabet **a** is entered the **case 'a'** is satisfied and since there are no statements to be executed in this **case** the control automatically reaches the next **case** i.e. **case 'A'** and executes all the statements in this **case**.

Note that here the order in which the cases are written is important.

(e)   Even if there are multiple statements to be executed in each **case** there is no need to enclose these within a pair of braces (unlike **if**, and **else**).

(f)   If we have no **default** case, then the program simply falls through the entire switch and continues with the next instruction (if any) that follows the control structure.

(g)   Is **switch** a replacement for **if**? Yes and no. Yes, because it offers a better way of writing programs as compared to **if**, and no because in certain situations we are left with no choice but to use **if**.The disadvantage of **switch** is that one cannot have a case in a **switch** which looks like...

```
case i <= 20 :
```

All that we can have after the case is an **int** constant or a **char** constant. Even a **float** is not allowed.

The advantage of **switch** over **if** is that it leads to a more structured program and the level of indentation is manageable, more so if there are multiple statements within each **case** of a **switch**.

(h)   The **break** statement when used in a **switch** takes the control outside the **switch**. However, use of **continue** will not take the control to the beginning of **switch** as one is likely to believe.

(i)   In principle, a **switch** may occur within another, but in practise it is rarely done. Such statements would be called nested **switch** statements.

(j)   The **switch** statement is very useful while writing menu driven programs. This aspect of switch is discussed in the exercise at the end of this chapter.

The *goto* Statement

Avoid **goto** statements! They make a C programmer's life miserable. There is seldom a legitimate reason for using **goto**, and its use is one of the reasons that programs become unreliable, unreadable, and hard to debug. And yet many programmers (especially those using BASIC) find **goto** seductive.

In a difficult programming situation it seems so easy to use a **goto** to take the control where you want to. However, almost always, there is a more elegant way of writing the same program using **if, for, while** and **switch**. These constructs are far more logical and easy to understand.

A **goto** statement can cause program control to end up almost anywhere in the program, for reasons that are often hard to unravel. Trust me, with good programming skills, **goto** can always be avoided. This is the first and last time that we are going to use **goto** in this book.

For sake of completeness of the book, here is how the **goto** is used. Consider the following program.

```
main( )
```

```
{
    int goals ;

    printf ( "Enter the number of goals scored against India" ) ;
    scanf ( "%d", &goals ) ;

    if ( goals <= 5 )
        goto sos ;
    else
    {
        printf ( "About time soccer players learnt C\n" ) ;
        printf ( "and said goodbye! adieu! to soccer" ) ;
        exit( ) ; /* terminates program execution */
    }

    sos:
        printf ( "To err is human!" ) ;
}
```

And here are two sample runs of the program...

```
Enter the number of goals scored against India 3
To err is human!
Enter the number of goals scored against India 7
About time soccer players learnt C
and said goodbye! adieu! to soccer
```

A few remarks about the program would make the things clearer.

- If the condition is satisfied the **goto** statement transfers control to the label 'sos', causing **printf( )** following **sos** to be executed.

- The label can be on a separate line or on the same line as the statement following it, as in,

  ```
  sos: printf ( "To err is human!" ) ;
  ```

- Any number of **goto**'s can take the control to the same label.

- The **exit( )** function is a standard library function which terminates the execution of the program. It is necessary to use this function since we don't want the statement

  ```
  printf ( "To err is human!" ) ;
  ```

  to get executed after execution of the **else** block.

- The big problem with **goto**'s is that when we do use them we can never be sure how we got to a certain point in our code. They obscure the flow of control. So as far as possible skip them. You can always get the job done without them.

- The only programing situation in favour of using **goto** is when we want to take the control out of the loop which is contained in several other loops. The following program illustrates this.

```
main( )
{
    int i, j, k ;

    for ( i = 1 ; i <= 3 ; i++ )
    {
        for ( j = 1 ; j <= 3 ; j++ )
        {
            for ( k = 1 ; k <= 3 ; k++ )
            {
                if ( i == 3 && j == 3 && k == 3 )
                    goto out ;
                else
                    printf ( "%d %d %d\n", i, j, k ) ;
            }
        }
    }
    out:
```

```
        printf ( "Out of the loop at last!" ) ;
}
```

Go through the program carefully and find out how it works. Also write down the same program without using **goto**.

Summary

This was a short chapter which made our knowledge of control instructions complete. Now you know how a **switch** works and while making decisions when to use **switch** and when to use **if**. Finally, you learnt about **goto** and why it should be avoided like plague. Armed with the basic knowledge of data types and control instructions, we are now prepared to explore more sophisticated feaures of C.

Exercise

[A]   What will be the output of the following programs:

(a)
```
main( )
{
    char suite = 3 ;
    switch ( suite )
    {
        case 1 :
            printf ( "\nDiamond" ) ;
        case 2 :
            printf ( "\nSpade" ) ;
        default :
            printf ( "\nHeart") ;
    }
    printf ( "\nI thought one wears a suite" ) ;
}
```

(b)   main( )

```
    {
        int k, j = 2 ;
        switch ( k = j + 1 )
        {
            case 0 :
                printf ( "\nTailor") ;
            case 1 :
                printf ( "\nTutor") ;
            case 2 :
                printf ( "\nTramp") ;
            default :
                printf ( "\nPure Simple Egghead!") ;
        }
    }

(c)    main( )
    {
        int i = 0 ;
        switch ( i )
        {
            case 0 :
                printf ( "\nTemple is a non-issue" ) ;
            case 1 :
                printf ( "\nAandhi is never stable" ) ;
            case 2 :
                printf ( "\nMandal will ruin India" ) ;
            case 3 :
                printf ( "\nWe want better politicians" ) ;
        }
    }

(d)    main( )
    {
        char ch = 'a' ;
        switch ( ch )
        {
            case 'a' :
```

```
            case 'b' :
                printf ( "\nYou entered b" ) ;
            case 'A' :
                printf ( "\na as in ashar" ) ;
        }
    }
```

(e)
```
main( )
{
    char i = '1' ;
    switch ( i )
    {
        case 0 :
            printf ( "\nFeeding fish" ) ;
        case 1 :
            printf ( "\nWeeding grass" ) ;
        case 2 :
            printf ( "\nmending roof" ) ;
        default :
            printf ( "\nJust to survive" ) ;
    }
}
```

[B]   Point out the errors, if any, in the following programs:

(a)
```
main( )
{
    int suite = 1 ;
    switch ( suite ) ;
    {
        case 0 ;
            printf ( "\nClub" ) ;
        case 1 ;
            printf ( "\nDiamond" ) ;
    }
}
```

(b)   main( )
```
main( )
{
    int temp ;
    scanf ( "%d", &temp ) ;
    switch ( temp )
    {
        case ( temp <= 20 ) :
            printf ( "\nOoooooohhhh! Damn cool!" ) ;
        case ( temp > 20 && temp <= 30 ) :
            printf ( "\nRain rain here again!" ) ;
        case ( temp > 30 && temp <= 40 ) :
            printf ( "\nWish I am at Everest" ) ;
        default :
            printf ( "\nGood old nagpur weather" ) ;
    }
}
```

(c)   main( )
```
main( )
{
    float a = 3.5 ;
    switch ( a )
    {
        case 0.5 :
            printf ( "\nThe art of C" ) ;
            break ;
        case 1.5 :
            printf ( "\nThe spirit of C" ) ;
            break ;
        case 2.5 :
            printf ( "\nSee through C" ) ;
            break ;
        case 3.5 :
            printf ( "\nSimply c" ) ;
    }
}
```

[C]   Write a menu driven program which has following options:

1. Factorial of a number
2. Prime or not
3. Odd or even
4. Exit

Make use of **switch** statement.

The outline of this program is given below:

```
/* A menu driven program */
main( )
{
    int choice ;
    while ( 1 )
    {
        printf ( "\n1. Factorial" ) ;
        printf ( "\n2. Prime" ) ;
        printf ( "\n3. Odd/Even" ) ;
        printf ( "\n4. Exit" ) ;
        printf ( "\nYour choice? " ) ;
        scanf ( "%d", &choice ) ;

        switch ( choice )
        {
            case 1 :
                /* logic for factorial of a number  */
                break ;
            case 2 :
                /* logic for deciding prime number */
                break ;
            case 3 :
                /* logic for odd/even */
                break ;
            case 4 :
                exit( ) ;
        }
    }
}
```

```
}
```

Note the following points :

(a) The statement **while** (1) puts the entire logic in an indefinite loop. This is necessary since the menu must keep reappearing on the screen once an item is selected and the appropriate action taken.

(b) **exit( )** is a standard library function. When it gets executed the program execution is immediately terminated. Note that a **break** would not have worked here because it would have taken the control only outside the **switch** and not outside the **while**.

5   *Functions*

Knowingly or unknowingly we rely on so many persons for so many things. Man is an intelligent species, but still cannot perform all of life's tasks all alone. He has to rely on others. You may call a mechanic to fix up your bike, hire a gardener to mow your lawn, or rely on a store to supply you groceries every month. A computer program (except for the simplest one) finds itself in a similar situation. It cannot handle all the tasks by itself. Instead, it requests other programlike entities - called 'functions' in C - to get its tasks done. In this chapter we will study these functions. We will look at a variety of features of these functions, starting with the simplest one and then working towards those which demonstrate the virility of C functions.

What is a Function

A function is a self-contained block of statements that perform a coherent task of some kind. Every C program can be thought of as a collection of these functions. As we noted earlier, using a function is something like hiring a person to do a specific job for you. Sometimes the interaction with this person is very simple; sometimes it's complex.

Suppose you have a task which is always performed exactly in the same way... say a bimonthly servicing of your motorbike. When you want it to be done, you go to the service station and say, "It's time, do it now". You don't need to give instructions, because the mechanic knows his job. You don't need to be told when the job is done. You assume the bike would be serviced in the usual way, the mechanic does it and that's that.

Let us now look at a simple C function which operates in much the same way as the mechanic. Actually, we will be looking at two things: a program that calls or activates the function and the function itself.

```
main( )
{
```

```
        message( ) ;
        printf ( "\nCry, and you stop the monotony!" ) ;
}
message( )
{
        printf ( "\nSmile, and the world smiles with you..." ) ;
}
```

And here's the output...

```
Smile, and the world smiles with you...
Cry, and you stop the monotony!
```

Here, through **main( )** we are calling the function **message( )**. What do we mean when we say that **main( )** 'calls' the function **message( )**? We mean that the control passes to the function **message( )**. The activity of **main( )** is temporarily suspended; it falls asleep while the **message( )** function wakes up and goes to work. When the **message( )** function runs out of statements to execute, the control returns to **main( )**, which comes to life again and begins executing its code at the exact point where it left off. Thus, **main( )** becomes the 'calling' function, whereas **message( )** becomes the 'called' function.

Looking at the function **message( )** now we can specify the general form of a function. Here it is...

```
function ( arg1, arg2, arg3 )
type arg1, arg2, arg3 ;
{
        statement 1 ;
        statement 2 ;
        statement 3 ;
        statement 4 ;
}
```

Though the function **message( )** didn't have any arguments within the pair of parentheses, some functions may have them. If the arguments are present, before beginning with the statements in the functions it is necessary to declare the type of the arguments through type declaration statements.

We would discuss these arguments later in the chapter. Before that let us spend some more time on simpler functions which do not have arguments. If you have grasped the concept of 'calling' a function you are prepared for a call to more than one functions. Consider the following example:

```
main( )
{
    printf ( "\nI am in main" ) ;
    italy( ) ;
    brazil( ) ;
    argentina( ) ;
}
italy( )
{
    printf ( "\nI am in italy" ) ;
}
brazil( )
{
    printf ( "\nI am in brazil" ) ;
}
argentina( )
{
    printf ( "\nI am in argentina" ) ;
}
```

The output of the above program when executed would be as under:

```
I am in main
I am in italy
I am in brazil
I am in argentina
```

From this program a number of conclusions can be drawn:

- Any C program contains at least one function.

- If a program contains only one function, it must be **main( )**.

- In a C program if there are more than one functions present, then one (and only one) of these functions must be **main( )**, because program execution always begins with **main( )**.

- There is no limit on the number of functions that might be present in a C program.

- Each function in a program is called in the sequence specified by the function calls in **main( )**.

- After each function has done its thing, control returns to **main( )**.When **main( )** runs out of function calls, the program ends.

As we have noted earlier the program execution always begins with **main( )**. Except for this fact all C functions enjoy a state of perfect equality. No precedences, no priorities, nobody is nobody's boss. One function can call another function it has already called but has in the meantime left temporarily in order to call a third function which will sometime later call the function that has called it, if you understand what I mean. No? Well, let's illustrate with an example.

```
main( )
{
    printf ( "\nI am in main" ) ;
    italy( ) ;
    printf ( "\nI am finally back in main" ) ;
}
italy( )
{
    printf ( "\nI am in italy" ) ;
```

```
      brazil( ) ;
      printf ( "\nl am back in italy" ) ;
}
brazil( )
{
      printf ( "\nl am in brazil" ) ;
      argentina( ) ;
}
argentina( )
{
      printf ( "\nl am in argentina" ) ;
}
```

And the output would look like...

```
I am in main
I am in italy
I am in brazil
I am in argentina
I am back in italy
I am finally back in main
```

Here, **main( )** calls other functions, which in turn call still other functions. Trace carefully the way control passes from one function to another. Since the compiler always begins the program execution with **main( )**, every function in a program must be called directly or indirectly by **main( )**. In other words, the **main( )** function drives other functions.

Let us now summarise what we have learnt so far.

(a)   C program is a collection of one or more functions.

(b)   A funcion gets called when the function name is followed by a semicolon. For example,

```
main( )
{
```

```
        argentina( ) ;
}
```

(c)   A function is defined when function name is followed by a pair
       of braces in which one or more statements my be present. For
       example,

```
argentina( )
{
    statement 1 ;
    statement 2 ;
    statement 3 ;
}
```

(d)   Any function can be called from any other function. Even
       main( ) can be called from other functions. For example,

```
main( )
{
    message( ) ;
}
message( )
{
    printf ( "\nCan't imagine life without C" ) ;
    main( ) ;
}
```

(e)   A function can be called any number of times. For example,

```
main( )
{
    message( ) ;
    message( ) ;
}
message( )
{
    printf ( "\nJewel Thief!!" ) ;
```

```
}
```

(f)   The order in which the functions are defined in a program and
        the order in which they get called need not necessarily be same.
        For example,

```
main( )
{
     message1( ) ;
     message2( ) ;
}
message2( )
{
     printf ( "\nBut the butter was bitter" ) ;
}
message1( )
{
     printf ( "\nMary bought some butter" ) ;
}
```

Here, even though **message1( )** is getting called before **message2( )**, still, **message1()** has been defined after **message2( )**. However, it is advisable to define the functions in the same order in which they are called. This makes the program easier to understand.

(g)   A function can call itself. Such a process is called 'recursion'. We would discuss this aspect of C functions later in this chapter.

(h)   A function can be called from other function, but a function cannot be defined in another function. Thus, the following program code would be wrong, since **argentina( )** is being defined inside another function, **main( )**.

```
main( )
{
```

```
        printf ( "\nI am in main" ) ;
        argentina( )
        {
            printf ( "\nI am in argentina" ) ;
        }
    }
```

(i)   There are basically two types of functions:

Library functions Ex. **printf( )**, **scanf( )** etc.
User defined functions Ex. **argentina( )**, **brazil( )** etc.

As the name suggests, library functions are nothing but commonly required functions grouped together and stored in what is called a Library. This library of functions is present on the disk and is written for us by people who write compilers for us. Almost always a compiler comes with a library of standard functions. The procedure of calling both types of functions is exactly same.

Why Use Functions

Why write separate functions at all? Why not squeeze the entire logic into one function, **main( )**? Two reasons:

(a)   Writing functions avoids rewriting the same code over and over. Suppose you have a section of code in your program that calculates area of a triangle. If, later in the program, you want to calculate the area of a different triangle, you won't like it if you are required to write the same instructions all over again. Instead, you would prefer to jump to a 'section of code' that calculates area and then jump back to the place from where you left off. This section of code is nothing but a function.

(b)   Using functions it becomes easier to write programs and keep track of what they are doing. If the operation of a program can be divided into separate activities, and each activity placed in a different function, then each could be written and checked more or less independently. Separating the code into modular functions also makes the program easier to design and understand.

What is the moral of the story? Don't try to cram the entire logic in one function. It is a very bad style of programming. Instead, break a program into small units and write functions for each of these isolated subdivisions. Don't hesitate to write functions that are called only once. What is important is that these functions perform some logically isolated task.

Passing Values between Functions

The functions that we have used so far haven't been very flexible. We call them and they do what they are designed to do. Like our mechanic who always services the motor-bike in exactly the same way, we haven't been able to influence the functions in the way they carry out their tasks. It would be nice to have a little more control over what functions do, in the same way it would be nice to be able to tell the mechanic, "Also change the engine oil, I am going for an outing". In short, now we want to communicate between the 'calling' and the 'called' functions.

The mechanism used to convey information to the function is the 'argument'. You have unknowingly used the arguments in the **printf( )** and **scanf( )** functions; the format string and the list of variables used inside the parentheses in these functions are arguments. The arguments are sometimes also called 'parameters'.

Consider the following program. In this program, in **main( )** we receive the values of **a, b** and **c** through the keyboard and then output the sum of **a, b** and **c**. However, the calculation of sum is done in a different function called **calsum( )**. If sum is to be calculated in **calsum( )** and values of **a, b** and **c** are received in **main( )**, then we must pass on these values to **calsum( )**, and once **calsum( )** calculates the sum we must return it from **calsum( )** back to **main( )**.

```
/* Sending and receiving values between functions */
main( )
{
    int a, b, c, sum ;

    printf ( "\nEnter any three numbers " ) ;
    scanf ( "%d %d %d", &a, &b, &c ) ;

    sum = calsum ( a, b, c ) ;

    printf ( "\nSum = %d", sum ) ;
}

calsum ( x, y, z )
int x, y, z ;
{
    int d ;

    d = x + y + z ;
    return ( d ) ;
}
```

And here is the output...

```
Enter any three numbers 10 20 30
Sum = 60
```

There are a number of things to note about this program:

(a)   In this program, from the function **main( )** the values of **a, b** and **c** are passed on to the function **calsum( )**, by making a call to the function **calsum( )** and mentioning **a, b** and **c** in the parentheses:

```
sum = calsum ( a, b, c ) ;
```

In the **calsum( )** function these values get collected in three variables **x, y** and **z**:

```
calsum ( x, y, z )
int x, y, z ;
```

(b) The variables **a, b** and **c** are called 'actual arguments', whereas the variables **x, y** and **z** are called 'formal arguments'. Any number of arguments can be passed to a function being called. However, the type, order and number of the actual and formal arguments must always be same.

Instead of using different variable names **x, y** and **z**, we could have used the same variable names **a, b** and **c**. But the compiler would still treat them as different variables since they are in different functions.

(c) There are two methods of declaring the formal arguments. The one that we have used in our program is known as Kernighan and Ritchie (or just K & R) method.

```
calsum ( x, y, z )
int x, y, z ;
```

Another method is,

```
calsum ( int x, int y, int z )
```

This method is more commonly used these days.

(d) In the earlier programs the moment closing brace (}) of the called function was encountered the control returned to the calling function. No separate **return** statement was necessary to send back the control.

This approach is fine if the called function is not going to return any meaningful value to the calling function. In the above program, however, we want to return the sum of **x, y** and **z.** Therefore, it is necessary to use the **return** statement.

The **return** statement serves two purposes:

(1) On executing the **return** statement it immediately transfers the control back to the calling program.
(2) It returns the value present in the parentheses after **return,** to the calling program. In the above program the value of sum of three numbers is being returned.

(e) There is no restriction on the number of **return** statements that may be present in a function. Also, the **return** statement need not always be present at the end of the called function. The following program illustrates these facts.

```
fun( )
{
    char ch ;

    printf ( "\nEnter any alphabet " ) ;
    scanf ( "%c", &ch ) ;

    if ( ch >= 65 && ch <= 90 )
        return ( ch ) ;
    else
        return ( ch + 32 ) ;
}
```

In this function different **return** statements will be executed depending on whether **ch** is capital or not.

(f) Whenever the control returns from a function some value is definitely returned. If a meaningful value is returned then it should be accepted in the calling program by equating the called function to some variable. For example,

```
sum = calsum ( a, b, c ) ;
```

(g) All the following are valid **return** statements.

```
return ( a ) ;
return ( 23 ) ;
return ( 12.34 ) ;
return ;
```

In the last statement a garbage value is returned to the calling function since we are not returning any specific value. Note that in this case the parentheses after **return** are dropped.

(h) If we want that a called function should not return any value, in that case, we must mention so by using the keyword **void** as shown below.

```
void display( )
{
    printf ( "\nHeads I win..." ) ;
    printf ( "\nTails you lose" ) ;
}
```

(i) A function can return only one value at a time. Thus, the following statements are invalid.

```
return ( a, b ) ;
return ( x, 12 ) ;
```

There is a way to get around this limitation, which would be discussed later in this chapter when we learn pointers.

(j)   If the value of a formal argument is changed in the called function, the corresponding change does not take place in the calling function. For example,

```
main( )
{
    int a = 30 ;
    fun ( a ) ;
    printf ( "\n%d", a ) ;
}

fun ( int b )
{
    b = 60 ;
    printf ( "\n%d", b ) ;
}
```

The ouput of the above program would be:

```
60
30
```

Thus, even though the value of **b** is changed in **fun( )**, the value of **a** in **main( )** remains unchanged. This means that when values are passed to a called function the values present in actual arguments are not physically moved to the formal arguments; just a photocopy of values in actual argument is made into formal arguments.

Scope Rule of Functions

Look at the following program:

```
main( )
{
    int i = 20 ;
```

```
        display ( i ) ;
    }

    display ( int j )
    {
        int k = 35 ;
        printf ( "\n%d", j ) ;
        printf ( "\n%d", k ) ;
    }
```

In this program is it necessary to pass the value of the variable **i** to the function **display( )**? Will it not become automatically available to the function **display( )**? No. Because by default the scope of a variable is local to the function in which it is defined. The presence of **i** is known only to the function **main( )** and not to any other function. Similarly, the variable **k** is local to the function **display( )** and hence it is not available to **main( )**. That is why to make the value of **i** available to **display( )** we have to explicitly pass it to **display( )**. Likewise, if we want **k** to be available to **main( )** we will have to return it to **main( )** using the **return** statement. In general we can say that the scope of a variable is local to the function in which it is defined.

Advanced Features of Functions

With a sound basis of the preliminaries of C functions, let us now get into their intricacies. Following advanced topics would be considered here.

(a)   Function Declaration and Prototypes
(b)   Calling functions by value or by reference
(c)   Recursion

Let us understand these features one by one.

Function Declaration and Prototypes

Any C function by default returns an **int** value. More specifically, whenever a call is made to a function, the compiler assumes that this function would return a value of the type **int**. If we desire that a function should return a value other than an **int**, then it is necessary to explicitly mention so in the calling function as well as in the called function. Suppose we want to find out square of a number using a function. This is how this simple program would look like:

```
main( )
{
    float a, b ;

    printf ( "\nEnter any number " ) ;
    scanf ( "%f", &a ) ;

    b = square ( a ) ;
    printf ( "\nSquare of %f is %f", a, b ) ;
}

square ( float x )
{
    float y ;

    y = x * x ;
    return ( y ) ;
}
```

And here are three sample runs of this program...

```
Enter any number 3
Square of 3 is 9.000000
Enter any number 1.5
Square of 1.5 is 2.000000
Enter any number 2.5
Square of 2.5 is 6.000000
```

The first of these answers is correct. But square of 1.5 is definitely not 2. Neither is 4 a square of 2.5. This happened because **any** C function, by default, always returns an integer value. Therefore, **even** though the function **square( )** calculates the square of 1.5 as 2.25, the problem crops up when this 2.25 is to be returned to **main( )**. **square( )** is not capable of returning a **float** value. How do we overcome this? The following program segment illustrates how to make **square( )** capable of returning a **float** value.

```
main( )
{
    float square( ) ;
    float a, b ;

    printf ( "\nEnter any number " ) ;
    scanf ( "%f", &a ) ;

    b = square ( a ) ;
    printf ( "\nSquare of %f is %f", a, b ) ;
}

float square ( float x )
{
    float y ;

    y = x * x ;
    return ( y ) ;
}
```

And here is the output...

```
Enter any number 1.5
Square of 1.5 is 2.250000
Enter any number 2.5
Square of 2.5 is 6.250000
```

Now the expected answers i.e. 2.25 and 6.25 are obtained. Note that the function **square( )** must be declared as **float** in **main( )** as well. The statement **float square( )** means that it is a function which will return a **float** value.

In practice you may seldom be required to return a value other than an **int**, but just in case you are required to, employ the above method. In some programming situations we want that a called function should not return any value. This is made possible by making use of the keyword **void**. This is illustrated in the following program.

```
main( )
{
    void gospel( ) ;
    gospel( ) ;
}

void gospel( )
{
    printf ( "\nViruses are electronic bandits..." ) ;
    printf ( "\nwho eat nuggets of information..." ) ;
    printf ( "\nand chunks of bytes..." ) ;
    printf ( "\nwhen you least expect..." ) ;
}
```

Here, the **gospel( )** function has been defined to return **void**; means it would return nothing. Therefore, it would just flash the four messages about viruses and return the control back to the **main( )** function.

Call by Value and Call by Reference

By now we are well familiar with how to call functions. But, if you observe carefully, whenever we called a function and passed something to it we have always passed the 'values' of variables to the called function. Such function calls are called 'calls by value'. By this what we mean is, on calling a function we are passing values of variables to it. The examples of call by value are shown below:

```
sum = calsum ( a, b, c ) ;
f = factr ( a ) ;
```

We have also learnt that variables are stored somewhere in memory. So instead of passing the value of a variable, can we not pass the location number (also called address) of the variable to a function? If we are able to do so it would become a 'call by reference'. What purpose a 'call by reference' serves we would find out a little later. First we must equip ourselves with knowledge of how to make a 'call by reference'. This feature of C functions needs atleast an elementary knowledge of 'pointers'. So let us first acquire the basics of pointers after which we would take up this topic once again.

An Introduction to Pointers

Which feature of C do beginners find most difficult to understand? The answer is easy: pointers. Other languages have pointers but few use them so frequently as C does. And why not? It is C's clever use of pointers that makes it the excellent language it is.

The difficulty beginners have with pointers has much to do with C's pointer terminology than the actual concept. For instance, when a C programmer says that a certain variable is a "pointer", what does that mean? It is hard to see how a variable can point to something, or in a certain direction.

It is hard to get a grip on pointers just by listening to programmer's jargon. In our discussion of C pointers, therefore, we will try to avoid this difficulty by explaining pointers in terms of programming concepts we already understand. The first thing we want to do is explain the rationale of C's pointer notation.

Pointer Notation

Consider the declaration,

    int i = 3 ;

This declaration tells the C compiler to:

(a)   Reserve space in memory to hold the integer value.
(b)   Associate the name **i** with this memory location.
(c)   Store the value 3 at this location.

We may represent **i**'s location in memory by the following memory map.

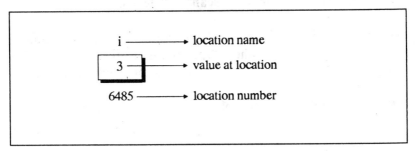

Figure 5.1

We see that the computer has selected memory location 6485 as the place to store the value 3. The location number 6485 is not a number to be relied upon, because some other time the computer may choose a different location for storing the value 3. The important point is, **i**'s address in memory is a number.

We can print this address number through the following program:

```
main( )
{
    int i = 3 ;
    printf ( "\nAddress of i = %u", &i ) ;
```

```
    printf ( "\nValue of i = %d", i ) ;
}
```

The output of the above program would be:

```
Address of i = 6485
Value of i = 3
```

Look at the first **printf( )** statement carefully. '&' used in this statement is C's 'address of' operator. The expression **&i** returns the address of the variable **i**, which in this case happens to be 6485. Since 6485 represents an address, there is no question of a sign being associated with it. Hence it is printed out using **%u**, which is a format specifier for printing an unsigned integer. We have been using the '&' operator all the time in the **scanf( )** statement.

The other pointer operator available in C is '*', called 'value at address' operator. It gives the value stored at a particular address. The 'value at address' operator is also called 'indirection' operator.

Observe carefully the output of the following program:

```
main( )
{
    int i = 3 ;

    printf ( "\nAddress of i = %u", &i ) ;
    printf ( "\nValue of i = %d", i ) ;
    printf ( "\nValue of i = %d", *( &i ) ) ;
}
```

The output of the above program would be:

```
Address of i = 6485
Value of i = 3
Value of i = 3
```

Note that printing the value of ***(&i)** is same as printing the value of **i**.

The expression **&i** gives the address of the variable **i**. This address can be collected in a variable, by saying,

    j = &i ;

But remember that **j** is not an ordinary variable like any other integer variable. It is a variable which contains the address of other variable (**i** in this case).

Since **j** is a variable the compiler must provide it space in the memory. Once again, the following memory map would illustrate the contents of **i** and **j**.

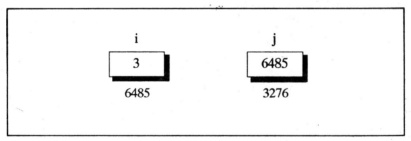

Figure 5.2

As you can see, **i**'s value is 3 and **j**'s value is **i**'s address.

But wait, we can't use **j** in a program without declaring it. And since **j** is a variable which contains the address of **i**, it is declared as,

    int *j ;

This declaration tells the compiler that **j** will be used to store the address of an integer value. In other words **j** points to an integer. How do we justify the usage of ***** in the declaration,

```
int *j ;
```

Let us go by the meaning of *****. It stands for 'value at address' . Thus, **int *j** would mean, the value at the address contained in **j** is an **int**.

Here is a program that demonstrates the relationships we have been discussing.

```
main( )
{
    int i = 3 ;
    int *j ;

    j = &i ;
    printf ( "\nAddress of i = %u", &i ) ;
    printf ( "\nAddress of i = %u", j ) ;
    printf ( "\nAddress of j = %u", &j ) ;
    printf ( "\nValue of j = %u", j ) ;
    printf ( "\nValue of i = %d", i ) ;
    printf ( "\nValue of i = %d", *( &i ) ) ;
    printf ( "\nValue of i = %d", *j ) ;
}
```

The output of the above program would be:

```
Address of i = 6485
Address of i = 6485
Address of j = 3276
Value of j = 6485
Value of i = 3
Value of i = 3
Value of i = 3
```

Work through the above program carefully, taking help of the memory locations of **i** and **j** shown earlier. This program summarises everything that we have discussed so far. If you don't understand the program's output, or the meanings of **&i**, **&j**, ***j** and ***(&i)**, re-read the last few pages. Everything we say about C pointers from here onwards will depend on your understanding these expressions thoroughly.

Look at the following declarations,

```
int *alpha ;
char *ch ;
float *s ;
```

Here, **alpha, ch** and s are declared as pointer variables, i.e. variables capable of holding addresses. Remember that, addresses (location nos.) are always going to be whole numbers, therefore pointers always contain whole numbers. Now we can put these two facts together and say: pointers are variables which contain addresses, and since addresses are always whole numbers, pointers would always contain whole numbers.

The declaration **float *s** does not mean that s is going to contain a floating point value. What it means is, s is going to contain the address of a floating point value. Similarly, **char *ch** means that **ch** is going to contain the address of a char value. Or in other words, the value at address stored in **ch** is going to be a **char.**

The concept of pointers can be further extended. Pointer, we know is a variable which contains address of another variable. Now this variable itself might be another pointer. Thus, we now have a pointer which contains another pointer's address. The following example should make this point clear.

```
main( )
{
    int i = 3, *j, **k ;

    j = &i ;
    k = &j ;
    printf ( "\nAddress of i = %u", &i ) ;
```

```
        printf ( "\nAddress of i = %u", j ) ;
        printf ( "\nAddress of i = %u", *k ) ;
        printf ( "\nAddress of j = %u", &j ) ;
        printf ( "\nAddress of j = %u", k ) ;
        printf ( "\nAddress of k = %u", &k ) ;
        printf ( "\nValue of j  = %u", j ) ;
        printf ( "\nValue of k  = %u", k ) ;
        printf ( "\nValue of i  = %d", i ) ;
        printf ( "\nValue of i  = %d", * ( &i ) ) ;
        printf ( "\nValue of i  = %d", *j ) ;
        printf ( "\nValue of i  = %d", **k ) ;
}
```

The output of the above program would be:

```
        Address of i = 6485
        Address of i = 6485
        Address of i = 6485
        Address of j = 3276
        Address of j = 3276
        Address of k = 7234
        Value of j = 6485
        Value of k = 3276
        Value of i = 3
        Value of i = 3
        Value of i = 3
        Value of i = 3
```

Figure 5.3 would help you in tracing out how the program prints the above output.

Remember that when you run this program the addresses that get printed might turn out to be something different than the ones shown in the figure. However, with these addresses too the relationship between **i**, **j** and **k** can be easily established.

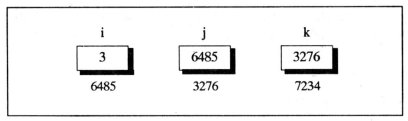

Figure 5.3

Observe how the variables **j** and **k** have been declared,

int i, *j, **k ;

Here, **i** is an ordinary **int**, **j** is a pointer to an **int** (often called an integer pointer), whereas **k** is a pointer to a integer pointer. We can extend the above program still further by creating a pointer to a pointer to an integer pointer. In principle, you would agree that likewise there can exist a pointer to a pointer's pointer's pointer's pointer. There is no limit on how far can we go on extending this definition. Possibly, till the point we can comprehend it. And that point of comprehension is usually a pointer to a pointer. Beyond this one rarely requires to extend the definition of a pointer. But just in case...

Back to Function Calls

Having had the first tryst with pointers let us now get back to what we had originally set out to learn - the two types of function calls: call by value and call by reference. Arguments can generally be passed to functions in one of the two ways:

(a)   sending the values of the arguments
(b)   sending the addresses of the arguments

In the first method the 'value' of each of the actual arguments in the calling function is copied into corresponding formal arguments of the called function. With this method the changes made to the formal arguments in the called function have no effect on the values of actual arguments in the calling function. The following program illustrates the 'Call by Value'.

```
main( )
{
    int a = 10, b = 20 ;

    swapv ( a, b ) ;
    printf ( "\na = %d b = %d", a, b ) ;
}

swapv ( int x, int y )
{
    int t ;

    t = x ;
    x = y ;
    y = t ;

    printf ( "\nx = %d y = %d", x, y ) ;
}
```

The output of the above program would be:

```
x = 20 y = 10
a = 10 b = 20
```

Note that values of **a** and **b** remain unchanged even after exchanging the values of **x** and **y**.

In the second method (call by reference) the addresses of actual arguments in the calling function are copied into formal arguments of the called function. This means that using these addresses we would have an access to the actual arguments and hence we would be able to manipulate them. The following program illustrates this fact.

```
main( )
{
    int a = 10, b = 20 ;

    swapr ( &a, &b ) ;
    printf ( "\na = %d b = %d", a, b ) ;
}

swapr( int *x, int *y )
{
    int t ;

    t = *x ;
    *x = *y ;
    *y = t ;
}
```

The output of the above program would be:

```
a = 20 b = 10
```

Note that this program manages to exchange the values of **a** and **b** using their addresses stored in **x** and **y**.

Usually in C programming we make a call by value. This means in general you cannot alter the actual arguments. But if desired, it can always be achieved through a call by reference.

Using a call by reference intelligently we can make a function return more than one value at a time, which is not possible ordinarily. This is shown in the program given below.

```
main( )
{
    int radius ;
    float area, perimeter ;
```

```
    printf ( "\nEnter radius of a circle " ) ;
    scanf ( "%d", &radius ) ;
    areaperi ( radius, &area, &perimeter ) ;

    printf ( "Area = %f", area ) ;
    printf ( "\nPerimeter = %f", perimeter ) ;
}

areaperi ( int r, float *a, float *p )
{
    *a = 3.14 * r * r ;
    *p = 2 * 3.14 * r ;
}
```

And here is the output...

```
Enter radius of a circle 5
Area = 78.500000
Perimeter = 31.400000
```

Here, we are making a mixed call, in the sense, we are passing the value of **radius** but, addresses of **area** and **perimeter**. And since we are passing the addresses, any change that we make in values stored at addresses contained in the variables **a** and **p,** would make the change effective in **main( )**. That is why when the control returns from the function **areaperi( )** we are able to output the values of **area** and **perimeter.**

Thus, we have been able to return two values from a called function, and hence, have overcome the limitation of the **return** statement, which can return only one value from a function at a time.

Recursion

In C, it is possible for the functions to call themselves. A function is called 'recursive' if a statement within the body of a function calls the same function. Sometimes called 'circular definition', recursion is thus the process of defining something in terms of itself.

A simple example of recursion is the function **rec( )** shown below, which computes the factorial value of an integer. As we know the factorial of a number is the product of all the integers between 1 and that number. For example, 3 factorial is 3 * 2 * 1, or 6. For the sake of understanding let us first look at the non-recursive function for calculating the factorial value of an integer.

```
main( )
{
    int a, fact ;

    printf ( "\nEnter any number " ) ;
    scanf ( "%d", &a ) ;

    fact = factorial ( a ) ;
    printf ( "Factorial value = %d", fact ) ;
}

factorial ( int x )
{
    int f = 1, i ;

    for ( i = x ; i >= 1 ; i-- )
        f = f * i ;

    return ( f ) ;
}
```

And here is the output...

```
Enter any number 3
Factorial value = 6
```

Work through the above program carefully, till you understand the logic of the program properly. Recursive factorial function can be understood only if you are thorough with the above logic.

Following is the recursive version of the function to calculate the factorial value.

```
main( )
{
    int a, fact ;

    printf ( "\nEnter any number " ) ;
    scanf ( "%d", &a ) ;

    fact = rec ( a ) ;
    printf ( "Factorial value = %d", fact ) ;
}

rec ( x )
int x ;
{
    int f ;

    if ( x == 1 )
        return ( 1 ) ;
    else
        f = x * rec ( x - 1 ) ;

    return ( f ) ;
}
```

And here is the output for four runs of the program...

```
Enter any number 1
Factorial value = 1
Enter any number 2
Factorial value = 2
```

```
Enter any number 3
Factorial value = 6
Enter any number 5
Factorial value = 120
```

Let us understand this recursive factorial function thoroughly. In the first run when the number entered through **scanf( )** is 1, let us see what action does **rec( )** takes. The value of **a** (i.e. 1) is copied into **x**. Since **x** turns out to be 1 the condition **if (x == 1)** is satisfied and hence 1 (which indeed is the value of 1 factorial) is returned through the **return** statement.

When the number entered through **scanf( )** is 2, the (**x == 1**) test fails, so we reach the statement,

```
f = x * rec ( x - 1 ) ;
```

And here is where we meet recursion. How do we handle the expression **x * rec (x - 1)**? We multiply **x** by **rec (x - 1)**. Since the current value of **x** is 2, it is same as saying that we must calculate the value (2 * rec (1)). We know that the value returned by **rec (1)** is 1, so the expression reduces to (2 * 1), or simply 2. Thus the statement,

```
x * rec ( x - 1 ) ;
```

evaluates to 2, which is stored in the variable **f**, and is returned to **main( )**, where it is duly printed as

```
Factorial value = 2
```

Now perhaps you can see what would happen if the value of **a** is 3, 4, 5 and so on.

In case the value of **a** is 5, **main( )** would call **rec( )** with 5 as its actual argument, and **rec( )** will send back the computed value. But before sending the computed value, **rec( )** calls **rec( )** and waits for a value to be returned. It is possible for the **rec( )** that has just been called to call yet another **rec( )**, the argument **x** being decreased in value by 1 for each of these recursive calls. We speak of this series of calls to **rec( )** as being different invocations of **rec( )**. These successive invocations of the same function are possible because the C compiler keeps track of which invocation calls which. These recursive invocations end finally when the last invocation gets an argument value of 1, which the preceeding invocation of **rec( )** now uses to calculate its own **f** value and so on up the ladder. So we might say what happens is,

> rec (5) returns (5 times rec (4),
>   which returns (4 times rec (3),
>   which returns (3 times rec (2),
>   which returns (2 times rec (1),
>   which returns (1)))))

Foxed? Well, that is recursion for you in its simplest garbs. I hope you agree that it's difficult to visualise how the control flows from one function call to another. Possibly Figure 5.4 would make the things a bit clearer.

Assume that the number entered through **scanf( )** is 3. Using the figure let's visualise what exactly happens when the recursive function **rec( )** gets called. Go through the figure carefully. The first time when **rec( )** is called from **main( )**, **x** collects 3. From here, since **x** is not equal to 1, the **if** block is skipped and **rec( )** is called again with the argument (**x** - 1), i.e. 2. This is a recursive call. Since **x** is still not equal to 1, **rec( )** is called yet another time, with argument (2 - 1). This time as **x** is 1, control goes back to previous **rec( )** with the value 1, and **f** is evaluated as 2.

Similarly, each **rec( )** evaluates its **f** from the returned value, and finally 6 is returned to main( ). The sequence would be grasped better by following the arrows shown in the figure. Let it be clear that while executing the program there do not exist so many copies of the function **rec( )**. These have been shown in the figure just to help you keep track of how the control flows during successive recursive calls.

```
from main( )
   |
   v
rec ( x )              rec ( x )              rec ( x )
int x ;                int x ;                int x ;
{                      {                      {
   int f ;                int f ;                int f ;

   if ( x == 1)           if ( x == 1)           if ( x == 1)
      return ( 1 ) ;          return ( 1 ) ;     ┌── return ( 1 ) ;
   else                   else                   else
      f = x * rec ( x - 1 ) ;   f = x * rec ( x - 1 ) ;      f = x * rec ( x - 1 ) ;

   return ( f ) ;         return( f ) ;          return ( f ) ;
}                      }                      }

to main ( )
```

Figure 5.4

Recursion may seem strange and complicated at first glance, but it is often the most direct way to code an algorithm - and, once you are familiar with recursion, the clearest way of doing so.

While writing recursive functions you must have an **if** statement somewhere in the recursive function to force the function to return without recursive call being executed. If you don't do this and you call the function, you will fall in an indefinite loop, and will never return from the called function. This is a very common error while writing recursive functions. My advice is to use **printf( )** statement liberally during the development of recursive function, so that you can watch what is going on and can abort execution if you see that you have made a mistake.

A word of advice... some people seem to think recursively more easily than others. If you feel comfortable with recursion, then use it. If you do not, use iterative methods like **for, while** or **do-while**.

Summary

In this chapter you have learnt how to use functions, how to write them, how the functions interact with one another, how to send them information using arguments, and how to use them to return values. You also learnt how to return non-integer values from a function, how recursive functions work and importantly you had your first tryst with the pointers and the pointer notations.

Exercise

Simple functions, Passing values between functions

[A]   What will be the output of the following programs:

(a)   main( )
```
main( )
{
    printf ( "\nOnly stupids use C?" ) ;
    display( ) ;
}
display( )
{
    printf ( "\nFools too use C!" ) ;
    main( ) ;
}
```

(b)   main( )
```
main( )
{
    printf ( "\nC to it that C survives" ) ;
    main( ) ;
}
```

(c)   main( )

```
main( )
{
    int i = 45, c ;
    c = check ( i ) ;
    printf ( "\n%d", c ) ;
}
check ( int ch )
{
    if ( ch >= 45 )
        return ( 100 ) ;
    else
        return ( 10 * 10 ) ;
}
```

(d)   main( )

```
main( )
{
    int i = 45, c ;
    c = multiply ( i * 1000 ) ;
    printf ( "\n%d", c ) ;
j
check ( int ch )
{
    if ( ch >= 40000 )
        return ( ch / 10 ) ;
    else
        return ( 10 ) ;
}
```

[B]   Point out the errors, if any, in the following programs:

(a)   main( )

```
main( )
{
    int i = 3, j = 4, k, l ;
    k = addmult ( i, j ) ;
    l = addmult ( i, j ) ;
```

```
            printf ( "\n%d %d", k, l ) ;
    }
    addmult ( int ii, int jj )
    {
        int kk, ll ;
        kk = ii + jj ;
        ll = ii * jj ;
        return ( kk, ll ) ;
    }
```

(b)
```
    main( )
    {
        int a ;
        a = message( ) ;
    }
    message( )
    {
        printf ( "\nViruses are written in C" ) ;
        return ;
    }
```

(c)
```
    main( )
    {
        float a = 15.5 ;
        char ch = 'C' ;
        printit ( a, ch ) ;
    }
    printit ( a, ch )
    {
        printf ( "\n%f %c", a, ch ) ;
    }
```

(d)
```
    main( )
    {
        message( ) ;
        message( ) ;
```

```
        }
        message( ) ;
        {
            printf ( "\nPraise worthy and C worthy are synonyms" ) ;
        }
```

(e)   main( )
```
       {
           let_us_c( )
           {
               printf ( "\nC is a Cimple minded language !" ) ;
               printf ( "\nOthers are of course no match !" ) ;
           }
       }
```

[C]   Answer the following:

(a)   Is this a correctly written function:

```
       sqr ( a ) ;
       int a ;
       {
           return ( a * a ) ;
       }
```

(b)   State whether the following statements are True or False:

1.   The variables commonly used in C functions are available to all functions in a program.

2.   To return the control back to the calling function we must use the keyword **return**.

3.   The same variable names can used in different functions, without any conflict.

4.   Every called function must contain a **return** statement.

5. A function may contain more than one **return** statements.

6. Each **return** statement in a function may return a different value.

7. A function can still be useful even if you don't pass any arguments to it and the function doesn't return any value back.

[D] Answer the following:

(a) Write a function to calculate the factorial value of any integer entered through the kevboard.

(b) Write a function **power (a, b)**, to calculate the value of **a** raised to **b**.

(c) Write a general purpose function to convert any given year into its roman equivalent. The following table shows the roman equivalents of decimal numbers:

Decimal	Roman	Decimal	Roman
1	i	100	c
5	v	500	d
10	x	1000	m
50	1		

Example:

Roman equivalent of 1988 is mdcccclxxxviii
Roman equivalent of 1525 is mdxxv

(d) Any year is entered through the keyboard. Write a function to determine whether the year is a leap year or not.

(e)   A positive integer is entered through the keyboard. Write a function to obtain the prime factors of this number.

For example, prime factors of 24 are 2, 2, 2 and 3, whereas prime factors of 35 are 5 and 7.

Function Prototypes, Call by Value/Reference, Pointers

[E]   What will be the output of the following programs:

(a)
```
main( )
{
     float area ;
     int radius = 1 ;
     area = circle ( radius ) ;
     printf ( "\n%f", area ) ;
}
circle ( int r )
{
     float a ;
     a = 3.14 * r * r ;
     return ( a ) ;
}
```

(b)
```
main( )
{
     void slogan( ) ;
     int c = 5 ;
     c = slogan( ) ;
     printf ( "\n%d", c ) ;
}
void slogan( )
{
     printf ( "\nOnly He men use C!" ) ;
}
```

[F]   Answer the following:

(a)   Write a function which receives a **float** and an **int** from **main( )**, finds the product of these two and returns the product which is printed through **main( )**.

(b)   Write a function which receives 5 integers and returns the sum, average and standard deviation of these numbers. Call this function from **main( )** and print the results in **main( )**.

[G]   What will be the output of the following programs:

(a)
```
main( )
{
    int i = 5, j = 2 ;
    junk ( i, j ) ;
    printf ( "\n%d %d", i, j ) ;
}
junk ( int i, int j )
{
    i = i * i ;
    j = j * j ;
}
```

(b)
```
main( )
{
    int i = 5, j = 2 ;
    junk ( &i, &j ) ;
    printf ( "\n%d %d", i, j ) ;
}
junk ( int *i, int *j )
{
    *i = *i * *i ;
    *j = *j * *j ;
}
```

(c)
```
main( )
{
```

```
        int i = 4, j = 2 ;
        junk ( &i, j ) ;
        printf ( "\n%d %d", i, j ) ;
    }
    junk ( int *i, int j )
    {
        *i = *i * *i ;
        j = j * j ;
    }
```

(d)   main( )
```
    {
        float a = 13.5 ;
        float *b, *c ;
        b = &a ;  /* suppose address of a is 1006 */
        c = b ;
        printf ( "\n%u %u %u", &a, b, c ) ;
        printf ( "\n%f %f %f %f %f", a, *(&a), *&a, *b, *c ) ;
    }
```

[H]   Point out the errors, if any, in the following programs:

(a)   main( )
```
    {
        int i = 135, a = 135, k ;
        k = pass ( i, a ) ;
        printf ( "\n%d", k ) ;
    }
    pass ( int j, int b )
    int c ;
    {
        c = j + b ;
        return ( c ) ;
    }
```

(b)   main( )

```
    {
        int p = 23, f = 24 ;
        jiaayjo ( &p, &f ) ;
        printf ( "\n%d %d", p, f ) ;
    }
    jiaayjo ( int q, int g )
    {
        q = q + q ;
        g = g + g ;
    }
```

(c)
```
    main( )
    {
        int k = 35, z ;
        z = check ( k ) ;
        printf ( "\n%d", z ) ;
    }
    check ( m )
    {
        int m ;
        if ( m > 40 )
            return ( 1 ) ;
        else
            return ( 0 ) ;
    }
```

(d)
```
    main( )
    {
        int i = 35, *z ;
        z = function ( &i ) ;
        printf ( "\n%d", z ) ;
    }
    function ( int *m )
    {
        return ( m + 2 ) ;
    }
```

[I]   What will be the output of the following programs:

(a)
```
main( )
{
    int i = 0 ;
    i++ ;
    if ( i <= 5 )
    {
        printf ( "\nC adds wings to your thoughts" ) ;
        exit( ) ;
        main( ) ;
    }
}
```

(b)
```
main( )
{
    static int i = 0 ;
    i++ ;
    if ( i <= 5 )
    {
        printf ( "\n%d", i ) ;
        main( ) ;
    }
    else
        exit( ) ;
}
```

[J]   Attempt the following:

(a)   A 5 digit positive integer is entered through the keyboard, write a function to calculate sum of digits of the 5 digit number:

     (1) Without using recursion
     (2) Using recursion

(b)   A positive integer is entered through the keyboard, write a program to obtain the prime factors of the number. Modify the function suitably to obtain the prime factors recursively.

(c)   Write a recursive function to obtain the first 25 numbers of a Fibonacci sequence. In a Fibonacci sequence the sum of two successive terms gives the third term. Following are the first few terms of the Fibonacci sequence:

1 1 2 3 5 8 13 21 34 55 89...

6   *Data Types Revisited*

A s seen in the first chapter the primary data types could be of three varieties: **char**, **int**, and **float**. It may seem odd to many, how C programmers manage with such a tiny set of data types. Fact is, the C programmers aren't really deprived. They can derive any number of data types from these five types. In fact, the number of data types that can be derived in C, is in principle, unlimited. A C programmer can always invent whatever data type he needs.

Not only this, the primary data types themselves could be of several types. For example, a **char** could be an **unsigned char** or a **signed char**. Or an **int** could be a **short int** or a **long int**. Sufficiently confusing? Well, let us take a closer look at these variations of primary data types in this chapter.

To fully define a variable one needs to mention not only its type but also its storage class. In this chapter we would be exploring the different storage classes and their relevance in C programming.

Integers, *long* and *short*

We had seen earlier that an integer constant is any number in the range -32768 to +32767. This is because an integer constant always occupies two bytes in memory and in two bytes we cannot store a number bigger than +32767 or smaller than -32768.

Remember that out of the two bytes used to store an integer, the highest bit (sixteenth bit) is used to store the sign of the integer. This bit is 1 if the number is negative, and 0 if the number is positive. Most of the times C programs can be managed within this generous range, but bigger ranges are available should you need them. C offers a variation of the integer data type that will provide what are called **long** integer values. **long** integers require twice the space in memory than ordinary **int**s do. Thus, **long** integers would occupy four bytes of memory. **long** variables which hold **long** integers are declared using the keyword **long**, as in,

```
long int i ;
long int abc ;
```

long integers cause the program to run a bit slower, but the range of values that we can use is expanded tremendously. The value of a **long** integer can vary from -2147483648 to +2147483647. More than this you should not need unless you are taking a world census.

If there are such things as **long**s, symmetry requires **short**s as well... integers which need less space in memory and thus help speed up program execution. **short** integer variables are declared as,

```
short int j ;
short int height ;
```

In fact, a **short int** is nothing but our ordinary **int**, which we were using all the time without knowing that it was a **short int**. C allows the abbreviation of **short int** to **int** and of **long int** to **long**. So the declarations made above can be written as,

```
long i ;
long abc ;
int j ;
int height ;
```

Naturally, most C programmers prefer this short-cut.

Sometimes we come across situations where the constant is small enough to be an **int**, but still we want to give it as much storage as a **long**. In such cases we add the suffix 'L' or 'l' at the end of the number. Thus 23 is an integer and would occupy two bytes, whereas 23L is a long integer and hence would occupy four bytes.

Integers, *signed* and *unsigned*

Sometimes, we know in advance that the value stored in a given integer variable will always be positive - when it is being used to only count things, for example. In such a case we can declare the variable to be **unsigned**, as in,

> unsigned int num_students ;

With such a declaration, the range of permissible integer values will shift from the range -32768 to +32767 to the range 0 to 65535. Thus, declaring an integer as **unsigned** almost doubles the size of the largest possible value that it can otherwise take. This so happens because on declaring the integer as **unsigned**, the sixteenth bit is now free and is not used to store the sign of the number. Note that an **unsigned** integer still occupies two bytes. In fact an **unsigned int** is nothing but a **short unsigned int**. Thus, all the following declarations are same:

> short unsigned int i ;
> unsigned int i ;
> unsigned i ;

The way there exists a **short unsigned int**, there also exists a **long unsigned int** which has a range of 0 to 4294967295 and occupies four bytes of memory.

By default a **short int** is a **signed short int** and a **long int** is a **signed long int**.

Chars, *signed* and *unsigned*

The way there are **signed** and **unsigned int**s (either **short** or **long**), similarly there are **signed** and **unsigned char**s, both occupying one byte each, but having different ranges. A **signed char** is same as our ordinary **char** and has a range from -128 to +127; whereas an unsigned char has a range from 0 to 255. Let us now see a program that illustrates this range:

```
main( )
{
    char ch = 291 ;
    printf ( "\n%d %c", ch, ch ) ;
}
```

What output do you expect from this program? Possibly, 291 and the character corresponding to it. Well, not really. Surprised? The reason is that ch has been defined as a char, and a char cannot take a value bigger than +127. Hence when value of ch exceeds +127, an appropriate value from the other side of the range is picked up and stored in ch. This value in our case happens to be 35, hence 35 and its corresponding character, #, gets printed out.

Here is another program which would make the concept clearer.

```
main( )
{
    char ch ;

    for ( ch = 0 ; ch <= 255 ; ch++ )
        printf ( "\n%d %c", ch, ch ) ;
}
```

This program should output ascii values and their corresponding characters. Well, No! This is an indefinite loop. The reason is that ch has been defined as a char, and a char cannot take values bigger than +127. Hence when value of ch is +127 and we perform ch++ it becomes -128 instead of +128. -128 is less than 255 hence the condition is still satisfied. Here onwards ch would take values like -127, -126, -125, ... -2, -1, 0, +1, +2, ... +127, -128, -127 etc. Thus the value of ch would keep oscillating between -128 to +127, thereby ensuring that the loop never gets terminated. How do you overcome this difficulty? Would declaring ch as an unsigned char solve the problem? Even this would not serve the purpose since when **ch** reaches a value 255, **ch++** would try to make it 256 which cannot be stored in an **unsigned char**. Thus the only alternative is to declare **ch** as an **int**. However, if we are bent upon writing the program using **unsigned char**, it can be done as shown below. Definitely less elegant, but workable all the same.

```
main( )
{
    unsigned char ch ;

    for ( ch = 0 ; ch <= 254 ; ch++ )
        printf ( "\n%d %c", ch, ch ) ;

    printf ( "\n%d %c", ch, ch ) ;
}
```

Floats and Doubles

A **float** occupies four bytes in memory and can range from -3.4e38 to +3.4e38. If this is insufficient then C offers a **double** data type which occupies 8 bytes in memory and has a range from -1.7e308 to +1.7e308. A variable of type **double** can be declared as,

```
double a, population ;
```

If the situation demands usage of real numbers which lie even beyond the range offered by **double** data type then there exists a **long double** which can range from -1.7e4932 to +1.7e4932. A **long double** occupies 10 bytes in memory.

You would see that most of the times in C programming one is required to use either **chars** or **ints** and cases where **floats**, **doubles** or **long doubles** would be used are indeed rare.

Let us now write a program which puts to use all the data types that we have learnt in this chapter. Go through the following program carefully, which shows how to use these different data types. Note the format specifiers used to input and output these data types.

```
main( )
{
    char c ;
    unsigned char d ;
    int i ;
    unsigned int j ;
    long int k ;
    unsigned long int m ;
    float x ;
    double y ;
    long double z ;

    scanf ( "%c %c", &c, &d ) ;
    printf ( "%c %c", c, d ) ;

    scanf ( "%d %u", &i, &j ) ;
    printf ( "%d %u", i, j ) ;

    scanf ( "%ld %lu", &k, &m ) ;
    printf ( "%ld %lu", k, m ) ;

    scanf ( "%f %lf %Lf", &x, &y, &z ) ;
    printf ( "%f %lf %Lf", x, y, z ) ;
}
```

Let us capture the essence of all the data types that we have learnt so far in a figure.

Data Type	Range	Bytes	Format
signed char	-128 to + 127	1	%c
unsigned char	0 to 255	1	%c
short signed int	-32768 to +32767	2	%d
short unsigned int	0 to 65535	2	%u
long signed int	-2147483648 to +2147483647	4	%ld
long unsigned int	0 to 4294967295	4	%lu
float	-3.4e38 to +3.4e38	4	%f
double	-1.7e308 to +1.7e308	8	%lf
long double	-1.7e4932 to 1.7e4932	10	%Lf

Figure 6.1 Datatypes in C

Storage Classes in C

We have already said all that needs to be said about constants, but we are not finished with variables. To fully define a variable one needs to mention not only its 'type' but also its 'storage class'. In other words, not only do all variables have a data type, they also have a 'storage class'.

We have not mentioned storage classes yet, though we have written several programs in C. We were able to get away with this because storage classes have defaults. If we don't specify the storage class of a variable in its declaration, the compiler will assume a storage class depending on the context in which the variable is used. Thus, variables have certain default storage classes.

From C compiler's point of view, a variable name identifies some physical location within the computer where the string of bits representing the variable's value is stored. There are basically two kinds of locations in a computer where such a value may be kept: Memory and CPU registers. It is the variable's storage class which determines in which of these two locations the value is stored.

Moreover, a variable's storage class tells us:

(a)   Where the variable would be stored.
(b)   What will be the initial value of the variable, if the initial value is not specifically assigned. (i.e. the default initial value).
(c)   What is the scope of the variable; i.e. in which functions the value of the variable would be available.
(d)   What is the life of the variable; i.e. how long would the variable exist.

There are four storage classes in C:

(a)   Automatic storage class
(b)   Register storage class
(c)   Static storage class
(d)   External storage class

Let us examine these storage classes one by one.

Automatic Storage Class

The features of a variable defined to have an automatic storage class are as under:

Storage	– Memory.
Default initial value	– An unpredictable value, which is often called a garbage value.
Scope	– Local to the block in which the variable is defined.
Life	– Till the control remains within the block in which the variable is defined.

Following program shows how an automatic storage class variable is declared, and the fact that if the variable is not initialised it contains a garbage value.

```
main( )
{
    auto int i, j ;
    printf ( "\n%d %d", i, j ) ;
}
```

The output of the above program could be..

1211 221

where, 1211 and 221 are garbage values of **i** and **j**. When you run this program you may get different values, since garbage values could be absolutely any values. So always make it a point that you initialise the automatic variables properly, otherwise you are likely to get unexpected results. Note that the keyword for this storage class is **auto** and not automatic.

Scope and life of an automatic variable is illustrated in the following program.

```
main( )
{
    auto int i = 1 ;
    {
        {
            {
                printf ( "\n%d ", i ) ;
            }
            printf ( "%d ", i ) ;
        }
        printf ( "%d ", i ) ;
    }
}
```

The output of the above program is:

1 1 1

This is because, all **printf( )** statements occur within the outermost block (a block is all statements enclosed within a pair of braces) in which **i** has been defined. It means the scope of **i** is local to the block in which it is defined.

The moment the control comes out of the block in which the variable is defined, the variable and its value is irretrievably lost. To catch my point, go through the following program.

```
main( )
{
    auto int i = 1 ;
    {
        auto int i = 2 ;
        {
            auto int i = 3 ;
            printf ( "\n%d ", i ) ;
        }
        printf ( "%d ", i ) ;
    }
    printf ( "%d", i ) ;
}
```

The output of the above program would be:

3 2 1

Note that the Compiler treats the three **i**'s as totally different variables, since they are defined in different blocks. Once the control comes out of the innermost block the variable **i** with value 3 is lost, and hence the **i** in the second **printf( )** refers to **i** with value 2. Similarly, when the control comes out of the next innermost block, the third **printf( )** refers to the **i** with value 1.

Understand the concept of life and scope of an automatic storage class variable thoroughly before proceeding with the next storage class.

Register Storage Class

The features of a variable defined to be of **register** storage class are as under:

Storage   – CPU registers.
Default initial value – Garbage value.
Scope   – Local to the block in which the variable is defined.
Life   – Till the control remains within the block in which the variable is defined.

A value stored in a CPU register can always be accessed faster than the one which is stored in memory. Therefore, if a variable is used at many places in a program it is better to declare its storage class as **register**. A good example of frequently used variables are loop counters. We can name their storage class as **register**.

```
main( )
{
    register int i ;

    for ( i = 1 ; i <= 10 ; i++ )
        printf ( "\n%d", i ) ;
}
```

Here, even though we have declared the storage class of **i** as **register**, we cannot say for sure that the value of **i** would be stored in a CPU register. Why? Because the number of CPU registers are limited (14 in case of a microcomputer), and they may be busy doing some other task. What happens in such an event... the variable works as if its storage class is **auto**.

We cannot use **register** storage class for all types of variables. For example, the following declarations are wrong:

```
register float q ;
register double a ;
register long c ;
```

This is because the CPU registers in a microcomputer are usually 16 bit registers and therefore cannot hold a **float** value or a **double** value, which require 4 and 8 bytes respectively for storing a value. However, if you use the above declarations you won't get any error messages. All that would happen is the compiler would treat the variables to be of **auto** storage class.

Static Storage Class

The features of a variable defined to have a **static** storage class are as under:

Storage   – Memory.
Default initial value   – Zero.
Scope   – Local to the block in which the variable is
                            defined.
Life   – Value of the variable persists between dif-
                            ferent function calls.

Compare the two programs and their output given in Figure 3.9 to understand the difference between the **automatic** and **static** storage classes.

The programs above consist of two functions **main( )** and **increment( )**. The function **increment( )** gets called from **main( )** thrice. Each time it increments the value of **i** and prints it. The only difference in the two programs is that one uses an **auto** storage class for variable **i**, whereas the other uses **static** storage class.

```
main( )                          main( )
{                                {
   increment( ) ;                   increment( ) ;
   increment( ) ;                   increment( ) ;
   increment( ) ;                   increment( ) ;
}                                }

increment( )                     increment( )
{                                {
   auto int i = 1 ;                 static int i = 1 ;
   printf ( "%d\n", i ) ;           printf ( "%d\n", i ) ;
   i = i + 1 ;                      i = i + 1 ;
}                                }

The output of the above programs  would be:

1                                1
1                                2
1                                3
```

Figure 6.2

Like **auto** variables, **static** variables are also local to the block in which they are declared. The difference between them is that **static** variables don't disappear when the function is no longer active. Their values persist. If the control comes back to the same function again the **static** variables have the same values they had last time around.

In the above example, when variable **i** is **auto**, each time **increment( )** is called it is re-initialised to one. When the function terminates, **i** vanishes and its new value of 2 is lost. The result: no matter how many times we call **increment( )**, **i** is initialised to 1 every time.

On the other hand, if **i** is **static**, it is initialised to 1 only once. It is never initialised again. During the first call to **increment( )**, **i** is incremented to 2. Because **i** is static, this value persists. The next time **increment( )** is called, **i** is not re-initialised to 1; on the contrary its old value 2 is still available. This current value of **i** (i.e. 2) gets printed and then **i = i + 1** adds 1 to **i** to get a value of 3. The third time **increment( )** is called, the current value of **i** (i.e. 3) gets printed and once again **i** is incremented. In short if the storage class is **static** then the statement **static int i = 1** is executed only once, irrespective of how many times the same function is called.

All this having been said, a word of advice: avoid using **static** variables unless you really need them. Because their values are kept in memory when the variables are not active, which means they take up space in memory that could otherwise be used by other variables.

External Storage Class

The features of a variable whose storage class has been defined as external are as follows:

Storage   – Memory.
Default initial value – Zero.
Scope   – Global.
Life   – As long as the program's execution doesn't come to an end.

External variables differ from those we have already discussed in that their scope is global, not local. External variables are declared outside all functions, yet are available to all functions that care to use them. Here is an example to illustrate this fact.

```
int i ;
main( )
{
    printf ( "\ni = %d", i ) ;
```

```
        increment( ) ;
        increment( ) ;
        decrement( ) ;
        decrement( ) ;
    }

    increment( )
    {
        i = i + 1 ;
        printf ( "\non incrementing i = %d", i ) ;
    }

    decrement( )
    {
        i = i - 1 ;
        printf ( "\non decrementing i = %d", i ) ;
    }
```

The output would be:

```
    i = 0
    on incrementing i = 1
    on incrementing i = 2
    on decrementing i = 1
    on decrementing i = 0
```

As is obivous from the above output, the value of **i** is available to the functions **increment( )** and **decrement( )** since **i** has been declared outside all functions.

Strictly speaking the function that uses an external variable should declare that variable external via the keyword **extern**, as shown below.

```
    int x = 21 ;
    main( )
```

```
{
    extern int x ;
    printf ( "\n%d", x ) ;
}
```

Then how come the previous program worked without using the keyword **extern** in **increment( )** or **decrement( )**. This is because use of **extern** inside a function is optional as long as as we declare it outside and above that function in the same source code file.

Another small issue. What will be the output of the following program?

```
int x = 10 ;
main( )
{
    int x = 20 ;

    printf ( "\n%d", x ) ;
    display( ) ;
}
display( )
{
    printf ( "\n%d", x ) ;
}
```

Here **x** is defined at two places, once outside **main( )** and once inside it. When the control reaches the **printf( )** in **main( )** which **x** gets printed? Whenever such a conflict arises it's the local variable which gets preference over the global variable. Hence the **printf( )** outputs 20. When **display( )**is called and control reaches the **printf( )** there is no such conflict. Hence this time the value of the global **x**, i.e. 10 gets printed.

Which to Use When

Dennis Ritchie has made available to the C programmer a number of storage classes with varying features, believing that the programmer is in a best position to decide which one of these storage classes is to be used when. We can make a few ground rules for usage of different storage classes in different programming situations with a view to:

(a)   economise the memory space consumed by the variables
(b)   improve the speed of execution of the program

The rules are as under:

-   Use **static** storage class only if you want the value of a variable to persist between different function calls. A typical application of this storage class is recursive functions.

-   Use **register** storage class for only those variables which are being used very often in a program. Reason is, there are very few CPU registers at our disposal and many of them might be busy doing something else. Make careful utilisation of the scarce resources. A typical application of **reigster** storage class is loop counters, which get used a number of times in a program.

-   Use **extern** storage class for only those variables which are being used by almost all the functions in the program. This would avoid unnecessary passing of these variables as arguments when making a function call. Declaring all the variables as **extern** would amount to a lot of wastage of memory space because these variables remain active throughout the life of the program.

-   If you don't have any of the express needs mentioned above, then use the **auto** storage class. In fact most of the times we end up using the **auto** variables, because often it so happens that once we have used the variables in a function we don't mind loosing them.

Summary

Now you know all the variations of the primary data types, namely **signed** and **unsigned char, long** and **short int, float, double** and **long double.** You are also aware of the format specifications for all these data types when they are used in **scanf( )** and **printf( )** statements.

Our understanding of the variables is now complete with the knowledge of storage classes like **auto, register, static** and **extern** as well as their utility.

Exercise

[A] What will be the output of the following programs:

(a)
```
main( )
{
    int i ;
    for ( i = 0 ; i <= 50000 ; i++ )
        printf ( "\n%d", i ) ;
}
```

(b)
```
main( )
{
    float a = 13.5 ;
    double b = 13.5 ;
    printf ( "\n%f %lf", a, b ) ;
}
```

(c)
```
int i = 0 ;
main( )
```

```
    {
        printf ( "\nmain's i = %d", i ) ;
        i++ ;
        val( ) ;
        printf ( "\nmain's i = %d", i ) ;
        val( ) ;
    }
    val( )
    {
        i = 100 ;
        printf ( "\nval's i = %d", i ) ;
        i++ ;
    }
```

(d)   ```
    main( )
    {
        int x, y, s = 2
        s *= 3 ;
        y = f (s) ;
        x = g (s) ;
        printf ("\n%d %d %d", s, y, x) ;
    }
    int t = 8 ;
    f (int a)
    {
        a += -5 ;
        t -= 4 ;
        return (a + t) ;
    }
    g (int a)
    {
        a = 1 ;
        t += a ;
        return (a + t) ;
    }
```

(e)    main( )
```

```
        {
            static int count = 5 ;
            printf ( "\ncount = %d", count-- ) ;
            if ( count != 0 )
                main( ) ;
        }
```

(f)   main( )
```
        {
            int i, j ;
            for ( i = 1 ; i < 5 ; i++ )
            {
                j = g ( i ) ;
                printf ( "\n%d", j ) ;
            }
        }
        g ( int x )
        {
            static int v = 1 ;
            int b = 3 ;
            v += x ;
            return ( v + x + b ) ;
        }
```

(g)   float x = 4.5 ;
```
        main( )
        {
            float y, float f( ) ;
            x *= 2.0 ;
            y = f ( x ) ;
            printf ( "\n%f %f", x, y ) ;
        }
        float f ( float a )
        {
            a += 1.3 ;
            x -= 4.5 ;
            return ( a + x ) ;
```

```
}
```

[B] Point out the errors, if any, in the following programs:

(a)
```
main( )
{
    long num ;
    num = 2 ;
    printf ( "\n%ld", num ) ;
}
```

(b)
```
main( )
{
    char ch = 200 ;
    printf ( "\n%d", ch ) ;
}
```

(c)
```
main( )
{
    unsigned a = 25 ;
    long unsigned b = 25l ;
    printf ( "\n%lu %u", a, b ) ;
}
```

(d)
```
main( )
{
    long float a = 25.345e454 ;
    unsigned double b = 25 ;
    printf ( "\n%lf %d", a, b ) ;
}
```

(e)
```
main( )
{
    float a = 25.345 ;
    float *b ;
    b = &a ;
```

```
    printf ( "\n%f %u", a, b ) ;
}
```

[C]   State whether the following statements are True or False:

(a) Storage for a register storage class variable is allocated each time the control reaches the block in which it is present.

(b) Most of the times we need to use automatic storage class variables.

(c) An extern storage class variable is not available to the functions that precedes its definition, unless the variable is explicitily declared in these functions.

(d) The value of an automatic storage class variable persists between various function invocations.

(e) If the CPU registers are not available, the register storage class variables are treated as static storage class variables.

(f) The register storage class variables cannot hold float values.

[D]   Following program calculates the sum of digits of the number 12345. Go through it and find out why is it necessary to declare the storage class of the variable **sum** as **static**.

```
main( )
{
    int a ;
    a = sumdig ( 12345 ) ;
    printf ( "\n%d", a ) ;
}
sumdig ( int num )
{
    static int sum ;
```

```
int a, b ;

a = num % 10 ;
b = ( num - a ) / 10 ;
sum = sum + a ;
if ( b != 0 )
    sumdig ( b ) ;
else
    return ( sum ) ;
}
```

7   The C Preprocessor

The C preprocessor is exactly what its name implies. It is a program that processes our source program before it is passed to the compiler. Preprocessor commands (often known as directives) form what can almost be considered a language within C language. We can certainly write C programs without knowing anything about the preprocessor or its facilities. But preprocessor is such a great convenience that virtually all C programmers rely on it. This is a capability that does not exist in many other higher level languages. This chapter explores the preprocessor directives and discusses the pros and cons of using them in programs.

Features of C Preprocessor

There are several steps involved from the stage of writing a C program to the stage of getting it executed. Figure 7.1 shows these different steps. You can observe from the figure that our program passes through several processors before it is ready to be executed. The input and output to each of these processors is shown in Figure 7.2.

Whenever we want to execute our programs in Quick C, we do so by hitting the function key F5. In Turbo C the same thing can be achieved using Ctrl F9. When we do this, preprocessing, compiling, linking as well as execution of the program is done automatically.

The preprocessor offers several features called preprocessor directives. Each of these preprocessor directives begin with a # symbol. The directives can be placed anywhere in a program but are most often placed at the beginning of a program, before **main( )**, or before the beginning of a particular function. We would learn the following preprocessor directives here:

(a) Macro expansion
(b) File inclusion

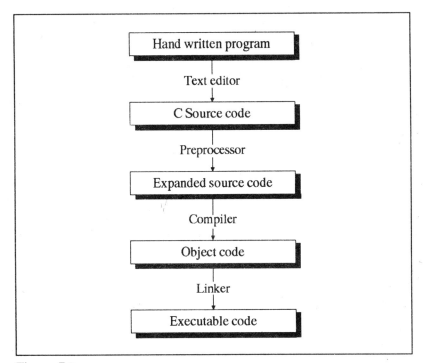

Figure 7.1

Processor	Input	Output
Editor	Program typed from keyboard	C source code containing program and preprocessor commands
Preprocessor	C source code file	Source code file with the preprocessing commands properly sorted out
Compiler	Source code file with preprocessing commands sorted out	Relocatable object code
Linker	Relocatable object code and the standard C library functions	Executable code in machine language

Figure 7.2

(c)   Conditional Compilation
(d)   Miscellaneous directives

Let us understand these features of preprocessor one by one.

Macro Expansion

Have a look at the following program.

```
#define UPPER 25
main( )
{
    int i ;
    for ( i = 1 ; i <= UPPER ; i++ )
        printf ( "\n%d", i ) ;
}
```

In this program instead of writing 25 in the **for** loop we are writing it in the form of UPPER, which has already been defined before **main( )** through the statement,

```
#define UPPER 25
```

This statement is called 'macro definition' or more commonly, just a 'macro'. What purpose does it serve? During preprocessing, the preprocessor replaces every occurrence of UPPER in the program with 25. Here is another example of macro definition.

```
#define PI  3.1415
main( )
{
    float r = 6.25 ;
    float area ;

    area = PI * r * r ;
    printf ( "\nArea of circle = %f", area ) ;
```

}

UPPER and PI in the above programs are often called 'macro templates', whereas, 25 and 3.1415 are called their corresponding 'macro expansions'.

When we compile the program, before the source code passes to the compiler it is examined by the C preprocessor for any macro definitions. When it sees the **#define** directive, it goes through the entire program in search of the macro templates; wherever it finds one, it replaces the macro template with the appropriate macro expansion. Only after this procedure has been completed is the program handed over to the compiler.

In C programming it is customary to use capital letters for macro template. This makes it easy for programmers to pick out all the macro templates when reading through the program.

Note that macro template and its macro expansion are separated by blanks or tabs. A space between # and **define** is optional. Remember that a macro definition is never to be terminated by a semicolon.

And now a million dollar question... why use **#define** in the above programs? What have we gained by substituting PI for 3.1415 in our program? Probably, we have made the program easier to read. Even though 3.1415 is such a common constant that it is easily recognizable, there are many instances where a constant doesn't reveal its purpose so readily. For example, as we will find out later, the phrase "\x1B[2J" causes the screen to clear. But which would you find easier to understand in the middle of your program "\x1B[2J" or "CLEARSCREEN"? Thus, we would use the macro definition

```
#define CLEARSCREEN "\x1B[2J"
```

Then wherever CLEARSCREEN appears in the program it would automatically be replaced by "\x1B[2J" before compilation begins.

There is perhaps a more important reason for using macro definition than mere readability. Suppose a constant like 3.1415 appears many times in your program. This value may have to be changed some day to 3.141592. Ordinarily, you would need to go through the program and manually change each occurrence of the constant. However if you have defined PI in a **#define** directive, you only need to make one change, in the **#define** directive itself:

```
#define PI 3.141592
```

Beyond this the change will be made automatically to all occurrences of PI before the beginning of compilation.

In short, it is nice to know that you would be able to change values of a constant at all the places in the program by just making a change in the **#define** directive. This convenience may not matter for small programs shown above, but with large programs macro definitions are almost indispensable.

But the same purpose could have been served had we used a variable **pi** instead of a macro template **PI**. A variable could also have provided a meaningful name for a constant and permitted one change to effect many occurrences of the constant. It's true that a variable can be used in this way. Then, why not use it? For three reasons it's a bad idea.

Firstly, it is inefficient, since the compiler can generate faster and more compact code for constants than it can for variables. Secondly, using a variable for what is really a constant encourages sloppy thinking and makes the program more difficult to understand: if something never changes, it is hard to imagine it as a variable. And thirdly, there is always a danger that the variable may get altered somewhere in the program, inadvertently; so it's no longer a constant that you think it is.

Thus, using **#define** can produce more efficient and more easily understandable programs. It is used extensively by C programmers as you will see in many programs in this book.

Following three examples show places where a **#define** directive is popularly used by C programmers.

A **#define** directive is many a times used to define operators as shown below.

```
#define AND &&
#define OR ||
main( )
{
    int f = 1, x = 4, y = 90 ;

    if ( ( f < 5 ) AND ( x <= 20 OR y <= 45 ) )
        printf ( "\nYour PC will always work fine..." ) ;
    else
        printf ( "\nIn front of the maintentance man" ) ;
}
```

A **#define** directive could be used even to replace a condition, as shown below.

```
#define AND &&
#define ARANGE ( a > 25 AND a < 50 )
main( )
{
    int a = 30 ;

    if ( ARANGE )
        printf ( "within range" ) ;
    else
        printf ( "out of range" ) ;
}
```

A **#define** directive could be used to replace even an entire C statement. This is shown below.

```
#define FOUND printf("The Yankee Doodle Virus") ;
main( )
{
    char signature ;

    if ( signature == 'Y' )
        FOUND
    else
        printf ( "Safe... as yet !" ) ;
}
```

Macros with Arguments

The macros that we have used so far are called simple macros. Macros can have arguments, just as functions can. Here is an example which illustrates this fact.

```
#define AREA(x) ( 3.14 * x * x )
main( )
{
    float r1 = 6.25, r2 = 2.5, a ;

    a = AREA ( r1 ) ;
    printf ( "\nArea of circle = %f", a ) ;
    a = AREA ( r2 ) ;
    printf ( "\nArea of circle = %f", a ) ;
}
```

Here's the output of the program...

```
Area of circle = 122.656250
Area of circle = 19.625000
```

In this program wherever the preprocessor finds the phrase **AREA(x)** it expands it into the statement (**3.14 * x * x**). However, that's not all that it does. The **x** in the macro template **AREA(x)** is an argument that matches the **x** in the macro expansion (**3.14 * x * x**). The statement **AREA(r1)** in the program causes the variable **r1** to be substituted for **x**. Thus the statement **AREA(r1)** is equivalent to:

```
( 3.14 * r1 * r1 )
```

After the above source code has passed through the preprocessor, what the compiler gets to work on will be this:

```
main( )
{
    float r1 = 6.25, r2 = 2.5, a ;

    a = 3.14 * 6.25 * 6.25 ;
    printf ( "Area of circle = %f\n", a ) ;
    a = 3.14 * 2.5 * 2.5 ;
    printf ( "Area of circle = %f", a ) ;
}
```

Here is another example of macros with arguments:

```
#define ISDIGIT(y) ( y >= 48 && y <= 57 )
main( )
{
    char ch ;

    printf ( "Enter any digit " ) ;
    scanf ( "%c", &ch ) ;

    if ( ISDIGIT(ch) )
        printf ( "\nYou entered a digit" ) ;
    else
        printf ( "\nIllegal input" ) ;
}
```

There are two points to remember while writing macros with arguments:

(a)   Be careful not to leave a blank between the macro template and its argument while defining the macro. For example, there should be no blank between **AREA** and **(x)** in the definition,
#define AREA(x) (3.14 * x * x)

If we were to write **AREA (x)** instead of **AREA(x)**, the **(x)** would become a part of macro expansion, which we certainly don't want. What would happen is, the template would be expanded to

(6.25) (3.14 * 6.25 * 6.25)

which won't run. Not at all what we wanted.

(b)   The entire macro expansion should be enclosed within parentheses. Here is an example of what would happen if we fail to enclose the macro expansion within parentheses.

```
#define SQUARE(n) n * n
main( )
{
    int j ;

    j = 64 / SQUARE(4) ;
    printf ( "j = %d", j ) ;
}
```

The output of the above program would be:

j = 64

whereas what we expected was j = 4.

What went wrong? The macro was expanded into

```
j = 64 / 4 * 4 ;
```

which yielded 64.

Macros Versus Functions

In the above example a macro was used to calculate the area of the circle. As we know, even a function can be written to calculate the area of the circle. Though macro calls are 'like' function calls, they are not really the same thing. Then what is the difference between the two?

In a macro call the preprocessor replaces the macro template with its macro expansion, in a stupid, unthinking, literal way. Whereas in a function call the control is passed to a function along with certain arguments, some calculations are performed in the function and a useful value is returned back from the function.

This brings us to a question: when is it best to use macros with arguments and when is it better to use a function? Usually macros make the program run faster but increases the program size, whereas functions make the program smaller and compact.

If we use a macro hundred times in a program, the macro expansion goes into our source code at hundred different places, thus increasing the program size. On the other hand, if a function is used, then even if it is called from hundred different places in the program, it would take the same amount of space in the program.

But passing arguments to a function and getting back the returned value does take time and would therefore slow down the program. This gets avoided with macros since they have already been expanded and placed in the source code before compilation.

Moral of the story is: if the macro is simple and sweet like in our examples, it makes a nice shorthand and avoids the overheads associated with function calls. On the other hand, if we have a fairly large macro and it is used fairly often, perhaps we ought to replace it with a function.

File Inclusion

The second preprocessor directive we'll explore in this chapter is file inclusion. This directive causes one file to be included in another. The preprocessor command for file inclusion looks like this:

```
#include "filename"
```

and it simply causes the entire contents of **filename** to be inserted into the source code at that point in the program. Of course this presumes that the file being included is existing. When and why this feature is used? It can be used in two cases:

(a)   If we have a very large program, the code is best divided into several different files, each containing a set of related functions. It is a good programming practise to keep different sections of a large program separate. These files are **#includ**ed at the beginning of main program file.

(b)   Many a times we need some functions or some macro definitions almost in all programs that we write. In such a case these commonly needed functions and macro definitions can be stored in a file, and that file can be included in every program we write, which would add all the statements in this file to our program as if we have typed them in.

It is common for the files which are to be included to have a .h extension. This extension stands for 'header file', possibly because it contains statements which when included go to the head of your program.

Actually there exist two ways to write **#include** statement. These are:

```
#include "filename"
#include <filename>
```

The meaning of each of these forms is given below:

#include "goto.c"   This command would look for the file **goto.c** in the current directory as well as the specified list of directories as mentioned in the include search path that might have been set up.

#include <goto.c>   This command would look for the file **goto.c** in the specified list of directories only.

Conditional Compilation

We can, if we want, have the compiler skip over part of a source code by inserting the preprocessing commands **#ifdef** and **#endif**, which have the general form:

```
#ifdef macroname
     statement 1 ;
     statement 2 ;
     statement 3 ;
#endif
```

If **macroname** has been **#defined**, the block of code will be processed as usual; otherwise not.

Where would **#ifdef** be used? When would you like to compile only a part of your program? In two cases:

(a)   To "comment out" obsolete lines of code. It often happens that a program is changed at the last minute to satisfy a client. This involves rewriting some part of source code to the client's satisfaction and delete the old code. But veteran programmers are familiar with the client who changes his mind and wants the old code back again just the way it was. Now you would definitely not like to retype the deleted code again.

One solution in such a situation is to put the old code within a pair of /* */ combination. But we might have already written a comment in the code that we are about to "comment out". This would mean we end up with nested comments. Obviously, this solution won't work since we can't nest comments in C.

Therefore the solution is to use conditional compilation as shown below.

```
main( )
{
    #ifdef OKAY
        statement 1 ;
        statement 2 ;  /* detects virus */
        statement 3 ;
        statement 4 ;  /* specific to stone virus */
    #endif

    statement 5 ;
    statement 6 ;
    statement 7 ;
}
```

Here, statements 1, 2, 3 and 4 would get compiled only if the macro OKAY has been defined, and we have purposefully omitted the definition of the macro OKAY. At a later date if we want that these statements should also get compiled all that we are required to do is to delete the **#ifdef** and **#endif** statements.

(b) A more sophisticated use of **#ifdef** has to do with making the programs portable, i.e. to make them work on two totally different computers. Suppose an organisation has two different types of computers and you are expected to write a program that works on both the machines. You can do so by isolating the lines of code that must be different for each machine by marking them off with **#ifdef**. For example:

```
main( )
{
    #ifdef PCAT
        code suitable for a PC/AT
    #else
        code suitable for a PC/XT
    #endif
    code common to both the computers
}
```

When you compile this program it would compile only the code suitable for a PC/XT and the common code. This is because the macro PCAT has not been defined. Note that the working of **#ifdef - #else - #endif** is similar to the ordinary **if - else** control instruction of C.

If you want to run your program on a PC/AT, just add a statement at the top saying,

```
#define PCAT
```

Sometimes, instead of **#ifdef** the **#ifndef** directive is used. The **#ifndef** (which means 'if not defined') works exactly opposite to **#ifdef**. The above example if written using **#ifndef**, would look like this:

```
main( )
{
    #ifndef PCAT
        code suitable for a PC/XT
    #else
        code suitable for a PC/AT
    #endif
```

```
        code common to both the computers
    }
```

#if and #elif Directives

The **#if** directive can be used to test whether an expression evaluates to a nonzero value or not. If the result of the expression is nonzero, then subsequent lines upto a **#else**, **#elif** or **#endif** are compiled, otherwise they are skipped.

A simple example of **#if** directive is shown below:

```
    main( )
    {
        #if TEST <= 5
            statement 1 ;
            statement 2 ;
            statement 3 ;
        #else
            statement 4 ;
            statement 5 ;
            statement 6 ;
        #endif
    }
```

If the expression, **TEST <= 5** evaluates to true then statements 1, 2, and 2 are compiled otherwise statements 4, 5 and 6 are compiled. In place of the expression **TEST <= 5** other expressions like (**LEVEL == HIGH || LEVEL == LOW**) or **ADAPTER == CGA** can also be used.

If we so desire we can have nested conditional compilation directives. An example which uses such directives is shown below.

```
    #if ADAPTER == MA
        code for monochrome adapter
```

```
#else
    #if ADAPTER == CGA
        code for colour graphics adapter
    #else
        #if ADAPTER == EGA
            code for enhanced graphics adapter
        #else
            #if ADAPTER == VGA
                code for video graphics array
            #else
                code for super video graphics array
            #endif
        #endif
    #endif
#endif
```

The above program segment can be made more compact by using another conditional compilation directive called **#elif**. The same program using this directive can be rewritten as shown below. Observe that by using the **#elif** directives the number of **endif**s used in the program get reduced.

```
#if ADAPTER == MA
    code for monochrome adapter
#elif ADAPTER == CGA
    code for colour graphics adapter
#elif ADAPTER == EGA
    code for enhanced graphics adapter
#elif ADAPTER == VGA
    code for video graphics array
#else
    code for super video graphics array
#endif
```

Miscellaneous Directives

There are two more preprocessor directives available, though they are not very commonly used. They are:

(a)   #undef
(b)   #pragma

#undef Directive

On some occasions it may be desirable to cause a defined name to become 'undefined'. This can be accomplished by means of the **#undef** directive. In order to undefine a macro which has been earlier **#defined**, the directive,

    #undef macro template

can be used. Thus the statement,

    #undef PCAT

would cause the definition of PCAT to be removed from the system. All subsequent **#ifdef PCAT** statements would evaluate to false. In practise seldom are we required to undefine a macro, but for some crooked reason if you are required to, then you know that there is something to fall back upon.

#pragma Directive

This directive is another special purpose directive that you can use to turn on or off certain features. Pragmas vary from one compiler to another. There are certain pragmas available with Microsoft C compiler which deal with formatting source listings and placing comments in the object file generated by the compiler. Turbo C compiler has got a pragma which allows you to write assembly language statements in your C program. The details of these pragmas are beyond the scope of this book.

Summary

You have learnt in this chapter yet another unique feature of C language that is not found in most other high-level programming languages. The preprocessor directives enable the programmer to write programs that are easy to develop, read, modify, and transport to a different computer system.

You have learnt when and how to effectively use the preprocessor directives **#define, #include, #ifdef - #else - #endif, #if and #elif.** The seldom used directives like **#undef** and **#pragma** have also been introduced.

Exercise

[A]   Answer the following:

(a)   What is a preprocessor directive

    1. a message from compiler to the programmer
    2. a message from compiler to the linker
    3. a message from programmer to the preprocessor
    4. a message from programmer to the microprocessor

(b)   Which of the following are correctly formed **#define** statements

```
#define  INCH PER FEET  12
#define  SQR (X) ( X * X )
#define  SQR(X)  X * X
#define  SQR(X)  ( X * X )
```

(c)   State True or False:

    1.   A macro must always be written in capital letters.

    2.   A macro should always be accomodated in a single line.

    3.   After preprocessing when the program is sent for compilation the macros are removed from the expanded source code.

(d)   How many **#include** directives may be there in a given program file?

(e)   What is the difference between the following two **#include** directives:

```
#include "conio.h"
#include <conio.h>
```

(f)   A header file is:

    1.   A file that contains standard library functions
    2.   A file that contains definitions and macros
    3.   A file that contains user defined functions
    4.   A file that is present in current working directory

[B]   What will be the output of the following program:

(a)
```
main( )
{
    int i = 2 ;
    #ifdef DEF
        i *= i ;
    #else
        printf ( "\n%d", i ) ;
    #endif
```

```
            }

(b)    #define PRODUCT(x) ( x * x )
       main( )
       {
            int i = 3, j ;
            j = PRODUCT( i + 1 ) ;
            printf ( "\n%d", j ) ;
       }

(c)    #define PRODUCT(x) ( x * x )
       main( )
       {
            int i = 3, j, k ;
            j = PRODUCT( i++ ) ;
            k = PRODUCT ( ++i ) ;

            printf ( "\n%d %d", j, k ) ;
       }
```

[C]   Attempt the following:

(a)   Write down macro definitions for the following:

   (1) To test whether a character entered is a small case letter or not.

   (2) To test whether a character entered is a upper case letter or not.

   (3) To test whether a character is an alphabet or not. Make use of the macros you defined in (1) and (2) above.

   (4) To obtain the bigger of two numbers.

(b)   Write macro definitions with arguments for calculation of area and perimeter of a triangle, a square and a circle. Store these macro definitions in a file called "areaperi.h". Include this file in your program, and call the macro definitions for calculating area and perimeter for different squares, triangles and circles.

8   *Arrays*

he C language provides a capability that enables the user to design a set of similar data types, called array. This chapter describes how arrays can be created and manipulated in C.

We should note that, in many C books and courses arrays and pointers are taught separately. I feel it is worthwhile to deal with these topics together. This is because pointers and arrays are so closely related that discussing arrays without discussing pointers would make the discussion incomplete and wanting. In fact all arrays make use of pointers internally. Hence it is all too relevant to study them together rather than as isolated topics.

What are Arrays

For understanding the arrays properly, let us consider the following program:

```
main( )
{
    int x ;
    x = 5 ;
    x = 10 ;
    printf ( "\nx = %d", x ) ;
}
```

No doubt, this program will print the value of **x** as 10. Why so? Because when a value 10 is assigned to **x**, the earlier value of **x** i.e. 5 is lost. Thus, ordinary variables (the ones which we have used so far) are capable of holding only one value at a time (as in the above example). However, there are situations in which we would want to store more than one value at a time in a single variable.

For example, suppose we wish to arrange the percentage marks obtained by 100 students in ascending order. In such a case we have two options to store these marks in memory:

(a)   Construct 100 variables to store percentage marks obtained by 100 different students. i.e. each variable containing one student's marks.

(b)   Construct one variable (called array or subscripted variable) capable of storing or holding all the hundred values.

Obviously, the second alternative is better. A simple reason for this is, it would be much easier to handle one variable than handling 100 different variables. Moreover, there are certain logics which cannot be dealt with, without the use of an array. Now a formal definition of an array: An array is a collective name given to a group of 'similar quantities'. These similar quantities could be percentage marks of 100 students, or salaries of 300 employees, or ages of 50 employees. What is important is that the quantities must be 'similar'. Each member in the group is referred to by its position in the group. For example, assume the following group of numbers which represent percentage marks obtained by five students.

per = { 48, 88, 34, 23, 96 }

If we want to refer to the second number of the group, the usual notation used is per$_2$. Similarly, the fourth number of the group is referred as per$_4$. However, in C, the fourth number is referred as **per[3]**. This is because in C the counting of elements begins with 0 and not with 1. Thus, in this example **per[3]** refers to 23 and **per[4]** refers to 96. In general, the notation would be **per[i]**, where, **i** can take a value 0, 1, 2, 3, or 4, depending on the position of the element being referred. Here **per** is the subscripted varaible (array), whereas **i** is its subscript.

Thus, an array is a collection of similar elements. These similar elements could be all **ints**, or all **floats**, or all **chars** etc. Usually, the array of characters is called a 'string', whereas an array of **ints** or **floats** is called simply an array. Remember that all elements of any given array must be of the same type. i.e. we cannot have an array of 10 numbers, of which 5 are **ints** and 5 are **floats**.

A Simple Program Using Array

Let us try to write a program to find average marks obtained by a class of 30 students in a test.

```
main( )
{
    float avg, sum = 0 ;
    int i ;
    int marks[30] ;  /* array declaration */

    for ( i = 0 ; i <= 29 ; i++ )
    {
        printf ( "\nEnter marks " ) ;
        scanf ( "%d", &marks[i] ) ;  /* store data in array */
    }

    for ( i = 0 ; i <= 29 ; i++ )
        sum = sum + marks[i] ;  /* read data from an array*/

    avg = sum / 30 ;
    printf ( "\nAverage marks = %f", avg ) ;
}
```

There is a lot of new material in this program, so let us take it apart slowly.

Array Declaration

To begin with, like other variables an array needs to be declared so that the compiler will know what kind of an array and how large an array we want. In our program we have done this with the statement:

```
int marks[30] ;
```

Here, **int** specifies the type of the variable, just as it does with ordinary variables and the word **marks** specifies the name of the variable. The

[30] however is new. The number 30 tells how many elements of the type **int** will be in our array. This number is often called the 'dimension' of the array. The bracket ([ ]) tells the compiler that we are dealing with an array.

Accessing Elements of an Array

Once an array is declared, let us see how individual elements in the array can be referred. This is done with subscript, the number in the brackets following the array name. This number specifies the element's position in the array. All the array elements are numbered, starting with 0. Thus, **marks[2]** is not the second element of the array but the third. In our program we are using the variable **i** as a subscript to refer to various elements of the array. This variable can take different values and hence can refer to the different elements in the array in turn. This ability to use variables as subscripts is what makes arrays so useful.

Entering Data into an Array

Here is the section of code that places data into the array:

```
for ( i = 0 ; i <= 29 ; i++ )
{
    printf ( "\nEnter marks " ) ;
    scanf ( "%d", &marks[i] ) ;
}
```

The **for** loop causes the process of asking for and receiving a student's marks from the user to be repeated 30 times. The first time through the loop, **i** has a value 0, so the **scanf( )** statement will cause the value typed to be stored in the array element **marks[0]**, the first element of the array. This process will be repeated until **i** becomes 29. This is last time through the loop, which is a good thing, because there is no array element like **marks[30]**.

In the **scanf( )** statement, we have used the "address of" operator (&) on the element **marks[i]** of the array, just as we have used it earlier on other variables (**&rate**, for example). In so doing, we are passing the address of this particular array element to the **scanf( )** function, rather than its value; which is what **scanf( )** requires.

Reading Data from an Array

The balance of the program reads the data back out of the array and uses it to calculate the average. The **for** loop is much the same, but now the body of the loop causes each student's marks to be added to a running total stored in a variable called **sum**. When all the marks have been added up, the result is divided by 30, the number of students, to get the average.

```
for ( i = 0 ; i <= 29 ; i++ )
    sum = sum + marks[i] ;

avg = sum / 30 ;
printf ( "\nAverage marks = %f", avg ) ;
```

To fix our ideas, let us revise whatever we have learnt about arrays:

(a) An array is a collection of similar elements.
(b) The first element in the array is numbered 0, so the last element is 1 less than the size of the array.
(c) An array is also known as a subscripted variable.
(d) Before using an array its type and dimension must be declared.
(e) However big an array its elements are always stored in contiguous memory locations. This is a very important point which we would discuss in more detail later on.

More on Arrays

Array is a very popular data type with C programmers. This is because of the convenience with which arrays lend themselves to programming. The features which make arrays so convenient to program would be discussed below, along with the possible pitfalls in using them.

Array Initialisation

So far we have used arrays that did not have any value in them to begin with. We managed to store values in them during program execution. Let us now see how to initialise an array while declaring it. Following are a few examples which demonstrate this.

```
int num[6] = { 2, 4, 12, 5, 45, 5 } ;
int n[ ] = { 2, 4, 12, 5, 45, 5 } ;
float press[ ] = { 12.3, 34.2 -23.4, -11.3 } ;
```

Note the following points carefully:

(a)   Till the array elements are not given any specific values, they are supposed to contain garbage values.

(b)   If the array is initialised where it is declared, mentioning the dimension of the array is optional as in the 2nd example above.

Array Elements in Memory

Consider the following array declaration:

```
int arr[8] ;
```

What happens in memory when we make this declaration? 16 bytes get immediately reserved in memory. 16, because each of the 8 integers would be 2 bytes long. And since the array is not being initialised, all eight values present in it would be garbage values. This so happens because the storage class of this array is assumed to be **auto**. If the storage class is declared to be **static** then all the array elements would have a default initial value as zero. Whatever be the initial values all the array elements would always be present in contiguous memory locations. This arrangement of array elements in memory is shown in Figure 8.1.

12	34	66	-45	23	346	77	90
4002	4004	4006	4008	4010	4012	4014	4016

Figure 8.1

Bounds Checking

In C there is no check to see if the subscript used for an array exceeds the size of the array. Data entered with a subscript exceeding the array size will simply be placed in memory outside the array; probably on top of other data, or on the program itself. This will lead to unpredictable results, to say the least, and there will be no error message to warn you that you are going beyond the array size. In some cases the computer may just hang. Thus, the following program may turn out to be suicidal.

```
main( )
{
    int num[40], i ;

    for ( i = 0 ; i <= 100 ; i++ )
        num[i] = i ;
}
```

Thus, to see to it that we do not reach beyond the array size is entirely the programmer's botheration and not the compiler's.

Passing Array Elements to A Function

Array elements can be passed to a function by calling the function by value, or by reference. In the call by value we pass values of array elements to the function, whereas in the call by reference we pass addresses of array elements to the function. These two calls are illustrated below:

```
/* Demonstration of call by value */
main( )
{
    int i ;
    int marks[ ] = { 55, 65, 75, 56, 78, 78, 90 ) ;

    for ( i = 0 ; i <= 6 ; i++ )
        display ( marks[i] ) ;
}

display ( int m )
{
    printf ( "%d ", m ) ;
}
```

And here's the output...

55 65 75 56 78 78 90

Here, we are passing an individual array element at a time to the function **display( )** and getting it printed in the function **display( )**. Note that since at a time only one element is being passed, this element is collected in an ordinary integer variable **m**, in the function **display( )** .

And now the call by reference.

```
/* Demonstration of call by reference */
main( )
```

```
{
    int i ;
    int marks[ ] = { 55, 65, 75, 56, 78, 78, 90 } ;

    for ( i = 0 ; i <= 6 ; i++ )
        disp ( &marks[i] ) ;
}

disp ( int *n )
{
    printf ( "%d ", *n ) ;
}
```

And here's the output...

55 65 75 56 78 78 90

Here, we are passing addresses of individual array elements to the function **display( )**. Hence, the variable in which this address is collected (**n**) is declared as a pointer variable. And since **n** contains the address of array element, to print out the array element we are using the 'value at address' operator (*****).

Read the following program carefully. The purpose of the function **disp( )** is just to display the array elements on the screen. The program is only partly complete. You are required to write the function **show( )** on your own. Try your hand at it.

```
main( )
{
    int i ;
    int marks[ ] = { 55, 65, 75, 56, 78, 78, 90 } ; '

    for ( i = 0 ; i <= 6 ; i++ )
        disp ( &marks[i] ) ;
}
```

```
disp ( int *n )
{
    show ( &n ) ;
}
```

Pointers and Arrays

To be able to see what pointers have got to do with arrays, let us first learn some pointer arithmetic. Consider the following example:

```
main( )
{
    int i = 3, *x ;
    float j = 1.5, *y ;
    char k = 'c', *z ;

    printf ( "\nValue of i = %d", i ) ;
    printf ( "\nValue of j = %f", j ) ;
    printf ( "\nValue of k = %c", k ) ;
    x = &i ;
    y = &j ;
    z = &k ;
    printf ( "\nOriginal address in x = %u", x ) ;
    printf ( "\nOriginal address in y = %u", y ) ;
    printf ( "\nOriginal address in z = %u", z ) ;
    x++ ;
    y++ ;
    z++ ;
    printf ( "\nNew address in x = %u", x ) ;
    printf ( "\nNew address in y = %u", y ) ;
    printf ( "\nNew address in z = %u", z ) ;
}
```

Suppose **i, j** and **k** are stored in memory at addresses 1002, 2004 and 5006, the output would be...

```
Value of i = 3
Value of j = 1.5
Value of k = c
Original address in x = 1002
Original address in y = 2004
Original address in z = 5006
New address in x = 1004
New address in y = 2008
New address in z = 5007
```

Observe the last three lines of the output. 1004 is original value in **x** plus 2, 2008 is original value in **y** plus 4, and 5007 is original value in **z** plus 1. This so happens because every time a pointer is incremented it points to the immediately next location of its type. That is why, when the integer pointer **x** is incremented, it points to an address two locations after the current location, since an **int** is always 2 bytes long. Similarly **y** points to an address 4 locations after the current location and **z** points 1 location after the current location. This is a very important result and can be effectively used while passing the entire array to a function.

The way a pointer can be incremented, it can be decremented as well, to point to earlier locations. Thus, the following operations can be performed on a pointer:

(a)   Addition of a number to a pointer. For example,

```
int i = 4, *j, *k ;
j = &i ;
j = j + 1 ;
j = j + 9 ;
k = j + 3 ;
```

(b)   Subtraction of a number from a pointer. For example,

```
int i = 4, *j, *k ;
j = &i ;
```

```
j = j - 2 ;
j = j - 5 ;
k = j - 6 ;
```

(c)   Subtraction of one pointer from another.

One pointer variable can be subtracted from another provided both variables point to elements of the same array. The resulting value indicates the number of bytes separating the corrseponding array elements. This is illustrated in the following program.

```
main( )
{
    int arr[ ] = { 10, 20, 30, 45, 67, 56, 74 } ;
    int *i, *j ;

    i = &arr[1] ;
    j = &arr[5] ;
    printf ( "%d %d", j - i, *j - *i ) ;
}
```

Here **i** and **j** have been declared as integer pointers holding addresses of first and fifth element of the array respectively.

Suppose the array begins at location 4002, then the elements **arr[1]** and **arr[5]** would be present at locations 4004 and 4012 respectively, since each integer in the array occupies two bytes in memory. The expression **j - i** would print a value 5 and not 10. This is because **j** and **i** are pointing to locations which are 5 integers apart. What would be the result of the expression ***j - *i**? 36, since ***j** and ***i** return the values present at addresses contained in the pointers **j** and **i**.

(d)   Comparison of two pointer variables.

Pointer variables can be compared provided both variables point to objects of the same data type. Such comparisons can be useful when both pointer variables point to elements of the same array. The comparison can test for either equality or inequality. Moreover a pointer variable can be compared with zero (usually expressed as NULL). The following program illustrates how the comparison is carried out.

```
main( )
{
    int arr [ ] = { 10, 20, 36, 72, 45, 36 } ;
    int *j, *k ;

    j = &arr [ 4 ] ;
    k = ( arr + 4 ) ;

    if ( j == k )
        printf ( "The two pointers point to the same location" ) ;
    else
        printf ( "The two pointers do not point to the same location" ) ;
}
```

A word of caution! Do not attempt the following operations on pointers... they would never work out.

(a)   Addition of two pointers
(b)   Multiplication of a pointer with a constant
(c)   Division of a pointer with a constant

Now we will try to correlate the following two facts, which we have learnt above:

(a)   Array elements are always stored in contiguous memory locations.
(b)   A pointer when incremented always points to an immediately next location of its type.

Suppose we have an array **num[ ]** = { 24, 34, 12, 44, 56, 17 }. The following figure shows how this array is located in memory.

24	34	12	44	56	17
4001	4003	4005	4007	4009	4011

Figure 8.2

Here is a program that prints out the memory locations in which the elements of this array are stored.

```
main( )
{
    int num[] = { 24, 34, 12, 44, 56, 17 } ;
    int i ;

    for ( i = 0 ; i <= 5 ; i++ )
    {
        printf ( "\nelement no. %d ", i ) ;
        printf ( "address = %u", &num[i] ) ;
    }
}
```

The output of this program would look like this:

```
element no. 0 address = 4001
element no. 1 address = 4003
element no. 2 address = 4005
element no. 3 address = 4007
element no. 4 address = 4009
element no. 5 address = 4011
```

Note that the array elements are stored in contiguous memory locations, each element occupying two bytes, since it is an integer array.

When you run this program, you make get different addresses, but what is certain is that each subsequent address would be 2 bytes greater than its immediate predecessor.

Our next two programs show ways in which we can access the elements of this array.

```
main( )
{
    int num[ ] = { 24, 34, 12, 44, 56, 17 } ;
    int i ;

    for ( i = 0 ; i <= 5 ; i++ )
    {
        printf ( "\naddress = %u ", &num[i] ) ;
        printf ( "element = %d", num[i] ) ;
    }
}
```

The output of this program would be:

```
address = 4001 element = 24
address = 4003 element = 34
address = 4005 element = 12
address = 4007 element = 44
address = 4009 element = 56
address = 4011 element = 17
```

This method of accessing array elements by using subscripted variables is already known to us. This method has in fact been given here for easy comparison with the next method, which accesses the array elements using pointers.

```
main( )
{
    int num[ ] = { 24, 34, 12, 44, 56, 17 } ;
    int i, *j ;
```

```
        j = &num[0] ;  /* assign address of zeroeth element */

        for ( i = 0 ; i <= 5 ; i++ )
        {
            printf ( "\naddress = %u ", j ) ;
            printf ( "element = %d", *j ) ;
            j++ ;  /* increment pointer to point to next location */
        }
    }
```

The output of this program would be:

```
        address = 4001 element = 24
        address = 4003 element = 34
        address = 4005 element = 12
        address = 4007 element = 44
        address = 4009 element = 56
        address = 4011 element = 17
```

In this program, to begin with we have collected the base address of the array (address of the 0th element) in the variable **j** using the statement,

```
        j = &num[0] ;  /* assigns address 4001 to j */
```

When we are inside the loop for the first time, **j** contains the address 4001, and the value at this address is 24. These are printed using the statements,

```
        printf ( "\naddress = %u ", j ) ;
        printf ( "element = %d", *j ) ;
```

On incrementing **j** it points to the next memory location of its type (that is location no. 4003). But location no. 4003 contains the second element of the array, therefore when the **printf( )** statements are executed for the second time they print out the second element of the array and its address (i.e. 34 and 4003)... and so on till the last element of the array has been printed.

Obviously, a question arises as to which of the above two methods should be used when? Accessing array elements by pointers is **always** faster than accessing them by subscripts. However, from the point of view of convenience in programming we should observe the following:

Array elements should be accessed using pointers if the elements are to be accessed in a fixed order, say from beginning to end, or from end to beginning, or every alternate element or any such definite logic.

Instead, it would be easier to access the elements using a subscript if there is no fixed logic in accessing the elements. However, in this case also, accessing the elements by pointers would work faster than subscripts.

Passing an Entire Array to A Function

In the previous section we saw two programs - one in which we passed individual elements of an array to a function, and another in which we passed addresses of individual elements to a function. Let us now see how to pass an entire array to a function rather than its individual elements. Consider the following example:

```
/* Demonstration of passing an entire array to a function */
main( )
{
    int num[ ] = { 24, 34, 12, 44, 56, 17 } ;
    dislpay ( &num[0], 6 ) ;
}

display ( int *j, int n )
{
```

```
int i ;

for ( i = 0 ; i <= n - 1 ; i++ )
{
    printf ( "\nelement = %d", *j ) ;
    j++ ;  /* increment pointer to point to next location */
}
}
```

Here, the **display( )** function is used to print out the array elements. Note that the address of the zeroeth element is being passed to the **display( )** function. The **for** loop is same as the one used in the earlier program to access the array elements using pointers. Thus, just passing the address of the zeroth element of the array to a function is as good as passing the entire array to the function. It is also necessary to pass the total number of elements in the array, otherwise the **display( )** function would not know when to terminate the **for** loop. Note that the address of the zeroth element (many a times called the base address) can also be passed by just passing the name of the array. Thus, the following two function calls are same:

```
display ( &num[0], 6 ) ;
display ( num, 6 ) ;
```

The Real Thing

If you have grasped the concept of storage of array elements in memory and the arithmetic of pointers, here is some real food for thought. Once again consider the following array.

24	34	12	44	56	17
4001	4003	4005	4007	4009	4011

Figure 8.3

This is how we would declare the above array in C,

    int num[ ] = { 24, 34, 12, 44, 56, 17 } ;

We also know that on mentioning the name of the array we get its base adddress. Thus, by saying ***num** we would be able to refer to the zeroth element of the array, that is, 24. One can easily see that ***num** and *(**num + 0**) both refer to 24.

Similarly, by saying *(**ñum + 1**) we can refer the first element of the array, that is, 34. In fact, this is what the C compiler does internally. When we say, **num[i]**, the C compiler internally converts it to *(**num + i**). This means that all the following notations are same:

    num[i]
    *(num + i)
    *(i + num)
    i[num]

And here is a program to prove my point.

```
/* Accessing array elements in different ways */
main( )
{
    int num[ ] = { 24, 34, 12, 44, 56, 17 } ;
    int i ;

    for ( i = 0 ; i <= 5 ; i++ )
    {
        printf ( "\naddress = %u ", &num[i] ) ;
        printf ( "element = %d %d", num[i], *( num + i ) ) ;
        printf ( "%d %d", *( i + num ), i[num] ) ;
    }
}
```

The output of this program would be:

```
address = 4001 element = 24 24 24 24
address = 4003 element = 34 34 34 34
address = 4005 element = 12 12 12 12
address = 4007 element = 44 44 44 44
address = 4009 element = 56 56 56 56
address = 4011 element = 17 17 17 17
```

More Than One Dimension

So far we have explored arrays with only one dimension. It is also possible for arrays to have two or more dimensions. The two dimensional array is also called a matrix.

Here is a sample program that stores roll number and marks obtained by a student side by side in a matrix.

```
main( )
{
    int stud[4][2] ;
    int i, j ;

    for ( i = 0 ; i <= 3 ; i++ )
    {
        printf ( "\n Enter roll no. and marks" ) ;
        scanf ( "%d %d", &stud[i][0], &stud[i][1] ) ;
    }

    for ( i = 0 ; i <= 3 ; i++ )
        printf ( "\n%d %d", stud[i][0], stud[i][1] ) ;
}
```

There are two parts to the program - in the first part through a **for** loop we read in the values of roll no. and marks, whereas, in second part through another **for** loop we print out these values.

Look at the **scanf( )** statement used in the first **for** loop:

```
scanf ( "%d %d", &stud[i][0], &stud[i][1] ) ;
```

In **stud[i][0]** and **stud[i][1]** the first subscript of the variable **stud**, is row number which changes for every student. The second subscript tells which of the two columns are we talking about... the zeroth column which contains the roll no. or the first column which contains the marks. Remember, the counting of rows and columns begin with zero. The complete array arrangement is shown below.

	col. no. 0	col. no. 1
row no. 0	1234	56
row no. 1	1212	33
row no. 2	1434	80
row no. 3	1312	78

Figure 8.4

Thus, 1234 is stored in **stud[0][0]**, 56 is stored in **stud[0][1]** and so on. The above arrangement highlights the fact that a two dimensional array is nothing but a collection of a number of one dimensional arrays placed one below the other.

In our sample program the array elements have been stored rowwise and accessed rowwise. However, you can access the array elements columnwise as well. Traditionally, the array elements are being stored and accessed rowwise, therefore we would also stick to the same strategy.

Initialising A 2-Dimensional Array

How do we initialise a two dimensional array? As simple as this...

```
int stud[4][2] = {
```

```
            { 1234, 56 },
            { 1212, 33 },
            { 1434, 80 },
            { 1312, 78 }
        } ;
```

or even this would work...

```
int stud[4][2] = { 1234, 56, 1212, 33, 1434, 80, 1312, 78 } ;
```

of course with a corresponding loss in readability.

It is important to remember that while initialising an array it is necessary to mention the second (column) dimension, whereas the first dimension (row) is optional.

Thus the declarations,

```
int arr[2][3] = { 12, 34, 23, 45, 56, 45 } ;
int arr[ ][3] = { 12, 34, 23, 45, 56, 45 } ;
```

are perfectly acceptable,

whereas,

```
int arr[2][ ] = { 12, 34, 23, 45, 56, 45 } ;
int arr[ ][ ] = { 12, 34, 23, 45, 56, 45 } ;
```

would never work.

Memory Map of A 2-Dimensional Array

Let us reiterate the arrangement of array elements in a two dimensional array of students, which contains roll nos. in one column and the marks in the other.

The array arrangement shown in Figure 8.4 is only conceptually true. This is because memory doesn't contain rows and columns. In memory whether it is a one-dimensional or a two-dimensional array the array elements are stored in one continuous chain. The arrangement of array elements of a two-dimensional array in memory is shown below:

s[0][0]	s[0][1]	s[1][0]	s[1][1]	s[2][0]	s[2][1]	s[3][0]	s[3][1]
1234	56	1212	33	1434	80	1312	78
5002	5004	5006	5008	5010	5012	5014	5016

Figure 8.5

We can easily refer to the marks obtained by the third student using the subscript notation as shown below:

printf ("Marks of third student = %d", stud[2][1]) ;

Can we not refer the same element using pointer notation, the way we did in one-dimensional arrays? Answer is yes. Only the procedure is slightly difficult to understand. So, read on...

Pointers and 2-Dimensional Arrays

The C language embodies an unusual but powerful capability: it can treat parts of arrays as arrays. More specifically, each row of a two dimensional array can be thought of as a one dimensional array. This is a very important fact if we wish to access array elements of a two dimensional array using pointers.

Thus, the declaration,

    int s[5][2] ;

can be thought of as setting up a one dimensional array of 5 elements, each of which is a one dimensional array 2 elements long. We refer to an element of a one dimensional array using a single subscript. Similarly, if we can imagine **s** to be a one dimensional array then we can refer to its zeroth element as **s[0]**, the next element as **s[1]** and so on. More specifically, **s[0]** gives the address of the zeroth one dimensional array, **s[1]** gives the address of the first one dimensional array and so on. This fact can be illustrated by the following program.

```
/* Demo: 2-D array is an array of arrays */
main( )
{
    int s[5][2] = {
                        { 1234, 56 },
                        { 1212, 33 },
                        { 1434, 80 },
                        { 1312, 78 }
                  } ;
    int i, j ;

    for ( i = 0 ; i <= 3 ; i++ )
        printf ( "\nAddress of %d th 1-D array = %u", s[i] ) ;
}
```

And here is the output...

```
Address of 0 th 1-D array = 5002
Address of 1 th 1-D array = 5006
Address of 2 th 1-D array = 5010
Address of 3 th 1-D array = 5014
```

Let's figure out how the program works. The compiler knows that **s** is an integer array. So each element of this array occupies 2 bytes. There are two elements in each row, so each row takes 4 bytes. Thus, each row starts 4 bytes further along than the last one. And, since each row is a one dimensional array, each of these one dimensional arrays starts 4 bytes further along than the last one, as can be seen in the memory map of the array shown below.

s[0][0]	s[0][1]	s[1][0]	s[1][1]	s[2][0]	s[2][1]	s[3][0]	s[3][1]
1234	56	1212	33	1434	80	1312	78
5002	5004	5006	5008	5010	5012	5014	5016

Figure 8.6

The compiler knows how many columns are there in the array **s**, since we specified this in the array declaration. So it interprets the expression **s[0]** as (**s + 0**), and **s[1]** as (**s + 1**). Therefore, (**s + 0**) is interpreted as address 5002, and (**s + 1**) is interpreted as address 5006 and so on.

Now, we have been able to reach each individual row. What remains is to be able to refer to individual elements of a row. Suppose we want to refer to the element **s[2][1]** using pointers. We know (from the above program) that **s[2]** would give the address 5010, the address of the second one dimensional array. Obviously (5010 + 1) would give the address 5012. Or (**s[2] + 1**) would give the address 5012. And the value at this address can be obtained by using the value at address operator, saying ***(s[2] + 1)**. But, we have already studied while learning one dimensional arrays that **num[i]** is same as ***(num + i)**. Similarly, ***(s[2] + 1)** is same as, ***(*(s + 2) + 1)**. Thus, all the following expressions refer to the same element,

```
s[2][1]
*( s[2] + 1 )
*( *( s + 2 ) + 1 )
```

Using these concepts the following program prints out each element of a two dimensional array using pointer notation.

```
/* Pointer notation to access 2-D array elements */
main( )
{
    int s[5][2] = {
                        { 1234, 56 },
                        { 1212, 33 },
                        { 1434, 80 },
                        { 1312, 78 },
                    } ;
    int i, j ;

    for ( i = 0 ; i <= 3 ; i++ )
    {
        printf ( "\n" ) ;
        for ( j = 0 ; j <= 1 ; j++ )
            printf ( "%d ", *( *( s + i ) + j ) ) ;
    }
}
```

And here is the output...

```
1234  56
1212  33
1434  80
1312  78
```

Three Dimensional Array

We aren't going to show a programming example that uses a three dimensional array. This is because, in practice, one rarely uses this array. However, an example of initialising a three dimensional array will consolidate your understanding of subscripts:

```
int arr[3][4][2] = {
                        {
                            { 2, 4 },
```

```
                    { 7, 8 },
                    { 3, 4 },
                    { 5, 6 }
            },
            {
                    { 7, 6 },
                    { 3, 4 },
                    { 5, 3 },
                    { 2, 3 }
            },
            {
                    { 8, 9 },
                    { 7, 2 },
                    { 3, 4 },
                    { 5, 1 },
            }
        } ;
```

A three dimensional array can be thought of as an array of arrays of arrays. The outer array has three elements, each of which is a two dimensional array of four one dimensional arrays, each of which contains five integers. In other words, a one dimensional array of two elements is constructed first. Then four such one dimensional arrays are placed one below the other to give a two dimensional array containing four rows. Then, three such two dimensional arrays are placed one behind the other to yield a three dimensional array containing three 2-dimensional arrays. In the array declaration note how the commas have been given. Figure 8.7 would possibly help you in visualising the situation better.

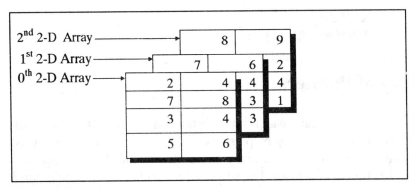

Figure 8.7

Again remember that the arrangement shown above is only conceptually true. In memory the same array elements are stored linearly as shown in Figure 8.8.

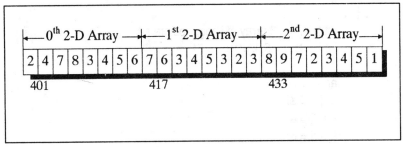

Figure 8.8

How would you refer to the array element 1 in the above array? The first subscript should be [2], since the element is in third two dimensional array; the second subscript should be [3] since the element is in fourth row of the two dimensional array; and the third subscript should be [1] since the element is in second position in the one dimensional array. We can therefore say that the element 1 can be referred as **arr[2][3][1]**. It may be noted here that the counting of array elements even for a 3-D array begins with zero. Can we not refer to this element using pointer notation? Of course, yes. For example, the following two expressions refer to the same element in the 3-D array:

```
arr[2][3][1]
*( *( *( arr + 2 ) + 3 ) + 1 )
```

Array of Pointers

The way there can be an array of **ints** or an array of **floats**, similarly there can be an array of pointers. Since a pointer variable always contains an address, an array of pointers would be nothing but a collection of addresses. The addresses present in the array of pointers can be addresses of isolated variables or addresses of array elements or any other addresses. All rules that apply to an ordinary array apply in toto to the array of pointers as well. I think a program would clarify the concept.

```
main( )
{
    int *arr[4] ;  /* array of integer pointers */
    int i = 31, j = 5, k = 19, l = 71, m ;

    arr[0] = &i ;
    arr[1] = &j ;
    arr[2] = &k ;
    arr[3] = &l ;

    for ( m = 0 ; m <= 3 ; m++ )
        printf ( "%d ", * ( arr[m] ) ) ;
}
```

Figure 8.9 shows the contents and the arrangement of the array of pointers in memory. As you can observe, **arr** contains addresses of isolated **int** variables **i, j, k** and **l**. The **for** loop in the program picks up the addresses present in **arr** and prints the values present at these addresses.

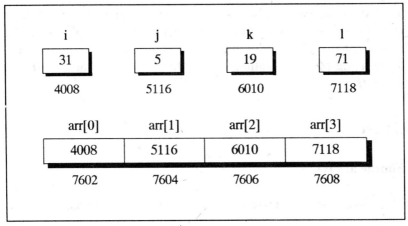

Figure 8.9

An array of pointers can even contain the addresses of other arrays.
The following program would justify this.

```
main( )
{
    int a[ ] = { 0, 1, 2, 3, 4 } ;
    int *p[ ] = { a, a + 1, a + 2, a + 3, a + 4 } ;

    printf ( "\n%u %u %d", p, *p, * ( *p ) ) ;
}
```

I would leave it for you to figure out the output of this program.

Summary

In this chapter we have learnt how to handle arrays in a variety of
forms. We have learnt how to declare arrays, how to initialise them
and how to access array elements using the subscript notation and the
pointer notation. We also took a look at the pointer arithmetic. We
have also investigated how to pass individual array elements to a
function or even how to pass entire array to a function.

We have covered one dimensional and two dimensional arrays and even peeked into three dimensional arrays. We have also seen the complicated topic of accessing array elements of a two dimensional array using pointer notation and finally the concept of an array of pointers.

Exercise

Simple arrays

[A] What will be the output of the following programs:

(a)
```
main( )
{
    int num[26], temp ;
    num[0] = 100 ;
    num[25] = 200 ;
    temp = num[25] ;
    num[25] = num[0] ,
    num[0] = temp ;
    printf ( "\n%d %d", num[0], num[25] ) ;
}
```

(b)
```
main( )
{
    int array[26], i ;
    for ( i = 0 ; i <= 25 ; i++ )
    {
        array[i] = 'A' + i ;
        printf ( "\n%d %c", array[i], array[i] ) ;
    }
}
```

(c)
```
main( )
{
    int sub[50], i ;
```

```
        for ( i = 0 ; i <= 48 ; i++ ) ;
        {
            sub[i] = i ;
            printf ( "\n%d", sub[i] ) ;
        }
    }
```

[B]   Point out the errors, if any, in the following program segments:

(a)   /* mixed has some char and some int values */
      int char mixed[100] ;

(b)   main( )
```
    {
        int a[10], i ;
        for ( i = 1 ; i <= 10 ; i++ )
        {
            scanf ( "%d", a[i] ) ;
            printf ( "%d", a[i] ) ;
        }
    }
```

(c)   main( )
```
    {
        int size ;
        scanf ( "%d", &size ) ;
        int arr[size] ;
        for ( i = 1 ; i <= size ; i++ )
        {
            scanf ( "%d", arr[i] ) ;
            printf ( "%d", arr[i] ) ;
        }
    }
```

[C]   Answer the following:

(a)   An array is a collection of

    1. different data types scattered throughout memory
    2. the same data type scattered throughout the memory
    3. the same data type placed next to each other in memory
    4. different data types placed next to each other in memory

(b)   Is this a correct array declaration?

    int num (25) ;

(c)   Which element of the array does this expression reference?

    num[4]

(d)   What is the difference between the 5's in these two expressions? (select the correct answer)

    int num[5] ;
    num[5] = 11 ;

    1. first is particular element, second is type
    2. first is array size, second is particular element
    3. first is particular element, second is array size
    4. both specify array size

(e)   State whether the following statements are True or False:

    1. The array **int num[26]** has twenty-six elements.
    2. The expression **num[1]** designates the first element in the array.
    3. The expression **num[27]** designates the twenty-eighth element in the array.

[D]   Attempt the following:

(a)   Twenty five numbers are entered from the keyboard into an array. Write a program to find out how many of them are positive, how many are negative, how many are even and how many odd.

(b)   Implement the following sorting algorithms on a set of 25 numbers. (Refer Figure 8.10 for the logic of the algorithms)

    -   Selection sort
    -   Bubble sort
    -   Insertion sort

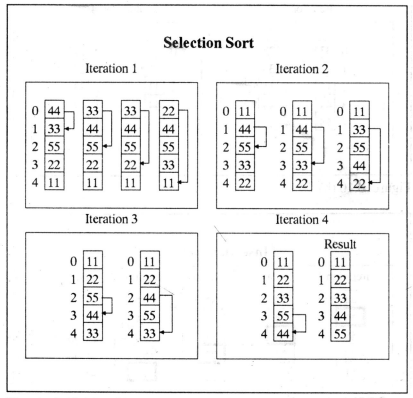

Figure 8.10 (a)

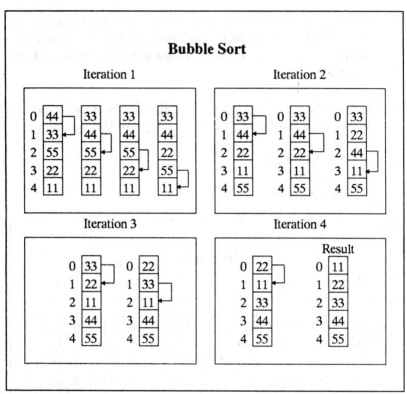

Figure 8.10 (b)

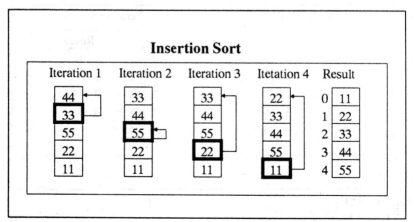

Figure 8.10 (c)

(c) Implement the following procedure to generate prime numbers from 1 to 100 into a program. This procedure is called sieve of Eratosthenes.

step 1   Fill an array **num[100]** with numbers from 1 to 100

step 2   Starting with the second entry in the array, set all its multiples to zero.

step 3   Proceed to the next non-zero element and set all its multiples to zero.

step 4   Repeat step 3 till you have set up the multiples of all the non-zero elements to zero

step 5   At the conclusion of step 4, all the non-zero entries left in the array would be prime numbers, so print out these numbers.

More on arrays, Arrays and pointers

[E] What will be the output of the following programs:

(a)
```
main( )
{
    int b[ ] = { 10, 20, 30, 40, 50 } ;
    int i ;
    for ( i = 0 ; i <= 4 ; i++ )
        printf ( "\n%d" *( b + i ) ) ;
}
```

(b)
```
main( )
{
    int b[ ] = { 0, 20, 0, 40, 5 } ;
    int i, *k ;
    k = b ;
    for ( i = 0 ; i <= 4 ; i++ )
    {
        printf ( "\n%d" *k ) ;
        k++ ;
    }
```

```
        }
(c)    main( )
       {
           int a[ ] = { 2, 4, 6, 8, 10 } ;
           int i ;
           change ( a, 5 ) ;
           for ( i = 0 ; i <= 4 ; i++ )
               printf( "\n%d", a[i] ) ;
       }
       change ( int *b, int n )
       {
           int i ;
           for ( i = 0 ; i < n ; i++ )
               *( b + i ) = *( b + i ) + 5 ;
       }

(d)    main( )
       {
           int a[5], i, b = 16 ;
           for ( i = 0 ; i < 5 ; i++ )
               a[i] = 2 * i ;
           f ( a, b ) ;
           for ( i = 0 ; i < 5 ; i++ )
               printf ( "\n%d", a[i] ) ;
           printf( "\n%d", b ) ;
       }
       f ( int *x, int y )
       {
           int i ;
           for ( i = 0 ; i < 5 ; i++ )
               *( x + i ) += 2 ;
           y += 2 ;
       }

(e)    main( )
```

```
{
    static int a[5] ;
    int i ;
    for ( i = 0 ; i <= 4 ; i++ )
        printf ( "\n%d", a[i] ) ;
}
```

(f)   main( )

```
{
    int a[5] = { 5, 1, 15, 20, 25 } ;
    int i, j, k = 1, m ;
    i = ++a[1] ;
    j = a[1]++ ;
    m = a[i++] ;
    printf ( "\n%d %d %d", i, j, m ) ;
}
```

[F]   Point out the errors, if any, in the following programs:

(a)   main( )

```
{
    int array[6] = { 1, 2, 3, 4, 5, 6 } ;
    int i ;
    for ( i = 0 ; i <= 25 ; i++ )
        printf ( "\n%d", array[i] ) ;
}
```

(b)   main( )

```
{
    int sub[50], i ;
    for ( i = 1 ; i <= 50 ; i++ )
    {
        sub[i] = i ;
        printf ( "\n%d" , sub[i] ) ;
    }
}
```

(c)   main( )
```
{
    int a[ ] = { 10, 20, 30, 40, 50 } ;
    int j ;
    j = a ;  /* store the address of zeroth element */
    j = j + 3 ;
    printf ( "\n%d" *j ) ;
}
```

(d)   main( )
```
{
    float a[ ] = { 13.24, 1.5, 1.5, 5.4, 3.5 } ;
    float *j ;
    j = a ;
    j = j + 4 ;
    printf ( "\n%d %d %d", j, *j, a[4] ) ;
}
```

(e)   main( )
```
{
    float a[ ] = { 13.24, 1.5, 1.5, 5.4, 3.5 } ;
    float *j, *k ;
    j = a ;
    k = a + 4 ;
    j = j * 2 ;
    k = k / 2 ;
    printf ( "\n%d %d", *j, *k ) ;
}
```

(f)   main( )
```
{
    int max = 5 ;
    float arr[max] ;
    for ( i = 0 ; i < max ; i++ )
        scanf ( "%f", &arr[i] ) ;
}
```

[G]   Answer the following:

(a)   What will happen if you try to put so many values into an array
      when you initialise it that the size of the array is exceeded?

      1. nothing
      2. possible system malfunction
      3. error message from the compiler
      4. other data may be overwritten

(b)   In an array **int arr[12]** the word **arr** represents the a_____
      of the array

(c)   What will happen if you put too few elements in an array when
      you initialise it?

      1. nothing
      2. possible system malfunction
      3. error message from the compiler
      4. unused elements will be filled with 0 's or garbage

(d)   What will happen if you assign a value to an element of an
      array whose subscript exceeds the size of the array?

      1. the element will be set to 0
      2. nothing, it's done all the time
      3. other data may be overwritten
      4. error message from the compiler

(e)   When you pass an array as an argument to a function, what
      actually gets passed?

      1. address of the array
      2. values of the elements of the array
      3. address of the first element of the array
      4. number of elements of the array

(f)   Which of these are reasons for using pointers?

1. To manipulate parts of an array
2. To refer to keywords such as **for** and **if**
3. To return more than one value from a function
4. To refer to particular programs more conveniently

(g)   If you don't initialise a static array, what will be the elements set to?

1. 0
2. an undetermined value
3. a floating point number
4. the character constant '\0'

(h)   State True or False:

Address of a floating point variable is always a whole number.

(i)   Which of the following is the correct way of declaring a float pointer:

1. float ptr ;
2. float *ptr ;
3. *float ptr ;
4. None of the above

(j)   Add the missing statement for the following program to print 35.

```
main( )
{
    int j, *ptr ;
    *ptr = 35 ;
    printf ( "\n%d", j ) ;
}
```

(k)   if **int s[5]** is a one dimensional array of integers, which of the
      following refers to the third element in the array?

      1. *(s + 2)
      2. *(s + 3)
      3. s + 3
      4. s + 2

[H]   Attempt the following:

(a)   Write a program which performs the following tasks:

      -   initialise an integer array of 10 elements in **main( )**
      -   pass the entire array to a function **modify( )**
      -   in **modify( )** multiply each element of array by 3
      -   return the control to **main( )** and print the new array
          elements in **main( )**

(b)   The screen is divided into 25 rows and 80 columns. The
      characters which are displayed on the screen are stored in a
      special memory called VDU memory (not to be confused with
      ordinary memory). Each character displayed on the screen
      occupies two bytes in VDU memory. The first of these bytes
      contains the ascii value of the character being displayed
      whereas the second byte contains the colour in which the
      character is displayed.

      For example, the ascii value of the character present on zeroth
      row and zeroth column on the screen is stored at location
      number 0xB8000000. Therefore the colour of this character
      would be present at location number 0xB8000000 + 1. Similar-
      ly ascii value of character in row 0, col 1 will be at location
      0xB8000000 + 2, and its colour at 0xB8000000 + 3.

      With this knowledge write a program which when executed
      would keep converting every capital letter on the screen to
      small case letter and every small case letter to capital letter.

The procedure should stop the moment the user hits a key from the keyboard.

This is an activity of a rampant Virus called Dancing Dolls. (For monochrome adapter, use 0xB0000000 instead of 0xB8000000).

More than one dimension

[I]   What will be the output of the following programs:

(a)   main( )
```
{
    int n[3][3] = {
                        2, 4, 3,
                        6, 8, 5,
                        3, 5, 1
                    };
    printf ( "\n%d %d %d", *n, n[3][3], n[2][2] ) ;
}
```

(b)   main( )
```
{
    int n[3][3] = {
                        2, 4, 3,
                        6, 8, 5,
                        3, 5, 1
                    };
    int i, *ptr ;
    ptr = n ;
    for ( i = 0 ; i <= 8 ; i++ )
        printf ( "\n%d", *( ptr + i ) ) ;
}
```

(c)   main( )
```
{
```

```
    int n[3][3] = {
                    2, 4, 3,
                    6, 8, 5,
                    3, 5, 1
            } ;
    int i, j ;
    for ( i = 0 ; i <= 2 ; i++ )
        for ( j = 0 ; j <= 2 ; j++ )
            printf ( "\n%d %d", n[i][j], *( *( n + i ) + j ) ) ;
}
```

[J]   Point out the errors, if any, in the following programs:

(a)   ```
main( )
{
    int twod[ ][ ] = {
                    2, 4,
                    6, 8
                } ;
    printf ("\n%d", twod) ;
}
```

(b)    ```
main( )
{
    int three[3][ ] = {
                    2, 4, 3,
                    6, 8, 2,
                    2, 3 ,1
                } ;
    printf ( "\n%d", three[1][1] ) ;
}
```

[K]   How will you initialise a three dimensional array **threed[3][2][3]**? How will you refer the first and last element in this array?

[L]   Attempt the following:

(a)   Write a program to pick up the largest number from any 5 row by 5 column matrix.

(b)   Write a program to obtain transpose of a 4 x 4 matrix. The transpose of a matrix is obtained by exchanging the elements of each row with the elements of the corresponding column.

(c)   Very often in fairs we come across a puzzle which contains 15 numbered square pieces, which can be moved horizontally or vertically. A possible arrangement of these pieces is shown below:

1	4	15	7
8	10	2	11
14	3	6	13
12	9	5	

Figure 8.11

As you can see there is a blank at bottom right corner. Implement the following procedure through a program:

Draw the boxes as shown above. Display the numbers in the above order. Allow the user to hit any of the arrow keys (up, down, left, or right).

If user hits say, right arrow key then the piece with a number 5 should move to the right and blank should replace the original position of 5. Similarly, if down arrow key is hit, then 13 should move down and blank should replace the original position of 13. If left arrow key or up arrow key is hit then no action should be taken.

The user would continue hitting the arrow keys till the numbers aren't arranged in ascending order.

Keep track of the number of moves in which the user manages to arrange the numbers in ascending order. The user who manages it in minimum number of moves is the one who wins.

How do we tackle the arrow keys? We cannot receive them using **scanf( )** function. Arrow keys are special keys which are identified by their 'scan codes'. Use the following function in your program. It would return the scan code of the arrow key being hit. Don't worry about how this function is written. We are going to deal with it later. The scan codes for the arrow keys are:

up arrow key - 72 down arrow key - 80
left arrow key - 75 right arrow key - 77

```
/* Returns scan code of the key that has been hit */
#include "dos.h"
getkey( )
{
    union REGS i, o ;

    while ( !kbhit( ) )
        ;
    i.h.ah = 0 ;
    int86 ( 22, &i, &o ) ;
    return ( o.h.ah ) ;
}
```

(d)   Those readers who are from an Engineering/Science back-ground may try, writing programs for following problems.

(1) Write a program to add two 6 x 6 matrices.
(2) Write a program to multiply any two 3 x 3 matrices.

(3) Write a program to sort all the elements of a 4 x 4 matrix.

(4) Write a program to obtain the determinant value of a 5 x 5 matrix.

9   *Puppetting On Strings*

261

In the last chapter you learnt how to define arrays of differing sizes and dimensions, how to initialise arrays, how to pass arrays to a function etc. With this knowledge under your belt, you should be ready ʻo handle strings, which are, simply put, a special kind of array. And strings, the ways to manipulate them, and how pointers are related to strings are going to be the topics of discussion in this chapter.

What are Strings

The way a group of integers can be stored in an integer array, similarly a group of characters can be stored in a character array. Character arrays are many a times also called strings. Most languages (like Basic, Fortran etc.) internally treat strings as character arrays, **but** somehow conceal this fact from the programmer. Character arrays or strings are used by programming languages to manipulate text such as words and sentences.

A string constant is a one dimensional array of characters terminated by a null ('\0'). For example,

```
char name[ ] = { 'H', 'A', 'E', 'S', 'L', 'E', 'R', '\0' } ;
```

Each character in the array occupies one byte of memory and the last character is always '\0'. What character is this? It looks like two characters, but it is actually only one character, with the \ indicating that what follows it is something special. '\0' is called null character. Note that '\0' and '0' are not same. Ascii value of '\0' is 0, whereas ascii value of '0' is 48. Figure 9.1 shows the way a character array is stored in memory. Note that the elements of the character array are stored in contiguous memory locations.

The terminating null ('\0') is important, because it is the only way the functions that work with a string can know where the string ends. In fact, a string not terminated by a '\0' is not really a string, but merely a collection of characters.

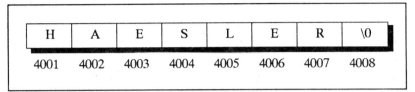

Figure 9.1

C concedes the fact that you would use strings very often and hence provides a shortcut for initialising strings. For example, the string used above can also be initialised as,

```
char name[ ] = "HAESLER" ;
```

Note that, in this declaration '\0' is not necessary. C inserts the null character automatically.

More about Strings

In what way are character arrays different than numeric arrays? Can elements in a character array be accessed in the same way as the elements of a numeric array? Do I need to take any special care of '\0'? Why numeric arrays don't end with a '\0'? Declaring strings is okay, but how do I manipulate them? Questions galore!! Well, let us settle some of these issues right away with the help of sample programs.

```
/* Program to demonstrate printing of a string */
main( )
{
    char name[ ] = "Klinsman" ;
    int i = 0 ;

    while ( i <= 7 )
    {
        printf ( "%c", name[i] ) ;
        i++ ;
```

```
        }
    }
```

And here is the output...

Klinsman

No big deal. We have initialised a character array, and then printed out the elements of this array within a **while** loop. Can we write the **while** loop without using the final value 7? We can; because we know that each character array always ends with a '\0'. Following program illustrates this.

```
main( )
{
    char name[ ] = "Klinsman" ;
    int i = 0 ;

    while ( name[i] != '\0' )
    {
        printf ( "%c", name[i] ) ;
        i++ ;
    }
}
```

And here is the output...

Klinsman

This program doesn't rely on the length of the string (number of characters in it) to print out its contents and hence is definitely more general than the earlier one. Here is another version of the same program; this one uses a pointer to access the array elements.

```
main( )
{
    char name[ ] = "Klinsman" ;
```

```
        char *ptr ;

        ptr = name ;  /* store base address of string */

        while ( *ptr != '\0' )
        {
            printf ( "%c", *ptr ) ;
            ptr++ ;
        }
}
```

As with the integer array, by mentioning the name of the array we get the base address (address of the zeroth element) of the array. This base address is stored in the variable **ptr** using,

```
    ptr = name ;
```

Once the base address is obtained in **ptr**, ***ptr** would yield the value at this address, which gets printed promptly through,

```
    printf ( "%c", *ptr ) ;
```

Then, **ptr** is incremented to point to the next character in the string. This derives from two facts: array elements are stored in contiguous memory locations and on incrementing a pointer it points to the immediately next location of its type. This process is carried out till **ptr** doesn't point to the last character in the string, that is, '\0'.

In fact, the character array elements can be accessed exactly in the same way as the elements of an integer array. Thus, all the following notations refer to the same element:

```
    name[i]
    *( name + i )
    *( i + name )
    i[name]
```

Even though there are so many ways (as shown above) to refer to the elements of a character array, rarely is any one of them used. This is because **printf( )** function has got a sweet and simple way of doing it, as shown below. Note that **printf( )** doesn't print the '\0'.

```
main( )
{
    char name[ ] = "Klinsman" ;
    printf ( "%s", name ) ;
}
```

The %s used in **printf( )** is a format specification for printing out a string. The same specification can be used to receive a string from the keyboard, as shown below.

```
main( )
{
    char name[25] ;

    printf ( "Enter your name " ) ;
    scanf ( "%s", name ) ;
    printf ( "Hello %s!", name ) ;
}
```

And here is a sample run of the program...

```
Enter your name Debashish
Hello Debashish!
```

Note that the declaration **char name[25]** sets aside 25 bytes under the array **name[ ],** whereas the **scanf( )** function fills in the characters typed at keyboard into this array until the enter key is hit. Once enter is hit, **scanf( )** places a '\0' in the array. Naturally, we should pass the base address of the array to the **scanf( )** function.

While entering the string using **scanf( )** we must be cautious about two things:

(a)   The length of the string should not exceed the dimension of the
       character array. This is because the C compiler doesn't perform
       bounds checking on character arrays. Hence, if you carelessly
       exceed the bounds there is always a danger of overwriting
       something important, and in that event, you would have
       nobody to blame but yourselves.

(b)   **scanf( )** is not capable of receiving multi-word strings. There-
       fore names such as 'Debashish Roy' would be unacceptable.
       The way to get around this limitation is by using the function
       gets( ). The usage of functions **gets( )** and its counterpart
       puts( ) is shown below.

```
main( )
{
    char name[25] ;

    printf ( "Enter your full name " ) ;
    gets ( name ) ;
    puts ( "Hello!" ) ;
    puts ( name ) ;
}
```

And here is the output...

```
Enter your name Debashish Roy
Hello!
Debashish Roy
```

The program and the output are self-explanatory except for the
fact that, **puts( )** can display only one string at a time (hence
the use of two **puts( )** in the program above). Also, on displaying a string, unlike **printf( )**, **puts( )** places the cursor on the
next line. Though **gets( )** is capable of receiving only one string
at a time, the plus point with **gets( )** is it can receive a
multi-word string.

Standard Library String Functions

With every C compiler a large set of useful string handling library functions are provided. The following figure lists the more commonly used functions along with their purpose.

Function	Use
strlen	Finds length of a string
strlwr	Converts a string to lowercase
strupr	Converts a string to uppercase
strcat	Appends one string at the end of another
strncat	Appends first n characters of a string at the end of another
strcpy	Copies a string into another
strncpy	Copies first n character of one string into another
strcmp	Compares two strings
strncmp	Compares first n characters of two strings
strcmpi	Compares two strings without regard to case ("i" denotes that this function ignores case)
stricmp	compares two strings without regard to case (identical to strcmpi)
strnicmp	Compares first n characters of two strings without regard to case
strdup	Duplicates a string
strchr	Finds first occurrence of a given character in a string
strrchr	Finds last occurrence of a given character in a string
strstr	Finds first occurrence of a given string in another string
strset	Sets all characters of string to a given character
strnset	Sets first n characters of a string to a given character
strrev	Reverses string

Figure 9.2

Out of the above list we shall discuss the functions **strlen( )**, **strcpy( )**, **strcat( )** and **strcmp( )**, since these are the most commonly used functions. This will also illustrate how the library functions in general handle strings. Let us study these functions one by one.

strlen( )

This function counts the number of characters present in a string. Its usage is illustrated in the following program.

```
main( )
{
    char arr[ ] = "Bamboozled" ;
    int len1, len2 ;

    len1 = strlen ( arr ) ;
    len2 = strlen ( "Humpty Dumpty" ) ;

    printf ( "\nstring = %s length = %d", arr, len1 ) ;
    printf ( "\nstring = %s length = %d", "Humpty Dumpty", len2 ) ;
}
```

The output would be...

```
string = Bamboozled length = 10
string = HumptyDumpty length = 13
```

Note that in the first call to the function **strlen( )**, we are passing the base address of the string, and the function in turn returns the length of the string. While calculating the length it doesn't count '\0'. Even in the second call,

```
len2 = strlen ( "Humpty Dumpty" ) ;
```

what gets passed to **strlen( )** is the address of the string and not the string itself. Can we not write a function **xstrlen( )** which imitates the standard library function **strlen( )**? Let us give it a try...

```
/* A look-alike of the function strlen( ) */
main( )
{
    char arr[ ] = "Bamboozled" ;
    int len1, len2 ;

    len1 = xstrlen ( arr ) ;
    len2 = xstrlen ( "Humpty Dumpty" ) ;

    printf ( "\nstring = %s length = %d", arr, len1 ) ;
    printf ( "\nstring = %s length = %d", "Humpty Dumpty", len2 ) ;
}

xstrlen ( char *s )
{
    int length = 0 ;

    while ( *s != '\0' )
    {
        length++ ;
        s++ ;
    }

    return ( length ) ;
}
```

The output would be...

```
string = Bamboozled length = 10
string = HumptyDumpty length = 13
```

The function **xstrlen( )** is fairly simple. All that it does is keep counting the characters till the end of string is not met. Or in other words keep counting characters till the pointer s doesn't point to '\0'.

strcpy( )

This function copies the contents of one string into another. The base addresses of the source and target strings should be supplied to this function. Here is an example of **strcpy( )** in action...

```
main( )
{
    char source[ ] = "Sayonara" ;
    char target[20] ;

    strcpy ( target, source ) ;
    printf ( "\nsource string = %s", source ) ;
    printf ( "\ntarget string = %s", target ) ;
}
```

And here is the output...

```
source string = Sayonara
target string = Sayonara
```

On supplying the base addresses, **strcpy( )** goes on copying the characters in source string into the target string till it doesn't encounter the end of source string ('\0'). It is our responsibility to see to it that the target string's dimension is big enough to hold the string being copied into it. Thus, a string gets copied into another, piecemeal, character by character. There is no short-cut for this. Let us now attempt to mimic **strcpy( )**, via our own string copy function, which we will call **xstrcpy( )**.

```
main( )
{
```

```
        char source[ ] = "Sayonara" ;
        char target[20] ;

        xstrcpy ( target, source ) ;
        printf ( "\nsource string = %s", source ) ;
        printf ( "\ntarget string = %s", target ) ;
    }

xstrcpy ( char *t, char *s )
{
    while ( *s != '\0' )
    {
        *t = *s ;
        s++ ;
        t++ ;
    }
    *t = '\0' ;
}
```

The output of the program would be...

```
    source string = Sayonara
    target string = Sayonara
```

Note that having copied the entire source string into the target string, it is necessary to place a '\0' into the target string, to mark its end.

strcat( )

This function concatenates the source string at the end of the target string. For example, "Bombay" and "Nagpur" on concatenation would result into a string "BombayNagpur". Here is an example of **strcat( )** at work.

```
    main( )
    {
```

```
        char source[ ] = "Folks!" ;
        char target[30] = "Hello" ;

        strcat ( target, source ) ;
        printf ( "\nsource string = %s", source ) ;
        printf ( "\ntarget string = %s", target ) ;
}
```

And here is the output...

```
        source string = Folks!
        target string = HelloFolks!
```

Note that the target string has been made big enough to hold the final string. I leave it to you to develop your own **xstrcat( )** on lines of **xstrlen( )** and **xstrcpy( )**.

strcmp( )

This is a function which compares two strings to find out whether they are same or different. The two strings are compared character by character until there is a mismatch or end of one of the strings is reached, whichever occurs first. If the two strings are identical, **strcmp( )** returns a value zero. If they're not, it returns the numeric difference between the ascii values of the non-matching characters. Here is a program which puts **strcmp( )** in action.

```
        main( )
        {
            char string1[ ] = "Jerry" ;
            char string2[ ] = "Ferry" ;
            int i, j, k ;

            i = strcmp ( string1, "Jerry" ) ;
            j = strcmp ( string1, string2 ) ;
            k = strcmp ( string1, "Jerry boy" ) ;
```

```
        printf ( "\n%d %d %d", i, j, k ) ;
}
```

And here is the output...

    0 4 -32

In the first call to **strcmp( )**, the two strings are identical - "Jerry" and "Jerry" - and the value returned by **strcmp( )** is zero. In the second call, the first character of "Jerry" doesn't match with the first character of "Ferry" and the result is 4, which is the numeric difference between ascii value of 'J' and ascii value of 'F'. In the third call to **strcmp( )** "Jerry" doesn't match with "Jerry boy", because the null character at the end of "Jerry" doesn't match the blank in "Jerry boy". The value returned is -32, which is the value of null character minus the ascii value of space i.e. '\0' minus ' ', which is equal to -32.

The exact value of mismatch will rarely concern us. All we usually want to know is whether or not the first string is alphabetically above the second string. If it is, a positive value is returned; if it isn't, a negative value is returned. Any non-zero value means there is a mismatch. Try to implement this procedure into a function **xstrcmp( )**.

Two Dimensional Array of Characters

In the last chapter we saw several examples of 2-dimensional integer arrays. Let's now look at a similar entity, but one dealing with characters. Our example program asks you to type your name. When you do so, it checks your name against a master list to see if you are worthy of entry to the palace. Here's the program...

```
#define FOUND 1
#define NOTFOUND 0
```

```
main( )
{
    char masterlist[6][10] = {
                                "akshay",
                                "parag",
                                "raman",
                                "srinivas",
                                "gopal",
                                "rajesh"
                            } ;
    int i, flag, a ;
    char yourname[10] ;

    printf ( "\nEnter your name " ) ;
    scanf ( "%s", yourname ) ;

    flag = NOTFOUND ;
    for ( i = 0 ; i <= 5 ; i++ )
    {
        a = strcmp ( &masterlist[i][0], yourname ) ;
        if ( a == 0 )
        {
            printf ( "Welcome, you can enter the palace" ) ;
            flag = FOUND ;
            break ;
        }
    }

    if ( flag == NOTFOUND )
        printf ( "Sorry, you are a trespasser" ) ;
}
```

And here is the output for two sample runs of this program...

```
Enter your name dinesh
Sorry, you are a trespasser
Enter your name raman
```

Welcome, you can enter the palace

Notice how the two dimensional character array has been initialised. The order of the subscripts in the array declaration is important. The first subscript gives the number of names in the array, while the second subscript gives the length of each item in the array.

Instead of initialising names, had these names been supplied from the keyboard, the program segment would have looked like this...

```
for ( i = 0 ; i <= 5 ; i++ )
    scanf ( "%s", &masterlist[i][0] ) ;
```

While comparing the strings through **strcmp( )**, note that the addresses of the strings are being passed to **strcmp( )**. As seen in the last section, if the two strings match, **strcmp( )** would return a value 0, otherwise it would return a non-zero value.

The variable **flag** is used to keep a record of whether the control did reach inside the **if** or not. To begin with, we set **flag** to NOTFOUND. Later through the loop if the names match, **flag** is set to FOUND. When the control reaches beyond the **for** loop, if **flag** is still set to NOTFOUND, it means none of the names in the **masterlist[ ][ ]** matched with the one supplied from the keyboard.

The names would be stored in the memory as shown in Figure 9.3. Note that each string ends with a '\0'. The arrangement as you can appreciate is similar to that of a two dimensional numeric array.

Here, 1001, 1011, 1021 etc. are the base addresses of successive names. As seen from the above pattern some of the names do not occupy all the bytes reserved for them. For example, even though 10 bytes are reserved for storing the name "akshay", it occupies only 7 bytes. Thus, 3 bytes go waste. Similarly, for each name there is some amount of wastage. In fact, more the number of names, more would be the wastage. Can this not be avoided? Yes, it can be... by using what is called an 'array of pointers', which is our next topic of discussion.

1001	a	k	s	h	a	y	\0			
1011	p	a	r	a	g	\0				
1021	r	a	m	a	n	\0				
1031	s	r	i	n	i	v	a	s	\0	
1041	g	o	p	a	l	\0				
1051	r	a	j	e	s	h	\0			

1060 (last location)

Figure 9.3

Array of Pointers to Strings

As we know, a pointer variable always contains an address. Therefore, if we construct an array of pointers it would contain a number of addresses. Let us see how the names in the earlier example can be stored in the array of pointers.

```
char *names[ ] = {
                  "akshay",
                  "parag",
                  "raman",
                  "srinivas",
                  "gopal",
                  "rajesh"
              };
```

In this declaration **names[ ]** is an array of pointers. It contains base addresses of respective names. That is, base address of "akshay" is stored in **names[0]**, base address of "parag" is stored in **names[1]** and so on. This is depicted in the following figure.

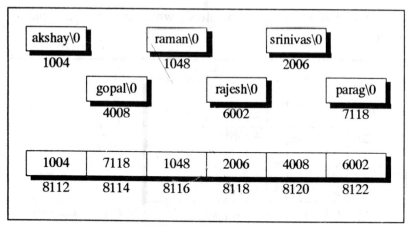

Figure 9.4

In the two dimensional array of characters, the strings occupied 60 bytes. As against this in array of pointers, the strings occupy only 41 bytes. Note that in two dimensional array of characters, the last name ended at location number 1060, whereas in array of pointers to strings, it ends at 1041. A substantial saving, you would agree. But realise that acually 19 bytes are not saved, since 10 bytes are sacrificed for storing the addresses in the array **names[ ]**. Thus, one reason to store strings in an array of pointers is to make a more efficient use of available memory.

Another reason to use an array of pointers to store strings is to obtain greater ease in manipulation of the strings. This is shown by the following programs. The first one uses a two dimensional array of characters to store the names, whereas the second uses an array of pointers to strings. The purpose of both the programs is very simple. We want to exchange the position of the names "raman" and "srinivas".

```
/* Exchange names using 2-D array of characters */
main( )
{
    char names[ ][10] = {
```

```
                              "akshay",
                              "parag",
                              "raman",
                              "srinivas",
                              "gopal",
                              "rajesh"
                         } ;
        int i ;
        char t ;

        printf ( "\nOriginal: %s %s", &names[2][0], &names[3][0] ) ;

        for ( i = 0 ; i <= 9 ; i++ )
        {
            t = names[2][i] ;
            names[2][i] = names[3][i] ;
            names[3][i] = t ;
        }

        printf ( "\nNew: %s %s", &names[2][0], &names[3][0] ) ;
    }
```

And here is the output...

```
    Original: raman srinivas
    New: srinivas raman
```

Note that in this program to exchange the names we are required to exchange corresponding characters of the two names. In effect, 10 exchanges are needed to interchange two names.

Let us see, if the number of exchanges can be reduced by using an array of pointers to strings. Here is the program...

```
    main( )
    {
        char *names[ ] = {
```

```
                              "akshay",
                              "parag",
                              "raman",
                              "srinivas",
                              "gopal",
                              "rajesh"
                        } ;
        char *temp ;

        printf ( "Original: %s %s", names[2], names[3] ) ;

        temp = names[2] ;
        names[2] = names[3] ;
        names[3] = temp ;

        printf ( "\nNew: %s %s", names[2], names[3] ) ;
}
```

And here is the output...

```
Original: raman srinivas
New: srinivas raman
```

The output is same as the earlier program. In this program all that we are required to do is exchange the addresses (of the names) stored in the array of pointers, rather than the names themselves. Thus, by effecting just one exchange we are able to interchange names. This makes handling strings very convenient.

Thus, from the point of view of efficient memory usage and ease of programming, an array of pointers to strings definitely scores over a two dimensional character array. That is why, even though in principle strings can be stored and handled through a two dimensional array of characters, in actual practise it is the array of pointers to strings which is more commonly used.

Limitation of Array of Pointers to Strings

When we are using a two dimensional array of characters we are at liberty to either initialise the strings where we are declaring the array, or receive the strings using **scanf( )** function. However, when we are using an array of pointers to strings we can initialise the strings at the place where we are declaring the array, but we cannot receive the strings from keyboard using **scanf( )**. Thus, the following program would never work out.

```
main( )
{
    char *names[6] ;
    int i ;

    for ( i = 0 ; i <= 5 ; i++ )
    {
        printf ( "\nEnter name " ) ;
        scanf ( "%s", names[i] ) ;
    }
}
```

The program doesn't work because, when we are declaring the array it is containing garbage values. And it would be definitely wrong to send these garbage values to **scanf( )** as the addresses where it should keep the strings received from the keyboard.

Summary

In this chapter we have examined strings, which are nothing but arrays of characters. We have seen how the strings are stored in memory, how to initialise strings, and how to access elements of a string using subscript and pointer notations. We have learnt two new functions to input and output strings: **gets( )** and **puts( )**; and four more functions **strlen( )**, **strcpy( )**, **strcat( )** and **strcmp( )** which can manipulate strings. More importantly we imitated some of these functions to learn how these standard library functions are written.

We also explored the topic of two dimensional array of characters, and a new data type for storing strings: the array of pointers to strings. Lastly we pointed out what are the benifits and limitations of these two approaches for storing strings.

Exercise

Simple strings

[A]   What will be the output of the following programs:

(a)
```
main( )
{
    char c[2] = "A" ;
    printf ( "\n%c", c[0] ) ;
    printf ( "\n%s", c ) ;
}
```

(b)
```
main( )
{
    char s[ ] = "Get organised! learn C!!" ;
    printf ( "\n%s", &s[2] ) ;
    printf ( "\n%s", s ) ;
    printf ( "\n%s", &s ) ;
    printf ( "\n%c", s[2] ) ;
}
```

(c)
```
main( )
{
    char s[ ] = "No two viruses work similarly" ;
    int i = 0 ;
    while ( s[i] != 0 )
    {
```

```
            printf ( "\n%c %c", s[i], *( s + i ) ) ;
            printf ( "\n%c %c", i[s], *( i + s ) ) ;
            i++ ;
        }
    }
```

(d)   main( )
```
    {
        char s[ ] = "Churchgate: no church no gate" ;
        char t[25] ;
        char *ss, *tt
        ss = s ;
        while ( *ss != '\0' )
            *ss++ = *tt++ ;
        printf ( "\n%s", t ) ,
    }
```

(e)   main( )
```
    {
        char s[ ] = "Mumbadevi" ;
        char t[25] ;
        char *ss, *tt ;
        ss = s ;
        while ( *ss++ = *tt++ ) ;
            printf ( "\n%s", t ) ;
    }
```

[B]   Point out the errors, if any, in the following programs:

(a)   main( )
```
    {
        int arr[ ] = { 'A', 'B', 'C', 'D' } ;
        int i ;
        for ( i = 0 ; i <= 3 ; i++ )
            printf ( "\n%d", arr[i] ) ;
    }
```

(b)
```
main( )
{
    char arr[8] = "Rhombus" ;
    int i ;
    for ( i = 0 ; i <= 7 ; i++ )
        printf ( "\n%d", *arr ) ;
        arr++ ;
}
```

[C] Answer the following:

(a) "A" is a _____ while 'A' is a _____.

(b) A string is terminated by a _____ character, which is written as _____.

(c) The array char **name[10]** can consist of a maximum of _____ characters.

(d) True or False:

The array elements are always stored in contiguous memory locations.

(e) Which is more appropriate for reading in a multi-word string?

gets( )   printf( )   scanf( )   puts( )

(f) If the string "Hackers have put us on hit list" is fed to the following set of **scanf( )** statements, what will be the contents of the array **s** in each case?

```
static char s[30] ;
scanf ( "%s", &s[2] ) ;
scanf ( "%s", s ) ;
scanf ( "%s", &s ) ;
scanf ( "%c", &s[2] ) ;
```

```
scanf ( "%c", &s ) ;
```

[D] Answer the following:

(a) Observe the purpose of the functions given in Figure 9.2 and write your own functions (like say, xstrlen, xstrupr etc.) which imitate these standard library functions.

(b) Following program uses certain functions. Observe the sample run of this program and write down the code for these user-defined functions.

```
main( )
{
    char mess[ ] = "Do not blame me, I never voted VP";
    char newmess[7] ;
    xleft ( mess, newmess, 6 ) ;
    printf ( "\n%s", newmess ) ;
    xright ( mess, newmess, 6 ) ;
    printf ( "\n%s", newmess ) ;
    xsubstr ( mess, newmess, 8, 5 ) ;
    printf ( "\n%s", newmess ) ;
}
```

The output of this program would be...

```
Do not
ted VP
blame
```

(c) Write a program that will print out all the rotations of a string typed into it. For example, the rotations of the word "space" are:

```
space      paces      acesp      cespa      espac
```

(d)   Write a program that replaces two or more consecutive blanks in a string by a single blank. For example, if the input is

Grim   return   to   the   planet   of   apes!!

the output should be

Grim return to the planet of apes!!

Two dimensional array, Array of pointers to strings

[E]   Answer the following:

(a)   How many bytes in memory will be occupied by the following array of pointers to strings? How many bytes would be required to store the same strings, if they are stored in a two dimensional character arrray?

```
char *mess[ ] = {
                    "Hammer and tongs",
                    "Tooth and nail",
                    "Spit and polish",
                    "You and C"
            };
```

(b)   Can an array of pointers to strings be used to collect strings from the keyboard? If not, why not?

[F]   Answer the following:

(a)   Write a program to count the number of 'e' in the following array of pointers to strings:

```
char *s[ ] = {
                    "We will teach you how to...",
                    "Move a mountain",
                    "Level a building",
```

```
                    "Erase the past",
                    "Make a million",
                    "...all through C!"
            } ;
```

(b)   Develop a program that receives the month and year from the keyboard as integers and prints the calendar in the following format.

March 1995						
Mon	Tue	Wed	Thu	Fri	Sat	Sun
		1	2	3	4	5
6	7	8	9	10	11	12
13	14	15	16	17	18	19
20	21	22	23	24	25	26
27	28	29	30	31		

Note that according to the Gregorian calendar 01/01/1900 was Monday. With this as the base the calendar should be generated.

(c)   Modify the above program suitably so that once the calendar for a particular month and year has been displayed on the screen, then using arrow keys the user must be able to change the calendar in the following manner:

Up arrow key : Next year, same month
Down arrow key : Previous year, same month
Right arrow key: Same year, next month
Left arrow key : Same year, previous month

If the escape key is hit then the procedure should stop.

Hint: Use the **getkey( )** function discussed in Chapter 8, problem number [L](c).

(d)   Write a program to reverse the strings stored in the following array of pointers to strings:

```
char *s[ ] = {
            "To err is human...",
            "But to really mess things up...",
            "One needs to know C!!"
        } ;
```

Hint: Write a function **xstrrev (string)** which should reverse the contents of one string. Call this function for reversing each string stored in **s**.

10 *Structures*

Why Use Structures

289

Which mechanic is good enough who knows how to repair only one type of vehicle? None. Same thing is true about C language. It wouldn't have been so popular had it been able to handle only all **ints**, or all **floats** or all **chars** at a time. In fact when we handle real world data, we don't usually deal with little atoms of information by themselves - things like integers, characters and such. Instead we deal with entities that are collections of things, each thing having its own attributes, just as the entity we call a 'book' is a collection of things such as title, author, call number, publisher, number of pages, date of publication etc. As you can see all this data is dissimilar, for example author is a string, whereas number of pages is an integer. For dealing with such collections, C provides a data type called 'structure'. A structure gathers together, different atoms of information that comprise a given entity. And structures is the topic of this chapter.

Why Use Structures

We have seen earlier how ordinary variables can hold one piece of information and how arrays can hold a number of pieces of information of the same data type. These two data types can handle a great variety of situations. But quite often we deal with entities that are collection of dissimilar data types.

For example, suppose you want to store data about a book. You might want to store its name (a string), its price (a float) and number of pages in it (an int). If data about say 3 such books is to be stored, then we can follow two approaches:

(a)   Construct individual arrays, one for storing names, another for storing prices and still another for storing number of pages.

(b)   Use a structure variable.

Let us examine these two approaches one by one. For the sake of programming convenience assume that the names of books would be single character long.

```
main( )
{
    char name[3] ;
    float price[3] ;
    int pages[3], i ;

    printf ( "\nEnter names, prices and no. of pages of 3 books\n" ) ;

    for ( i = 0 ; i <= 2 ; i++ )
        scanf ( "%c %f %d", &name[i], &price[i], &pages[i] );

    printf ( "\nAnd this is what you entered\n" ) ;
    for ( i = 0 ; i <= 2 ; i++ )
        printf ( "%c %f %d\n", name[i], price[i], pages[i] );
}
```

And here is the sample run...

```
Enter names, prices and no. of pages of 3 books
A  100.00  354
C  256.50  682
F  233.70  512

And this is what you entered
A  100.000000  354
C  256.500000  682
F  233.700000  512
```

This approach no doubt allows you to store names, prices and number of pages. But as you must have realised, it is an unwieldy approach that obscures the fact that you are dealing with a group of characteristics related to a single entity: the book.

The program becomes more difficult to handle as the number of items relating to the book go on increasing. For example, we would be required to use a number of arrays, if we also decide to store name of the publisher, date of purchase of book etc. To solve this problem, C provides a special data type... the structure.

A structure contains a number of data types grouped together. These data types may or may not be of the same type. The following example illustrates the use of this data type.

```
main( )
{
    struct book
    {
        char name ;
        float price ;
        int pages ;
    } ;
    struct book b1, b2, b3 ;

    printf ( "\nEnter names, prices & no. of pages of 3 books\n" ) ;
    scanf ( "%c %f %d", &b1.name, &b1.price, &b1.pages ) ;
    scanf ( "%c %f %d", &b2.name, &b2.price, &b2.pages ) ;
    scanf ( "%c %f %d", &b3.name, &b3.price, &b3.pages ) ;

    printf ( "\nAnd this is what you entered" ) ;
    printf ( "\n%c %f %d", b1.name, b1.price, b1.pages ) ;
    printf ( "\n%c %d %f", b2.name, b2.price, b2.pages ) ;
    printf ( "\n%c %d %f", b3.name, b3.price, b3.pages ) ;
}
```

And here is the output...

```
Enter names, prices and no. of pages of 3 books
A 100.00 354
C 256.50 682
F 233.70 512
```

```
And this is what you entered
A 100.000000 354
C 256.500000 682
F 233.700000 512
```

This program demonstrates two fundamental aspects of structures:

(a)   declaration of a structure
(b)   accessing of structure elements

Let us now look at these concepts one by one.

Declaring A Structure

In our example program, the following statement declares the structure type:

```
struct book
{
     char name ;
     float price ;
     int pages ;
} ;
```

This statement defines a new data type called **struct book**. Each variable of this data type will consist of a character variable called **name**, a float variable called **price** and an integer variable called **pages**. The general form of a structure declaration statement is given below:

```
struct <structure name>
{
     structure element 1 ;
     structure element 2 ;
     structure element 3 ;
```

```
      ......
      ......
   } ;
```

Once the new strutcture data type has been defined one or more
variables can be declared to be of that type. For example the variables
b1, b2, b3 can be declared to be of the type **struct book**, as,

```
   struct book b1, b2, b3 ;
```

This statement sets aside space in memory. It makes available space
to hold all the elements in the structure: in this case, 7 bytes... one for
name, four for **price** and two for **pages.** These bytes are always in
adjacent memory locations.

If we so desire, we can combine the declaration of the structure type
and the structure variables in one statement.

For example,

```
   struct book
   {
       char name ;
       float price ;
       int pages ;
   } ;
   struct book b1, b2, b3 ;
```

is same as...

```
   struct book
   {
       char name ;
       float price ;
       int pages ;
   } b1, b2, b3 ;
```

or even...

```
struct
{
    char name ;
    float price ;
    int pages ;
} b1, b2, b3 ;
```

Like primary variables and arrays, structure variables can also be initialised where they are declared. The format used is quite similar to that used to initiate arrays.

```
struct book
{
    char name[10] ;
    float price ;
    int pages ;
} ;
struct book b1 = { "Basic", 130.00, 550 } ;
struct book b2 = { "Physics", 150.80, 800 } ;
```

Note the following points while declaring a structure type:

(a)   The closing brace in the structure type declaration must be followed by a semicolon.

(b)   It is important to understand that a structure type declaration does not tell the compiler to reserve any space in memory. All a structure declaration does is, it defines the 'form' of the structure.

(c)   Usually structure type declaration appears at the top of the source code file, before any variables or functions are defined. In very large programs they are usually put in a separate header file, and the file is included (using the preprocessor directive **#include**) in whichever program we want to use this structure type.

Accessing Structure Elements

Having declared the structure type and the structure variables, let us see how the elements of the structure can be accessed.

In arrays we can access individual elements of an array using a subscript. Structures use a different scheme. They use a dot (.) operator. So to refer to **pages** of the structure defined in our sample program we have to use,

    b1.pages

Similarly, to refer to **price** we would use,

    b1.price

Note that before the dot there must always be a structure variable and after the dot there must always be a structure element.

How Structure Elements are Stored

Whatever be the elements of a structure, they are always stored in contiguous memory locations. This can be illustrated by the following program:

```
/* Memory map of structure elements */
main( )
{
    struct book
    {
        char name ;
        float price ;
        int pages ;
    } ;
    struct book b1 = { 'B', 130.00, 550 } ;
```

```
        printf ( "\nAddress of name = %u", &b1.name ) ;
        printf ( "\nAddress of price = %u", &b1.price ) ;
        printf ( "\nAddress of pages = %u", &b1.pages ) ;
    }
```

Here is the output of the program...

```
    Address of name = 1001
    Address of price = 1002
    Address of pages = 1006
```

Actually the structure elements are stored in memory as shown in the following figure:

b1.name	b1.price	b1.pages
'B'	130.00	550

Figure 10.1

Array of Structures

Our sample program showing usage of structure is rather simple minded. All it does is, it receives values into various structure elements and output these values. But that's all we intended to do anyway... show how structure types are created, how structure variables are declared and how individual elements of a structure variable are referenced.

In our sample program, to store data of 100 books we would be required to use 100 different structure variables from **b1** to **b100**, which is definitely not very convenient. A better approach would be to use an array of structures. Following program shows how to use an array of structures.

```
/* Usage of an array of structures */
main( )
{
    struct book
    {
        char name ;
        float price ;
        int pages ;
    } ;

    struct book b[100] ;
    int i ;

    for ( i = 0 ; i <= 99 ; i++ )
    {
        printf ( "\nEnter name, price and pages " ) ;
        scanf ( "%c %f %d", &b[i].name, &b[i].price, &b[i].pages ) ;
    }

    for ( i = 0 ; i <= 99 ; i++ )
        printf ( "\n%c %f %d", b[i].name, b[i].price, b[i].pages ) ;
}
```

Now a few comments about the program:

(a)   Notice how the array of structures is declared...

```
struct book b[100] ;
```

This provides space in memory for 100 structures of the type **struct book**.

(b)   The syntax we use to reference each element of the array **b** is similar to the syntax used for arrays of **ints** and **chars**. For example, we refer to zeroth book's price as **b[0].price**. Similarly, we refer first book's pages as **b[1].pages**.

(c)   It should be appreciated what careful thought Dennis Ritchie has put into C language. He first defined array as a collection of similar elements; then realised that dissimilar data types which are often found in real life cannot be handled using arrays, therefore created a new data type called structure. But even using structures programming convenience could not be achieved, because a lot of variables (**b1** to **b100** for storing data about hundred books) needed to be handled. And therefore he allowed us to create an array of structures; an array of similar data types which themselves are a collection of dissimilar data types. Hats off to the genius!

(d)   In an array of structures all elements of the array are stored in adjacent memory locations. Since each element of this array is a structure, and since all structure elements are always stored in adjacent locations you can very well visualise the arrangement of array of structures in memory. In our example, **b[0]**'s **name**, **price** and **pages** in memory would be immediately followed by **b[1]**'s **name**, **price** and **pages**, and so on.

Additional Features of Structures

Let us now explore the intricacies of structures with a view of programming convenience. We would highlight these intricacies with suitable examples:

(a)   The values of a structure variable can be assigned to another structure variable of the same type using the assignment operator. It is not necessary to copy the structure elements piecemeal. Obviously, programmers prefer assignment to piecemeal copying. This is shown in the following example.

```
main( )
```

```
        {
            struct employee
            {
                char name[10] ;
                int age ;
                float salary ;
            } ;
            struct employee e1 = { "Sanjay", 30, 5500.50 } ;
            struct employee e2, e3 ;

            /* piece-meal copying */
            strcpy ( e2.name, e1.name ) ;
            e2.age = e1.age ;
            e2.salary = e1.salary ;

            /* copying all elements at one go */
            e3 = e2 ;

            printf ( "\n%s %d %f", e1.name, e1.age, e1.salary ) ;
            printf ( "\n%s %d %f", e2.name, e2.age, e2.salary ) ;
            printf ( "\n%s %d %f", e3.name, e3.age, e3.salary ) ;
        }
```

The output of the program would be...

```
Sanjay 30 5500.500000
Sanjay 30 5500.500000
Sanjay 30 5500.500000
```

Ability to copy the contents of all structure elements of one variable into the corresponding elements of another structure variable is rather surprising, since C does not allow assigning the contents of one array to another just by equating the two. As we saw earlier, for copying arrays we have to copy the contents of the array element by element.

This copying of all structure elements at one go has been possible only because the structure elements are stored in contiguous memory locations. Had this not been so, we would have been required to copy structure variables element by element. And who knows, had this been so, structures would not have become popular at all.

(b)   One structure can be nested within another structure. Using this facility complex data types can be created. The following program shows nested structures at work.

```
main( )
{
    struct address
    {
        char phone[15] ;
        char city[25] ;
        int pin ;
    } ;

    struct emp
    {
        char name[25] ;
        struct address a ;
    } ;
    struct emp e = { "jeru", "531046", "nagpur", 10 };

    printf ( "\nname = %s phone = %s", e.name, e.a.phone ) ;
    printf ( "\ncity = %s pin = %d", e.a.city, e.a.pin ) ;
}
```

And here is the output...

```
name = jeru phone = 531046
city = nagpur pin = 10
```

Notice the method used to access the elements of a structure that is a part of another structure. Here, the dot operator is used twice, as in the expression,

e.a.pin or e.a.city

Of course, the nesting process need not stop at this level. We can nest a structure within a structure, within another structure, which is in still another structure and so on... till the time we can comprehend the structure ourselves. Such construction however gives rise to variable names that can be surprisingly self descriptive, for example:

maruti.engine.bolt.large.qty

This clearly signifies that we are referring to the quantity of large sized bolts which fit on an engine of a maruti car.

(c) Like an ordinary variable, a structure variable can also be passed to a function. We may either pass individual structure elements or the entire structure at one go. Let us examine both the approaches one by one using suitable programs.

```
/* Passing individual structure elements */
main( )
{
    struct book
    {
        char name[25] ;
        char author[25] ;
        int callno ;
    } ;
    struct book b1 = { "Let us C", "YPK", 101 } ;

    display ( b1.name, b1.author, b1.callno ) ;
}
```

```
display ( char *s, char *t, int n )
{
    printf ( "\n%s %s %d", s, t, n ) ;
}
```

And here is the output...

Let us C YPK 101

Observe that in the declaration of the structure, **name** and **author** have been declared as arrays. Therefore, when we call the function **display( )** using,

```
display ( b1.name, b1.author, b1.callno ) ;
```

we are passing the base addresses of the arrays **name** and **author**, but the value stored in **callno**. Thus, this is a mixed call: a call by reference as well as a call by value.

It can be immediately realised that to pass individual elments would become more tedious as the number of structure elements go on increasing. A better way would be to pass the entire structure variable at a time. This method is shown in the following program.

```
struct book
{
    char name[25] ;
    char author[25] ;
    int callno ;
} ;

main( )
{
    struct book b1 = { "Let us C", "YPK", 101 } ;
    display ( b1 ) ;
}
```

```
display ( struct book b )
{
    printf ( "\n%s %s %d", b.name, b.author, b.callno ) ;
}
```

And here is the output...

Let us C YPK 101

Note that here the calling of function **display( )** becomes quite compact,

```
display ( b1 ) ;
```

Having collected what is being passed to the **display( )** function, the question comes, how do we define the formal arguments in the function. We cannot say,

```
struct book b1 ;
```

because the data type **struct book** is not known to the function **display( )**. Therefore, it becomes necessary to define the structure type **struct book** outside **main( )**, so that it becomes known to all functions in the program.

(d)   The way we can have a pointer pointing to an **int**, or a pointer pointing to a **char**, similarly we can have a pointer pointing to a **struct**. Such pointers are known as 'structure pointers'.

Let us look at a program which demonstrates the usage of a structure pointer.

```
main( )
{
    struct book
    {
```

```
            char name[25] ;
            char author[25] ;
            int callno ;
    } ;
    struct book b1 = { "Let us C", "YPK", 101 } ;
    struct book *ptr ;

    ptr = &b1 ;
    printf ( "\n%s %s %d", b1.name, b1.author, b1.callno ) ;
    printf ( "\n%s %s %d", ptr->name, ptr->author, ptr->callno ) ;
}
```

The first **printf( )** is as usual. The second **printf( )** however is peculiar. We can't use **ptr.name** or **ptr.callno** because **ptr** is not a structure variable but a pointer to a structure, and the dot operator requires a structure variable on its left. In such cases C provides an operator **->**, called an arrow operator to refer to the structure elements. Remember that on the left hand side of the '.' structure operator, there must always be a structure variable, whereas on the left hand side of the '->' operator there must always be a pointer to a structure. The arrangement of the structure variable and pointer to structure in memory is shown in the figure given below.

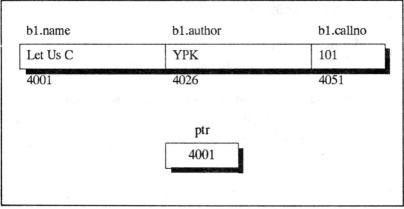

Figure 10.2

Can we not pass the address of a structure variable to a function? We can. The following program demonstrates this.

```
/* Passing address of a structure variable */
struct book
{
    char name[25] ;
    char author[25] ;
    int callno ;
} ;

main( )
{
    struct book b1 = { "Let us C", "YPK", 101 } ;
    display ( &b1 ) ;
}

display ( struct book *b )
{
    printf ( "\n%s %s %d", b->name, b->author, b->callno ) ;
}
```

And here is the output...

```
Let us C YPK 101
```

Again note that to access the structure elements using pointer to a structure we have to use the '->' operator.

Also the structure **struct book** should be declared outside **main( )** such that this data type is available to **display( )** while declaring pointer to the structure.

Uses of Structures

Where are structures useful? The immediate application that comes to the mind is Database Management. That is, to maintain data about employees in an organisation, books in a library, items in a store, financial accounting transactions in a company etc. But mind you, use of structures stretches much beyond database management. They can be used for a variety of applications like:

- (a) changing the size of the cursor
- (b) clearing the contents of the screen
- (c) placing the cursor at appropriate position on screen
- (d) drawing any graphics shape on the screen
- (e) receiving a key from the keyboard
- (f) checking the memory size of the computer
- (g) finding out the list of equipment attached to the computer
- (h) formatting a floppy
- (i) hiding a file from the directory
- (j) displaying the directory of a disk
- (k) sending the output to printer
- (l) interacting with the mouse

And that is certainly a very impressive list! At least impressive enough to make you realise how important a data type a structure is and to be thorough with it if you intend to program any of the above applications. Some of these applications are illustrated in Chapter 17.

Summary

In this chapter we have covered the use of structures, which allow us to combine several variables of different types into a single entity. We have also examined the features of structures which lead to programming convenience. We concluded the chapter by making you aware of what different applications the structure can be put to.

308   Let Us C

Exercise

[A]   What will be the output of the following programs:

(a)
```
main( )
{
    struct gospel
    {
        int num ;
        char mess1[50] ;
        char mess2[50] ;
    } m ;

    m.num = 1 ;
    strcpy ( m.mess1, "If all that you have is hammer" ) ;
    strcpy ( m.mess2, "Everything looks like a nail" ) ;

    /* assume that the strucure is located at address 1004 */
    printf ( "\n%u %u", &m.num, m.mess1, m.mess2 ) ;
}
```

(b)
```
struct gospel
{
    int num ;
    char mess1[50] ;
    char mess2[50] ;
} m1 =   { 2, "If you are driven by success",
                "make sure that it is a quality drive"
            } ;
main( )
{
    struct gospel m2, m3 ;
    m2 = m1 ;
    m3 = m2 ;
    printf ( "\n%d %s %s", m1.num, m2.mess1, m3.mess2 ) ;
}
```

[B]   Point out the errors, if any, in the following programs:

(a)
```
main( )
{
    struct employee
    {
        char name[25] ;
        int age ;
        float bs ;
    } ;
    struct employee e ;
    strcpy ( e.name, "Hacker" ) ;
    age = 25 ;
    printf ( "\n%s %d", e.name, age ) ;
}
```

(b)
```
main( )
{
    struct
    {
        char name[25] ;
        char language[10] ;
    } ;
    struct employee e = { "Hacker", "C" } ;
    printf ( "\n%s %d", e.name, e.language ) ;
}
```

(c)
```
struct virus
{
    char signature[25] ;
    char status[20] ;
    int size ;
} v[2] = {
            "Yankee Doodle", "Deadly", 1813,
            "Dark Avenger",  "Killer", 1795
        } ;
```

```
main( )
{
    int i ;
    for ( i = 0 ; i <=1 ; i++ )
        printf ( "\n%s %s", v.signature, v.status ) ;
}
```

(d)   ```
       struct s
       {
           char ch ;
           int i ;
           float a ;
       } ;
       main( )
       {
           struct s var = { 'C', 100, 12.55 } ;
           f (var) ;
           g (&var) ;
       }
       f (struct s v)
       {
           printf ("\n%c %d %f", v -> ch, v -> i, v -> a) ;
       }
       g (struct s *v)
       {
           printf ("\n%c %d %f", v.ch, v.i, v.a) ;
       }
       ```

(e)    ```
       struct s
       {
           int i ;
           struct s *p ;
       } ;
       main( )
       {
           struct s var1, var2 ;
       ```

```
        var1.i = 100 ;
        var2.i = 200 ;
        var1.p = &var2 ;
        var2.p = &var1 ;
        printf ( "\n%d %d", var1.p -> i, var2.p -> i ) ;
}
```

[C] Answer the following:

(a) Ten floats are to be stored in memory. What would you prefer, an array or a structure?

(b) Given the statement,

   maruti.engine.bolts = 25 ;

   which of the following is true?

   1. structure bolts is nested within structure engine
   2. structure engine is nested within structure maruti
   3. structure maruti is nested within structure engine
   4. structure maruti is nested within structure bolts

(c) State True or False:

   1. All structure elements are stored in contiguous memory locations.

   2. An array should be used to store dissimilar elements, and a structure to store similar elements.

   3. In an array of structures, not only are all structures stored in contiguous memory locations, but the elements of individual structures are also stored in contiguous locations.

(d)   struct time
   {

```
        int hours ;
        int minutes ;
        int seconds ;
    } t ;
    struct time *tt ;
    tt = &t ;
```

Looking at the above declarations, which of the following refers to **seconds** correctly:

1. tt.seconds
2. (*tt).seconds
3. time.t
4. tt -> seconds

11   Input/Output In C

As mentioned in the first chapter, Dennis Ritchie wanted C to remain compact. In keeping with this intention he deliberately omitted everthing related with Input/Output (I/O) from his definition of the langauge. Thus, C simply has no provision for receiving data from any of the input devices (like say keyboard, floppy etc.), nor for sending data to the output devices (like say VDU, floppy etc.). Then how do we manage I/O, and how is it that we were we able to use **printf( )** and **scanf( )** if C has nothing to offer for I/O? This is what we intend to explore in this chapter.

Types of I/O

Though C has no provision for I/O, it of course has to be dealt with at some point or the other. There is not much use writing a program that spends all it's time telling itself a secret. Each Operating System has it's own facility for inputting and outputting data from and to the files and devices. It's a simple matter for a system programmer to write a few small programs that would link the C compiler for particular Operating system's I/O facilities.

The developers of C Compilers do just that. They write several standard I/O functions and put them in libraries. Though these functions are not part of C's formal definiton, they have become a standard feature of C langauge, and have been imitated more or less faithfully by every designer of a DOS based or a UNIX based C compiler. Whatever version of C you are using it's almost certain that you have access to such a library of I/O functions.

Do understand that the I/O facilities with different operating systems would be different. Thus, the way DOS displays output on screen would be different than the way UNIX does it. Fortunately, the **printf( )** function that we use on a DOS based C compiler works even with a UNIX based C compiler. This is because, the standard library function **printf( )** for DOS based C compiler has been written keeping in mind the way DOS outputs characters to screen. Similarly, the **printf( )** function for a UNIX based compiler has been written keeping in mind the way UNIX outputs characters to screen. We as users do not have to bother about which **printf( )** has been written in what manner. We should just use **printf( )** and it would take care of the rest of the details. Same is true about all other standard library functions available for I/O.

There are numerous library functions available for I/O. These can be classified into three broad categories:

(a) Console I/O functions - functions to receive input from keyboard and write output to VDU.

(b) Disk I/O functions - functions to perform I/O operations on a floppy disk or hard disk.

(c) Port I/O functions - functions to perform I/O operations on various ports.

Let us now take a close look at each of these categories of I/O functions.

Console I/O Functions

Console I/O functions can be further classified into two categories: formatted and unformatted console I/O functions. The basic difference between them is that the formatted functions allow the input read from the keyboard or the output displayed on the VDU to be formatted as per our requirements. For example, if values of average marks and percentage marks are to be displayed on the screen, then the details like where this output would appear on the screen, how many spaces would be present between the two values, the number of places after the decimal points etc. can be controlled using formatted functions. The functions available under each of these two categories are shown in Figure 11.1. Now let us discuss these console I/O functions in detail.

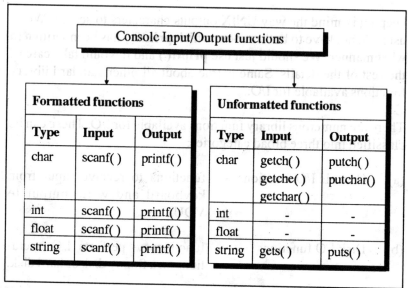

Figure 11.1

Formatted Console I/O Functions

As can be seen from Figure 6.1 the functions **printf( )**, and **scanf( )** fall under the category of formatted console I/O functions. These functions allow us to supply the input in a fixed format and let us obtain the output in the specified form. Let us discuss these functions one by one.

We have talked a lot about **printf( )**, used it regularly, but without having introduced it formally. Well, better late than never. It's general form looks like this...

    printf ("format string", list of variables) ;

The format string can contain:

- characters that are simply printed as they are
- conversion specifications that begin with a **%** sign

- escape sequences that begin with a \ sign

For example, look at the following program:

```
main( )
{
    int avg = 346 ;
    float per = 69.2 ;

    printf ( "Average = %d\nPercentage = %f", avg, per ) ;
}
```

The output of the program would be...

```
Average = 346
Percentage = 69.200000
```

How does **printf( )** function interpret the contents of the format string. For this it examines the format string from left to right. So long as it doesn't come across either a % or a \ it continues to dump the characters that it encounters, on to the screen. In this example **Average =** is dumped on the screen. The moment it comes across a conversion specification in the format string it picks up the first variable in the list of variables and prints its value in the specified format. In this example, the moment **%d** is met the variable **avg** is picked up and its value is printed. Similarly, the moment an escape sequence is met it takes the appropriate action. In this example, the moment \n is met it places the cursor at the beginning of the next line. This process continues till the end of format string is reached.

Conversion Specifications

The **%d** and **%f** used in the **printf( )** are called conversion characters. They tell **printf( )** to print the value of **avg** as a decimal integer and the value of per as a float. Following is the list of conversion characters that can be used with the **printf( )** funcion.

Data type		Conversion character
Integer	short signed	%d or %i
	short unsigned	%u
	long signed	%ld
	long unsigned	%lu
	unsigned hexadecimal	%x
	unsigned octal	%o
Real	float	%f
	double	%lf
character	signed character	%c
	unsigned character	%c
string		%s

Figure 11.2

We can provide following optional specifiers in the conversion specifications.

Specifier	Description
dd	digits specifying field width
.	decimal point separating field width from precision (precision stands for the number of places after the decimal point)
dd	digits specifying precision
-	minus sign for left justifying the output in the specified field width

Figure 11.3

Now a short explaination about these conversion specifications. The field width specifier tells **printf( )** how many columns on screen should be used while printing a value. For example, **%10d** says, "print the variable as a decimal integer in a field of 10 columns." If the value to be printed happens not to fill up the entire field, the value is right justified and is padded with blanks on the left. If we include the minus sign in conversion specification (as in **%-10d**), this means left justification is desired and the value will be padded with blanks on the right. Here is an example which should make this point clear.

```
main( )
{
    int weight = 63 ;

    printf ( "\nweight is %d kg", weight ) ;
    printf ( "\nweight is %2d kg", weight ) ;
    printf ( "\nweight is %4d kg", weight ) ;
    printf ( "\nweight is %6d kg", weight ) ;
    printf ( "\nweight is %-6d kg", weight ) ;
}
```

The output of the program would look like this ...

```
                      1         2         3
Columns   0123456789012345678901234567890
          weight  is 63 kg
          weight  is 63 kg
          weight  is   63 kg
          weight  is      63 kg
          weight  is 63      kg
```

Specifying the field width can be useful in creating tables of numeric values, as the following program demonstrates.

```
main( )
{
    printf ( "\n%f %f %f", 5.0, 13.5, 133.9 ) ;
    printf ( "\n%f %f %f", 305.0, 1200.9, 3005.3 ) ;
}
```

And here is the output...

>   5.000000 13.500000 133.900000
>   305.000000 1200.900000 3005.300000

Even though the numbers have been printed, the numbers have not been lined up properly and hence are hard to read. A better way would be something like this...

```
main( )
{
    printf ( "\n%10.1f %10.1f %10.1f", 5.0, 13.5, 133.9 ) ;
    printf ( "\n%10.1f %10.1f %10.1f", 305.0, 1200.9, 3005.3 );
}
```

This results into a much better output...

>   01234567890123456789012345678901
>   5.0   13.5   133.9
>   305.0   1200.9   3005.3

The conversion specifications could be used even while displaying string of characters. The following program would clarify this point:

```
/* Formatting strings with printf( ) */
main( )
{
    char firstname1[ ] = "Sandy" ;
    char surname1[ ] = "Malya" ;
    char firstname2[ ] = "AjayKumar" ;
    char surname2[ ] = "Gurubaxani" ;

    printf ( "\n%20s%20s", firstname1, surname1 ) ;
    printf ( "\n%20s%20s", firstname2, surname2 ) ;
}
```

And here's the output...

```
01234567890123456789012345678901234567890123456789 0
            Sandy              Malya
         AjayKumar          Gurubaxani
```

The conversion specification **%20s** reserves 20 columns for printing a string and then prints the string in these 20 columns with right justification. This helps lining up names of different lengths properly. Obviously, the format **%-20s** would have left justified the string.

Escape Sequences

We saw earlier how the newline character, **\n**, when inserted in a **printf( )**'s format string, takes the cursor to the beginning of the next line. The newline character is an 'escape sequence', so called because the backslash symbol (\) is considered an 'escape' character: it causes an escape from the normal interpretation of a string, so that the next character is recognised as one having a special meaning.

The following example shows usage of **\n** and a new escape sequence **\t**, called 'tab'. A **\t** moves the cursor to the next tab stop. A 80 column screen usually has 10 tab stops. In other words, the screen is divided into 10 zones of 8 columns each. Printing a tab takes the cursor to the beginning of next printing zone. For example, if cursor is positioned in column 5, then printing a tab takes it to column 8.

```
main( )
{
    printf ( "You\tmust\tbe\tcrazy\nto\thate\tthis\tbook" ) ;
}
```

And here's the output...

```
          1       2       3       4
01234567890123456789012345678901234567890
You     must    be      crazy
to      hate    this    book
```

The cursor jumps over eight columns when it encounters the '\t' character. This is another useful technique for lining up columns of output. Most compilers allow the user to change the number of print zones available on the screen, thereby changing the tab width.

The **\n** character causes a new line to begin following 'crazy'. The tab and newline are probably the most commonly used escape sequences, but there are others as well. The following figure shows a complete list of these escape sequences.

Esc. Seq.	Purpose	Esc. Seq.	Purpose
\n	New line	\t	Tab
\b	Backspace	\r	Carriage return
\f	Form feed	\a	Alert
\'	Single quote	\"	Double quote
\\	Backslash		

Figure 11.4

The first few of these escape sequences are more or less self-explanatory. **\b** moves the cursor one position to the left of its current position. **\r** takes the cursor to the beginning of the line in which it is currently placed. **\a** alerts the user by sounding the speaker inside the computer. Form feed advances the computer stationery attached to the printer to the top of the next page. Characters that are ordinarily used as delimiters... the single quote, double quote, and the backslash can be printed by preceding them with the backslash. Thus, the statement,

```
printf ( "He said, \"Let's do it!\"" ) ;
```

will print...

He said, "Let's do it!"

So far we have been describing **printf( )**'s specification as if we are forced to use only **%d** for an integer, only **%c** for a char, only **%s** for a string and so on. This is not true at all. In fact, **printf( )** uses the specification that we mention and attempts to perform the specified conversion, and does its best to produce a proper result. Sometimes the result is nonsensical, as in case when we ask it to print a string using **%d**. Sometimes the result is useful, as in the case we ask **printf( )** to print ascii value of a character using **%d**. Sometimes the result is disastrous and the entire program blows up.

The following program shows a few of these conversions, some sensible, some weird.

```
main( )
{
    char ch = 'z' ;
    int i = 125 ;
    float a = 12.55 ;
    char s[ ] = "hello there !" ;

    printf ( "\n%c %d %f", ch, ch, ch ) ;
    printf ( "\n%s %d %f", s, s, s ) ;
    printf ( "\n%c %d %f",i ,i, i ) ;
    printf ( "\n%f %d\n", a, a ) ;
}
```

And here's the output ...

```
z 122 -9362831782501783000000000000000000000000000000.000000
hello there ! 3280 -9362831782501783000000000000000000000000000.000000
} 125 -936283178250178300000000000000000000000000000.000000
12.550000 0
```

I will leave it to you to analyse the results by yourselves. Some of the conversions you would find are quite sensible.

Let us now turn our attention to **scanf( )**. **scanf( )** allows us to enter data from keyboard that will be formatted in a certain way.

The general form of **scanf( )** statement is as follows:

```
scanf ( "format string", list of addresses of variables ) ;
```

For example:

```
scanf ( "%d %f %c", &c, &a, &ch ) ;
```

Note that we are sending addresses of variables (addresses are obtained by using '**&**' the 'address of' operator) to **scanf( )** function. This is necessary because the values received from keyboard must be dropped into variables corresponding to these addresses. The values that are supplied through the keyboard must be separated by either blank(s), tab(s), or newline(s). Do not include these escape sequences in the format string.

All the format specifications that we learnt in **printf( )** function apply for **scanf( )** function as well.

sprintf( ) and *sscanf( )* Functions

The **sprintf( )** function works similar to the **printf( )** function except for one small difference. Instead of sending the output to the screen as **printf( )** does, this function writes the output to an array of characters. The following program illustrates this.

```
main( )
{
    int i = 10 ;
    char ch = 'A' ;
    float a = 3.14 ;
    char str[20] ;
```

```
        printf ( "\n%d %c %f", i, ch, a ) ;
        sprintf ( str, "%d %c %f", i, ch, a ) ;
        printf ( "\n%s", str ) ;
}
```

In this Program the **printf( )** prints out the values of **i, ch** and **a** on the screen, whereas **sprintf( )** stores these values in the character array **str**. Since the string **str** is present in memory what is written into **str** using **sprintf( )** doesn't get displayed on the screen. Once **str** has been built, its contents can be displayed on the screen. In our program this was achieved by the second **printf( )** statement.

The counterpart of **sprintf( )** is the **sscanf( )** function. It allows us to read characters from a string and to convert and store them in C variables according to specified formats. The **sscanf( )** function comes in handy for in-memory conversion of characters to values. You may find it convenient to read in strings from a file and then extract values from a string by using **sscanf( )**. The usage of **sscanf( )** is same as **scanf( )**, except that the first argument is the string from which reading is to take place.

Unformatted Console I/O Functions

There are several standard library functions available under this category - those which can deal with a single character and those which can deal with a string of characters. For openers let us look at those which handle one character at a time.

So far for input we have consistently used the **scanf( )** function. However, for some situations the **scanf( )** function has one glaring weakness... you need to hit the Enter key before the function can digest what you have typed. However, we often want a function that will read a single character the instant it is typed without waiting for the Enter key to be hit. **getch( )** and **getche( )** are two functions which serve this purpose. These functions return the character that has been most recently typed. The 'e' in **getche( )** function means it echoes (displays) the character that you typed to the screen. As against this **getch( )** just returns the character that you typed without echoing it on the screen. **getchar( )** works similarly and echos the character that you typed on the screen, but unfortunately requires Enter key to be typed following the character that you typed. The difference between **getchar( )** and **fgetchar( )** is that the former is a macro whereas the latter is a function. Here is a sample program which illustrates the use of these functions.

```
main( )
{
    char ch ;

    printf ( "\nPress any key to continue" ) ;
    getch( ) ; /* will not echo the character */

    printf ( "\nType any character" ) ;
    ch = getche( ) ; /* will echo the character typed */

    printf ( "\nType any character" ) ;
    getchar( ) ; /* will echo character, must be followed by enter key */
    printf ( "\nContinue Y/N" ) ;
    fgetchar( ) ; /* will echo character, must be followed by enter key */
}
```

And here is a sample run of this program...

```
Press any key to continue
Type any character B
Type any character W
Continue Y/N Y
```

putch( ) and **putchar( )** form the other side of the coin. They print a character on the screen. As far as the working of **putch( ) putchar( )** and **fputchar( )** is concerned it's exactly same. The following program illustrates this.

```
main( )
{
    char ch = 'A' ;

    putch ( ch ) ;
    putchar ( ch ) ;
    fputchar ( ch ) ;
    putch ( 'Z' ) ;
    putchar ( 'Z' ) ;
    fputchar ( 'Z' ) ;
}
```

And here is the output...

```
AAAZZZ
```

The limitation of **putch( )**, **putchar( )** and **fputchar( )** is that they can output only one character at a time.

gets( ) and *puts( )*

gets( ) receives a string from the keyboard. Why is it needed? Because **scanf( )** function has some limitations while receiving string of characters, as the following example illustrates...

```
main( )
{
    char name[50] ;

    printf ( "\nEnter name " ) ;
    scanf ( "%s", name ) ;
    printf ( "%s", name ) ;
}
```

And here is the output...

```
Enter name Jonty Rhodes
```

Jonty

Surprised? Where did "Rhodes" go? It never got stored in the array **name[ ]**, because the moment the blank was typed after "Jonty" **scanf( )** assumed that the name being entered has ended. The result is that there is no way (at least not without a lot of trouble on the programmer's part) to enter a multi-word string into a single variable (**name** in this case) using **scanf( )**. The solution to this problem is to use **gets( )** function. As said earlier, it gets a string from the keyboard. It is terminated when an Enter key is hit. Thus, spaces and tabs are perfectly acceptable as part of the input string. More exactly, **gets( )** gets a newline (**\n**) terminated string of characters from the keyboard and replaces the **\n** with a **\0**.

The **puts( )** function works exactly opposite to **gets( )** function. It outputs a string to the screen.

Here is a program which illustrates the usage of these functions:

```
main( )
{
    char footballer[40] ;

    puts ( "Enter name" ) ;
    gets ( footballer ) ; /* sends base address of array */
    puts ( "Happy footballing!" ) ;
    puts ( footballer ) ;
}
```

Following is the sample output:

```
Enter name
Jonty Rhodes
Happy footballing!
Jonty Rhodes
```

Why did we use two **puts( )** functions to print "Happy footballing!" and "Jonty Rhodes"? Because, unlike **printf( )**, **puts( )** can output only one string at a time. If we attempt to print two strings using **puts( )**, only the first one gets printed. Similarly, unlike **scanf( )**, **gets( )** can be used to read only one string at a time.

Disk I/O Functions

Having dealt with the various Console Input/Output (I/O) functions like **printf( )**, **scanf( )**, **getch( )** etc., let us now turn our attention to Disk I/O. Disk I/O operations are performed on entities called files. There are a large number of standard library functions available for performing Disk or file I/O. These functions can be broadly divided into two categories:

(a)   High level file I/O functions (also called standard I/O or stream I/O functions)
(b)   Low level file I/O functions (also called system I/O functions)

High level disk I/O functions are more commonly used in C programs, since they are easier to use than low level disk I/O functions. There is one basic difference between high level and low level disk I/O functions. High level disk I/O functions do their own buffer management, whereas in low level disk I/O functions, buffer management has to be done explicitly by the programmer.

We will take up a detailed discussion of what is a buffer, how is it managed in high level and low level disk I/O functions when we become familiar with both types of functions. At this stage we can just say that low disk level I/O is harder to program than high level disk I/O. However, low level disk I/O is more efficient both in terms of operation and the amount of memory used by the program. The following figure shows the detailed classification of disk I/O functions.

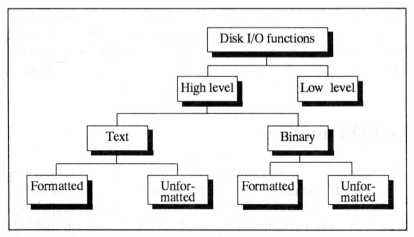

Figure 11.5

As you can see the high level file I/O functions are further categorised into text and binary. This classification arises out of the mode in which a file is opened for input or output. Which of these two modes is used to open the file determines:

(a)   How newlines (\n) are stored.
(b)   How end of file is indicated.
(c)   How numbers are stored in the file.

We will look at these differences at a later stage in this chapter. Let us now directly jump to writing programs which perform file I/O in high level, unformatted, text mode.

Our first program will read a file and count how many characters, spaces, tabs and newlines are present in the file. We will first list the program and show what it does, and then dissect it line by line. Here is the listing.

```
/* Count chars, spaces, tabs and newlines in a file */
# include "stdio.h"
main( )
{
```

```
FILE *fp ;
char ch ;
int nol = 0, not = 0, nos = 0, noc = 0 ;

fp = fopen ( "PR1.C", "r" ) ;

while ( 1 )
{
    ch = fgetc ( fp ) ;

    if ( ch == EOF )
        break ;

    noc++ ;

    if ( ch == ' ' )
        nob++ ;

    if ( ch == '\n' )
        nol++ ;

    if ( ch == '\t' )
        not++ ;
}

fclose ( fp ) ;

printf ( "\nNumber of characters = %d", noc ) ;
printf ( "\nNumber of blanks = %d", nob ) ;
printf ( "\nNumber of tabs = %d", not ) ;
printf ( "\nNumber of lines = %d", nol ) ;
}
```

And here is a sample run...

```
Number of characters = 125
Number of blanks = 25
```

Number of tabs = 13
Number of lines = 22

The above statistics are true for a file "PR1.C", which we had on our disk. You may give any other filename and obtain different results. More important than the actual statistics, is how the program calculates these. So let us now take a look at how it does it.

Opening A File

Before we can write information to a file on a disk or read it, we must open the file. Opening a file establishes a link between the program and the operating system, about, which file we are going to access and how. We provide the operating system with the name of the file and whether we plan to read or write to it. The link between our program and the operating system is a structure called **FILE** which has been defined in the header file "stdio.h" (standing for standard input/output header file). Therefore, it is necessary to always include this file when we are doing high level disk I/O. When we request the operating system to open a file, what we get back (if the request is indeed granted), is a pointer to the structure **FILE**. That is why, we make the following declaration before opening the file,

    FILE *fp ;

Each file we open will have its own **FILE** structure. The **FILE** structure contains information about the file being used, such as its current size, its location in memory etc. More importantly it contains a character pointer which points to the character that is about to get read.

Now let us understand the following statements,

    FILE *fp ;
    fp = fopen ("PR1.C", "r") ;

fp is a pointer variable, which contains address of the structure **FILE** which has been defined in the header file "stdio.h".

fopen( ) will open a file "PR1.C" in 'read' mode, which tells the C compiler that we would be reading the contents of the file. Note that "r" is a string and not a character; hence the double quotes and not single quotes. In fact, **fopen( )** performs three important tasks when you open the file in "r" mode:

(a)   Firstly it searches on the disk the file to be opened.

(b)   If the file is present, it loads the file from the disk into memory. Of course if the file is very big, then it loads the file part by part.

        If the file is absent, **fopen( )** returns a NULL. NULL is a macro defined in "stdio.h" which indicates that you failed to open the file.

(c)   It sets up a character pointer (which is part of the FILE structure) which points to the first character of the chunk of memory where the file has been loaded.

Reading from A File

Once the file has been opened for reading using **fopen( )**, as we have seen the file's contents are brought into memory (partly or wholly) and a pointer points to the very first character. To read the file's contents from memory there exists a function called **fgetc( )**. This has been used in our sample program through,

```
ch = fgetc ( fp ) ;
```

fgetc( ) reads the character from current pointer position, advances the pointer position so that it now points to the next character, and returns the character that is read, which we collected in the variable **ch**. Note that once the file has been opened, we no longer refer to the file by its name, but through the file pointer **fp**.

We have used the function **fgetc( )** within an indefinite **while** loop. There has to be a way to break out of this **while**. When shall we break out... the moment we reach the end of file. But what is end of file? End of file is signified by a special character, whose ascii value is 26. This character is inserted beyond the last character in the file, when it is created. This character can also be generated from the keyboard by typing ctrl Z.

While reading from the file, when **fgetc( )** encounters this special character, instead of returning the character that it has read, it returns the macro EOF. The EOF macro has been defined in the file "stdio.h". In place of the function **fgetc( )** we could have as well used the macro **getc( )** with the same effect.

In our sample program, we go on reading each character from the file till end of file is met. As each character is being read we keep running totals of number of characters, number of blanks, number of tabs and number of lines read. Note that the end of the line is marked by a **\n**. Once out of the loop, we print these running totals.

Trouble in Opening A File

There is a possibility that when we try to open a file using the function **fopen( )**, the file may not be opened. While opening the file in "r" mode, this may happen because the file being opened may not be present on the disk at all. And you obviously cannot read a file which doesn't exist. Similarly, while opening the file for writing, **fopen( )** may fail due to a number of reasons, like, disk space may be insufficient to open a new file, or the disk may be write protected and so on.

Crux of the matter is that it is important for any program that accesses disk files to check whether a file has been opened successfully before trying to read or write to the file. If the file opening fails due to any of the several reasons mentioned above, the **fopen( )** function returns a value NULL (defined in "stdio.h" as **#define NULL 0**). Here is how this can be handled in a program...

```
#include "stdio.h"
main( )
{
    FILE *fp ;

    fp = fopen ( "PR1.C", "r" ) ;
    if ( fp == NULL)
    {
        puts ( "cannot open file" ) ;
        exit( ) ;
    }
}
```

Closing The File

When we have finished reading from the file, we need to close it. This is done using the function **fclose( )** through the statement,

```
fclose ( fp ) ;
```

This deactivates the file and hence it can no longer be accessed using **getc( )**. Once again we don't use the filename but the file pointer **fp**.

File Opening Modes

In our first program on disk I/O we have opened the file in read ("r") mode. However, "r" is but one of the several modes in which we can open a file. Following is a list of all possible modes in which a file can be opened. The tasks performed by **fopen( )** when a file is opened in each of these modes are also mentioned.

"r"   Searches file. If the file exists, loads it into memory and sets up a pointer which points to the first character in it. If the file doesn't exist it returns NULL.

        Operations possible - reading from the file.

"w"   Searches file. If the file exists, its contents are overwritten. If the file doesn't exist, a new file is created. Returns NULL, if unable to open file.

       Operations possible - writing to the file.

"a"   Searches file. If the file exists, loads it into memory and sets up a pointer which points to the first character in it. If the file doesn't exist, a new file is created. Returns NULL, if unable to open file.

       Oprations possible - appending new contents at the end of file.

"r+"   Searches file. If it exists, loads it into memory and sets up a pointer which points to the first character in it. If file doesn't exist it returns NULL.

       Operations possible - reading existing contents, writing new contents, modifying existing contents of the file.

"w+"   Searches file. If the file exists, its contents are destroyed. If the file doesn't exist a new file is created. Returns NULL, if unable to open file.

       Operations possible - writing new contents, reading them back and modifying existing contents of the file.

"a+"   Searches file. If the file exists, loads it into memory and sets up a pointer which points to the first character in it. If the file doesn't exist, a new file is created. Returns NULL, if unable to open file.

       Operations possible - reading existing contents, appending new contents to end of file. Cannot modify existing contents.

A File-copy Program

We have already used the function **fgetc( )** which reads characters from a file. Its counterpart is a function called **fputc( )** which writes characters to a file. As a practical use of these character I/O functions we can copy the contents of one file into another, as demonstrated in the following example. This program takes the contents of a text file and copies them into another text file, character by character.

```c
#include "stdio.h"
main( )
{
    FILE *fs, *ft ;
    char ch ;

    fs = fopen ( "pr1.c", "r" ) ;
    if ( fs == NULL )
    {
        puts ( "Cannot open source file" ) ;
        exit( ) ;
    }

    ft = fopen ( "pr2.c", "w" ) ;
    if ( ft == NULL )
    {
        puts ( "Cannot open target file" ) ;
        fclose ( fs ) ;
        exit( ) ;
    }

    while ( 1 )
    {
        ch = fgetc ( fs ) ;

        if ( ch == EOF )
            break ;
        else
```

```
                        fputc ( ch, ft ) ;
                }

            fclose ( fs ) ;
            fclose ( ft ) ;
        }
```

I hope most of the stuff in the program can be easily understood, since it has already been dealt with in the earlier section. What is new is only the function **fputc( )**. Let us see how it works.

Writing to A File

The **fputc( )** function is similar to the **putch( )** function, in the sense that both output characters. However, **putch( )** function always writes to the VDU, whereas, **fputc( )** writes to the file. Which file? The file signifed by **ft**. The writing process continues till all characters from the source file have been written to the target file, following which the **while** loop terminates.

Note that our sample file-copy program is capable of copying only text files. To copy files with extension .EXE or .COM, we need to open the files in binary mode, a topic which would be dealt with in sufficient detail later on.

A Closer Look at *fclose( )*

Closing the file has several effects. First any characters remaining in the buffer are written to the disk. What buffer? We didn't say anything about the buffer before since it is invisible to the programmer when using high level disk I/O functions. However, buffer is necessary even if it is invisible.

Consider, for example, how inefficient it would be to actually access the disk every time we want to write a character to it. Every time we write something to a disk, it takes some time for the disk drive to position the read/write head correctly. On a floppy disk system, the drive motor has to actually start rotating the disk from a standstill every time the disk is accessed. If this is to be done for every character we write to the disk, it would take a long time to perform disk I/O. This is where a buffer comes in.

When you send a character off to a file by using **fputc( )**, the character is actually stored in a buffer - an area in memory, rather than being immediately written to the disk. When the buffer is full, its contents are written to the disk at once. Or if the program knows that the last character to be written to the disk has been received in the buffer, but it is still not full, it forces the buffer to be written to the disk by 'closing' the file.

A major advantage of using the high level disk I/O functions is that these activities take place automatically, the programmer doesn't need to worry about them.

Another purpose that **fclose( )** serves is, it frees the link used by the particular file, and the associated buffers, so that these are available for other files.

Using *argc* and *argv*

To execute the above file-copy program we are required to first type the program, compile it, and then execute it. This program can be improved in two ways:

(a)   There should be no need to compile the program everytime to use the file-copy utility. It means the program must be executable at command prompt (A> or C> if you are using MS-DOS, $ if you are using Unix).

(b)   Instead of the program prompting us to enter the source and target filenames, we must be able to supply them at command prompt, in the form:

C>filecopy PR1.C PR2.C

where, PR1.C is the source filename and PR2.C is the target filename.

The first improvement is simple. In MS-DOS, the executable file (the one which can be executed at DOS prompt and has an extension .EXE) can be created in Turbo C by using the key F9 to compile the program. In Quick C the same can be achieved by using the option Alt RCX.

Under Unix this is not required since in Unix every time we compile a program we always get an executable file.

The second improvement is possible by passing the source filename and target filename to the function **main( )**. This is illustrated below:

```
#include "stdio.h"
main ( int argc, char *argv[ ] )
{
    FILE *fs, *ft ;
    char ch ;

    if ( argc != 3 )
    {
        puts ( "Insufficient arguments" ) ;
        exit( ) ;
    }

    fs = fopen ( argv[1], "r" ) ;
    if ( fs == NULL)
    {
        puts ( "Cannot open source file" ) ;
        exit( ) ;
    }
```

```
ft = fopen ( argv[2], "w" ) ;
if ( ft == NULL )
{
    puts ( "Cannot open target file" ) ;
    fclose ( fs ) ;
    exit( ) ;
}

while ( 1 )
{
    ch = fgetc ( fs ) ;

    if ( ch == EOF )
        break ;
    else
        fputc ( ch, ft ) ;
}

fclose ( fs ) ;
fclose ( ft ) ;
}
```

The arguments that we pass on to **main( )** at the command prompt
are called command line arguments. The function **main( )** can have
two arguments, traditionally named as **argc** and **argv**. Out of these,
argv is an array of pointers to strings and **argc** is an **int** whose value
is equal to the number of strings to which **argv** points. When the
program is executed, the strings on the command line are passed to
main( ). More precisely, the strings at the command line are stored
in memory and address of the first string is stored in **argv[0]**, address
of the second string is stored in **argv[1]** and so on. The argument **argc**
is set to the number of strings given on the command line. For
example, in our sample program, if at the command prompt we give,

    filcopy PR1.C PR2.C

then,

argc would contain 3
argv[0] would contain base address of the string "filecopy"
argv[1] would contain base address of the string "PR1.C"
argv[2] would contain base address of the string "PR2.C"

Whenever we pass on the arguments to **main( )**, it is a good habit to check whether the correct number of arguments have been passed on to **main( )** or not. In our program this has been done through,

```
if ( argc != 3 )
{
    printf ( "Insufficient arguments" ) ;
    exit( ) ;
}
```

Rest of the program is same as the earlier file-copy program. **This program is better than the earlier file-copy program on three counts:**

(a)   There is no need to recompile the program everytime we want to use this utiltiy. It can be executed at command prompt.
(b)   Once an executable file is created nobody with malicious intensions can tamper with your C source code program.
(c)   We are able to pass source file name and target file name to **main( )**, and utilise them in **main( )**.

One final comment... the **while** loop that we have used in our program can be written in a more compact form, as shown below:

```
while ( ( ch = fgetc ( fs ) ) != EOF )
    fputc ( ch, ft ) ;
```

This avoids the usage of an indefinite loop and a **break** statement to come out of this loop. Here, first **fgetc (fs)** gets the character from the file, assigns it to the variable **ch**, and then **ch** is compared against **EOF**. Remember that it is necessary to put the expression

```
ch = fgetc ( fs )
```

within a pair of parentheses, so that first the character read is assigned to variable **ch** and then it is compared with **EOF**.

There is one more way of writing the **while** loop. It is shown below:

```
while ( !feof ( fs ) )
{
    ch = fgetc ( fs ) ;
    fputc ( ch, ft ) ;
}
```

Here, **feof( )** is a macro which reutrns a 0 if end of file is not reached. Hence we use the ! operator to negate this 0 to the truth value. When the end of file is reached **feof( )** returns a non-zero value, ! makes it 0 and since now the condition evaluates to false the **while** loop gets terminated.

Note that the following three methods for opening a file are same, since, essentially a base address of the string (pointer to a string) is being passed to **fopen( )**.

```
fs = fopen ( "PR1.C" , "r" ) ;
fs = fopen ( filename, "r" ) ;
fs = fopen ( argv[1] , "r" ) ;
```

String (line) I/O in Files

For many purposes, character I/O is just what is needed. However, in some situations the usage of functions which read or write entire strings might turn out to be more efficient.

Reading or writing strings of characters from and to files is as easy as reading and writing individual characters. Here is a program that writes strings to a file using the function **fputs( )**.

```
/* Receives strings from keyboard and writes them to file */
```

```
#include "stdio.h"
main( )
{
    FILE *fp ;
    char s[80] ;

    fp = fopen ( "POEM.TXT", "w" ) ;
    if ( fp == NULL )
    {
        puts ( "Cannot open file" ) ;
        exit( ) ;
    }

    printf ( "\nEnter a few lines of text:\n" ) ;
    while ( strlen ( gets(s) ) > 0 )
    {
        fputs ( s, fp ) ;
        fputs ( "\n" ) ;
    }

    fclose ( fp ) ;
}
```

And here is a sample run of the program...

```
Enter a few lines of text:
Shining and bright, they are forever,
so true about diamonds,
more so of memories,
especially yours !
```

Note that each string is terminated by hitting enter. To terminate the execution of the program, hit enter at the beginning of a line. This creates a string of zero length, which the program recognises as the signal to close the file and exit.

We have set up a character array to receive the string; the **fputs( )** function then writes the contents of the array to the disk. Since **fputs( )** does not automatically add a newline character to the end of the string, we must do this explicitly to make it easier to read the string back from the file.

Here is a program that reads strings from a disk file.

```
/* Reads strings from the file and displays them on screen */
#include "stdio.h"
main( )
{
    FILE *fp ;
    char s[80] ;

    fp = fopen ( "POEM.TXT", "r" ) ;
    if ( fp == NULL )
    {
        puts ( "Cannot open file" ) ;
        exit( ) ;
    }

    while ( fgets ( s, 79, fp ) != NULL )
        printf ( "%s" , s ) ;

    fclose ( fp ) ;
}
```

And here is the output...

```
Shining and bright, they are forever,
so true about diamonds,
more so of memories,
especially yours !
```

The function **fgets( )** takes three arguments. The first is the address where the string is stored, and the second is the maximum length of the string. This argument prevents **fgets( )** from reading in too long a string and overflowing the array. The third argument, as usual, is the pointer to the structure **FILE**. When all the lines from the file have been read, we attempt to read one more line, in which case **fgets( )** returns a NULL.

The Awkward Newline

We had earlier written a program that counts the total number of characters present in a file. If we use that program to count the number of characters present in the above poem (stored in the file "POEM.TXT"), it would give us the character count as 101. The same file if seen in the directory, would be reported by MS-DOS to contain 105 characters.

This discrepancy occurs because of the difference in the way C and DOS represent the end of line. In C the end of line is signalled by single character, the **\n**. In DOS, on the other hand, the end of line is marked by two characters, a carriage return (**\r**), and the linefeed (which is same as the C newline, **\n**).

When your program writes a C text file to disk, DOS causes all the newlines to be converted into carriage return-linefeed combinations. When your program reads in a text file, the carriage return-linefeed combinations are converted back into a single newline character.

Thus, DOS oriented programs like DIR command would count two characters at the each end of line, while C oriented programs, like our character count program, will count one. In our poem there are four lines, therefore there is a discrepancy of four characters.

A Brief Review

So far we have learnt four functions for disk I/O. These can be categorised as shown below.

Category	Functions
High level, Text, Unformatted, Character I/O	getc( ), putc( ) fgetc( ), fputc( ) Here, **getc( )** and **putc( )** are macros, whereas **fgetc( )** and **fputc( )** are their function versions.
High level, Text, Unformatted, String I/O	**fgets( )**, **fputs( )**
High level, Text, Unformatted, int I/O	No standard library function
High level, Text, Unformatted, float I/O	No standard library function

Figure 11.6

Formatted Disk I/O Functions

So far we have dealt with reading and writing only characters and strings. There exist no standard library functions to read or write numbers under the category of high level, unformatted, text I/O functions.

For formatted reading and writing of characters, strings, integers, floats, there exist two functions, **fscanf( )** and **fprintf( )**. Here is a program which illustrates the use of these functions...

```
#include "stdio.h"
main( )
{
    FILE *fp ;
    char another = 'Y' ;
    char name[40] ;
    int age ;
    float bs ;
```

```
fp = fopen ( "EMPLOYEE.DAT", "w" ) ;
if ( fp == NULL )
{
    puts ( "Cannot open file" ) ;
    exit( ) ;
}

while ( another == 'Y' )
{
    printf ( "\nEnter name, age and basic salary\n" ) ;
    scanf ( "%s %d %f", name, &age, &bs ) ;
    fprintf ( fp, "%s %d %f\n", name, &age, &bs ) ;

    printf ( "Another employee (Y/N) " ) ;
    fflush ( stdin ) ;
    another = getche( ) ;
}
fclose ( fp ) ;
}
```

And here is the output of the program...

```
Enter name, age and basic salary
Anil 34 1550.55
Another employee (Y/N) Y
Enter name, age and basic salary
Sanjay 24 1200.75
Another employee (Y/N) Y
Enter name, age and basic salary
Ramesh 26 2000.65
Another employee (Y/N) N
```

The key to this program is the function **fprintf( )**, which writes the values of three variables to the file. This function is similar to **printf( )**, except that a FILE pointer is included as the first argument. As in **printf( )**, we can format the data in a variety of ways, by using

fprintf( ). In fact all the format conventions of **printf( )** function work with **fprintf( )** as well.

Perhaps you are wondering what for have we used the function **fflush( )**. The reason is to get rid of a peculiarity of **scanf( )**. After supplying data for one employee, we would hit the enter key. What **scanf( )** does is it assigns name, age and salary to appropriate variables and keeps the enter key unread in the keyboard buffer. So when it's time to supply Y or N for the question 'Another employee (Y/N)', **getch( )** will read the enter key from the buffer thinking that user has entered the enter key. To avoid this problem we use the function **fflush( )**. It is designed to remove or 'flush out' any data remaining in the buffer. The argument to **fflush( )** must be the buffer which we want to flush out. Here we use 'stdin', which means buffer related with standard input device the keyboard.

Now suppose, we want to read back the names, ages and basic salaries of different employees which we stored through the earlier program into the file "EMPLOYEE.DAT". Following program does just this:

```
#include "stdio.h"
main( )
{
    FILE *fp ;
    char name[40] ;
    int age ;
    float bs ;

    fp = fopen ( "EMPLOYEE.DAT", "r" ) ;
    if ( fp == NULL )
    {
        puts ( "Cannot open file" ) ;
        exit( ) ;
    }

    while ( fscanf ( fp, "%s %d %f", name, &age, &bs ) != EOF )
        printf ( "\n%s %d %f", name, &age, &bs ) ;
```

```
            fclose ( fp ) ;
      }
```

And here is the output...

```
      Anil 34 1550.550000
      Sanjay 24 1200.750000
      Ramesh 26 2000.650000
```

This program uses the **fscanf( )** function to read the data from the disk. This function is similar to **scanf( )**, except that, as with **fprintf( )**, a pointer to **FILE** is included as the first argument.

Standard DOS Devices

To perform reading or writing operations on a file we need to use the function **fopen( )**, which sets up a file pointer to refer to this file. MS-DOS also predefines pointers for five standard files. To access these pointers we need not use **fopen( )**. These standard file pointers are shown in Figure 11.7

Standard File pointer	Description
stdin	standard input device (keyboard)
stdout	standard output device (VDU)
stderr	standard error device (VDU)
stdaux	standard auxiliary device (serial port)
stdprn	standard printing device (parallel printer)

Figure 11.7

Thus the statement **ch = fgetc (stdin)** would read a character from the keyboard rather than from a file. We can use this statement without any any need to use **fopen( )** or **fclose( )** function calls.

The following program shows this technique at work. This program reads a file from the disk and prints it on the printer.

```
/* Print file contents on printer */
#include "stdio.h"
main( )
{
    FILE *fp ;
    char ch ;

    fp = fopen ( "poem.txt", "r" ) ;

    if ( fp == NULL )
    {
        printf ( "Cannot open file" ) ;
        exit( ) ;
    }

    while ( ( ch = fgetc ( fp ) ) != EOF )
        fputc ( ch, stdprn ) ;

    fclose ( fp ) ;
}
```

The statement **fputc (ch, stdprn) ;** writes a character read from the file to the printer. Note that although we opened the file on the disk we didn't open **stdprn,** the printer. Standard files and their use in redirection has been dealt with in more details in the last section of this chapter.

Note that these standard file pointers have been defined in the file "stdio.h". Therefore, it is necessary to include this file in the program which uses these standard file pointers.

Text Mode Versus Binary Mode

As we have seen earlier, the high level disk I/O functions can be categorised as text and binary. This classification arises out of the mode in which a file is opened. There are three main areas where text and binary mode files are different. These are:

(a)   Handling of newlines
(b)   Representation of end of file
(c)   Storage of numbers

Let us explore these three differences.

Text Versus Binary Mode: Newlines

We have already seen that, in text mode, a newline character is converted into the carriage return-linefeed combination before being written to the disk. Likewise, the carriage return-linefeed combination on the disk is converted back into a newline when the file is read by a C program. However, if a file is opened in binary mode, as opposed to text mode, these conversions will not take place.

As an example, let us revise our character count program to open a file in binary mode and see what effect it has on the count of characters present in the file. As you may recall, the earlier character count program had counted fewer characters in the file than the DOS DIR ommand. This was because DIR counted each end of line as two characters, while our program counted it as one. The following program would eliminate this discrepancy.

```
#include "stdio.h"
main( )
{
    FILE *fp ;
    char ch ;
    int noc = 0 ;
```

```
fp = fopen ( "POEM.TXT", "rb" ) ;
if ( fp == NULL )
{
    puts ( "Cannot open file" ) ;
    exit( ) ;
}

while ( 1 )
{
    ch = getc ( fp ) ;

    if ( ch == EOF )
        break ;

    noc++ ;
}

fclose ( fp )
printf ( "\nNumber of characters = %d", noc ) ;
}
```

And here is the output...

```
Number of characters = 105
```

There is only one difference between this program and the earlier character count program; we have opened the file in binary mode by using "rb" as an argument to **fopen( )**.

While opening the file in text mode we can use either "r" or "rt", but since, text mode is the default mode we usually drop the 't'. Using this program the character count would turn out to be 105, exactly same as that reported by the DIR command. There are four lines in our poem. Therefore, there are four carriage return-linefeed combinations in the file, signifying the end of four lines. Each counts as one in text mode, but two in binary mode, hence the difference of four characters. In binary mode the conversion of carrriage return-linefeed combination into newline or vice versa **does not** take place.

Text Versus Binary Mode: End of File

The second difference between text and binary modes is in the way the end-of-file is detected. In text mode, a special character, whose ascii value is 26, is inserted after the last character in the file to mark the end of file. If this character is detected at any point in the file, the read function would return the EOF signal to the program.

As against this, there is no such special character present in the binary mode files to mark the end of file. The binary mode files keep track of the end of file from the number of characters present in the directory entry of the file.

There is a moral to be derived from the end of file marker of text mode files. If a file stores numbers in binary mode, it is important that binary mode only be used for reading the numbers back, since one of the numbers we store might well be the number 26 (hexadecimal 1A). If this number is detected while we are reading the file by opening it in text mode, reading would be terminated prematurely at that point.

Thus the two modes are not compatible. See to it that the file that has been written in text mode is read back only in text mode. Similarly, the file that has been written in binary mode must be read back only in binary mode.

Text Versus Binary Mode: Storage of Numbers

The only function that is available for storing numbers in a disk file is the **fprintf( )** function. It is important to understand how numerical data is stored on the disk by **fprintf( )**. Text and characters are stored one character per byte, as we would expect. Are numbers stored as they are in memory, two bytes for an integer, four bytes for a float, and so on? No.

Numbers are stored as srtings of characters. Thus, 1234, even though it occupies two bytes in memory, when transferred to the disk using **fprintf( )**, it would occupy four bytes, one byte per character. Similarly, the floating point number 1234.56 would occupy 7 bytes on disk. Thus, numbers with more digits would require more disk space.

Hence if large amount of numerical data is to be stored in a disk file, using text mode may turn out to be inefficient. The solution is to open the file in binary mode and use those functions (**fread( )** and **fwrite( )** which are discussed later) which store the numbers in binary format. It means each number would occupy same number of bytes on disk as it occupies in memory.

Record I/O in Files

So far we have seen programs which write characters, strings or numbers to a file. If we desire to write a combination of these, that is a combination of dissimilar data types, what should we do? Use structures. Following program illustrates the use of structures for writing records of employees.

```c
/* Writing records to a file using structure */
#include "stdio.h"
main( )
{
    FILE *fp ;
    char another = 'Y' ;
    struct emp
    {
        char name[40] ;
        int age ;
        float bs ;
    } ;
    struct emp e ;

    fp = fopen ( "EMPLOYEE.DAT", "w" ) ;
```

```
        if ( fp == NULL )
        {
            puts ( "Cannot open file" ) ;
            exit( ) ;
        }

        while ( another == 'Y' )
        {
            printf ( "\nEnter name, age and basic salary: " ) ;
            scanf ( "%s %d %f", e.name, &e.age, &e.bs ) ;
            fprintf ( fp, "%s %d %f\n", e.name, e.age, e.bs ) ;

            printf ( "Add another record (Y/N) " ) ;
            fflush ( stdin ) ;
            another = getche( ) ;
        }

        fclose ( fp ) ;
    }
```

And here is the output of the program...

```
Enter name, age and basic salary: Sunil 34 1250.50
Add another record (Y/N) Y
Enter name, age and basic salary: Sameer 21 1300.50
Add another record (Y/N) Y
Enter name, age and basic salary: Rahul 34 1400.55
Add another record (Y/N) N
```

I suppose the program is self explanatory. We are just reading the data into a structure variable using **scanf( )**, and dumping it into a disk file using **fprintf( )**. The user can input as many records as he desires. The procedure ends, when the user supplies 'N' for the question 'Add another record (Y/N)'.

The above program has two disadvantages:

(a)   The numbers (basic salary) would occupy more number of bytes, since the file has been opened in text mode. This is because when the file is opened in text mode, each number is stored as a character string.

(b)   If the number of fields in the structure increase (say, by adding address, house rent allowance etc.), writing structures using **fprintf( )**, or reading them using **fscanf( )**, becomes quite clumsy.

Before we go on to eliminate these disadvantages, let us first complete the program that reads the employee records created by the above program. Here is how it can be done...

```
/* Read records from a file using structure */
#include "stdio.h"
main( )
{
    FILE *fp ;
    struct emp
    {
        char name[40] ;
        int age ;
        float bs ;
    } ;
    struct emp e ;

    fp = fopen( "EMPLOYEE.DAT", "r") ;

    if ( fp == NULL )
    {
        puts ( "Cannot open file" ) ;
        exit( ) ;
    }

    while ( fscanf ( fp, "%s %d %f", e.name, &e.age, &e.bs ) != EOF )
        printf ( "\n%s %d %f", e.name, e.age, e.bs ) ;
```

```
            fclose ( fp ) ;
        }
```

And here is the output of the program...

```
        Sunil 34 1250.500000
        Sameer 21 1300.500000
        Rahul 34 1400.500000
```

Let us now see a more efficient way of reading/writing records (structures). This makes use of two functions **fread( )** and **fwrite( )**. We will write two programs, first one would write records to the file and the second would read these records from the file and display them on the screen.

```
/* Receiving records from keyboard and writing them to a file in binary
mode */
#include "stdio.h"
main( )
{
    FILE *fp ;
    char another = 'Y' ;
    struct emp
    {
        char name[40] ;
        int age ;
        float bs ;
    } ;
    struct emp e ;

    fp = fopen ( "EMP.DAT", "wb" ) ;

    if ( fp == NULL)
    {
        puts ( "Cannot open file" ) ;
        exit( ) ;
```

```
        }

        while ( another == 'Y' )
        {
            printf ( "\nEnter name, age and basic salary: " ) ;
            scanf ( "%s %d %f", e.name, &e.age, &e.bs ) ;
            fwrite ( &e, sizeof ( e ), 1, fp ) ;

            printf ( "Add another record (Y/N) " ) ;
            fflush ( stdin ) ;
            another = getche( ) ;
        }

        fclose ( fp ) ;
    }
```

And here is the output...

```
    Enter name, age and basic salary: Suresh 24 1250.50
    Add another record (Y/N) Y
    Enter name, age and basic salary: Ranjan 21 1300.60
    Add another record (Y/N) Y
    Enter name, age and basic salary: Harish 28 1400.70
    Add another record (Y/N) N
```

Most of this program is similar to the one that we wrote earlier, which used **fprintf( )** instead of **fwrite( )**. Note, however, that the file "EMP.DAT" has now been opened in binary mode.

The information obtained about the employee from the keyboard is placed in the structure variable **e**. Then, the following statement writes the structure to the file:

```
    fwrite ( &e, sizeof ( e ), 1, fp ) ;
```

Here, the first argument is the address of the structure to be written to the disk.

The second argument is the size of the structure in bytes. Instead of counting the bytes occupied by the structure ourselves, we let the program do it for us by using the **sizeof( )** operator. **sizeof( )** operator gives the size of the variable in bytes. This keeps the program unchanged in event of change in the elements of the structure.

The third argument is the number of such structures that we want to write at one time. In this case, we want to write only one structure at a time. Had we had an array of structures, for example, we might have wanted to write the entire array at once.

The last argument is the pointer to the file we want to write to.

Now, let us write the program to read back the records written to the disk by the earlier program.

```
/* Read records from binary file and display them on VDU */
#include "stdio.h"
main( )
{
    FILE *fp ;
    struct emp
    {
        char name[40] ;
        int age ;
        float bs ;
    } ;
    struct emp e ;

    fp = fopen ( "EMP.DAT", "rb" ) ;

    if ( fp == NULL )
    {
        puts ( "Cannot open file" ) ;
        exit( ) ;
    }
```

```
        while ( fread ( &e, sizeof ( e ), 1, fp ) == 1 )
            printf ( "\n%s %d %f", e.name, e.age, e.bs ) ;

        fclose ( fp ) ;
    }
```

Here, the **fread( )** function causes the data read from the disk to be placed in the structure variable **e**. The format of **fread( )** is same as that of **fwrite( )**. The function **fread( )** returns the number of records read. Ordinarily, this should correspond to the third argument, the number of records we asked for... 1 in this case. If we have reached the end of file, since **fread( )** cannot read anything, it returns a 0. By testing for this situation, we know when to stop reading.

As you can now appreciate, any database management application in C must make use of **fread( )** and **fwrite( )** functions, since they store numbers more efficiently, and make writing/reading of structures quite easy. Note that even if the number of elements belonging to the structure increases, the format of **fread( )** and **fwrite( )** remains same.

Making It All Make Sense

So far we have learnt record I/O in bits and pieces. However, in any serious database management application, we will have to combine all that we have learnt in a proper manner to make sense. I have attempted to do this in the following menu driven program. There is a provision to Add, Modify, List and Delete records, the operations which are imperative in any database management. Following comments would help you in understanding the program easily:

Addition of records must always take place at the end of existing records in the file, much in the same way you would add new records in a register manually.

-       Listing records means displaying the existing records on the screen. Naturally, records should be listed from first record to last record.

-       While modifying records, first we must ask the user which record he intends to modify. Instead of asking the record number to be modified, it would be more meaningful to ask for the name of the employee whose record is to be modified. On modifying the record, the existing record gets overwritten by the new record.

-       In deleting records, except for the record to be deleted, rest of the records must first be written to a temporary file, then the original file must be deleted, and the temporary file must be renamed back to original.

-       Observe carefully the way the file has been opened, first for reading & writing, and if this fails (the first time you run this program it would certainly fail, because that time the file is not existing), for writing and reading. It is imperative that the file should be opened in binary mode.

-       Note that the file is being opened only once and closed only once, which is quite logical.

-       cls( ) function clears the contents of the screen and **gotorc( )** places the cursor at appropriate position on the screen. These functions should be stored in the file "goto.c", and this file must be included at the top of the program using **#include**. These functions are given at the end of the menu-driven program. Type them as they are in the file "goto.c". You would not be able to understand the details of these functions till you are through with Chapter 17. For the time being just manage to use them.

```
/* A menu-driven program for elementary database management */
#include "stdio.h"
```

```
main( )
{
    FILE *fp, *ft ;
    char another, choice ;
    struct emp
    {
        char name[40] ;
        int age ;
        float bs ;
    } ;
    struct emp e ;
    char empname[40] ;
    long int recsize ;

    fp = fopen ( "EMP.DAT", "rb+" ) ;

    if ( fp == NULL )
    {
        fp = fopen ( "EMP.DAT", "wb+" ) ;

        if ( fp == NULL )
        {
            puts ( "Cannot open file" ) ;
            exit( ) ;
        }
    }

    recsize = sizeof ( e ) ;

    while ( 1 )
    {
        cls( ) ;

        gotorc ( 10, 30 ) ;
        printf ( "1. Add Records" ) ;
        gotorc ( 12, 30 ) ;
        printf ( "2. List Records" ) ;
```

```
        gotorc ( 14, 30 ) ;
        printf ( "3. Modify Records" ) ;
        gotorc ( 16, 30 ) ;
        printf ( "4. Delete Records" ) ;
        gotorc ( 18, 30 ) ;
        printf ( "0. Exit" ) ;
        gotorc ( 20, 30 ) ;
        printf ( "Your choice" ) ;

        fflush ( stdin ) ;
        choice = getche( ) ;

        switch ( choice )
        {
            case '1' :

                fseek ( fp, 0 , SEEK_END ) ;
                another = 'Y' ;

                while ( another == 'Y' )
                {
                    printf ( "\nEnter name, age and basic sal. " ) ;
                    scanf ( "%s %d %f", e.name, &e.age, &e.bs ) ;
                    fwrite ( &e, recsize, 1, fp ) ;
                    printf ( "\nAdd another Record (Y/N) " ) ;
                    fflush ( stdin ) ;
                    another = getche( ) ·
                }

                break ;

            case '2' :

                rewind ( fp ) ;

                while ( fread ( &e, recsize, 1, fp ) == 1 )
                    printf ( "\n%s %d %f", e.name, e.age, e.bs ) ;
```

```
            break ;

    case '3' :

            another = 'Y' ;
            while ( another == 'Y' )
            {
                printf ( "\nEnter name of employee to modify " ) ;
                scanf ( "%s", empname ) ;

                rewind ( fp ) ;
                while ( fread ( &e, recsize, 1, fp ) == 1 )
                {
                    if ( strcmp ( e.name, empname ) == 0 )
                    {
                        printf ( "\nEnter new name, age & bs" ) ;
                        scanf ( "%s %d %f", e.name, &e.age,
                                    &e.bs ) ;
                        fseek ( fp, - recsize, SEEK_CUR ) ;
                        fwrite ( &e, recsize, 1, fp ) ;
                        break ;
                    }
                }

                printf ( "\nModify another Record (Y/N) " ) ;
                fflush ( stdin ) ;
                another = getche( ) ;
            }

            break :

    case '4' :

            another = 'Y' ;
            while ( another == 'Y' )
            {
```

```
                    printf ( "\nEnter name of employee to delete " ) ;
                    scanf ( "%s", empname ) ;

                    ft = fopen ( "TEMP.DAT", "wb" ) ;

                    rewind ( fp ) ;
                    while ( fread ( &e, recsize, 1, fp ) == 1 )
                    {
                        if ( strcmp ( e.name, empname ) != 0 )
                            fwrite ( &e, recsize, 1, ft ) ;
                    }

                    fclose ( fp ) ;
                    fclose ( ft ) ;

                    remove ( "EMP.DAT" ) ;
                    rename ( "TEMP.DAT", "EMP.DAT" ) ;

                    fp = fopen ( "EMP.DAT", "rb+" ) ;

                    printf ( "Delete another Record (Y/N) " ) ;
                    fflush ( stdin ) ;
                    another = getche( ) ;
                }
                break ;

            case '0' :
                fclose ( fp ) ;
                exit( ) ;
        }
    }
}
```

Type the following two functions in the file **goto.c**. The first one clears the screen, whereas the second places the cursor at desired position on the screen.

```
#include "dos.h"
cls( )
{
        union REGS i, o ;

        i.h.ah = 6 ;
        i.h.al = 0 ;
        i.h.ch = 0 ;
        i.h.cl = 0 ;
        i.h.dh = 24 ;
        i.h.dl = 79 ;
        i.h.bh = 7 ;
        int86 ( 16, &i, &o ) ;
}

gotorc ( int r, int c )
{
        union REGS i, o ;

        i.h.ah = 2 ;
        i.h.bh = 0 ;
        i.h.dh = r ;
        i.h.dl = c ;
        int86 ( 16, &i, &o ) ;
}
```

To understand how this program works, you need to be familiar with the concept of pointers. A pointer is initiated whenever we open a file. On opening a file a pointer is set up which points to the first record in the file. On using the functions **fread( )** or **fwrite( )**, the pointer moves to the beginning of next record. On closing a file the pointer is deactivated.

The **rewind( )** function places the pointer to the beginning of the file, irrespective of where it is present right now.

Note that the pointer movement is of utmost importance since **fread( )** always reads that record where the pointer is currently placed. Similarly, **fwrite( )** always writes the record where the pointer is currently placed.

The **fseek( )** function lets us move the pointer from one record to another. In the program above, to move the pointer to the previous record from its current position, we used the function,

        fseek (fp, -recsize, SEEK_CUR) ;

Here, **-recsize** moves the pointer back by **recsize** bytes from the current position. **SEEK_CUR** is a macro defined in "stdio.h".

Similarly, the following **fseek( )** would place the pointer beyond the last record in the file.

        fseek (fp, 0, SEEK_END) ;

In fact **-recsize** or 0 are just the offsets which tell the compiler by how many bytes should the pointer be moved from a particular position. The third argument could be either **SEEK_END**, **SEEK_CUR** or **SEEK_SET**. All these act as a reference from which the pointer should be offset. **SEEK_END** means move the pointer from the end of the file, **SEEK_CUR** means move the pointer with reference to its current position and **SEEK_SET** means move the pointer with reference to the beginning of the file.

If we wish to know where the pointer is positioned right now, we can use the function **ftell( )**. It returns this position as a **long int** which is an offset from the beginning of the file. The value returned by **ftell( )** can be used in subsequent calls to **fseek( )**. A sample call to **ftell( )** is shown below:

        position = ftell (fp) ;

where **position** is a **long int**

Detecting Errors in Reading/Writing

Not at all times when we perform a read or write operation on a file are we successful in doing so. Naturally there must be a provision to test whether our attempt to read/write was successful or not.

The standard library function **ferror( )** reports any error that might have occurred during a read/write operation on a file. It returns a zero if the read/write is successful and a non-zero value in case of a failure. The following program illustrates the usage of **ferror( )**.

```
#include "stdio.h"
main( )
{
    FILE *fp ;
    char ch ;

    fp = fopen ( "TRIAL", "w" ) ;

    while ( !feof ( fp ) )
    {
        ch = fgetc ( fp ) ;
        if ( ferror( ) )
        {
            printf ( "Error in reading file" ) ;
            break ;
        }
        else
            printf ( "%c", ch ) ;
    }

    fclose ( fp ) ;
}
```

In this program the **fgetc( )** function would obviously fail first time around since the file has been opened for writing whereas **fgetc( )** is attempting to read from the file. The moment the error occurs

ferror( ) returns a non-zero value and the **if** block gets executed. Instead of printing the error message using **printf( )** we can use the standard library function **perror( )** which prints the error message specified by the compiler. Thus in the above program the **perror( )** function can be used as shown below.

```
if ( ferror( ) )
{
        perror ( "TRIAL" ) ;
        break ;
}
```

Note that when the error occurs the error message that is displayed is:

```
TRIAL: Permission denied
```

This means we can precede the system error message with any message of our choice. In our program we have just displayed the filename in place of the error message.

Low Level Disk I/O

In low level disk I/O, data cannot be written as individual characters, or as strings or as formatted data, as is possible using high level disk I/O functions. There is only one way data can be written or read in low level disk I/O functions... as a buffer full of bytes.

Writing a buffer full of data resembles the **fwrite( )** function. However, unlike **fwrite( )**, the programmer must set up the buffer for the data, place the appropriate values in it before writing, and take them out after reading. Thus, the buffer in the low level I/O functions are very much a part of the program, rather than being invisible as in high level disk I/O functions.

Low level disk I/O functions offer following advantages :

(a)   Since these functions parallel the methods that MS- DOS uses
      to write to the disk, they are more efficient than the high level
      disk I/O functions.

(b)   Since there are fewer layers of routines to go through, low level
      I/O functions operate faster than their high level counterparts.

Let us now write a program that uses low level disk input/output
functions.

A Low Level File-copy Program

Earlier we had written a program to copy the contents of one file to
another. The limitation of the program as mentioned earlier, was that,
it could copy only the text files and not the .EXE or .COM files.

Here is a program that copies even .EXE files or .COM files, in
addtion to text files.

```
/* File-copy program which copies text, .com and .exe files */
#include "fcntl.h"
#include "types.h"
#include "stat.h"

main ( int argc, char *argv[ ] )
{
        char buffer[512] ;
        int inhandle, outhandle, bytes ;

        inhandle = open ( argv[1], O_RDONLY | O_BINARY ) ;
        if ( inhandle == -1 )
        {
            puts ( "Cannot open file" ) ;
            exit( ) ;
        }
```

```
        outhandle = open ( argv[2], O_CREAT | O_BINARY | O_WRONLY,
                                 S_IWRITE ) ;
        if ( inhandle == -1 )
        {
            puts ( "Cannot open file" ) ;
            close ( inhandle ) ;
            exit( ) ;
        }

        while ( 1 )
        {
            bytes = read ( inhandle, buffer, 512 ) ;

            if ( bytes > 0 )
                write ( outhandle, buffer, bytes ) ;
            else
                break ;
        }

        close ( inhandle ) ;
        close ( outhandle ) ;
    }
```

Declaring The Buffer

The first difference that you will notice in this program is that we declare a character buffer,

```
    char buffer[512] ;
```

This is the buffer in which the data read from the disk will be placed. The size of this buffer is important for efficient operation. Depending on the operating system, buffers of certain sizes are handled more efficiently than others. In MS-DOS the optimum buffer size is 512 bytes.

Opening A File

We have opened two files in our program, one is the source file from which we read the information, and the other is the target file into which we write the information read from the source file.

As in high level disk I/O, the file must be opened before we can access it. This is done using the statement,

```
inhandle = open ( argv[1], O_RDONLY | O_BINARY ) ;
```

We open the file for the same reason as we did in high level disk I/O: to establish communication with operating system about the file. As usual, we have to supply to **open( )**, the filename and the mode in which we want to open the file. The possible file opening modes are given below:

O_APPEND	-	Opens a file for appendng
O_CREAT	-	Creates a new file for writing (has no effect if file already exsts)
O_RDONLY	-	Creates a new file for reading only
O_RDWR	-	Creates a file for both reading and writing
O_WRONLY	-	Creates a file for writing only
O_BINARY	-	Creates a file in binary mode
O_TEXT	-	Creates a file in text mode

These 'O-flags' are defined in the file "fcntl.h". So this file must be included in the program while usng low level disk I/O. Note that the file "stdio.h" is not necessary for low level disk I/O. When two or more O-flags are used together, they are combined using the bitwise OR operator (|). Chapter 18 discusses bitwise operators in detail.

The other statement used in our program to open the file is,

```
outhandle = open ( argv[2], O_CREAT | O_BINARY | O_WRONLY,
                    S_IWRITE ) ;
```

Note that since the target file is not existing when it is being opened we have used the O_CREAT flag, and since we want to write to the file and not read from it, therefore we have used O_WRONLY. And finally, since we want to open the file in binary mode we have used O_BINARY.

Whenever O_CREAT flag is used, another argument must be added to **open( )** function to indicate the read/write status of the file to be created. This argument is called 'permission argument'. Permission arguments could be any of the following:

S_IWRITE   -   Writing to the file permitted
S_IREAD   -   Reading from the file permitted

To use these permissions, both the files "types.h" and "stat.h" must be **#includ**ed in the program alongwith "fcntl.h".

File Handles

Instead of returning a FILE pointer as **fopen( )** did, in low level disk I/O, **open( )** returns an integer value called 'file handle'. This is a number assigned to a particular file, which is used thereafter to refer to the file. If **open( )** returns a value of -1, it means that the file couldn't be successfully opened.

Interaction between Buffer and File

The following statement reads the file or as much of it as will fit into the buffer:

    bytes = read (inhandle, buffer, 512) ;

The **read( )** function takes three arguments. The first argument is the file handle, the second is the address of the buffer and the third is the maximum number of bytes we want to read.

The **read( )** function returns the number of bytes actually read. This is an important number, since it may very well be less than the buffer size (512 bytes), and we will need to know just how full the buffer is before we can do anything with its contents. In our program we have assigned this number to the variable **bytes**.

For copying the file, we must use both the **read( )** and the **write( )** functions in a **while** loop. The **read( )** function returns the number of bytes actually read. This is assigned to the variable **bytes**. This value will be equal to the buffer size (512 bytes) until the end of file, when the buffer will only be partially full. The variable **bytes** therefore is used to tell **write( )**, as to how many bytes to write from the buffer to the target file.

Note that when large buffers are used they must be made global variables, otherwise stack overflow occurs.

'O Redirection in DOS

The MS-DOS operating system incorporates (in versions 2.2 and later) a powerful feature that allows a program to read and write files, even when such capability has not been incorporated in the program. This is done through a process called 'redirection'.

Normally a C program receives its input from the standard input device, which is assumed to be the keyboaqrd, and sends its output to the standard output device, which is assumed to be the VDU. In other words, DOS makes certain assumptions about where input should come from amd where output should go. Redirection permits us to change these assumptions.

For example, using redirection the output of the program which normally goes to the VDU can be sent to the disk or the printer without really making a provision for it in the program. This is often a more convenient and flexible approach than providing a separate function in the program to write to the disk or printer. Similarly, redirection can be used to read information from disk file directly into a program, instead of receiving the input from keyboard.

If you're using Turbo C, a convenient way to use redirection is to compile a .EXE file and execute it from the DOS prompt, inserting the redirection symbols at appropriate places. Let us understand this process with the help of a program.

Redirecting The Output

Let's see how we can redirect the output of a program, from the screen to a file. We'll start by considering the simple program shown below:

```
/* File name: util.c */
#include "stdio.h"
main( )
{
    char ch ;
    while ( ( ch = getc ( stdin ) ) != EOF )
        putc ( ch, stdout ) ;
}
```

On compiling this program we would get an executable file UTIL.EXE. Normally, when we execute this file, the **putc( )** function will cause whatever we type to be printed on screen, until we don't type Ctrl Z, at which point the program will terminate, as shown in the following sample run. The Ctrl Z character is often called end of file character.

```
C>UTIL.EXE
perhaps I had a wicked childhood,
perhaps I had a miserable youth,
but somewhere in my wicked miserable past,
there must have been a moment of truth ^Z
C>
```

Now let's see what happens when we invoke this program from DOS in a different way, using redirection:

```
C>UTIL.EXE > POEM.TXT
C>
```

Here we are causing the output to be redirected to the file POEM.TXT. Can we prove that this the output has indded gone to the file POEM.TXT? Yes, by using the TYPE command in DOS as follows:

```
C>TYPE POEM.TXT
perhaps I had a wicked childhood,
perhaps I had a miserable youth,
but somewhere in my wicked miserable past,
there must have been a moment of truth
C>
```

There's the result of our typing sitting in the file. The redirection operator, '>', causes any output intended for the screen to be written to the file whose name follows the operator.

Note that the data to be redirected to a file doesn't need to be typed by a user at the keyboard; the program itself can generate it. Any output normally sent to the screen can be redirected to a disk file. As an example consider the following program for generating the Ascii table on screen:

```
/* File name: ascii.c*/
main( )
{
    int ch ;

    for ( ch = 0 ; ch <= 255 ; ch++ )
        printf ( "\n%d %c", ch, ch ) ;
}
```

When this program is compiled and then executed at DOS promot using the redirection operator,

C>ASCII.EXE > TABLE.TXT

the output is written to the file. This can be a useful capability any time you want to capture the output in a file, rather than displaying it on the screen.

DOS predefines a number of filenames for its own use. One of these names in PRN, which stands for the printer. Output can be redirected to the printer by using this filename. For example, if you invoke the ascii.exe program this way:

C>ASCII.EXE > PRN

the Ascii table will be printed on the printer.

Redirecting The Input

We can also redirect input to a program so that, instead of reading a character from the keyboard, a program reads it from a file. Let us now see how this can be done.

To redirect the input, we need to have a file containing something to be displayed. Suppose we use a file called NEWPOEM.TXT containing the following lines:

Let's start at the very beginning,
A very good place to start!

We'll assume that using some text editor these lines have been placed in the file NEWPOEM.TXT. Now, we use the input redirection operator '<' before the file, as shown below:

C>UTIL.EXE < NEWPOEM.TXT
Let's start at the very beginning,

A very good place to start!
C>

The lines are printed on the screen with no further effort on our part. Using redirection we've made our program UTIL.C perform the work of the DOS TYPE command.

Both Ways At Once

Redirection of input and output can be used together; the input for a program can come from a file via redirection, at the same time it's output can be redirected to a file. In DOS nomenclature, we can say that in such a case the program acts as a filter. The following command demonstrates this process.

C>UTIL < NEWPOEM.TXT > POETRY.TXT

In this case our program recevies the redirected input from the file NEWPOEM.TXT and instead of sending the output to the screen it would redirect it to the file POETRY.TXT.

Similarly to send the contents of the file NEWPOEM.TXT to the printer we can use the following command:

C>UTIL < NEWPOEM.TXT > PRN

While using such multiple redirections don't try to send output to the same file from which you are receiving input. This is because the output file is erased before it's written to. So by the time we manage to receive the input from a file it is already erased.

Redirection can be a powerful tool for developing utility programs to examine or alter data in files. Thus, redirection is used to establish a relationship between a program and a file. Another DOS operator can be used to relate two programs directly, so that the output of one is fed directly into another, with no files involved. This is called

'piping', and is done using the operator '|', called pipe. We won't
pursue this topic, but you can read about it in the DOS manual.

Summary

This chapter appears to be quite intimidating... so many functions,
with different purposes! But it's only a matter of time before one
becomes comfortable with these functions. Let me tell you that I/O
is still more complex. We have only covered the highlights, but you
perhaps have got an insight which would encourage you to explore
further on your own.

We have seen that there are basically three types of I/O: console I/O,
disk I/O and port I/O. we have dealt with the first two in detail,
whereas the third is outside the scope of this book. In console I/O we
learnt functions for formatted and unformatted I/O. In disk I/O we
saw that there are two main families of file handling functions: high
level and low level. High level functions are easier to use. but low
level functions are more efficient. We also examined the differences
between files stored in text and binary mode.

We ended the chapter with a look at the redirection capabilites of
MS-DOS and how they can be explored through C programs.

Exercise

Console I/O

[A]   What will be the output of the following programs:

```
(a)    main( )
       {
            char s[ ] = "Aw what the heck" ;
            printf ( "\n%s", s ) ;
            printf ( "\n%s", s[3] ) ;
```

```
            printf ( "\n%s", &s[3] ) ;
    }
```

(b)
```
    main( )
    {
        printf ( "\n%s", "Bit by bit I take a byte..." ) ;
        printf ( "\n%s", "As quiet flows the Don corleone" ) ;
    }
```

(c)
```
    char *m[ ] = {
                    "Our soccer is pathetic",
                    "Our politics is a scoundrels game",
                    "Our economy is Ram bharose",
                    "Prices have blown through the roof top",
                    "C seems to be the only plus point!!"
                } ;
    main( )
    {
        int i ;
        for ( i = 0 ; i <= 4 ; i++ )
            printf ( "\n%s", m[i] ) ;
    }
```

(d)
```
    char p[ ] = "The sixth sick sheikh's sixth ship is sick" ;
    main( )
    {
        int i = 0 ;
        while ( p[i] != '\0' )
        {
            putch ( p[i] ) ;
            i++ ;
        }
    }
```

[B] Point out the errors, if any, in the following programs:

(a)   main( )
```
{
    char name[40], prof[25] ;
    puts ( "Enter name of your favourite footballer" ) ;
    scanf ( "%s", name ) ;
    puts ( "Enter your profession" ) ;
    scanf ( "%s", &prof[0] ) ;
}
```

(b)   main( )
```
{
    char message[25] ;
    puts ( "Enter any message\n" ) ;
    gets ( "%s", message ) ;
}
```

(c)   main( )
```
{
    char key ;
    puts ( "press any key..." ) ;
    scanf ( "%c", &key ) ;
}
```

(d)   main( )
```
{
    char s[ ] = "Viruses at last" ;
    printf ( "\n%s", &s[0] ) ;
    printf ( "\n%s", &s[5] ) ;
}
```

(e)   main( )
```
{
    char *mess[5] ;
    for ( i = 0 ; i < 5 ; i++ )
        scanf ( "%s", mess[i] ) ;
}
```

(f)   main( )
```
{
    int i ;
    float j ;
    scanf ( "%d\n%f", &i, &j) ;
}
```

[C]   Answer the following:

(a)   To receive the string "We have got the guts, you get the glory!!" in an array **char str[100]** which of the following functions would you use?

    1.   scanf ("%s", str) ;
    2.   gets (str) ;
    3.   getche (str) ;
    4.   fgetchar (str) ;

(b)   Which function would you use if a single key is to be received through the keyboard?

    1.   scanf( )
    2.   gets( )
    3.   getche( )
    4.   getchar( )

(c)   If an integer is to be entered through the keyboard, which function would you use?

    1.   scanf( )
    2.   gets( )
    3.   getche( )
    4.   getchar( )

(d)   If a character string is to be received through the keyboard which function would work faster?

1. scanf( )
2. gets( )

(e)   What is the difference between **getchar( )**, **fgetchar( )**, **getch( )** and **getche( )**?

(f)   The format string of a **printf( )** function can contain:

1.   characters, conversion specifications and escape sequences
2.   character, integers and floats
3.   strings, integers and escape sequences
4.   Inverted commas, percentage sign and backslash character

(g)   A field width specifier in a **printf( )** function:

1.   controls the margins of the program listing
2.   specifies the maximum value of a number
3.   controls the size of type used to print numbers
4.   specifies how many columns will be used to print the number

[D]   Answer the following:

(a)   Write down two functions **xgets( )** and **xputs( )** which work similar to the standard library functions **gets( )** and **puts( )**.

(b)   Write down a function **getint( )** which would receive a numeric string from the keyboard, convert it to an integer number and return the integer to the calling function. A sample usage of **getint( )** is shown below:

```
main( )
{
    int a ;
    a = getint( ) ;
    printf ( "you entered %d", a ) ;
```

```
        }
```

Disk I/O, *argc*, *argv*

[E]   Point out the errors, if any, in the following programs:

(a)   main( )
```
        {
            FILE *fp ;
            fp = fopen ( "TRY.C", "r" ) ;
            fclose ( fp ) ;
        }
```

(b)   main( )
```
        {
            FILE fp ;
            fp == fopen ( "YOURS", "w" ) ;
            fclose ( fp ) ;
        }
```

(c)   #include "stdio.h"
```
        main( )
        {
            FILE *fp ;
            char c ;
            fp = fopen ( "TRY.C" ,"r") ;
            if ( fp == null )
            {
                puts ( "Cannot open file" ) ;
                exit( ) ;
            }
            while ( ( c = getc ( fp ) ) != EOF )
                putch ( c ) ;
            fclose ( fp ) ;
        }
```

(d)   #include "stdio.h"
```
main( )
{
    FILE *fp, *ft ;
    fp = fopen ( "TRY.C" , "r" ) ;
    fp = fopen ( "TRIAL.C", "r" ) ;
    fclose ( fp, ft ) ;
}
```

(e)   main(int ac, char *av[ ])
```
{
    printf ( "\n%d", ac ) ;
    printf ( "\n%s", av[0] ) ;
}
```

[F]   Answer the following:

(a)   The macro FILE is defined in which of the following files:

1. stdlib.h
2. stdio.c
3. io.h
4. stdio.h

(b)   State True or False:

1. The disadvantage of High Level Disk I/O functions is that the programmer has to manage the buffers.
2. If a file is opened for reading it is necessary that the file must exist.
3. If a file opened for writing already exists its contents would be overwritten.
4. For opening a file in append mode it is necessary that the file should exist.

(c)   On opening a file for reading which of the following activities are performed:

1. The disk is searched for existence of the file.
2. The file is brought into memory.
3. A pointer is set up which points to the first character in the file.
4. All the above.

(d)   Which of the following are the correct ways of opening a file

1.
```
#include "stdio.h"
main( )
{
    FILE *t ;
    char filename[30] ;
    scanf ( "%s", filename ) ;
    t = fopen ( filename, "r" ) ;
    fclose ( t ) ;
}
```

2.
```
#include "stdio.h"
main( )
{
    FILE *t ;
    t = fopen ( "jazz.c", "r" ) ;
    fclose ( t ) ;
}
```

3.
```
#include "stdio.h"
main ( int argc, char *argv[ ] )
{
    FILE *t ;
    t = fopen ( argv[1], "r" ) ;
    fclose ( t ) ;
}
```

4. All the above.

[G] Answer the following:

(a) Write a program to count the number of words in a given text file.

(b) Write a program to store every character typed at the keyboard into a file. The procedure should come to an end as soon as the character ~ is hit from the keyboard.

(c) Write a program to remove all blank lines from a file.

(d) Write a program to remove all comments from a C program file.

(e) Write a program to display the contents of a text file on the screen. Make following provisions:

Display the contents inside a box drawn with opposite corner co-ordinates being (1, 0) and (23, 79). Display the name of the file whose contents are being displayed, and the page numbers in the zeroth row. The moment one screenful of file has been displayed, flash a message 'Press any key...' in 24th row. When a key is hit, the next page's contents should be displayed, and so on till the end of file.

(f) Write a program to encrypt/decrypt a file using:

(1) An offset cipher: In an offset cipher each character from the source file is offset with a fixed value and then written to the target file.
For example, if character read from the source file is 'A', then convert this into a new character by offsetting 'A' by a fixed value, say 128, and then writing the new character to the target file.

(2) A substitution cipher: In this each character read from the source file is substituted by a corresonding predetermined character and this character is written to the target file. For example, if character 'A' is read from the source file, and if we have decided that every 'A' is to be substituted by '!', then a '!' would be written to the target file in place of every 'A' Similarly, every 'B' would be substituted by '5' and so on.

(g) A file opened in Document mode in Wordstar stores each word with its last character being stored as the ascii value of the character plus 128. As against this a Non-document mode file is stored as a normal file. Write down a program which would convert a Document mode file into a Non-document mode file.

String I/O, Formatted disk I/O, Text and binary modes

[H] Point out the errors, if any, in the following programs:

(a)
```
main( )
{
    FILE *fp ;
    char str[80] ;
    fp = fopen ( "TRY.C", "r" ) ;
    while ( fgets ( str, 80, fp ) != EOF )
        fputs ( str ) ;
    fclose ( fp ) ;
}
```

(b)
```
main( )
{
    FILE *fp ;
    char str[80] ;

    fp = fopen ( "MYPROG.C", "r" ) ;
    while ( fgets ( str, fp ) != EOF )
```

```
                printf ( "\n%s" , str ) ;
                fclose ( fp ) ;
        }

(c)     main( )
        {
                FILE *fp ;
                char name[25] ;
                int age ;

                fp = fopen ( "YOURS", "r" ) ;
                while ( fscanf ( fp, "%s %d", name, &age ) != NULL )
                fclose ( fp ) ;
        }
```

[I]   Answer the following:

(a)   Is it necessary that a file created in text mode must always be
       opened in text mode for subsequent operations?

(b)   State True or False:

       A file opened in binary mode and read using **fgetc( )** would
       report the same number of characters in the file as reported by
       DOS's DIR command.

(c)   While using the statement,

       fp = fopen ("myfile.c", "r") ;

       what happens if,

       - myfile.c does not exist on the disk
       - myfile.c exists on the disk

(d)   What is the purpose of the library function **fflush( )**?

(e)   While using the statement,

```
fp = fopen ( "myfile.c", "wb" ) ;
```

what happens if,

- myfile.c does not exist on the disk.
- myfile.c exists on the disk

(f)   A floating point array contains percentage marks obtained by students in an examination. To store these marks in a file "marks.c", in which mode would you open the file and why?

[J]   Answer the following:

(a)   Given below are two programs written in dBASE. The first one is poorly written. Contents-wise both the programs are same, but the second one has been properly indented (the IF's & ENDIF's, the DOWHILE's & ENDDO's, the DO CASE's & ENDCASE's have been properly lined up).

Program One

```
* A sample dbase program
INPUT "Enter any number" TO N
DO WHILE ( .T. )
IF ( N > 30 )
A = 25
ELSE
A = 30
ENDIF
INPUT "Enter any number" TO CODE
DO CASE
CASE CODE = 1
B = 100
CASE CODE = 2
B = 200
```

```
CASE CODE = 3
B = 300
CASE CODE = 4
B = 400
ENDCASE
ENDDO
```

Program Two

```
* A sample dbase program
INPUT "Enter any number" TO N
DO WHILE ( .T. )
    IF ( N > 30 )
        A = 25
    ELSE
        A = 30
    ENDIF
    INPUT "Enter any number" TO CODE
    DO CASE
        CASE CODE = 1
            B = 100
        CASE CODE = 2
            B = 200
        CASE CODE = 3
            B = 300
        CASE CODE = 4
            B = 400
    ENDCASE
ENDDO
```

Write a program which would receive as input the first program from a source file and output the properly indented second progran into a target file.

(b)   Write a program which prints out only those lines from a file which are containing more then 80 character. Also print out the line numbers of these lines.

(c)   Write a program that will concatenate two files: that is, append the contents of one file at the end of another and write the result into a third file. You must be able to execute the command at DOS prompt as follows:

```
C>CONCAT source1.txt source2.txt target.txt
```

(d)   A file contains a C program, but by mistake a novice has typed it out in capitals. It's a long program, therefore you cannot afford to have it retyped. Write a utility which reads this program and converts it to an appropriate small-case program and writes it to a target file. Use functions **fgets( )** and **fputs( )**.

Record I/O, Low level disk I/O

[K]   Point out the errors, if any, in the following programs:

(a)
```
main( )
{
    FILE *fp ;
    char names[20] ;
    int i ;
    fp = fopen ( "students.c", "wb" ) ;
    for ( i = 0 ; i <= 10 ; i++ )
    {
        puts ( "\nEnter name " ) ;
        gets ( name ) ;
        fwrite ( name, size of ( name ), 1, fp ) ;
    }
    close ( fp ) ;
}
```

(b)
```
main( )
{
    FILE *fp ;
    char name[20] = "Ajay" ;
    int i ;
```

```
            fp = fopen ( "students.c", "r" ) ;
            for ( i = 0 ; i <= 10 ; i++ )
                  fwrite ( name, sizeof ( name ), 1, fp ) ;
            close ( fp ) ;
      }
```

(c)   ```
      #include "fcntl.h"
      main( )
      {
            int fp ;
            fp = open ("pr22.c", "r") ;
            if (fp == -1)
                  puts ("cannot open file") ;
            else
                  close (fp) ;
      }
      ```

(d)   ```
      main( )
      {
            int fp ;
            fp = fopen ( "students.c", READ | BINARY ) ;
            if ( fp == -1 )
                  puts ( "cannot open file" ) ;
            else
                  close ( fp ) ;
      }
      ```

[L]   Answer the following:

(a)   In the file "STUD.DAT" there are 100 records with the following structure:

```
struct students
{
      int rollno ;
      float permarks ;
} ;
```

In another file "STUDENTS.DAT" there are 100 records with the following structure:

```
struct studinfo
{
    int rollno , centreno ;
    char branch[10];
    float per ;
} ;
```

However, in this file in all the 100 records no entry exists in the field **per**. Write a program to copy the percentage marks from the file "STUD.DAT" into the file "STUDENTS.DAT". See to it that data other than the percentage marks in "STUDENTS.DAT" remains undisturbed. Note that the roll numbers present in the two files are not necessarily in the same order.

(b) There are 100 records present in a file with the following structure:

```
struct
{
    char itemcode[6], itemname[20] ;
    int qty ;
} ;
```

Write a program to read these records, arrange them in ascending order and write them in to a target file.

(c) Write a program to list the contents of a database file (created through dBASE).
Before you set out to write the program the following information will be useful:
Each dBASE III plus database file has the following components: Header in the first 32 bytes, a structure of variable length (i.e. description about the fields) and actual data.

Header is organised in the following manner:

Byte nos.	Information stored
1	Type of file (0x3, 0x83)
2-4	Date of last updation (yy/dd/mm format)
5-8	Total no. of records in database
9-10	No. of bytes in the file header
11-12	No. of bytes per record
13-15	Reserved
16-28	Reserved for multiuser
29-32	Reserved

Structure which contains information about the various fields present in the database file begins at 33rd byte and contains the following information. Details of each field occupies 32 bytes, thus the structure is a mutiple of 32 bytes. This structure is as shown below:

Byte nos.	Information stored
1-11	Name of field padded with Ascii zeros
12	Field type in Ascii
13-16	Reserved
17	Length of field (binary)
18	No. of decimal places (binary)
19-20	Reserved for multiuser
21	Work area identification
22-23	Reserved for multiuser
24	Flag for set fields
25-31	Reserved area
32	Field separator (0x0D)

12 *Fundamental Computer Concepts*

With what we have learnt so far we are ready for bigger things. In this chapter we are going to change our focus from C language to C's interaction with the IBM compatible microcomputers. This doesn't mean that we have imbibed everything that C has to offer. Some key topics like bitwise operators and union data type still remain unexplored. These would be covered in later chapters. You now know enough, however, to begin exploring some of the features of the IBM PC family of computers in order to put C to work in real world programming situations.

Unfortunately, we cannot straightaway begin by writing programs. We need to know our PC in and out before we do that. I thought it appropriate that we should begin by first understanding the philosophy of the PC, the Operating System fundamentals and details about the devices like disks, VDU and keyboard. Therefore, I have divided the material into five chapters:

(a)   Fundamental Computer Concepts
(b)   Operating System Fundamentals
(b)   Disk Basics
(c)   VDU Basics
(c)   Keyboard Basics

Once we are through with these basics we would be better off to explore the capabilities of PC using C. The reader is requested to read the chapters in the afore-mentioned order to appreciate them better.

If we are to understand the PC thoroughly, where do we begin? Just open the CPU box and have a look at the circuitry. Let us begin this chapter with a peek into the CPU box.

Inside the CPU

There are basically six models which comprise the IBM PC family of microcomputers. They are, a PC, a PC/XT, a PC/AT, a PC/AT386, a PC/AT486 and a Pentium. The differences arise out of the micrprocessor which drives the microcomputer, the input/output units used, and the memory size. Figure 12.1 shows these differences. Note that the memory size that has been mentioned is as per the standard configuration marketed by a number of vendors, and may change as per the user's requirements. Similarly, the capacities of floppy disk drive (fdd) and hard disk drive (hdd), the type of video display unit (vdu) and keyboard (kb) may change from installation to istallation. The details are too intricate to be included in this figure.

Type	μp	I/O devices	Memory	OS used
PC	8088	kb, vdu, 2 fdd	256 kb	DOS
PC/XT	8088	kb, vdu, 1 fdd, 1 hdd	640 kb	DOS
PC/AT	80286	kb, vdu, 1 fdd, 1 hdd	1 mb	DOS/Unix
PC/AT 386	80386	kb, vdu, 1 fdd, 1 hdd	4 mb	DOS/Unix
PC/AT486	80486	kb, vdu, 1 fdd, 1 hdd	8 mb	DOS/Unix
Pentium	Pentium	kb, vdu, 1 fdd, 1 hdd	16 mb	DOS/Unix

Figure 12.1

All members of the PC family of computers consist of a microprocessor, memory chips and several smart or programmable circuit chips. All the main circuit components that make the computer work are located on a mother board, whereas other important parts are located on expansion boards, which can be plugged into the mother board.

Following is the the list of major components present on the mother board along with their functions in brief:

(a) Microprocessor

The microprocessor chip carries out two basic functions. Firsly, it performs numerical computations and logical comparisons using CPU registers. Secondly, it transfers data, addresses and control signals, using 'buses'.

(b)   Math co-processor

This is a dedicated processor which is capable of performing complex arithmetic. It may or may not be present on the mother board. If present, it takes substanital load off the microprocessor's shoulder and thereby accelerates the operations.

(c)   Memory chips

These are used for storage of data, instructions and intermediate & final results.

(d)   Support chips

Some of these chips control external devices, such as the disk drives or the video display unit, while other support chips help the microprocessor to carry out its tasks.

(e)   Built-in programs

These are the programs which are hard wired into the mother board at the time of manufacturing. These are often called ROM programs.

(f)   Expansion slots

These are the slots present on the mother board, into which controller cards for various input/ouput devices are plugged in. For example, the hard disk controller card which drives the hard disk is plugged into one of the expansion slots. Likewise, the display adapter that drives the monitor is also plugged into one of the expansion slots.

From the programmers point of view, the major difference in the various models of the microcomputer lies in the type of microprocessor it uses. Let us therefore examine the different types of microprocessors.

The Microprocessor

The microprocessor is the heart of all the PCs. The microprocessor carries out variety of computations, numeric comparisons, and data transfers in response to programs stored in memory. The microprocessor is also called Central Processing Unit, or simply CPU.

The CPU controls the computer's basic operation by sending and receiving control signals, memory addresses, and data from one part of the computer to another. The control signals, addresses and data are carried from one part to another through a 'bus'. A bus refers to a group of interconnecting electronic pathways that connect one part of the computer to another.

Actually speaking, a CPU consists of an Arithmetic Logic Unit to perform arithmetic and comparisons, Control Unit to control other units of the computer and Memory chips to store information. The microprocessor usually consists of an Arithmetic Logic Unit and a Control Unit. So a microprocessor may not be a complete CPU in itself. But with the widespread use of microprocessors, they have come to be called CPUs.

To enable the flow of data between the microprocessor and the memory there is a set of wires. This set of wires is called 'data bus'. Each wire in this bus carries a bit of data at a time (either zero or one in the form of an electric pulse). If the data bus has 8 wires then 8 bits or 1 byte of data can flow in it at a time and this is called a 8-bit data bus. Similarly, we have 16-bit and 32-bit data buses which can carry 16 and 32 bits at a time respectively.

A microprocessor with a 32-bit data bus is faster than the one with a 16-bit data bus. This is because in the former, four bytes of data are brought to the microprocessor at a time, while in the latter only 2 bytes of data are brought at a time.

If a microprocessor with a 32-bit data bus is faster than the one with a 16-bit data bus, then why not have a 32-bit data bus instead of a 16-bit data bus? This is not possible because the microprocessors are designed that way. A microprocessor with a provision for connecting only a 16-bit data bus cannot be connected with a 32-bit data bus.

Hence, each type of microprocessor can be distinguished by the width of the data bus that it is connected to. A microprocessor with a provision for 16-bit data bus is called a 16-bit microprocessor, the one with a provision for 32-bit data bus is called a 32-bit microprocessor and so on.

So given a set of microprocessors, one can easily grade them according to their speeds based on the width of their data bus. But this may not always be possible because the data bus width is not the only criterion by which speed of the microprocessor can be decided.

Consider the microprocessors named intel 8085 and intel 8088. Both have a 8-bit data bus. But the 8088 microprocessor is much faster than 8085. This is because internally the 8088 can process 16 bits at a time while the 8085 can process only 8 bits. So the 8088 will process 2 bytes in one operation whereas the 8085 would do it in 2 operations (one byte at a time). Hence 8088 is faster than 8085. It is for this reason that a 8088 microprocessor cannot be called an 8-bit microprocessor. Instead it is called an 8/16-bit microprocessor. The 8 represents the data bus width and the 16 represents the internal processing capability.

It should be noted that a 16-bit microprocessor may or may not be twice as fast as a 8-bit microprocessor due to a various other factors, which are too involved to be discussed here.

The way the data bus width decides the amount of data that can flow between the microprocessor and memory at a time, the address **bus** width determines the amount of memory that is accessible to the microprocessor. Thus, a 16-bit address bus can allow access to a maximum of 64 kb, since along a address bus 2^{16} various location numbers can be passed. Bigger the address bus width more is the addressable memory available with the microprocessor. While working in real mode the 8086 family of microprocessors can use only a 20-bit adrress bus, thereby limiting the addressable space to only 2^{20} bytes or 1 mb.

IBM range of PC compatibles are based on 8086 family of microprocessors like 8088 (PC, PC/XT), 80286 (PC/AT), or a 80386 (PC/AT386). A brief introduction of these common microprocessors follows.

The 8088 Microprocessor

The 8088 is a 16-bit microprocessor that controls the standard IBM PCs. For the microprocessor to carry out its basic task of data transfer and processing, internally, 14 registers provide a working area (28 bytes in size) that the microprocessor utilises for temporarily storing data, memory addresses, instruction pointers, and status and control flags. Through these registers the 8088 can access 1 mb of memory.

The 8086 Microprocessor

This differs from the 8088 micrprocessor in that it uses a full 16-bit data bus as against the 8-bit bus used by 8088.

The 80286 Microprocessor

Used with PC/AT, the 80286 is empowered with special features that makes the program execution faster as compared to that of a 8086. One of these features worth mentioning is multitasking (performing several tasks simultaneously).

The 80286 can run in either of the two operating modes: Real mode and Protected mode. In real mode, the 80286 works exactly like a 8086. In protected mode, however, the 80286 reserves a predetermined amount of memory for an executing program, preventing this memory from being used by any other program. This means that several programs can run simultaneously without the risk of one program accidently changing another program's memory area.

The 80386 Microprocessor

This is a faster and more powerful microprocessor as compared to a 80286. Like a 80286 this microprocessor also supports Real and Protected mode programming. It however has two important advantages over a 80286:

(a)   The 80386 is a 32-bit microprocessor with 32-bit registers. It can therefore perform computations and address memory 32 bits at a time instead of 16 bits at a time.
(b)   The 80386 offers a more flexible memory management than a 80286.

The following figure captures the essence of all that we have said about microprocessors so far.

Microprocessor	Data Bus	Address Bus	Max. Memory	Mode of operation
8088 (PC, XT)	8 bits	20 bits	1 mb	Real
8086 (PC, XT)	16 bits	20 bits	1 mb	Real
80286 (AT)	16 bits	24 bits	16 mb	Real/Protected
80386 (AT386)	32 bits	32 bits	4096 mb	Real/Protected
80486 (AT486)	32 bits	32 bits	244 mb	Real/Protected
Pentium	64 bits	64 bits	2^{44} mb	Real/Protected

Figure 12.2

Math Co-processor

There are many applications in which we expect the computer to do complex arithmetic operations. Ordinarily these operations are performed by the microprocessor. Naturally, a lot of valuable time of microprocessor is consumed in performing complex arithmetic as a result of which the other tasks which need microprocessor's attention get delayed. The overall result is decrease in speed of operation. In such a case use of math co-processor becomes ideal. It is a dedicated processor which does the arithmetic so that the microprocessor remains free to cater to other jobs. The math co-processor, if installed on the mother board must be compatible with the microprocessor. That is, a 8088 microprocessor can support only a intel 8087 math co-processor, a 80286 microprocessor can support only a 80287 math co-processor and so on.

Memory Chips

Memory chips can store data, instructions and intermediate & final results. The memory is organised into bytes, each byte capable of storing one character of information. Each byte of memory has an address or location number which uniquely identifies it. The size of memory is measured either in kilobytes (kb), megabytes (mb), gigabytes (gb) or terabytes (tb). Following conversions could come in handy at a later stage:

```
8 bits = 1 byte
1024 bytes = 1 kb
1024 kb = 1 mb
1024 mb = 1 gb
1024 gb = 1 tb
```

Memory could be of two types: RAM (Random Access Memory) or ROM (read only memory). Out of these, RAM is used for holding data, instructions and results. The RAM has two important characteristics:

- The data present in RAM can be easily read and modified through programs.

- This memory is volatile. It means its contents are lost on swithcing off the computer.

ROM or Read Only Memory contains instructions (built in programs) which are permanently recorded in memory at the time of manufacturing and cannot be changed by us. Secondly, ROM is not volatile, so turning off the computer doesn't wipe out its contents.

Support Chips

The overall operations of a computer are too complex to be controlled by the microprocessor alone. Therefore the microprocessor delgates certain tasks to chips called support chips. These support chips may be responsible for controlling the flow of information to and from various input/output devices like VDU and disk drives. Examples of support chips are:

- clock chip which generates signals that are needed to drive the microprocessor

- CRT controller chip which controls the VDU

- programmable peripheral interface chip which controls the speaker of the computer

- DMA chip which allows interaction with disk drive

- interrupt controller chip which supervises the operation of interrupts.

Built-in Programs

These are stored in the ROM chips and consist of routines which are fundamental to the very working of the computer. This consists of programs which check and intialise the standard and non-standard equipment attached to your computer, perform memory test every time you put on a computer, interact with the I/O devices etc. We are going to deal with these programs in later chapters.

Expansion Slots

The very name suggests that these are provided for expanding the capabilities of the computer. Suppose you want to upgrade a PC to a PC/XT, all that you are required to do is remove the floppy disk drive and its controller card and insert a hard disk drive and plug in the controller card of the hard disk in one of the expansion slots. Similarly, if you wish to change over from a monochrome VDU to a coloured one, replace the VDU and plug in a controller card which can drive the colour monitor. The number of expansion slots present on the mother board vary from 4 to 8.

Memory Revisited

When PCs came into existence memory capacity of 64 kb was considered to be sufficient. However, as new softwares came into being the memory requirement started growing. So came PCs with 256 kb and 512 kb memory. Softwares which were memory hungry were born soon and they required 640 kb memory to work comfortably. And soon the software developers started demanding more memory. While working in real mode the 8086 family of microprocessors use only a 20-bit address bus, thereby limiting the maximum memory accessible to only 1 mb. To overcome this limit of 1 mb two schemes came into existence: Expanded Memory and Extended memory. A brief explanation about the different types of memories is given below.

Conventional Memory

The regular RAM memory in your PC is called conventional or "base" memory. This was as little as 16 kb in earliest models of PCs.

Most now come with at least 640 kb. The hardware in a PC or XT allows a maximum of 1 mb. PC hardware that is 486-based can handle as much as 4096 mb - 4 gb. But the software in both standard PCs and high-powered 486-based PCs typically allows a maximum of 640 kb.

High Memory

The 384 kb of memory addresses above the DOS limit of 640 kb are called high memory or reserved memory. Your regular programs and data can't use high memory the way they use conventional memory. In fact, under regular circumstances, they are barred from using it at all. And any RAM chips that would have been at those addresses in high memory are automatically detoured to the reserved uses. That 384 kb was reserved by the programmers who created DOS for:

(a)   BIOS and other ROMs
(b)   Video memory
(c)   Future uses

Expanded Memory

The first major scheme for slipping around the DOS 640 kb limit on memory was expanded memory; it's still one of the most important. Expanded memory still forces programs to deal only with conventional memory, or with borrowed parts of high memory, but it swaps information from other memory in and out of these conventional addresses.

With the right software and hardware to handle this swapping of memory information, a PC can have as much as 32 mb more memory. Only programs that are written to understand expanded memory can use these megabytes, but there are quite a few available today which do.

Expanded memory can be slower than conventional memory, but that's a minor price to pay for getting so many megabytes. And in fact, under certain circumstances such as multitasking, swapping even more of conventional memory in and out in expanded memory fashion - a practice known as backfilling - can be faster than traditional conventional memory.

Extended Memory

Extended memory is memory at the addresses directly above 1 mb. That is, it's the memory above conventional and high memory. It is not the same thing as expanded memory. (It's too bad the names are so similar.) Expanded memory swaps information in and out of conventional memory; extended memory holds its own information. Extended memory works on any PCs built around the 286, 386, or 486 chips. These days many of the these systems ship with enough memory chips to fill 2 mb, 4 mb, or more.

Unfortunately, DOS limits what you can do with this memory - that pesky 640 kb will appear. But any PC can use it for caching or spooling. And some new software called DOS Extenders, special programs that push a 286, 386, or 486 processor into protected mode, can use as much as 16 mb of extended memory directly, almost as if it was conventional memory. Other operating systems such as OS/2 and Unix can also use extended memory. Extended memory can also be used as expanded memory through the magic of emulation. An emulator program can set up software registers and the other necessities of the expanded memory specification, and then tell your PC to treat extended meory as expanded. It won't be as fast as expanded memory that has real, hardware registers, but it will do the same jobs. One such emulator is the popular EMM386.EXE file that comes with DOS.

Figure 12.3 shows the organisation of various types of memory.

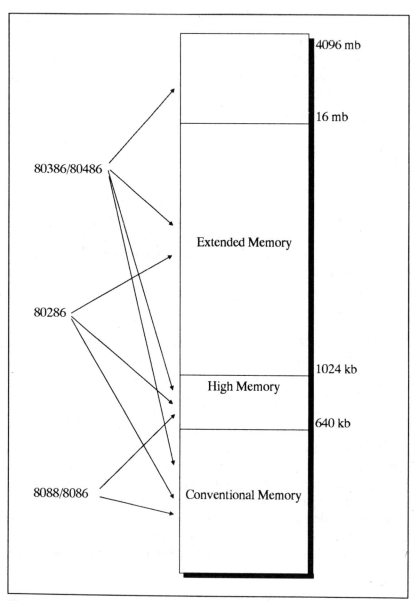

Figure 12.3

Summary

In this chapter we had a short guided tour inside the computer. We learnt the overall anatomy of the PC and its various vital components like micrprocessor, math co-processor, memory chips, support chips etc. It might appear at first glance why is this necessary in a C book. But it is my strong conviction that unless and until these bare minimum details are known to a C programmer he cannot interact with the hardware beyond a certain extent. Moreover, one comes to know what is happening inside the computer and how, as a result of which we are able to see the things in better light.

Exercise

[A]   Pick up the correct alternative for each of the following:

(a)   Which of the following are not housed on the mother board
      (1) Memory chips
      (2) Support chips
      (3) Disk Drive
      (4) Microprocessor

(b)   Which of the following doesn't belong to Intel 8086 family of microprocessor
      (1) 8086
      (2) 8088
      (3) 80286
      (4) 68000

(c)   Which of the following is a math co-processor
      (1) 8088
      (2) 8087
      (3) 8086
      (4) 80286

(d)   Which microprocessor is used in PC/AT
        (1) 8088
        (2) 8086
        (3) 80286
        (4) 8085

(e)   Which of the following task is not done by the microprocessor
        (1) Arithmetic operations
        (2) Logical comparision operations
        (3) Store data in CPU registers
        (4) Write information to disk

(f)   A computer which has 8086 as its CPU is called
        (1) 8/16-bit computer
        (2) 16/32-bit computer
        (3) 16-bit computer
        (4) 8-bit computer

(g)   Typically, a PC/AT has got
        (1) 2 Floppy disk drives
        (2) 2 Hard disk drives
        (3) 1 Floppy disk drive, 1 Hard disk dirve
        (4) None of the above

(h)   Programs stored in which of the following memories cannot
        be erased
        (1) RAM
        (2) ROM
        (3) Cache memory
        (4) Virtual memory

(i)   Which out of the following is the fastest microprocessor
        (1) 8086
        (2) 80286
        (3) 80386
        (4) 8088

(j)   Which of the following microprocessor cannot work in Real as well as in Protected mode
(1) 8088
(2) 80286
(3) 80386
(4) 80486

(k)   A 32-bit microprocessor can at a time handle
(1) 32 bits
(2) 32 bytes
(3) 32 kilobytes
(4) 32 megabytes

(l)   Pick the odd one out
(1) PC
(2) PC/XT
(3) Minicomputer
(4) PC/AT

(m)   If 9 bytes of data are required for processing in how many parts would an 8-bit data bus bring the data from memory
(1) 8 parts of 1 byte each
(2) 72 parts of 1 bit each
(3) 9 parts of 1 bit each
(4) 9 parts of 1 byte each

(n)   Which of the following is wrong about a 32-bit data bus
(1) It has 4 wires
(2) It has 32 wires
(3) 32 bits can flow at a time
(4) 4 bytes of data can flow at a time

(o)   A microprocessor which has a 8-bit data bus is a
(1) 8-bit microprocessor
(2) 16-bit microprocessor
(3) 32-bit microprocessor
(4) 8-byte microprocessor

414

(p) Which of a following is not a support chip
 (1) Microprocessor
 (2) Programmable peripheral interface chip
 (3) Keyboard controller chip
 (4) Interrupt controller chip

(q) Which of the following is not true about a math co-processor
 (1) It has numbers like 8087, 80287, 80387
 (2) It is present on each and every computer
 (3) It improves the speed of the computer
 (4) It does the arithmetic operations so that microprocessor can pay attention to other tasks

(r) A 8/16-bit microprocessor has got
 (1) a 8-bit data path and 16-bit internal processing capability
 (2) a 16-bit data path and 8-bit internal processing capability
 (3) a 8-byte data path and 16-byte internal processing capability
 (4) a 16-byte data path and 8-byte internal processing capability

[B] State True or false:

 (a) Disk drives are plugged into expansion slots.
 (b) Programs stored in RAM are permanent and cannot be modified.
 (c) To a 16-bit microprocessor a 32-bit data bus can be connected.
 (d) New data cannot be stored in RAM during program execution.
 (e) A data bus is a set of wires connecting the microprocessor and memory through which data flows.
 (f) Every PC needs to have a math co-processor.
 (g) If while executing a program the power goes off, all the instructions and data in the memory will be lost.
 (h) A PC/XT uses a 80186 microprocessor whereas a PC/AT uses a 80286 microprocessor.

13 Operating System Fundamentals

415

Operating System software (OS) is a class of programs which manage the resources of the computer, processes commands, and controls program execution. As the foundation of all computer operations, it is the most complex program executed on the computer, yet must also be the most reliable. In this chapter we first introduce the concept of OS software in general and then examine the details of the operating system of our interest - MS-DOS - with which we wish to interact through C programs.

Functions of OS

Any operating system, irrespective of whether it is being used on a microcomputer, minicomputer or mainframe computer plays three basic roles:

(a) As a 'manager', the operating system determines who will use the printer, disk, VDU, keyboard and other peripheral units and when they will use them. When an error is discovered, the operating system reports the error to the user. The operating system also manages the use of memory, controls timing of events, and controls the priorities of various requests.

(b) As a 'command processor', the operating system reads commands from the user, verifies their accuracy, loads what is needed from the disk and initiates the execution of the user command.

(c) As a 'controller', the operating system, at least to some extent, must always be in control of the system resources. If a program crashes from any type of error, control should return to the operating system, which then determines the type of error.

An operating system can be a Single-user OS, a Multiuser OS or a Multitasking OS.

A single user OS caters to a single user and all the resources are available to this user at all times. Microsoft's Disk Operating System (MS-DOS) is one such OS.

A multiuser OS is one that supports several users at a time. Most OS's for minicomputers and mainframe computers are multiuser OS. Unix and Xenix are the popular multiuser OSs.

A multitasking OS is the one that supports several tasks at a time, but only a single user. Windows and OS/2 are examples of multitasking OSs.

The following table shows the popularly used operating systems.

Type of Computer	Operating system used
Microcomputer	MS-DOS, Windows
Minicomputer	Unix
Mainframe	Unix, TOPS 20, CICS

Figure 13.1

We would now focus our attention on MS-DOS, one of the most popular operating system ever written.

Roots of MS-DOS

Way back in early eighties when a 8080 based 8-bit microcomputer was in use, it was being run on an OS called CP/M-80 or Control Program for Microcomputers. It was written by a man named Gary Kildall of Digital Research Corporation. CP/M-80 soon became the world's fastest selling OS.

When IBM decided to enter the Microcomputer market, they decided to base their computers on Intel's 8088 microprocessor. This is one of the several 8086 family of microprocessors. IBM had two main goals... it wanted an OS quickly and it wanted the OS to support the existing base of application programs.

IBM contacted Digital Research and Microsoft, neither of which had a 16-bit OS ready. However, Tim Patterson of Seattle Computer Products had written a 16-bit OS called 86-DOS. This OS to a large extent mimicked the CP/M-80 OS.

Microsoft purchased 86-DOS from Seattle Computer Products and promptly christened it as MS-DOS version 1.0. So when the IBM PC was released in the market in 1981, it was supported by MS-DOS 1.0. Soon a host of applications like Wordstar, dBASE III were developed by third party software houses based on MS-DOS 1.0.

With later releases of IBM PC's, IBM decided to make available to users three OS's, MS-DOS, CP/M-86 (a new and improved version of CP/M-80 with features similar to MS-DOS 1.0) and the UCSD-p OS. However, by that time MS-DOS had already won the race, and soon CP/M-86 and UCSD-p died their natural death. Therefore, we would base the rest of our discussion of OS on MS-DOS.

The Kingdom of DOS

The operating system used on 8086 family of microprocessors comes in two parts:

(a)   ROM software
(b)   DOS software

Out of these, the ROM (Read Only Memory) software is chip-based. That is, the programs which form the ROM software are hard-wired into the chips at the time of manufacturing, and hence cannot be modified or erased. As against this the DOS software is disk-based.

That is the programs belonging to DOS software are present on the disk in the form of files.

The ROM software consists of a number of functions (often called as routines). These can be divided into four types:

(a) ROM startup routines

These routines have a role to play when the computer is switched on.

(b) ROM-BIOS routines

BIOS stands for Basic I/O System. These routines have capabilities to interact with the hardware.

(c) ROM extension routines

These routines are an extension of ROM startup routines and they check and initialise non-standard equipment when computer is switched on.

(d) ROM BASIC routines

These routines form the core routines of Basic language.

Each of these would be discussed in sufficient detail after we see the components of DOS software.

The DOS software is divided into three parts which are stored in three different files on a disk (floppy or hard disk). The disk which contains all the three files is called a bootable disk. The three files are IO.SYS, MSDOS.SYS and COMMAND.COM.

On some of the systems instead of IO.SYS and MSDOS.SYS, files called IBMBIO.COM and IBMDOS.COM may be present. Out of these three files IO.SYS and MSDOS.SYS do not appear in the directory since their status is hidden. What are hidden files, how to unhide them, how to hide normal files will be discussed in the next chapter.

Let us now examine what are the contents of each of these files.

(a) IO.SYS

This file contains two important modules:

(1) Device drivers for devices like printer, VDU, keyboard, etc. There may be a few more new drivers to drive new equipment attached to the computer. All these drivers together are often called 'Disk BIOS'.

(2) SYSINIT module which loads the file MSDOS.SYS from the disk into memory.

(b) MSDOS.SYS

This file is also called DOS kernel. It is a link between the BIOS and our (application) programs, providing the logical interface for the application program, isolating the program from the physical aspects of the system, intricacies of the hardware and its internal working in detail. This kernel contains DOS service routines that are called by application programs using software interrupts. The DOS functions though similar to the ROM-BIOS routines, provide sophisticated and efficient control over the I/O operations than the ROM-BIOS routines do, especially with regard to disk file operations. The kernel has four major roles to play:

(1) Process control: wherein the kernel does the management of the program that is being executed. Process control includes loading the program requested by the user from the disk into memory, initiating the execution of the loaded

program and performing operating system recovery when program execution is terminated.

(2) Memory Management: refers to allocation of memory for application programs and managing it. This is necessary since different application programs have varying memory demands.

(3) Application Program Interface (API): It provides the programmer an interface to the hardware. This interface is hardware independent. It is just like an agent, an intelligent and a seasoned one, to whom any application programmer asks to interact with the hardware, for the simple reason that the programmer either has limited knowledge of interacting with the hardware or he prefers to rely on this interface (API) to get the particular work done without much of a headache... of course at the expense of speed. The programmer can write programs to directly interface with hardware, which would no doubt work faster than API, but for that he must have an indepth knowledge of working of hardware, otherwise he may land into trouble.

(4) File Management System: This portion of DOS kernel is the larger portion of MS-DOS and manages the reading and writing of the files.

(c)   COMMAND.COM: This file contains command processor, best known as shell. It is the user's interface to the Operating System.

This file contains special class of programs that are running under the control of MS-DOS. The command processor is responsible for carrying out user commands including loading and execution of application programs. The COMMAND.COM program makes use of other system resources that are contained in ROM-BIOS, IO.SYS and MSDOS.SYS.

COMMAND.COM consists of two distinct parts:

(1) Resident portion: As the name suggests once DOS has been loaded into memory, resident portion of COMMAND.COM resides in memory till we don't switch off the computer. It contains routines to process ctrl C's, critical errors and the job of termination of application programs. Resident portion also issues the error messages and is responsible for the familiar prompt: Abort, Retry, Ignore? It also contains code required to reload the transient portion of COMMAND.COM when necessary.

(2) Transient portion: It is the temporary portion of COMMAND.COM. It may or may not remain in memory at all times. If an application program falls short of memory, the transient portion of COMMAND.COM is erased and this memory is made available to application program.

The transient portion is responsible for issuing the DOS prompts, A, B or C, and for reading the commands from the keyboard or from batch files and then causing them to be executed. A batch file is a file which contains a batch or group of DOS commands.

We saw earlier that if the application program is big the transient portion gets erased and this space is utilised by application program. When application program terminates, the resident portion of the COMMAND.COM does a checksum of the transient portion to see if it has been destroyed by the application program that has just finished its execution. If it finds that transient portion has been erased then it fetches a fresh copy of it from the disk and places it in memory.

ROM Software

Software plays a vital role in the operation of computer. If some part of the software that is frequently needed, and is of utmost importance for any computer, it is permanently built into computer. It leads to computer operations becoming easier and efficient. And that is what the ROM programs are all about.

ROM stands for Read Only Memory; memory that is permanently recorded in the circuitry of the computer (ROM chips) that cannot be erased, changed or lost.

The advantage of these fundamental programs (software) is that they are always there, available to you and need not be loaded in to memory from the disks and hence help computer system operate efficiently.

Because they are permanent, the ROM programs are often the foundation upon which the other programs (including DOS) are built.

The ROM programs are stored in a ROM chip and they tell the system how to get started when the power is turned on and how to use various devices once the system starts running.

ROM software can be divided into four major categories. These are:

(a) ROM startup routines: these do the work of getting the computer started.

(b) ROM-BIOS routines: This is a collection of routines which provide support services for the continuing operation of computer.

(c) ROM BASIC routines: these provide the core of the Basic programming language.

(d)   ROM Extension routines: these are programs that are added to the main ROM when certain optional equipment is added to the computer.

Now let us take a closer look at each of these routines.

ROM Startup Routines

The first job of the ROM programs is to supervise the startup of the computer. This supervision process can be grouped into three stages:

(a)   POST (power on self test): The POST routines perform a quick reliability test of the computer and the ROM programs. This step is very important to make sure that the computer is ready. These routines check the integrity of the entire system and the status of I/O devices like keyboard, monitor etc.

(b)   Initialisation process: Following tasks are performed during this process:

-     A routine sets up a table of addresses called Interrupt Vector Table (IVT) in RAM at low end of memory. These addresses are addresses of Interrupt Service Routines stored inside the ROM-BIOS.
-     Another initialisation routine determines what equipment is attached to the computer and then places a record of it at a fixed location in memory.
-     The initialisation routines also check for new equipment. If they find any, they momentarily transfer control to the ROM extension routines, which initialise the new equipment and hand over the control back to ROM startup routines. The initialisation routines then continue executing the remaining startup routines.

(c)   After the execution of POST routines, initialisation routines and ROM extension routines, the final part of the startup procedure is left to the bootstrap loader program.

The bootstrap loader program is a short routine which attempts to read disk bootstrap program from the first sector of the disk. The purpose and working of disk bootstrap program is dealt in detail in Chapter 14. If the disk bootstrap program is successfully read into memory, the ROM Bootstrap startup procedure ends and the disk bootstrap program takes over the control.

The disk bootstrap program subsequently loads IO.SYS from the disk into memory. Then IO.SYS loads MSDOS.SYS into memory, and finally MSDOS.SYS loads COMMAND.COM into memory. Following this the DOS prompt (A, B, or C) is displayed.

ROM-BIOS Routines

ROM-BIOS stands for Read Only Memory's Basic Input/Output System. In the narrowest sense it means a bunch of device control programs.

ROM-BIOS is a collection of routines that are part of the hardware of your computer system and is supplied by the computer manufacturer as part of the hardware. Since these routines are permanently recorded and stored in ROM chips, they are often referred to as 'firmware' of the system.

The ROM-BIOS is that part of the ROM that is in active use whenever computer is at work. Its job is to provide the fundamental services that are needed for the operation of the computer. For the most part, the ROM-BIOS controls the computer's peripheral devices such as display screen, keyboard and disk drives. It consists of BIOS routines that translate a simple command, such as 'read something from the disk' into all steps necessary to actually execute the command.

BIOS works in two directions in a two sided process, linking the program execution in RAM with the hardware. Let us see how. One side of the BIOS receives request from programs (either application programs or even DOS) to perform standard ROM-BIOS I/O services. The request made to BIOS gives detailed information as to which device is to be used and for what purpose (how these requests are made, we will see in detail when we learn about interrupts). The other side of BIOS, then communicates with the computer's hardware devices like display screen, disk drives and so on, using detailed command codes fixed for a particular device. This process is shown in the figure given below:

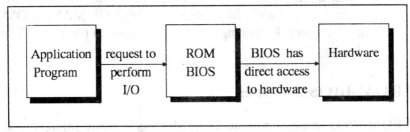

Figure 13.2

This side of ROM-BIOS also handles any hardware interrupt that a device generates to get attention. For example, whenever a key is pressed the keyboard generates an interrupt to let the ROM-BIOS know that a key has been hit. (Interrupts are the signals made to the microprocesser asking it to stop whatever it is doing at that moment and start executing the program whose location in the memory is specified when the signals are passed).

ROM BASIC Routines

ROM BASIC acts in two ways. Firstly, it provides the core of the BASIC langauge, which includes most of the commands and the underlying foundation (such as memory management) that BASIC uses. The disk based BASIC (interpreted basic) relies on ROM BASIC to get much of its work done. So, whenever it is in use it makes use of the ROM BASIC programs.

The second role of ROM BASIC comes into play when the booting fails. In such an event, the computer switches control to the ROM BASIC interpreter.

However, these days the computer manufacturers have dispensed with this ROM-BASIC chip (possibly to cut down the cost), therefore if booting fails we don't land into BASIC mode, but get a familiar message...

$\longrightarrow$

-- Non System disk --
Insert system disk and press any key

ROM Extension Routines

Since the original ROM-BIOS could not include support programs for future hardware, ROM Extensions are necessary. Non-standard equipment like hard disk, EGA monitor etc. if installed on your system are checked and initialised by ROM extension software. The PC was designed to allow installable extensions to the built in software in ROM. This additional ROM is usually stored on an adapter card that can be plugged into the empty expansion slots on the mother board.

What Happens at Boot-time

The process of switching on the computer is many a times referred to as 'booting' of the computer. The word comes from the phrase 'picking somebody up by his bootstraps'. And this is what you literally do when you put on the computer...wake it up and get it up and ready. While booting the computer needs to read some information from the disk. The disk which contains this information is known as a bootable disk.

The floppy disks and fixed disks (hard disks) come in variety of formats. Regardless of their formats, all the disks are potentially bootable; i.e. they can contain the information necessary to get an Operating System running at the time you start your computer. There is nothing special about a bootable disk; it is just the one that contains files that lets the ROM to load the Operating System. As you must have guessed these files are IO.SYS, MSDOS.SYS and COMMAND.COM.

Let us now see what exactly happens at boot time. The entire procedure is given below, stepwise:

(a)   The POST routines perform a reliability test on the other ROM programs to find whether they are in order or not.

(b)   The ROM startup routines set up addresses of ROM-BIOS routines in Interrupt Vector Table at low end of memory.

(c)   ROM startup routines check and initialise the standard equipment (like keyboard, vdu, floppy Disk drive and printer) and stores a list of this equipment at a fixed location in memory.

(d)   The ROM startup routines perform a memory check and stores the memory size value at a fixed location in memory. Typically this value is 256, 512 or 640.

(e)   The ROM startup routines check for non-standard equipment attached to the computer. If found, they momentarily transfer control to ROM extension routines. The ROM extension routines initialise the non standard equipment (like Hard disk) and hand over the control back to ROM startup routines.

(f)   One of the ROM startup routines called Bootstrap Loading Program loads the Disk Bootstrap Program from the Boot Sector of the disk into memory. Boot sector is sector number 1 on side 0 track 0 of the disk.

(g)   The disk bootstrap program loads the file IO.SYS from the disk into memory. IO.SYS contains two modules, Disk BIOS and SYSINIT.

(h)   The SYSINIT module loads the file MSDOS.SYS from disk into memory.

(i)   MSDOS.SYS loads the file COMMAND.COM into memory. COMMAND.COM contains two modules, Resident portion and Transient portion.

(j)   The transient portion of COMMAND.COM executes the file AUTOEXEC.BAT, if it is present on the disk.

(k)   The transient portion of COMMAND.COM finally displays the DOS prompt.

What is Where

ROM software is permanently recorded in memory, whereas DOS software get loaded into memory during boot-time. But where in memory? Well, Figure 13.3 shows it all. For convenience the contents in brief of each item in the figure are mentioned below:

(a) IVT   -   contains addresses of ROM-BIOS routines

(b) BIOS data area   -   contains the memory size, a list of standard equipment attached to your computer and some more useful information

(c) IO.SYS   -   Disk BIOS and SYSINIT

(d) MSDOS.SYS   -   contains routines for process control, memory management, Application Program Interface and file & disk management system

(e) COMMAND.COM   – contains two distinct parts, Resident portion and Transient portion

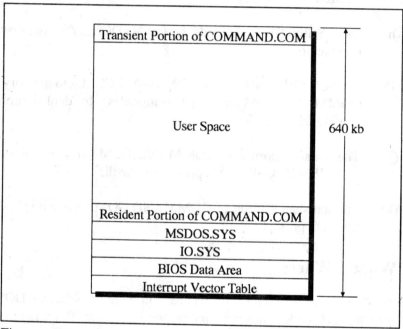

Figure 13.3

In the boot-time operations that we have mentioned in the earlier section we have purposefully omitted a few vital steps. For understanding these steps one needs to know the disk basics, which is the topic of our next chapter. A more comprehensive discussion of boot-time operations would be taken up in the next chapter.

Summary

In this chapter you learnt the purpose of any operating system in general. You also learnt how MS-DOS came into existence, what are the various components of ROM and DOS software and what is the purpose of each. You also learnt how these components get loaded into memory when the computer is switched on.

Exercise

[A]   Pick up the correct alternative for each of the following:

(a)   Which of the following is NOT true about an Operating System
   (1) It acts as a manager
   (2) It acts as a command processor
   (3) It acts as a controller
   (4) It acts as a compiler

(b)   Which of the following is NOT true about an Operating System
   (1) Single user
   (2) Batch processing
   (3) Multi user
   (4) Multi tasking

(c)   MS-DOS is a
   (1) Single user operating system
   (2) Multi user operating system
   (3) Multi tasking operating system
   (4) None of the above

(d)   OS/2 is a
   (1) Single user operating system
   (2) Multi user operating system
   (3) Multi tasking operating system
   (4) None of the above

(e)   Who was the originator of MS-DOS
   (1) Tim Patterson
   (2) Gary Kildall
   (3) Dennis Ritchie
   (4) Ken Thompson

(f)   Which of the following operating systems are supported on
       IBM Compatible microcomputers
       (1) Unix
       (2) Xenix
       (3) MS-DOS
       (4) All the above

(g)   At a time how many operating system can be at work on a
       computer
       (1) Only one
       (2) Two
       (3) Three
       (4) Four

(h)   Pick the odd one out
       (1) IO.SYS
       (2) MSDOS.SYS
       (3) ROM-BIOS
       (4) COMMAND.COM

(i)   Which of the following are components of IO.SYS
       (1) API and Disk BIOS
       (2) Disk BIOS and SYSINIT
       (3) SYSINIT and API
       (4) SYSINIT and Kernel

(j)   Which of the following belongs to COMMAND.COM
       (1) Shell Portion
       (2) Kernel Portion
       (3) Batch file Portion
       (4) Resident Portion

(k)   Which of the following is responsible for displaying the DOS
       prompt
       (1) Resident portion of COMMAND.COM
       (2) Transient portion of COMMAND.COM
       (3) SYSINIT module of IO.SYS

(4) AUTOEXEC.BAT

(l) Which of the following remains in memory temporarily
(1) Resident portion of COMMAND.COM
(2) Transient portion of COMMAND.COM
(3) API
(4) Disk BIOS

(m) Which of the following is responsible for loading of transient portion of COMMAND.COM
(1) Resident portion of COMMAND.COM
(2) MSDOS.SYS
(3) SYSINIT module of IO.SYS
(4) Bootstrap loader

(n) Non-standard equipment attached to the computer is checked and initialised by
(1) ROM startup software
(2) ROM extension software
(3) ROM BIOS software
(4) ROM Basic software

(o) Which of the following allows us to interact with the hardware
(1) ROM startup software
(2) ROM extension software
(3) ROM BIOS software
(4) ROM Basic software

(p) Bootstrap loader program is a program belonging to:
(1) ROM startup software
(2) ROM extension software
(3) ROM BIOS software
(4) ROM Basic software

[B] State True or False:

(a) Transient portion of COMMAND.COM is loaded on the top of resident portion of COMMAND.COM.

(b) Bootstrap loader program and disk bootstrap program are one and the same.

(c) Interrupt Vector Table contains addresses of ROM-BIOS routines.

(d) The file AUTOEXEC.BAT is executed by transient portion of COMMAND.COM.

(e) Commands like DIR, COPY, DEL are interpreted by the program stored in the file IO.SYS.

(f) These days the microcomputers do not contain ROM Basic software.

(g) Integrity check of the ROM routines is done every time we switch on the computer.

(h) ROM-BIOS software cannot be modified by a user.

(i) ROM software is chip-based whereas DOS software is disk-based.

[C] The memory size of your computer is stored at location numbers 0x413 and 0x414. Write a program to pickup this memory size and display it on the screen. What can you conclude if this value doesn't turn out to be a standard value?

14   *Disk Basics*

B y far the most widely used storage medium in the 8086 family of computers are the floppy disks and the fixed disks (hard disks). Floppy disks and Hard disks come in various sizes and capacities but they all work basically in the same way: Information is magnetically encoded on their surface in patterns. These patterns are determined by the disk drive and the software that controls the drive.

Although the type of storage device is important, it is the way the stored information is laid out and managed that concerns C programmers most. In this chapter we would therefore focus our attention on how information is organised and stored on floppy disks and hard disks.

Physical Structure of the Disk

To understand how data is organised on the disk, let us first consider the physical structure of the disk and the drive mechanism that reads from and writes to it. We will start with floppy diskes, but both floppy disks and fixed disks have the same basic geometry.

Inside the square plastic jacket of a floppy disk is a circular platter made of tough plastic material. This plastic disk is coated with magnetic material. A disk drive stores data on the disk by writing and reading magnetically encoded patterns that represent digital data. Since both sides of the disk are coated, both the sides can be used to store data.

A floppy disk drive contains a motor that rotates the disk at a constant speed. The drive has two read/write heads, one on each side of the disk. The heads are mounted on an arm that moves them in unison to any position towards or away from the centre of the disk.

The geometry of a fixed disk is similar to that of a floppy disk. Fixed disks rotate at a much higher speed, so the platters are made of magnetically coated metal, and not flexible plastic. Also, fixed disks consist a stack of several platters that rotate together, so fixed disk drives have multple read/write heads - one for each disk surface.

Information is always stored on the disk surface in a series of concentric circles, called 'tracks'. Each track is further divided into segments called 'sectors'. This process of dividing the disk into tracks and sectors is called 'formatting of disk'. Any new disk has to be first formatted before writing any information to it.

Had this scheme of tracks and sectors not been used, it would have lead to delays in:

(a)   searching the information to be read from the disk.
(b)   searching the empty space for writing new information to the disk.

This division of a disk into tracks and sectors speeds up the operations of reading data from the disk as well as writing data to it.

As we had seen earlier, the process of reading information or writing information is done by a read/write head inside the disk drive. To read/write information from/to disk, the disk has to rotate and the appropriate sector on the appropriate track has to come below the read/write head.

Locating a particular track on the disk surface is a relatively uncomplicated matter. The disk drive merely moves the read/write head to the position where the specified track is located, much like the way in which the needle of a record player is positioned on a location of a specific song on the record. The only difference being, the needle moves in an angle, whereas the read/write head moves linearly.

For locating a sector, a small hole on the floppy disk called 'sector hole' is made use of. This sector hole marks the location of the first sector, and all other sectors are referred to with reference to this hole.

The amount of information that can be stored on each side of disk depends on the number of tracks, number of sectors and size of each sector. How many tracks, how many sectors and what sector size depends upon the way in which the disk is formatted, which is under software control. This is the reason why a same disk can be formatted in a number of ways. Let us see in what different ways can a disk be formatted.

Floppy Disk Formats

We have seen earlier that the division of floppy into tracks and sectors is known as formatting a diskette. Unless and until a new disk is formatted, no information can be stored on it.

MS-DOS recognises a variety of formats. These were introduced along with each new version of DOS. Fortunately, all the formats are upwardly compatible. So even though a single sided disk is obsolete today, if one so desires he can comfortably use it even today. There is a guarantee that DOS would support it. Figure 14.1 shows the various formats supported by DOS, their specifications and the version of DOS with which they came into existence.

DOS version	Format ID	sides	tracks/ side	sectors/ track	Capacity	Media Desc.
1.0	S8	1	40	8	160 kb	FE
1.1	D8	2	40	8	320 kb	FF
2.0	S9	1	40	9	180 kb	FC
2.0	D9	2	40	9	360 kb	FD
3.0	QD15	2	80	15	1.2 mb	F9
3.3	QD18	2	80	18	1.44mb	F0

Figure 14.1

In Figure 14.1 the format ID is the usual way in which we refer a particular format, whereas media descriptor is the way DOS identifies a particular format.

Fixed Disk Formats

As on floppy disk, the data on fixed disks in organised in cylinders, sides and sectors. Think of a cylinder as a stack of tracks at a given position of read/write head. It may be recalled here that a fixed disk contains a number of platters. Figure 14.2 shows the popular fixed disk formats.

Fixed disk type	sides	tracks / side	sectors / track	bytes / sector	Capacity
Typical PC/XT Fixed disk	4	614	17	512	20 mb
Typical PC/AT Fixed disk	8	614	17	512	40 mb

Figure 14.2

Logical Structure of Floppy Disk

Regardless of the capacity of the disk we use, all disks are logically formatted in the same way; the disk's sides, tracks and sectors are identified numerically with the same notation, and certain sectors are always reserved for special programs that DOS uses to manage disk operations.

Every floppy disk is divided into four separate areas. These are:

(a)   Boot sector
(b)   File Allocation Table

(c)   Directory
(d)   Data space

The size of each area on the disk varies form format to format but the structure and the order of these areas on the diskettes remains same. Let us now dvelve more deeply in these four areas.

The Boot Sector

The Boot sector on the floppy disk contains two things, namely, Boot parameters and the disk bootstrap program. The purpose of the disk bootstrap program is to load DOS files from the disk into memory. Whether the disk bootstrap program would be used or not depends on whether the disk is being used for booting the computer or not.

The boot parameters are used by DOS at the time a read or write operation is performed on the disk. This is because the boot parameters contain vital information about how the disk has been formatted. From format to format the values of the boot parameters may change, but their order remains same. The list of boot parameters is given in Figure 14.3. Apart from the first 11 bytes in the list of boot parameters, the rest form what is known as BIOS parameter block (BPB).

The Root Directory

The root directory of a D9 disk occupies 7 sectors. However, depending on the format type used, the number of sectors reserved for storing directory entries may vary.

The root directory contains a series of 32-byte entries. Each of these 32-byte entries are either a filename, a sub-directory name or the volume label of the disk. If it's a file entry then it contains information about file's size, it's starting location on the disk, it's size, and it's date and time of creation. This information is present in the order shown in Figure 14.4.

Description	Length	Typical D9 disk values
Jump instruction	3 bytes	EB 34 90
System ID	8 bytes	IBM 3.0
No. of bytes per sector	2 bytes	512
No. of sectors per cluster	1 byte	2
No. of sectors in reserved area	2 bytes	1
No. of copies of FAT	1 byte	2
Max. no. of root directory entries	2 bytes	112
Total no. of sectors	2 bytes	720
Media descriptor	1 byte	FD
No. of sectors per FAT	2 bytes	2
No. of sectors per track	2 bytes	9
No. of sides	2 bytes	2
No. of hidden sectors	2 bytes	0

Figure 14.3

Description	Size	Format
Filename	8 bytes	ASCII characters
Extension	3 bytes	ASCII characters
Attribute	1 byte	bit coded
Reserverd for future use	10 bytes	unused, zeroes
Time	2 bytes	encoded
Date	2 bytes	encoded
Starting cluster number	2 bytes	integer
Size	4 bytes	long integer

Figure 14.4

Note the following points.

(a) Filename can be less than or equal to 8 characters. If it is less than 8 characters long then it is padded with blanks on the right. Usually blanks within a filename are not allowed.

(b) Extension or the family name can be maximum 3 characters long. If it less than 3 characters it is padded with blanks. While a filename must have atleast one character, the extension can be all blanks.

(c) When the directory contains a volume label entry, the filename and extension fields are treated as one combined field of 11 bytes. In this case embedded blanks are permitted.

(d) In the attribute byte each bit represents either the type of the file or whether the entry is a volume label entry or a sub directory name entry. The meaning of each bit is given in Figure 14.5.

Bit numbers								Meaning
7	6	5	4	3	2	1	0	
.	.	.	.	.	.	.	1	Read only
.	.	.	.	.	.	1	.	Hidden
.	.	.	.	.	1	.	.	System
.	.	.	.	1	.	.	.	Volume label entry
.	.	.	1	.	.	.	.	Sub-directory entry
.	.	1	.	.	.	.	.	Archive bit
.	1	.	.	.	.	.	.	Unused
1	.	.	.	.	.	.	.	Unused

Figure 14.5

If bit 0 is set to 1 then the file can only be read, it cannot be modified or deleted.

If bit 1 is 1 then the file is hidden and will not be shown in the directory. Vice versa, if bit 1 is 0, then the file will be shown in the directory as a normal file.

If bit 2 is 1, it means the file is an operating system file. For example, the files MSDOS.SYS, IO.SYS and COM-MAND.COM are operating system files.

Bit 3 marks the directory entry as a volume label entry. The label itself is stored in the filename and extension fields, the size and the starting cluster fields are not used, but the date and time fields are.

Bit 4 identifies the directory entry as the sub-directory name.

Bit 5 is called an archive bit. It is advisable to make backup copies of important files from the hard disk regularly. But the number of files that are present on the hard disk are usually quite large. Moreover, you won't like to backup of those files which haven't changed since they were last backed up. But how do we know which file has changed and which hasn't, since the last backup. This is where archive bit has a role to play.

DOS sets the archive bit to 1 whenever a file is created or modified. On backing up this file using the BACKUP command of DOS, this bit is set to 0. So next time you try to backup files from the hard disk, BACKUP command backs up only those files for whom this bit is 1. This is beacuse if the files have not changed since the last backup operation then this bit would certainly be still 0.

(e)   Following the attribute byte, there are 10 unused bytes set aside for possible future use. All ten bytes are usually set to 0.

(f)   The time at which the file was created or last modified is stored
        as a 2 byte entry. Similarly, the date on which the file was
        created or last modified is also stored as a 2 byte entry. Note
        that both these entries are in encoded form. This encoding is
        done to reduce the number of bytes occupied by date and time.
        Had the date like 10/10/90 been stored as string it would have
        occupied atleast 8 bytes. Therefore, a formula is applied on this
        date to reduce it to a two byte number. Similarly, the time entry
        is also reduced to a two byte number. The scheme used for
        encoding is discussed in Chapter 18.

(g)   The starting cluster number indicates the place where the file
        begins in the data space of the disk . For volume label entry the
        starting cluster number is 0.

(h)   The file size entry contains the exact file size in bytes.

(i)   Total no. of bytes available on root directory sectors is given
        by, number of sectors * bytes per sectors. For a typical 360 kb
        diskette, this turns out to be equal to 7 * 512.

        As we have seen, each directory entry of a file occupies 32
        bytes. Thus, the maximum number of files that can be stored
        in the root directory of a 360 kb diskette = (7 * 512) / 32 =
        112.

        Thus, the maximum number of files that can be stored on a
        particular type of disk depends on the number of sectors
        allocated for the root directory, which varies from disk to disk.
        For example, in 1.2 mb disk there are 14 sectors allocated for
        root directory and with 512 bytes per sector, this type of
        diskette can easily store a maximum of 224 files in its root
        directory.

The Data Space

All files and sub-directories are stored in this area. It occupies the last and largest part of each disk. DOS allocates space to files one cluster at a time. Remember that a cluster is nothing but a group of sectors that DOS allocates to a file at a time. How many sectors form a cluster depends upon how the disk has been formatted.

As a file is being created, or an existing file is extended, the file's allocated space grows. When more space is needed, DOS allocates another cluster to the file.

Under ideal conditions, a file is stored in one contiguous block of space. However, a file might be broken into several non-contiguous blocks, especially if information is added to an existing file or a new file is stored in the space left by an erased file. So don't be surprised if one file is scattered throughout the disk. This file fragmentation slows down the access to the file's contents to some degree.

The File Allocation Table

The FAT maps the usage of data space of the disk. It contains information about the space used by each individual file, the unused disk space and the space that is unusable due to defects in the disk. Since FAT contains vital information, two copies of FAT are stored on the disk, just in case one gets destroyed, the other can be used. A FAT entry can contain any of the following:

- Unused cluster
- Reserved cluster
- Bad cluster
- Last cluster in the file
- Next cluster number in the file

There is one entry in the FAT for each cluster in the files area. If the value in a FAT entry doesn't mark an unused, reserved or defective cluster, then the cluster corresponding to the FAT entry is part of a file, and the value in the FAT entry would indicate the next cluster in the file.

This means that the space that belongs to a given file is mapped by a chain of FAT entries, each of which points to the next entry in the chain. The first cluster number in the chain is the starting cluster number in the file's directory entry. When a file is created or extended, DOS allocates clusters to the file by searching the FAT for unused clusters and adding them to the chain. Vice versa, when a file is deleted, DOS frees the clusters that had been allocated to the file by clearing the corresponding FAT entries (by setting them to 0). The FAT chain for a file ends with an entry 0xFFFF in the FAT.

The first two entries (0 and 1) in the FAT are reserved for use by DOS. Therefore, cluster number 2 corresponds to the first cluster in the data space of the disk.

Figure 14.6 shows a FAT chain for a file called ICIT.PRG

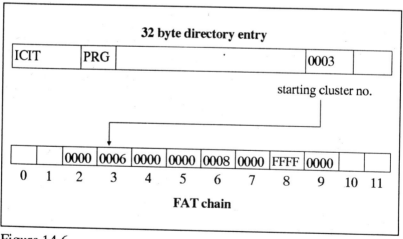

Figure 14.6

How Fixed Disks Differ

Physically, there are more than one platters in a fixed disk. Still, data is organised on fixed disks by track (cylinder), head, and sector number, just as it is on floppy disks.

Since hard disks are typically of high capacity the number of files stored on it are very high. If all these files are stored in the root directory then to manage these files would become quite tedious. Therefore, the files on a hard disk are usually split into various sub-directories. For example, in the root directory there could be a sub-directory containing all dbase programs, another sub-directory containing all C programs, still another containing all wordprocessing files, and so on. Within a sub-directory there can be still more sub-directories. Each sub-directory is linked to its parent directory, which can be a root directory or another sub-directory, thus forming a tree like structure, as shown in Figure 14.7.

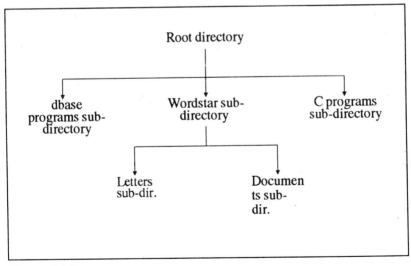

Figure 14.7

A sub-directory is stored in the disk's data space, just like any other file. The entries in the sub-directory are identical to those in the root directory, except that a sub-directory is not limited in size. Like an ordinary file, a sub-directory can grow without bounds as long as there is disk space available. Sub-directories can be created with any type of disk. However, since sub-directories take up precious data space, they are primarily intended for use with high-capacity hard disks; their use with floppy disks are usually avoided.

Since the storage capacity of a fixed disk is relatively large, some users prefer to use only part of the disk space for DOS and to use other portions of the disk for other operating systems. This is called partitioning of fixed disk. As many as four partitions are allowed by DOS. Each partition's data can be kept completely separate from the data in the other partitions. Each partition can contain its own boot sector and operating system.

The fixed disks also have a boot sector, FAT, Directory and Data space. However unlike floppy diskettes, side 0, track 0, sector 1 of the fixed disk contains a partition table and a master boot program. The partition table is 64 bytes long. It contains information about where each partition is located on the disk. The partition table also indicates which is the bootable partition. The first sector in the bootable partition is the boot sector which contains the boot parameters and the disk bootstrap program, which is used to load the operating system into memory.

Detailed Boot-time Operations

Now that we are armed with the knowledge of organisation of floppy disk and the hard disk, it is time we explored the boot time operations in more detail. The entire procedure can be divided into following distinct steps:

(a) The POST routines perform a reliability test of the other ROM programs to find whether they are in order or not.

(b)   A ROM startup routine sets up the Interrupt Vector Table, with the addresses of ROM BIOS routines.

(c)   A ROM startup routine performs RAM test and stores the base memory size value at locations 0x413 and 0x414.

(d)   ROM startup routines check and initialise the standard equipment (like Keyboard, VDU, Floppy Disk Drive and Printer) and stores a list of this equipment in memory at location 0x410.

(e)   The ROM startup routines check for non-standard equipment attached to the computer. If found, they momentarily transfer control to ROM extension routines. The ROM extension routines initialise the non standard equipment (like Hard disk) and hands over the control back to ROM startup routines.

(f)   A ROM startup routine reads from CMOS RAM (in case of AT and above) the system boot up sequence. Usually this sequence is A:,C: indicating that the system would first attempt to boot from A drive and if it fails to do so then it would attempt to boot from C drive. This sequence can however be changed.

In case of an XT the booting sequence is always A:,C: and this sequence cannot be changed.

(g)   A ROM startup routine called Bootstrap Loader loads the contents of side 0, track 0, sector 1 of the first drive in the system boot up sequence. Now there are two possibilities:

(1) The first drive in the system boot up sequence is drive A.
(2) The first drive in the system boot up sequence is drive C.

Let us now study the booting from these drives separately.

Booting from A Floppy Disk

(1)   The Bootstrap Loader Program is a short and primitive pro-
       gram, smart enough to move the head of the disk drive to track
       0, and read the contents of the first physical sector of the disk
       into memory, at a predetermined location and pass control to
       it.

       Side 0, track 0, sector 1 of floppy disk contains Boot
       Parameters and a Disk Bootstrap Program. Hence the
       Bootstrap Loader loads these into memory hands over the
       control to them.

       In the boot parameters the first three bytes contain a jump
       instruction. This instruction causes the control to jump to the
       Disk Bootstrap Program, bypassing the Boot Parameters which
       are placed after the jump instruction.

       The Disk Bootstrap Program's task is to load the file IO.SYS
       into memory. But it is handicapped because it doesn't know
       the exact location of IO.SYS on the disk which depends upon:

       -    Number of copies of FAT on the disk
       -    Number of sectors occupied by each copy of FAT
       -    Number of sectors occupied by the directory

       As we had seen earlier these parameters vary from one type of
       disk to another. This is where the Boot Parameters come to the
       rescue of Disk Bootstrap Program. Using the data in Boot
       Parameters it calculates the exact location of IO.SYS. Once
       this location has been found out, the actual loading of Operat-
       ing System into the memory starts.

(2)   The Disk Bootstrap Program first examines whether the file
       IO.SYS is present on the disk or not. If present it loads the file
       into memory and passes control to it. If absent, it flashes the
       familiar message:

Non system disk.Insert system disk and press any key

On inserting the system disk and hitting a key it loads IO.SYS from this disk. As soon as IO.SYS is loaded the Disk Bootstrap Program is wiped out from memory.

(3)   IO.SYS consists of two modules: Disk BIOS and SYSINIT. The SYSINIT module loads the file MSDOS.SYS from disk into memory and passes control to it.

(4)   MSDOS.SYS builds some internal data structures and work areas and then returns the control to SYSINIT.

SYSINIT loads a file CONFIG.SYS file from root directory of the floppy. This optional file can contain a variety of commands that enable the user to customize the working environment. For instance the user may specify the number of disk buffers, the maximum number of files that can be opened, etc. If it is found, the entire CONFIG.SYS file is loaded into memory and each command in it is executed one line at a time.

(5)   SYSINIT then loads Resident Portion of the file COMMAND.COM into memory. Once Resident Portion is loaded the SYSINIT module is discarded from memory and control is handed over to Resident Portion.

(6)   The Resident Portion of COMMAND.COM loads the Transient Portion of COMMAND.COM into high end of memory. High end here means the top of base memory. The high end would vary from computer to computer since different computers are likely to have different base memory sizes. The Resident portion figures out the high end from the base memory size stored at locations 0x413, 0x414 during RAM test.

The Transient portion of COMMAND.COM executes the file AUTOEXEC.BAT, if it is present in the root directory.

(7)   The Transient portion of COMMAND.COM finally displays the DOS prompt.

Booting from A Hard Disk

While booting from a hard disk steps (a) through (g) given above remain same. Rest of the steps are as follows:

(1)   Since capacity of hard disks is huge logical partitions are created on it to accommodate different operating systems. The information about where each partition begins and ends, the size of each partition, etc. is stored in a partition table in side 0, track 0, sector 1. This sector also contains a Master Boot Program. The partition table is 64 bytes long. The partition table also indicates which is the bootable partition. The ROM Bootstrap Loading program loads the partition table and the Master boot program into memory and passes control to it.

(g)   The Master boot program finds out which is the bootable partition, loads the boot sector (containing Boot Parameters and Disk bootstrap program) from the bootable partition and passes control to it.

(h)   Once the Disk Bootstrap Program receives the control the rest of the booting procedure is same as in case of booting from a floppy disk.

Figure 14.8 shows the booting procedure from a floppy disk and a hard disk for easy comparison.

One Last Thing about Disks

Just to make our life that much more difficult, the way ROM-BIOS refers individual sector on a disk is different than the way DOS refers

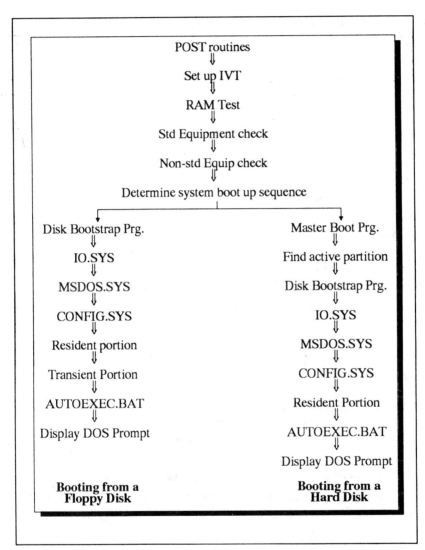

Figure 14.8

it. The ROM-BIOS functions refer sectors by their three dimensional-
locations (side number, track number and sector number), whereas,
DOS refers them by their sequential logical sector numbers.

While using BIOS services remember that,

-   Tracks are numbered from outermost track, increasing towards the innermost track, starting with 0.

-   Sides are also numbered from 0 onwards.

-   Sectors are numbered from 1 onwards.

Thus any location on the disk can be referred to by a unique combination of side, track and sector number.

DOS however doesn't recognise sides, tracks and sectors. Instead, DOS sees a disk as a linear sequence of logical sectors. The sequence of logical sectors begins with the first sector on the disk: side 0, track 0, sector 1 (boot sector) is DOS logical sector 0 . Similarly, side 0, track 0, sector 2 is DOS logical sector 1 and so on. Note that, the last sector in side 0, track 0 is followed by first sector in side 1, track 0 and so on.

Conversion of a sector number from BIOS to DOS or vice versa can be done using following formulae.

```
DOS sector number = ( BIOS sector no - 1 )
                  + ( BIOS side * sectors / track )
                  + ( BIOS track * sectors per track * sides per disk )

BIOS sector = ( 1 + DOS sector number ) % ( sectors per track )
BIOS track = ( DOS sector no. / ( sectors per track * sides per disk )
BIOS side = ( DOS sector no. / sectors per track ) % ( sides per disk )
```

Summary

In this chapter we learnt the physical and logical formats in which floppy disks and hard disks are organised. We also explored the contents of boot sector, the directory and the file allocation table. We examined the purpose of maintaining sub-directories and partitions on hard disks. We fininshed the chapter with detailed boot time operations while booting from a floppy disk and from a hard disk.

Exercise

[A]   Pick up the correct alternative for each of the following:

(a)   DOS identifies the way a disk has been formatted by
    (1) Format ID
    (2) Media descriptor
    (3) Number of tracks on the disk
    (4) Number of sectors on the disk

(b)   The boot sector of a disk contains
    (1) Disk bootstrap program
    (2) Bootstrap loader program
    (3) Directory entries
    (4) Information about when the disk was formatted

(c)   Length of each directory entry is
    (1) 34 bytes
    (2) 32 bytes
    (3) 36 bytes
    (4) 8 bytes

(d)   A cluster represents
    (1) A group of tracks
    (2) A group of sectors
    (3) Total number of tracks present on the disk
    (4) Total number of sectors present on the disk

(e)   The date field in the directory entry is
    (1) 2 bytes long
    (2) 8 bytes long
    (3) 6 bytes long
    (4) None of the above

(f)   Maximum length of a volume lable entry is
        (1) 8 bytes
        (2) 3 bytes
        (3) 11 bytes
        (4) None of the above

(g)   The status of the files IO.SYS and MSDOS.SYS is usually
        (1) Read/Write
        (2) System and Hidden
        (3) Read only
        (4) System, Read only and Hidden

(h)   Where a particular file begins in the data space is indicated by
        (1) Starting cluster number
        (2) FAT entry of the file
        (3) Boot parameters of the file
        (4) None of the above

(i)   The entry of starting cluster of a file is present in
        (1) Boot parameters
        (2) Directory
        (3) File allocation table
        (4) Data space

(j)   On hard disk side 0, track 0, sector 1 contains
        (1) Disk bootstrap
        (2) Directory
        (3) File allocation table
        (4) Partition table and master boot program

(k)   The size of a partition table on hard disk is
        (1) 64 bytes
        (2) 32 bytes
        (3) 16 bytes
        (4) 64 bits

(l)   Partition table contains information about

(1) Where the different partitions of the disk begin
(2) Where the different partitions of the disk end
(3) Which is the bootable partition
(4) All the above

(m) While booting from the hard disk the disk bootstrap program is loaded into memory by
(1) Master boot program
(2) Bootstrap loader program
(3) COMMAND.COM
(4) IO.SYS

(n) If a virus is to infect your disk, which is the possible place where it would lodge itself
(1) Boot sector
(2) File allocation table
(3) Directory
(4) Data space

[B] State whether the following statements are True or False:

(a) All diskettes can be made bootable.
(b) A bootable diskette is one which contains operating system files.
(c) The place where IO.SYS and MSDOS.SYS files can be present on the disk is fixed.
(d) BIOS refers to a sector by its logical number whereas DOS refers to it by side number, track number and sector number.
(e) All disk formats are upwardly compatible.
(f) Innermost track on the floppy disk is track number 0.
(g) Like a hard disk, a floppy disk can also be partitioned.
(h) On a hard disk more than one operating system can be present.
(i) A hard disk must always be partitioned.
(j) Number of sectors occupied by directory and file allocation table changes from format to format.

[C]   Write a program to read the boot parameters from the boot sector of a floppy disk and display them on the screen.

Hint: Use the standard library function **_bios_disk**( ) if you are using Quick C and the function **absread**( ) if you are using Turbo C.

15 VDU Basics

For most computer users, the two most important components of the computer system are the video display unit (VDU) and the keyboard. Many of them believe that VDU and the keyboard is the computer. And with VDU and keyboard being the human interface to the computer, they aren't too much wrong. It has been observed that the decision of customers who purchase software, is more often than not strongly influenced by how the screens have been designed in the software. Jazzier the screen, more appeal it carries for the users. Your monitor provides the link between you and your computer. Although you can get rid of your printer, disk drives, etc. you cannot sacrifice the monitor. Without it, you would be operating blind!

Components of VDU

The video system consists of two basic components:

(a) A video screen on which we actually see the images either in text or in graphics.

(b) A video display adapter which is a special printed circuit board that plugs into one of the several expansion slots present on the mother board of the computer (refer Figure 15.1). A video display adapter is sometimes simply referred as a video card.

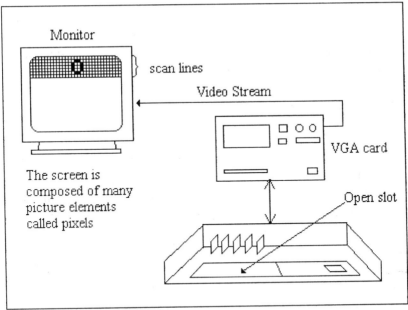

Figure 15.1

How are the images, either text or graphics, produced on the screen? The microprocessor does not have the ability to send signals necessary to produce the images on the screen. This task is performed by the display adapter. The display adapter acts as an agent between the microprocessor and the video screen. The display adapter consists of:

(a) Special memory called VDU memory.
(b) Circuitry which transfers the contents of the VDU memory on to the screen.

The microprocessor writes the information to be displayed on the screen into the VDU memory, whereas the display adapter circuitry transfers this information from VDU memory on to the screen. Therefore, we can describe the image displayed on the screen as a 'memory mapped display'. Each address in VDU memory corresponds to a specific location on the screen. The display adapter circuitry repeatedly (50 to 70 times a second) reads information from VDU memory and places it on the screen, making the images displayed on the screen clear and steady. This process is called 'refreshing the screen', and the rate at which the display adapter refreshes the screen is called 'refresh rate'. Low refresh rates cause the screen to flicker contributing to eye strain. The higher the refresh rate better it is for your eyes.

Let us now see what exactly happens when we try to display a message on the screen using **printf( )**. Firstly, the **printf( )** function calls a DOS or ROM-BIOS routine. This routine places the message to be displayed in the VDU memory. The display adapter circuitry transfers this message to the screen repeatedly, so that the image persists on the screen.

Figure 15.2 shows the exact location of VDU memory in 1 MB memory map. Note that the first megabyte of memory is divided into 16 blocks of 64 KB each. These blocks are numbered from 0 to 15. Out of these, blocks A and B are reserved for unconventional and conventional VDU memory respectively. Which out of these two blocks would be used depends on the type of display adapter used on your computer. In fact, types of display adapters is the topic of our next section.

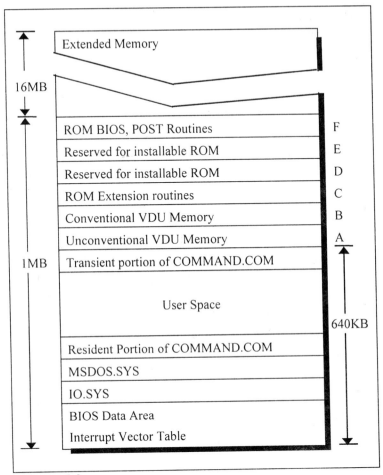

Figure 15.2

Display Adapters

A number of display adapters are available with varying capabilities. The 8086 family of microprocessors usually support the following display adapters:

(a) Monochrome Adapter (MA)

(b) Hercules Adapter
(c) Color Graphics Adapter (CGA)
(d) Enhanced Graphics Adapter (EGA)
(e) Multicolor Graphics Adapter (MCGA)
(f) Video Graphics Array (VGA)
(g) Super Video Graphics Array (SVGA)
(h) Extended Graphics Adapter (XGA)

Although clear differences exist between these different adapters, their strong family resemblance should encourage one to consider what they have in common before worrying about their differences.

Most of these adapters can be programmed in two fundamentally different modes, text mode and graphics mode. The lone exception is MA, which operates only in text mode. CGA and MA are usually called conventional display adapters and use B block of VDU memory, whereas MCGA, EGA, VGA, SVGA and XGA are called unconventional display adapters and use A block of VDU memory.

In text mode one can display only text characters (ASCII value 0 to 255), whereas, graphics mode is mainly used for complex drawings. However, in graphics mode, text characters can also be drawn in a variety of shapes and sizes.

The CGA, MCGA, EGA, VGA, SVGA and XGA can operate both in text and graphics mode to produce drawings and characters in several formats and colors. By contrast, MA can operate only in text mode and that too only in one color. EGA, VGA, SVGA and XGA offer better performance as regards the clarity and sharpness of the image and graphics and color capabilities as compared to MA, CGA or Hercules.

Let us now have a look at each of these adapters in brief.

Monochrome Adapter (MA)

The simplest and the first available adapter is the MA. This adapter can display only text (in single color) and has no graphics displaying capability. Originally this drawback only prevented the users from playing video games, but today, even the most serious business software uses graphics and color to great advantage. Hence, MA is no longer suitable, though it offers clarity and high resolution.

Hercules Adapter

The Hercules card emulates the MA but can also operate in a graphics mode. Because of its graphics capabilities the Hercules card became somewhat of a standard for monochrome systems.

Color Graphics Adapter (CGA)

For several years CGA was the most common display adapter, although its capabilities are quite limited from today's perspective. This adapter can display text as well as graphics. In text mode it operates in 25 row by 80 column mode with 16 colors. In graphics mode two resolutions are available: medium resolution graphics mode (320 x 200), with four colors available from a palette of 16; and two-color high resolution mode (640 x 200).

One drawback of CGA card is that it produces flicker and snow. **Flicker** is the annoying tendency of the text to flash as it moves up or down. **Snow** is the flurry of bright dots that can appear anywhere on the screen.

Enhanced Graphics Adapter (EGA)

The EGA was introduced by IBM in 1984 as an alternative to the CGA card. The EGA could emulate most of the functions and all the display modes of CGA as well as MA. The EGA offered higher resolution and was not plagued with the snow and flicker problems of the CGA. In addition to the monochrome and color displays designed for the MA and the CGA, the EGA could use the enhanced color monitor capable of displaying 640 x 350 pixels in 16 colors from a palette of 64.

The EGA card has several internal registers. A serious limitation of the EGA card is that it supports write operations to most of its internal registers, but no read operations. As a result, it is not possible for the software to detect and preserve the state of the adapter, which makes EGA unsuited for memory resident applications or for multitasking environments like Windows and OS/2.

Multicolor Graphics Adapter (MCGA)

The MCGA was designed to emulate the CGA card and to maintain compatibility with all the CGA modes. In addition to the text and graphics modes of the CGA, MCGA has two new graphics modes: a 640 x 480 pixel mode in 2 colors and a 320 x 200 pixel mode in 256 colors. The MCGA system was short-lived since soon after its launch IBM started supplying the VGA card.

Video Graphics Array (VGA)

The VGA card supports all the display modes of MA, CGA, MCGA and EGA. In addition VGA supports a graphics mode of 640 x 480 pixels resolution in 16 colors.

Super Video Graphics Array (SVGA)

The SVGA designation refers to enhancements to the VGA standard by independent vendors. Unlike display adapters discussed so far, the SVGA does not refer to a card that meets a particular specification but to a group of cards that have different capabilities. For example, one card may offer resolutions 800 x 600 and 1024 x 768, whereas, another card may not only offer the same resolutions but also provide more color choices in each resolution. These cards have different capabilities, but still both of them are classified as SVGA. Since each SVGA card has different capabilities, you need special device driver programs for driving them. This means that unlike VGA cards - which can have a single driver that works with all VGA cards, regardless of the vendor - each SVGA card must have a corresponding driver.

Extended Graphics Array (XGA)

The XGA evolved from the VGA an provides greater resolution, more colors and much better performance. The XGA has a graphics processor and bus mastering. Being a bus-master adapter means that the XGA can take control of the system as though it were the mother board. In essence, a bus master is an adapter with its own processor that can execute operations independent of the mother board. The XGA offers two new modes: 640 x 480 pixel mode with 65536 colors and 1024 x 768 pixel mode with 256 colors.

Display Screens (Monitors)

The type of the video screen, or monitor, that might be used has an important effect on program design. Many monitors cannot produce color or graphics, and some produce poor quality images. Moreover, each display adapter supports only certain types of display monitors. A variety of monitors can be used with 8086 family of computers. The major categories are:

(a) Monochrome monitors
(b) Composite monochrome monitors
(c) Composite color monitors
(d) TV sets
(e) RGB monitors
(f) VGA mono monitors
(g) VGA color monitors

Let us now examine the capabilities of each type of monitor.

Monochrome Monitors

These monitors are designed to display high resolution text, but no Graphics. These monitors work only with MA. Graphics images cannot be displayed on these types of monitors unless a special adapter like a Hercules Adapter is used with them.

Composite Monochrome Monitors

These monitors were among the most widely used monitors at one time. They were used with a CGA and provided a fairly good (not as good as monochrome monitor) one color image (usually green, amber or soft-white). A composite monochrome monitor could display text and graphics, but not color.

Composite Color Monitors

These monitors produce text, graphics and colors but have serious limitations. A 80-column display is often unreadable, only certain color combinations work well, and graphics resolution is of low quality.

TV Sets

Although the television set (color or black and white) is technically same as the composite color monitor, it usually produces an even lower quality image than the dedicated composite color monitor. Text displays must be in 40 column or even 20 column mode to ensure that the text is readable.

RGB Monitors

The RGB monitors are considered best of both the worlds. They combine the high quality text display of the monochrome monitor with the high resolution graphics and color. RGB stands for Red - Green - Blue. These monitors operate on three input signals that encode the primary colors Red, Green and Blue. The RGB monitors are compatible with the CGA and EGA cards.

VGA Mono Monitors

These monitors produce monochrome output on the VGA or MCGA system. These are used as a less expensive alternative to the standard VGA systems.

VGA Color Monitors

These monitors are based on analog instead of digital signals. These are the color monitors typically used in computers equipped with the VGA cards.

Video Display Modes

Just as an artist can choose from a variety of media when creating a picture (oils, etching, watercolors etc.), so a programmer can choose from a variety of modes, or formats. Each mode provides a

Mode	MDA	CGA	MCGA	EGA	VGA	SVGA	XGA	
0		✓	✓	✓	✓	✓	✓	
1		✓	✓	✓	✓	✓	✓	
2		✓						
			✓	✓	✓	✓	✓	
3		✓						
			✓	✓	✓	✓	✓	
4		✓	✓	✓	✓	✓	✓	
5		✓	✓	✓	✓	✓	✓	
6		✓	✓	✓	✓	✓	✓	
7	✓							
8-C				✓	✓	✓	✓	
D				✓	✓	✓	✓	
E				✓	✓	✓	✓	
F				✓	✓	✓	✓	
10h				✓	✓	✓	✓	
11h			✓		✓	✓	✓	
12h					✓	✓	✓	
13h			✓		✓	✓	✓	
14h							✓	
52h								
53h								
6Ah						✓		
72h								
73h								
100h						✓		
101h						✓		
102h						✓		
103h						✓		
104h						✓		
105h						✓		
106h						✓		
107h						✓		

Figure 15.3

Pixels horiz.	Pixels vert.	Max. pages	Display seg	Description
320	200	8	B800	Text, 25 rows x 40 cols, monochrome
320	200	8	B800	Text, 25 rows x 40 cols, 16 colors
640	200	4	B800	Text, 25 rows x 80 cols, monochrome
640	200	8	B800	
640	200	4	B800	Text, 25 rows x 80 cols, 16 colors
640	200	8	B800	
320	200	1	B800	Graphics, 4 colors
320	200	1	B800	Graphics, monochrome
640	200	1	B800	Graphics, 2 colors
720	350	1	B000	Text, 25 rows x 80 cols, monochrome
720	350	8	B000	
				PCjr and Invalid modes
320	200	8	A000	Graphics, 16 colors
640	200	4	A000	Graphics, 16 colors
640	350	2	A000	Graphics, 2 colors
640	350	2	A000	Graphics, 16 colors
640	480	1	A000	Graphics, 2 colors
640	480	1	A000	Graphics, 16 colors
320	200	1	A000	Graphics, 256 colors
640	400	4	B800	Text, 25 rows x 132 cols, 16 colors
640	480	1	A000	Graphics, 16 colors
640	480	1	A000	Graphics, 16 colors
800	600	1	A000	Graphics, 16 colors
640	480	1	A000	Graphics, 16 colors
640	475	1	None	Text, 25 rows x 80 cols
640	400	1	A000	Graphics, 256 colors
640	480	1	A000	Graphics, 256 colors
800	600	1	A000	Graphics, 16 colors
800	600	1	A000	Graphics, 256 colors
1024	768	1	A000	Graphics, 16 colors
1024	768	1	A000	Graphics, 256 colors
1024	1024	1	A000	Graphics, 16 colors
1024	1024	1	A000	Graphics, 256 colors

different combination of display characteristics. These characteristics include:

(a) whether text or graphics is to be displayed
(b) the amount of text to be displayed in one line
(c) the resolution
(d) the number of possible colors

Each mode requires certain hardware (monitor and display adapter) and programming approaches. Each and every mode will not be supported by a particular combination of monitor and display adapter. All the modes (approximately 34) are basically of two types, text and graphics. Figure 15.3 lists the various available modes, along with the number of colors, resolution and the maximum number of VDU pages that it can support. Figure 15.3 also shows which modes are supported by which adapter.

In India at most of the installations one finds one of the following three combinations of video systems:

(a) VGA monochrome monitor and VGA adapter
(b) VGA color monitor and VGA adapter
(c) VGA color monitor and SVGA adapter

When you first turn the computer on, it will boot up in mode 3. This is a text-only mode. To draw graphics you are required to switch to another mode available with the adapter.

We will now briefly discuss the various graphics elements like resolution, colors, etc. and how do they come together to make each of the above modes.

Resolution

Graphics images on the screen are built up from tiny dots called picture elements or 'pixels'. The display resolution is defined by the number of rows (called scan lines) from top to bottom, and number of pixels from left to right on each scan line.

Each mode uses a particular resolution. For example, mode 4 uses a resolution of 200 scan lines, each containing 320 pixels across. This is often referred to as '320 x 200' resolution.

In general, higher the resolution, more pleasing is the picture. Higher resolution means a sharper, clearer picture, with less pronounced 'staircase' effect on lines drawn diagonally and better looking text characters. On the other hand, higher resolution also means more memory requirement for the display.

Text or Graphics

All modes are fundamentally of two types, text or graphics. Some modes display only text, some support more number of colors, whereas some are made only for graphics. As seen earlier, the display adapter continuously dumps the contents of the VDU memory on the screen. Most text modes use B block in the memory map, whereas most graphics modes use the A block.

The amount of memory required to represent a character on screen in text mode and a pixel in graphics mode varies from mode to mode. Figure 15.4 shows the resolution and the amount of memory required do display a fundamental element in each mode.

Mode No.	Type	Resolution	Memory Required
3	Text	80 x 25	2 bytes per char
5	Graphics	320 x 200	2 bits per pixel
6	Graphics	640 x 200	1 bit per pixel
7	Text	80 x 25	2 bytes per char
12h	Graphics	640 x 480	1 bit per pixel
13h	Graphics	320 x 200	1 byte per pixel

Figure 15.4

In mode 6 each pixel displayed on the screen occupies one bit in VDU memory. Since this bit can take only two values, either 0 or 1, only two colors can be used with each pixel. In mode 5, two bits are used to represent one pixel. These two bits can generate four values (00, 01, 10 and 11) and hence a pixel can be drawn in four possible colors. In modes 18 and 19 a pixel can be drawn in 16 and 256 colors respectively. How these colors are generated is discussed in a later section in this chapter.

As seen from Figure 15.4, text modes need two bytes in VDU memory to represent one character on screen. Of these two bytes the first byte contains the ASCII value of the character being displayed, whereas the second byte is the attribute byte. The attribute byte controls the color in which the character is being displayed.

How does the character actually get displayed on the screen? The ASCII value present in VDU memory must be translated into a character and drawn on the screen. This drawing is done by a character generator that is part of the display adapter. The CGA has a character generator that uses 8 scan lines and 8 pixels in each of these scan lines to produce a character on screen; whereas the MA's character generator uses 9 scan lines and 14 pixels in each of these scan lines to produce a character. This larger format of MA makes the characters generated by MA much sharper and hence easier to read.

On older display adapters like MA and CGA, the character generator is located in ROM (Read Only Memory). EGA and VGA do not have a character generator ROM. Instead, character generator data is loaded into plane 2 of display RAM. This feature makes it easy for custom character sets to be loaded. Multiple character sets (up to 4 for EGA and up to 8 for VGA) may reside in RAM simultaneously. A set of BIOS services are available for easy loading of character sets. Each character set can contain 256 characters. Either one or two character sets may be active giving these adapters the capability to display up to 512 different characters on the screen simultaneously. When two character sets are active, a bit in each character attribute byte selects which character set will be used for that character. Using a ROM-BIOS service we can select the active character set. Each character in the standard character set provided with the EGA is 8 pixels wide and 14 pixels tall. Since VGA has higher resolution, it provides a 9 pixel wide by 16 pixels tall character set. Custom character set can also be loaded using BIOS VDU services (refer appendix B).

The graphics modes can also display characters, but they are produced quite differently. The graphics modes can only store information bit-by-bit and characters are no exception... they must be drawn one bit at a time. The big advantage of this method is that one can design characters of desired style, shape and size.

Colors in Text Mode

In mode 3, for each character on screen there are two bytes in VDU memory, one containing the ASCII value of the character and other containing its attribute. The attribute byte controls the color of the character. The attribute byte contains three components: the foreground color (color of the character itself), the background color (color of the area not covered by the character) and the blinking component of the character. The following figure shows the breakup of the attribute byte:

Bits								**Purpose**
7	6	5	4	3	2	1	0	
.	.	.	.	.	.	.	1	Blue component of f/g color
.	.	.	.	.	.	1	.	Green component of f/g color
.	.	.	.	.	1	.	.	Red component of f/g color
.	.	.	.	1	.	.	.	Intensity component of f/g color
.	.	.	1	.	.	.	.	Blue component of b/g color
.	.	1	.	.	.	.	.	Green component of b/g color
.	1	.	.	.	.	.	.	Red component of b/g color
1	.	.	.	.	.	.	.	Blinking component

Figure 15.5

The first four bits can produce 16 different colors, whereas the Red, Green and Blue components of background colors can produce 8 different colors. Figure 15.6 shows which bit setting will produce what color.

Color	Components			
	Intensity	Red	Green	Blue
Black	0	0	0	0
Blue	0	0	0	1
Green	0	0	1	0
Cyan	0	0	1	1
Red	0	1	0	0
Magenta	0	1	0	1
Brown	0	1	1	0
White	0	1	1	1
Light Black	1	0	0	0
Light Blue	1	0	0	1
Light Green	1	0	1	0
Light Cyan	1	0	1	1
Light Red	1	1	0	0
Light Magenta	1	1	0	1
Yellow	1	1	1	0
Intense White	1	1	1	1

Figure 15.6

(a) foreground color (color of the character itself)
(b) background color (color of the area not covered by the character)
(c) blinking component of the character

Thus, if the bit settings of the attribute byte are, say, 00010100, then the character produced would be of red color on a blue background. Similarly, 10001110 would produce a yellow character on a black background, and the character would blink on the screen.

The MA doesn't support any colors. However, effects shown in Figure 15.7 can be obtained by setting up the attribute byte.

Effect	Setting Required
Normal characters	Black b/g and white f/g
Reverse video characters	White b/g and black f/g
Invisible characters	Black b/g and black f/g
Underlined characters	Black b/g and blue f/g

Figure 15.7

Thus, the bit setting 01110000 would produce a black character on a white background. The color combinations other than the ones mentioned above would produce the normal white-on-black characters.

Colors in Graphics Mode

So far we have seen how to set color in text modes. Setting color in graphics modes is quite different. In the graphics mode each pixel on the screen has a color associated with it. There are important differences here as compared to setting color is text mode. First, the pixels cannot blink. Second, each pixel is a discrete dot of color, there is no foreground and background... each pixel is simply one color or another. The number of colors that each adapter can support and the way each adapter generates these colors is drastically different. Here we would examine the color used by CGA, EGA and VGA.

Colors in CGA

The Color Graphics Adapter (CGA) supports two graphics modes: 320 x 200 medium resolution graphics mode and 640 x 200 high resolution graphics mode. The former supports four colors, whereas, the latter supports only two. In fact, the low resolution graphics mode supports two different sets of four colors each. These sets of colors are called palettes. It is possible to switch to a second set of 4 totally different colors than the first 4. The provision of palettes is made to keep memory requirement minimum while making available the facility of maximum colors. Mode 5 of CGA supports palette 0 and palette 1. The following figure shows the colors present in each palette.

Palette	Bits	Color
0	00	Black (may be changed to any of the 16 colors)
0	01	Green
0	10	Red
0	11·	Brown
1	00	Black (may be changed to any of the 16 colors)
1	01	Cyan
1	10	Magenta
1	11	Light gray

Figure 15.8

Colors in EGA

The EGA adapter has several registers which together make up the programming interface. Some of these register are responsible for determining the number of colors that EGA can support. EGA's display memory is organised in four planes. Each plane provides one bit of data for each pixel. The bits for a given pixel from each of the four planes are combined into a nibble that identifies one of the 16 palette registers. Each palette register is 8 bits long. Of these, 6 bits are used to represent color as shown in the following figure.

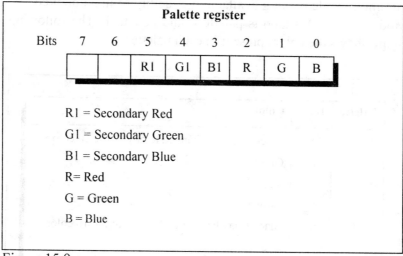

Figure 15.9

These six bits can represent 64 different colors. But, since there are only 16 palette registers they can contain only 16 out of the possible 64 values. Hence an EGA can display at a time only 16 out of the possible 64 colors. To be more specific, a 4-bit pixel value of 0 causes a 6-bit value stored in palette register 0 to be sent to the display as the color of that pixel. Likewise, a pixel value of 1 causes the contents of palette register 1 to be sent to the display. Since there are only 4 input bits, only 16 colors are available at any time. And since there are 6 output bits these 16 colors can be mapped to any of the 64 colors.

Of the lower six bits of the palette register, the secondary red, green and blue are less-intense versions of red, green and blue, although there exact effects vary from monitor to monitor .

Figure 15.10 sums up the color generation scheme used in an EGA.

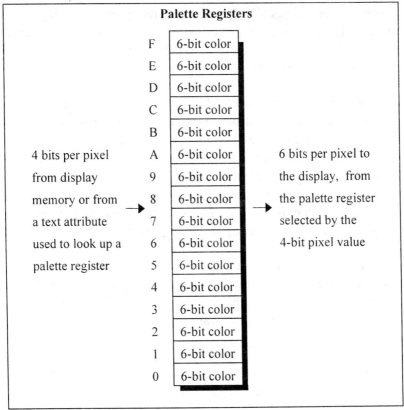

	Palette Registers	
	F	6-bit color
	E	6-bit color
	D	6-bit color
	C	6-bit color
	B	6-bit color
4 bits per pixel	A	6-bit color
from display	9	6-bit color
memory or from	8	6-bit color
a text attribute	7	6-bit color
used to look up a	6	6-bit color
palette register	5	6-bit color
	4	6-bit color
	3	6-bit color
	2	6-bit color
	1	6-bit color
	0	6-bit color

6 bits per pixel to the display, from the palette register selected by the 4-bit pixel value

Figure 15.10

Colors in VGA

The VGA card was introduced by IBM in April 1987. Unlike earlier VDU standards, which were digital, the VGA is an analog system. Why are displays going from digital to analog when most other electronic systems are going digital? For example, compact disk players, newer VCRs and camcorders have digital picture storage. With a digital Television set, you can watch several channels on a single screen by splitting the screen or placing a picture within another picture. Then why did IBM decide to change the video to analog? The answer is color. A digital display generates different colors by using the red, green and blue electron beams. In addition an intensity signal is used to display each color at one of the two intensity levels. This gives rise to a capability to generate 16 colors (2^4).

An analog display works like digital displays that use RGB electron beams to construct various colors, but each color in the analog system can be displayed at varying levels of intensity - 64 levels, in the case of the VGA. This versatility provides 2,62,144 possible colors (64^3). In computer graphics the color is often important than the resolution, because the human eye perceives the picture that has more colors as being more realistic. IBM moved graphics into analog to enhance the color capabilities.

With the fundamentals out of the way let us know see how colors are generated in VGA. In VGA too, there are 4 planes - red, green, blue and intensity, with one bit from each of these planes contributing towards 1 pixel value.

The 4-bit pixel value from the display memory is used as the address of 1 of the 16 palette registers. For example, a pixel value of 0 selects the palette register 0, a pixel value of 1 selects register 1, and so on. Once the palette register has been chosen the 6-bit value in it is combined with a 2-bit value from a color select register, resulting into a 8-bit value. This 8-bit value is used as the address of 1 of the 256 DAC (Digital to Analog Converter) registers. Each DAC register contains an 18-bit value which represents the color. The 18-bit value is organised as 6-bit red, green and blue color components. This value is sent to the analog conversion circuitry which converts it into three proportional analog signals and sends them to the monitor. Since each DAC register is 18-bit long, a pixel can have any of the 2,62,144 values (2^{18}).

VGA supports several graphics modes. The two popular ones are: 640 x 480, 16 color mode and a 320 x 200, 256 color mode. In the former, the color select register bits always have a value 0. Hence, in this mode only the first 64 DAC registers get used. As a result, only 64 out of the possible 2,62,144 color values can be used. And since there are only 16 palette registers, only 16 out of the 64 DAC registers can get selected. Thus, in this graphics mode we can use any 16 out of the 2,62,144 colors.

In the 256 color mode, the 2-bits from the color select register can take values like 00, 01, 10, 11. This combined with 64 possible values from the palette registers permit us to select 1 of the 256 DAC registers. As a result, we can use 256 out of the possible 2,62,144 color values.

The translation of a 4-bit color value into a 18-bit DAC register value is shown in Figure 15.11.

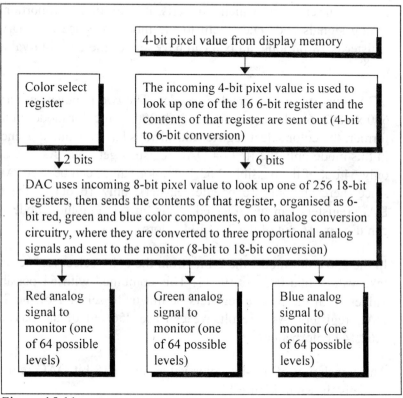

Figure 15.11

In summary, we cannot speak of 'color' at any point in the color translation process until the output stage of DAC. The 4-bit pixel value in memory, the 6-bit value in the palette registers and the 8-bit value sent to the DAC are all addresses, not colors. For example, a pixel with a 4-bit value of 0 is not black, it is address 0 of the palette register. If this palette register contains a value 0x3F then this value is not the white color but a value which would be combined with the 2 bits from the color select register to give a 8-bit value. Suppose the 2-bit value is 0 then the 8-bit value would remain 3Fh. This value is also not the white color. It is the address of the DAC register. It is the value stored in the DAC register 0x3F which represents the color. Suppose the value stored in the DAC register 0x3F is 63 then the pixel would be displayed in color 63. Thus, a pixel value of 0 in display memory can become color 63 when displayed on the screen. In short, it isn't color until the DAC says it's color.

We saw that EGA permits a choice of 16 out of 64 colors, whereas a VGA permits 16 out of 2,62,144 colors. So do we gain anything in switching over to VGA? Yes. We get a wider variety of colors to choose from and that too at a resolution better than what EGA can offer.

Video Pages

From Figure 15.3 it can be seen that mode number 3 permits a maximum of 4 video pages for a CGA and 8 for adapters like EGA and VGA. Let us now find out what are these video pages. Since in mode 3 each character displayed on the screen takes 2 bytes in display memory, a total of 2000 characters (25 x 80) would require 4000 bytes, or roughly 4 KB. As adapters come with more memory than 4 KB, if only the first 4 KB of the adapter memory is used then the rest would lie unutilised. To avoid this the display memory is split into several chunks of 4 KB each (for mode 3). These chunks of memory are called video pages or sometimes VDU pages. Thus, there are four video pages in mode 3, numbered from 0 to 3. At any given time, contents of one page are displayed on the screen. Information can be written into the displayed page or any of the other pages. Using this technique we can build a screen on an invisible page while another page is being displayed, then switch to the new page when appropriate time comes. Switching screen images this way makes them appear to regenerate instantaneously.

This technique is often used in writing menu-driven programs, where a different menu is written on each page. As a result, to switch over from one menu to another, all that we are required to do is to switch over to an appropriate page, where the menu is already written and ready to be displayed. This is obviously a better procedure than erasing the existing menu and writing a new menu.

In graphics modes too, the display memory is split into video pages. The maximum number of pages permitted depends on the bits required to store information of one pixel and the amount of display memory available.

Writing to VDU Memory in Text Mode

There are 3 ways of displaying characters on the screen.

(a) Using standard library functions
(b) Using ROM-BIOS or DOS routines
(c) Writing characters directly into VDU memory

The last option works faster than the other two, because, the standard library functions or ROM-BIOS/DOS routines ultimately write the characters to be displayed into VDU memory. Obviously, if we are able to write characters directly into VDU memory we would be able to bypass the standard library functions as well as the ROM-BIOS/DOS routines.

We know that above the 640 KB RAM, there are 2 blocks (block A and Block B) of 64 KB each. The B block is further divided into two parts of 32 KB each. The first 32 KB are used by the MA, rest by CGA/EGA/VGA. To be able to write directly to VDU memory, one must first know the address of the beginning of the VDU memory block. This beginning address for MA is 0xB0000 and that for CGA/EGA/VGA is 0xB8000.

Each character present on the screen has two bytes corresponding to it in the VDU memory. The first byte contains the ASCII value of the character, whereas the next byte contains the attribute (color) of the character. For example, using a VGA if 'A' is displayed in 0th row, 0th column on the screen, then address 0xB8000 contains the ASCII value of 'A', whereas the immediately adjacent address contains the attribute of 'A',

Thus, if one character occupies two bytes in VDU memory, 80 characters of 0th row will be represented by first 160 bytes from 0xB8000 onwards. Similarly, one screenful of characters would need 4000 bytes (80 x 25 x 2).

Using this concept let us now write a program which fills the entire screen with 'A's by writing this character directly into VDU memory.

```
/* Screenful of 'A's */
main( )
{
    int i ;
    char far *vidmem = 0xB8000000 ;

    for ( i = 0 ; i <= 3999 ; i = i + 2 )
        * ( vidmem + i ) = 'A' ;
}
```

The variable **vidmem** has been defined as a **far** pointer since we are trying to access the memory which is beyond the data segment of our program.

Now suppose we want to change the attribute of all characters on the screen to 112, it can be done using the following program.

```
/* Changing screen attributes */
main( )
{
    int i ;
    char far *vidmem = 0xB8000000 ;

    for ( i = 1 ; i <= 3999 ; i = i + 2 )
        * ( vidmem + i ) = 112 ;
}
```

Now it's time for something more complicated. The following program draws a filled box on the screen and displays a message in it.

```
char far *vidmem = 0xB8000000 ;
main( )
{
    int r, c, i ;
    char message[ ] = "Al Italia!!" ;

    for ( r = 5 ; r <= 20 ; r++ )
    {
        for ( c = 5 ; c <= 50 ; c++ )
            write2vdu ( ' ', 64, r, c ) ;
    }

    c = 10 ;
    for ( i = 0 ; i <= 10 ; i++ )
    {
        write2vdu ( message[i], 77, 10, c ) ;
        c++ ;
    }
```

```
}

write2vdu ( char ch, char attr, int row, int col )
{
    char far *v ;
    v = vidmem + row * 160 + col * 2 ;
    *v = ch ;
    v++ ;
    *v = attr ;
}
```

In the above example, a separate function **write2vdu( )** has been
called from the **main( )**. To it we have sent character to be
displayed (**ch**), its attribute (**attr**) and the row & column where it
is to be displayed. Upon receiving the arguments, the character
and its attribute are stored at appropriate locations in the VDU
memory. Work through the function **write2vdu( )** carefully till
you have analysed the whole process.

VDU Related Jargon

Frequently, one comes across confusing and conflicting
terminologies related with the VDU. This involves interlaced and
non-interlaced monitors, multisync monitors, energy saving
monitors, active matrix LCD display, etc. Let us now try to
demystify this jargon.

Multisync Monitor

Some monitors have a fixed refresh rate, whereas, others may
support a range of frequencies. This multiple frequency support
provides built in compatibility with future video standards. A
monitor that supports many video standards is called a multiple-
frequency monitor. Different vendors call multiple-frequency

monitor by different names, including multisync, multifrequency, multiscan and asynchronous monitors.

FST Monitor

The traditional screen is curved, meaning that it bulges outwards from the middle of the screen. This design is consistent with the vast majority of cathode ray tube designs, including your television set. FST stands for flat square tube. The flat screen results in less glare and a higher quality, more accurate image. The disadvantage is that the technology required to produce flat-screen displays is more expensive, resulting in higher prices for the monitors.

Interlaced and Non-Interlaced Monitors

In non-interlaced (conventional) monitors the electron beam sweeps the screen in lines from top to bottom one line after the other, completing the screen in one pass. In interlaced monitors too, the electron beam sweeps the screen from top to bottom, but it does so in two passes, sweeping the odd lines first and the even lines second. This technique provides more stable images.

Energy Saving Monitors

Monitor is one of the most power-hungry computer components. Hence, putting off the monitor if it is idle for a specific period of time can save energy. Many PC manufacturers are trying to meet Environmental Protection Agency's (EPA's) Energy Store Requirements. Any PC-monitor that consumes less than 70 watts can use the Energy Star logo. There are different energy saving standards available for monitors, By far the most popular amongst these is Video Electronic Standards Associations Display Power Management Signal (VESA-DPMS) specifications.

Active Matrix LCD Display

Instead of using the CRT technology, the laptop computers make use of Liquid Crystal Diode (LCD) displays. These displays have low glare flat screens and low power requirements (5 watts versus nearly 60 watts for an ordinary monitor). There are 3 LCD choices: passive-matrix monochrome, passive-matrix color and active-matrix color. The actual differences between these types is beyond the scope of this book.

Exercise

[A] Pick up the correct alternative for each of the following:

(a) Pick the odd one out

MA
CGA
EGA
VGA

(b) Which of the following is the best video system combination

(1) MA with monochrome monitor
(2) CGA with composite monochrome monitor
(3) VGA with RGB monitor
(4) SVGA with RBG monitor

(c) Which of the following would display a message on the screen fastest

(1) Using printf( )function
(2) Using puts( ) function
(3) Using ROM-BIOS services
(4) Directly writing to VDU memory

(d) Which of the following is not capable of displaying graphics

(1) MA
(2) CGA
(3) EGA
(4) VGA

(e) In CGA text mode each character is constructed using

(1) 8 scan lines and 8 pixels per scan line
(2) 9 scan lines and 14 pixels per scan line
(3) 14 scan lines and 9 pixels per scan line
(4) 200 scan lines and 640 pixels per scan line

(f) In the text mode each character displayed on the screen occupies _____ bytes in VDU memory

(1) 2
(2) 4
(3) 6
(4) 1

(g) In CGA high resolution graphics mode each pixel displayed on the screen occupies _____ in VDU memory

(1) 1 bit
(2) 1 byte
(3) 2 bytes
(4) 2 bits

(h) Out of the 64 kb of conventional VDU memory block, CGA uses only

(1) 16 bits
(2) 16 kb
(3) 64 kb
(4) 32 kb

[B] Answer the following:

(a) What do you mean by refresh rate? Is it true that higher the refresh rate better is the image on the screen?

(b) What is the purpose of the display adapter? Where is it present in the computer?

(c) Why is it that in text mode there is only one font available, whereas in graphics mode characters can be displayed in a variety of fonts?

(d) What attribute byte would you use if a message is to be displayed with brown background and yellow coloured characters?

(e) When we change over from one mode to another do the screen's current contents remain intact?

[C] Answer the following:

(a) In the following program the displaymenu( ) function is supposed to write a given menu on a given VDU page by directly writing it in VDU memory. You are required to write the function displaymenu( ). Make it as general as as you can.

```
char *filemenu[ ] = {
                    "Rename file",
                    "Copy file",
                    "Delete file",
                    "Display file"
              };

char *dirmenu[ ] = {
                    "Make directory",
                    "Change directory",
                    "Remove directory"
                    "List directory"
              };
    main( )
    {
```

```
    int row = 5, col = 20, vdupage, num ;

    num = 4 ;  /* number of menu items */
    vdupage = 0 ;
    displaymenu ( filemenu, row, col, vdupage, num ) ;
    vdupage = 1 ;
    displaymenu ( dirmenu, row, col, vdupage, num ) ;
}
```

(b) Write a general purpose function writestring( ) which will display a message on the screen by writing it directly into VDU memory. The function should be capable of displaying the message in the attribute which is sent to it.

(c) Write a program which continuously keeps changing the capital letters present on the screen into small case letters and small case letters present on the screen into capitals. You are not allowed to use printf( ), putchar( ), puts( ) or putch( ).

16   *Keyboard Basics*

Operation of Keyboard
Shift and Toggle Keys
Exercise

H ow many programs have you come across which make use of arrow keys, function keys, or control and shift keys. Almost all professional level software makes use of these keys one way or the other. Naturally these keys are of interest to a C programmer. This chapter explains you how these keys can be tackled. The first part of the chapter explains how the keyboard interacts with the computer. The second part deals with how the computer treats the keyboard information and makes it available to our programs.

Operation of Keyboard

The keyboard is an important component of the computer system. The keyboard unit contains a dedicated microprocessor. The main duty of the microprocessor is to watch the keys and report to the main computer whenever a key is pressed or released. If any key is pressed continuously, the keyboard microprocessor sends out a repeat action at specific intervals. The keyboard microprocessor also has a buffer that can store keys that are hit at times when the main computer is busy doing something else and is not in a position to accept them the moment they are hit.

A key if pressed for more than 0.5 seconds causes an auto repeat action to begin. That is, if you keep a key pressed for more than 0.5 seconds, the key automatically gets repeated and the repeat rate is about 10 characters per seconds. This 0.5 seconds duration is often called 'typematic delay' and the repeat action that follows is known as 'typematic rate'.

The typematic delay and the repeat rate are built into the hardware. In some keyboards, for example the one attached to a PC/AT, one can modify the typematic rate and typematic delay by programming the keyboard microprocessor.

Each time you press a key on the keyboard, the keyboard circuits transmit a sequence of one or more 8-bit numbers to the computer, through the connector cable. This sequence of 8-bits is called 'Scan code', and it uniquely identifies the key you pressed. The scan code can be thought of as a position code. Each key present on the keyboard has a unique scan code.

The keyboard produces different scan codes, depending on whether the key was pressed or released. Whenever you press a key the scan code byte contains a number ranging from 1 to 83. When you release the key, the keyboard generates a scan code which is 128 higher than the scan code generated when the key was pressed. For example, when we press the letter A, the keyboard generates the scan code 30; when we release it, the keyboard generates the scan code 158 (30 + 128).

The keyboard control circuitry on the computer's mother board monitors the keyboard for input. The keyboard controller generates an interrupt (a signal to stop the current activity of the microprocessor) each time it receives a scan code from the keyboard. The ROM-BIOS contains the corresponding routine which reads this scan code from the keyboard controller and then processes it.

The ROM-BIOS routine translates scan code into a two-byte sequence. The first byte contains the ascii value corresponding to the key pressed. The second byte contains the scan code of the key hit. If usual keys such as alphabets, digits or special symbols are hit then the first byte contains ascii value of the key hit, whereas the second byte contains the appropriate scan code. However, if special keys, such as function keys and numeric keypad keys are hit then the first byte contains a value 0, whereas the second byte contains the scan code of the key. Here is a simple program which reports the ascii code and scan code of the key that you hit from the keyboard.

```
main( )
{
    char ch ;

    printf ( "Press any key... " ) ;
```

```
ch = getch( ) ;

if ( ch == 0 )
{
    printf ( "\nascii code = %d", ch ) ;
    ch = getch( ) ;
    printf ( "\nscan code = %d", ch ) ;
}
else
    printf ( "\nascii code = %d", ch ) ;
}
```

Two sample runs of the program are shown below. Since we are using the function **getch( )** the character hit will not be echoed on the screen. Assume that in the first run the key z is hit, whereas in the second run the key F1 is hit.

```
Press any key
ascii code = 90
Press any key
ascii code = 0
scan code = 59
```

The same program can be written more effectively when we get the knowledge of interrupts and registers in the next chapter.

The translation by the ROM-BIOS of the scan codes which are sent to it is done carefully, checking first the status of the shift and toggle keys and then correspondingly interpreting the key or the key-combination pressed. We would be discussing these shift keys and toggle keys in the coming paragraphs.

The ROM-BIOS functions place the translated byte-pairs in a queue, which is kept in low memory and these byte pairs remain there until they are requested by a program. The ROM-BIOS uses a special buffer to store keyboard actions that have been processed. This buffer has the default capacity to store 15 characters but that can be changed by incorporating an appropriate command in the file CONFIG.SYS. If the characters are entered too fast and the buffer overflows, the computer will give a familiar beep sound and the extra characters will be lost.

Shift and Toggle Keys

We will now have a look at the shift keys and the toggle keys which are important for correct interpretation of the scan codes.

Shift Keys

The Ctrl, Shift, and Alt are known as shift keys. These keys change the shift state and hence change the meaning of the keys pressed along with them. For example, whenever you press Shift p, you get capital P; when you press Ctrl-C, you generate the "break" character.

The best example of the shift keys is when we use Alt key in combination with the number keys from the numeric keypad. For instance, Try pressing Alt 65 combination. Keep Alt key pressed, hit 6 and 5 from numeric keypad, and then release the Alt key. You would observe that the character A would be generated.

Toggle Keys

The two toggle keys, Caps-Lock and Num-Lock also affect the keyboard's shift state. When activated, Caps-Lock reverses the shift state of the alphabet keys; it does not affect the other keys. Likewise, the Num-Lock key disables the cursor control functions of the numeric keypad.

The difference between the shift keys and the toggle keys in changing the status is that the toggle keys (caps-lock and num-lock) are activated with a single keystroke and remain active until released by another keystroke.

The shift key and toggle key information is kept by the ROM-BIOS in memory locations 0x417 and 0x418 (refer Figure 16.1).

Byte 0x417

Bit numbers								Meaning
7	6	5	4	3	2	1	0	
1	.	.	.	.	.	.	.	Insert state
.	1	.	.	.	.	.	.	Caps Lock
.	.	1	.	.	.	.	.	Num Lock
.	.	.	1	.	.	.	.	Scroll Lock
.	.	.	.	1	.	.	.	Alt pressed
.	.	.	.	.	1	.	.	Ctrl pressed
.	.	.	.	.	.	1	.	Left Shift pressed
.	.	.	.	.	.	.	1	Right Shift pressed

Byte 0x418

Bit numbers								Meaning
7	6	5	4	3	2	1	0	
1	.	.	.	.	.	.	.	Insert pressed
.	1	.	.	.	.	.	.	Caps Lock pressed
.	.	1	.	.	.	.	.	Num Lock pressed
.	.	.	1	.	.	.	.	Scroll Lock pressed
.	.	.	.	1	.	.	.	Hold state active
.	.	.	.	.	1	.	.	Sys Req key pressed
.	.	.	.	.	.	1	.	Left Alt key pressed
.	.	.	.	.	.	.	1	Right Alt key pressed

Figure 16.1

The information stored in these two bytes is used to keep track of the current status (on/off) of the shift and toggle keys and whether or not they are pressed.

For example, the bits of the byte 0x417 keep track of the status of the keys, whereas the bits of the byte 0x418 only monitor whether the keys are pressed or not. These bits monitor the Ctrl, Alt, Shift, Caps-Lock, Num-Lock, Ins, and Scroll-Lock keys.

When you press a shift or a toggle key the corresponding bit of one of these bytes is altered. When the ROM-BIOS receives the release scan code of the shift key, it switches the status bit back to its original shift state.

Thus, when we press the keys Shift a, the ROM-BIOS performs the following steps:

- Since shift key is pressed, it puts ON the corresponding bit in 0x417.

- Having received the scan code of a, it first checks the status of the Shift key from the byte 0x417. Here, since it finds the bit on it puts the ascii value of capital a in the memory.

- The moment the shift key is released the release scan code sets the bit for shift key in byte 0x417 to off, so that subsequent keystrokes are interpreted accordingly.

Remember that keys like Ins, Caps-Lock, Num-Lock and Scroll-Lock key has 2 bits to store its information, one bit in each byte. The bit in byte 0x417 tells whether the status is on or off and the bit in byte 0x418 tells whether it is currently pressed or not.

Whenever the ROM-BIOS receives the scan code for an ordinary keystroke such as the letter a or an up arrow key, it first checks the shift status and then translates the key to an appropriate 2-byte code.

While the ROM-BIOS is translating scan codes, it checks for certain key combinations, such as Ctrl-Alt-Del, Ctrl-Break, Shift-PrtSc, and Ctrl-Num-Lock combinations. These five command-like key actions cause the ROM-BIOS to perform a specific task immediately. For example, Ctrl-Alt-Del combination reboots the computer, Shift-Prtsc prints the contents of the screen on the printer and so on.

Figure 16.2 shows scan codes of various keys and key combinations. This would come in quite handy while handling the specials keys in serious programming applications.

Scan Code	Key	Scan code	Key	Scan code	Key
1	Escape	117	Ctrl/End	31	Alt/S
15	Tab	118	Ctrl/Pgdn	32	Alt/D
71	Home	119	Ctrl/Home	33	Alt/F
72	Up arrow	132	Ctrl/PgUp	34	Alt/G
73	PgUp	16	Alt/Q	35	Alt/H
75	Left arrow	17	Alt/W	36	Alt/J
77	Right arrow	18	Alt/E	37	Alt/K
79	End	19	Alt/R	38	Alt/L
80	Down arrow	20	Alt/T	44	Alt/Z
81	PgDn	21	Alt/Y	45	Alt/X
82	Ins	22	Alt/U	46	Alt/C
83	Del	23	Alt/I	47	Alt/V
114	Ctrl/PrtSc	24	Alt/O	48	Alt/B
115	Ctrl/left	25	Alt/P	49	Alt/N
116	Ctrl/right	30	Alt/A	50	Alt/M
59-68	F1-F10	104-113	Alt/F1-F10	94-103	Ctrl-F1-F10
84-93	Sh/F1-F10	120-129	Alt/1-0		

Figure 16.2

Summary

This chapter throws light on how the keyboard interacts with the computer and how the information sent by keyboard is managed by the computer. We learnt that every key has got a code for its position called scan code. On hitting any key ROM-BIOS generates a two byte sequence, first byte containing the ascii value and second containing the scan code value. For special keys the ascii value byte contains zero. We also learnt how ROM-BIOS tackles shift and toggle keys using the information stored in bytes 0x417 and 0x418.

Exercise

[A]   Answer the following:

(a)   What are the actions of following key combinations?

    (1) Ctrl-Alt-Del
    (2) Ctrl-C
    (3) Shift-PrtSc
    (4) Ctrl-Num Lock

(b)   What is the difference between shift keys and toggle keys?

(c)   What are the contents of the two-byte sequence generated on hitting a key?

(d)   What do you mean by 'Typematic Rate' and 'Typematic Delay'? Can these be changed through a program?

(e)   Is it true that two different scan codes are generated, one on pressing a key and another on releasing it?

(f)   How do you type out graphics characters on the screen?

(g)   If the caps lock is right now ON and you hit the key combination shift A, how would this combination be interpreted by the computer using bytes 0x417 and 0x418?

(h)   If a program is being executed and you hit 2-3 keys, how would these keys be tackled? Where would these keys be stored? Maximum how many keys can be stored?

[B]   Answer the following:

(a)   Write a program which puts on a capital lock. Make use of the coding scheme given earlier for bytes 0x417 and 0x418.

(b)   Write a function which allows the user to hit a key from the keyboard. If an ordinary key is hit the function should return the ascii code of the key hit, whereas if a special key is hit, the function should return the scan code of the key.

17 *Interaction With Hardware Through C*

Of Approaches
    ROM-BIOS Versus High Level Language Functions
    ROM-BIOS Philosophy
The CPU Registers
Interrupts and Interrupt Vector Table
Invoking ROM-BIOS Functions
*Union*s
    Union of Structures
The *int86( )* Function
    Finding Memory Size
    Using the Declarations in *dos.h*
    Positioning Cursor on the Screen
Interrupts to Access ROM-BIOS Services
DOS Function Requests
Exercise

G enerally speaking, the more you know about how your computer works, the more effective you will be at writing programs for it. High level languages like BASIC, COBOL, FORTRAN etc, are not designed to include every possible function that you might need while programming - though admittedly some are better than the other. At some point, you will want to go deeper into your system and use some of the routines the languages them-selves use, or perhaps go even deeper and program at the hardware level. In this chapter we will explore various approaches that can be used to interact with the hardware through C. We would also highlight which approach is best suited for reliable and safe interaction.

We would also examine a data type called 'union' and how it can be used for interaction with hardware.

Of Approaches

A basic good feature of any programmer worth his salt is: he should never fall short of ideas. He must know more than one way to approach a problem. Therefore, when we set out to interact with the hardware through C, we must also know which approaches could be used. There are several ways to interact with the hardware. These are as under:

(a)   Using high level language functions
(b)   Using ROM-BIOS functions (routines)
(c)   Using DOS functions (routines) stored in the files IO.SYS and MSDOS.SYS
(d)   Directly programming the hardware

You may decide to employ any one of these approaches in your programs, but the one which directly programs the hardware would run fastest. At the same time this is the one which is most unreliable. Reason being there are many pitfalls in directly programming the hardware. For one, one must have a detailed knowledge of the hardware one is trying to program. Secondly, the programs that we write for one type of hardware may not be portable to another computer which has a different hardware.

For example, if we decide to directly program the disk drive controller card, we have to have the knowledge about, the type of the disk drive, in which direction it rotates, at what speed it rotates, how to move the read/write head to accurately read the information and so on... pretty heady stuff indeed! Moreover, there is no guarantee that the program that you write for one drive would work with the other, since the drives come in a number of varieties. So directly programming the hardware is the path which only the experts should tread on.

There is a saying that 'software cannot destroy hardware'. I disagree. While directly programming the hardware you may mess up things to such an extent that the drive head goes and sits in some irretrievable position, or worse still your monitor may blow, or a transformer may burn. Yes, believe me!

The programs which use 'high level language functions' to interact with the hardware are no doubt most reliable, but work very slowly. Moreover, you are limited by what the function has been designed to do. You may feel cramped as a result of this, since in certain cases you may want a function to do one thing for you, whereas the function has not been programmed to do this at all.

So, the moral of the story is that the two approaches 'directly programming the hardware' and 'using high level language functions' are two extremes. The golden mean is to either use 'ROM-BIOS functions' or the 'DOS functions'. Let us examine why is this so.

The most important reason why we should use ROM-BIOS and DOS functions is: whether we want or we don't these functions always occupy some space in memory. This is because they are always present in memory whenever the computer is on. Common sense tells us that we better use THEM.

Some of the ROM-BIOS functions overlap with their DOS counter-parts. For example, to write something to a disk, there exists a ROM-BIOS function as well as a DOS function. Naturally, the question arises which one should we prefer?

The ROM-BIOS functions work directly with the hardware and peripheral devices, performing some of the system's most fundamental tasks, such as reading data from the disk or writing data to the screen. DOS functions are often built from these basic functions and enhanced to make a particular process more efficient.

This is not to say that you should always use ROM-BIOS functions since they are available. DOS or the high level languages often provide the same services as the ROM-BIOS functions, but in a form that is easier to use in your programs. However, when a program needs more direct access to the hardware, than what DOS functions or the high level language functions can provide, ROM-BIOS functions are usually the answer.

ROM-BIOS Versus High Level Language Functions

As we had seen in the Chapter 7, the C program before it is ready to run has to be compiled and linked with standard library functions. Have a look at Figure 17.1. It illustrates how the user-defined functions and the high level language functions (standard library functions) are linked together on compilation to form an executable code.

From Figure 17.1 you can observe that the high level language functions have a role to play in the executable file, which is stored on the disk. Contrary to this, the ROM-BIOS functions never add to the size of the executable file. This is because the ROM-BIOS functions never get compiled and linked as ordinary high level language functions do. Thus, the EXE file of the program which use ROM-BIOS functions would be much smaller in size as compared to the size of EXE file of the program which uses high level language functions.

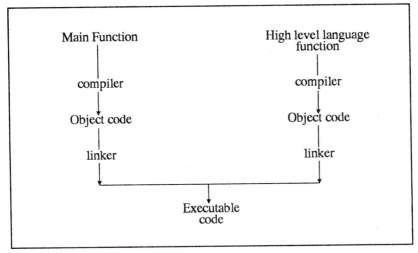

Figure 17.1

However, to use the ROM-BIOS functions in your programs is certainly not the simplest of tasks. This is due the fact that unlike ordinary functions, ROM-BIOS functions do not have names. So we cannot call them the way we call ordinary functions by names. Then how do we call them? For this we will have to understand the philosophy behind the ROM-BIOS functions.

ROM-BIOS Philosophy

To invoke any C function we just call it by its name in our program. For example, in the program given below we call the function **display( )** from **main( )**, just by mentioning its name, followed by a semicolon.

```
main( )
{
    int i = 3 ;
    display ( i ) ;
}
```

```
display ( int j )
{
    printf ( "%d", j ) ;
}
```

However, calling ROM-BIOS functions is not so simple, because, as we mentioned, ROM-BIOS functions do not have names. So how do we call them? By obtaining their addresses, and passing control to these addresses. But remembering addresses of all ROM-BIOS functions is a near impossible task. Fortunately, we are spared from this task. The addresses of ROM-BIOS functions are stored in the Interrupt Vector Table (IVT) in low memory area. Thus, to invoke a BIOS function, all that we need to do is: obtain the address of this function from the IVT and somehow manage to pass the control to this address to execute the ROM-BIOS routine.

At the specific moment when the ROM-BIOS function is called, the microprocessor is usually busy doing something; and the microprocessor is capable of performing only one task at a time. Therefore, its current activity must be interrupted before the control can be passed to the ROM-BIOS routine. When the microprocessor stops its current activity temporarily, and passes control to the ROM-BIOS routine, we say that 'an interrupt has occurred'. Once the ROM-BIOS routine has been executed the microprocessor resumes its original interrupted task.

Thus, all ROM-BIOS functions are invoked through 'interrupts'. Each interrupt instruction selects a particular address in the IVT and passes control to this address. This design makes it possible for any program to use a ROM-BIOS function without knowing its specific memory location. There are numerous ROM-BIOS functions available. They have been divided into subject categories, each with its own controlling interrupt. For example, all functions related with VDU are grouped under interrupt number 16, all functions related with printer are grouped under interrupt number 23 and so on.

One secret of successful programming with ROM-BIOS functions is a clear understanding of the concept of addressing scheme of 8086 family of micoprocessors, Registers, Interrupts and Interrupt Vector Table. For understanding the addressing scheme the reader is referred to Appendix F at the end of this book, whereas the other concepts are discussed in the next section.

The CPU Registers

The microprocessors have their own internal storage locations which are used to temporarily hold the data. These storage locations are known as 'registers'. The strategy of the microprocessor is to move whatever data is to be processed, from memory to a register, process the data, and then return the result to memory. In some languages, such as C, it is possible to access these registers, to store values in them or to retrieve values stored in them.

The 8086 family of microprocessors (the 8088, 8086, 80286 and 80386) uses a variety of 16-bit registers to aid the microprocessor in efficiently executing and performing arithmetic and logical comparison operations, as well as to receive instructions and pass data to and from the memory.

There are in all fourteen registers, each with a special use. These registers are grouped as under:

(a)   Scratch-Pad Registers:

These are also known as data registers. These are four in number and are used by the programs to temporarily hold the intermediate results and operands of arithmetic and logical comparison operations. The various scrach-pad registers are:

AX - Accumulator
BX - Base
CX - Count

DX - Data

Each of these 16-bit registers can be subdivided and separately used as two 8-bit registers. The high order 8-bit registers are known as AH, BH, CH, and DH, and the low order 8-bit registers are known as AL, BL, CL, and DL.

(b)   Segment Registers:

The 8086 microprocessor family refers to any memory location in terms of a 16-bit segment value and a 16-bit offset within the segment (this addressing scheme is discussed in detail in Appendix F). Out of these two, specific segments of memory are identified by segment registers, whereas offsets within a segment are identified by offset registers. There are four segments in memory, therefore, there are four segment registers. These are as under:

-    The CS register identifies the code segment, which contains the program being executed.
-    The DS and ES registers identify the data segment and the extra segment, where data used in programs is stored.
-    The SS register identifies the stack segment.

(c)   Offset Registers:

Five offset registers which contain the offset within a segment, are used in conjunction with the segment registers to pinpoint an address in memory.

The Instruction Pointer (IP), also called the program counter contains the offset within the code segment where the current program is executing. It is used with CS segment register to track the location of the next instruction to be executed.

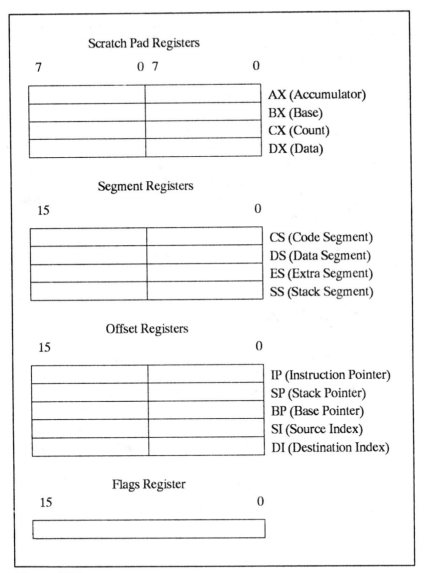

Figure 17.2

The stack registers, called the stack pointer (SP) and the base pointer (BP) provide the offset within the stack segment.

The index registers, called source index (SI) and destination index (DI) are for general purpose addressing of data (usually data strings).

(d)   Flags Register:

The flags register is used to indicate whether a particular process or operation was successfully carried out or not. For example, while formatting a disk, whether the formatting of each individual track was successful or not is reported through the flags register. There are nine 1-bit flags in the 16-bit flags register, whereas 7 bits are unused.

Figure 17.2 shows the 14 CPU registers present in the 8086 family of microprocessors.

Interrupts and Interrupt Vector Table

An interrupt is a signal to the microprocessor that its immediate attention is needed. The moment the interrupt draws the microprocessor's attention, the microprocessor's normal work is interrupted and hence the name, interrupt. In other words, an interrupt is the signal which when generated asks the microprocessor to stop whatever it is doing at that moment (when the signal is issued) and execute some other task.

The signal may be generated through either software or hardware. For example, the **int86( )** function in C generates a software interrupt, whereas, on hitting a key from the keyboard, a hardware interrupt is generated.

Every interrupt (be it a software or a hardware interrupt) has got a specific number. For example, on hitting a key from the keyboard, interrupt number 9 is generated, whereas when the timer of the computer ticks, interrupt number 8 is generated. The 8086 family supports totally 256 interrupts, numbered from 0 o 255.

When a hardware or a software interrupt occurs, the microprocessor stops its current processing activity, and executes a small memory resident routine called Interrupt Service Routine (ISR). Each interrupt has got its corresponding ISR. Once the ISR has performed its task, the microprocessor resumes the task that was interrupted when the interrupt occurred.

The addresses of various ISR's are stored in low area of memory, in Interrupt Vector Table (IVT). Each address is four bytes long and is in the form segment:offset. Thus, the first four byte entry in the IVT is the address of the ISR which is to be executed if interrupt number 0 occurs. Similarly, the second four byte entry in the IVT is the address of the ISR which is to be executed if interrupt number 1 occurs, an so on.

Thus, when an interrupt occurs the microprocessor performs the following steps:

- It first finds out what is the number of the generated interrupt.

- Having found out the interrupt number, it multiplies this number by four (since each address is IVT is 4 bytes long), then goes to the Interrupt Vector Table (IVT) and finds out the address of the corresponding ISR.

- The moment the address of the ISR to be executed is found, the contents of the various registers of the microprocessor are saved onto a stack (this process is called pushing register values onto the stack)

- The registers are setup with appropriate values necessary for execution of ISR, and then the ISR is executed.

- Once the ISR has been executed, the values which were earlier pushed onto the stack, are now popped off from the stack back into the CPU registers, and the micrprocessor resumes its interrupted activity.

Let us examine the above activities with some real life situation, like say hitting a key from the keyboard.

- When a key is hit from the keyboard, interrupt number 9 occurs.

- Nine is multiplied by four, resulting into 36. The microprocessor now goes to location numbers 36, 37, 38, 39 in IVT and picks up the address of the corresponding ISR.

- On obtaining the address of the ISR, it saves the existing register values on the stack.

- Registers are set up with new values required by the ISR, and control is passed to the ISR, which then gets executed.

- Once the ISR is executed, the old register values are popped back into the registers from the stack, and the interrupted task is resumed.

Note that we can replace an existing ISR with a new one, by storing the address of our ISR at an appropriate place in the IVT. In fact, this is what a computer virus does.

Invoking ROM-BIOS Functions

Armed with the knowledge of registers, interrupts and IVT let us now proceed with invoking of the ROM-BIOS functions. We would be required to perform the following steps to call a ROM-BIOS function:

(a)   Make an interrupt to occur.
(b)   Find out the number of the interrupt that has occurred.
(c)   Obtain from IVT the address of the ISR which services this interrupt.
(d)   Push the curent values of CPU registers onto the stack.
(e)   Place new values in CPU registers as required by the ROM-BIOS function being called.
(f)   Execute the ROM-BIOS function.

(g)   Pop the values from the stack back into the CPU registers.

(h)   Resume the interrupted task.

Out of the above, except for steps (a) and (e) all other steps are performed by the microprocessor itself. So our task is to just place the values needed by the ROM-BIOS routine into the registers and make a software interrupt to occur. As seen earlier the software interrupt can be caused by using the standard library function **int86( )**, which also manages to place values in CPU registers, as required by the ROM-BIOS function.

The ROM-BIOS functions have been written in such a manner that, some functions expect values to be placed in registers AX, BX, CX etc., whereas some functions expect a different value in high byte (AH) of AX register, and a different value in low byte (AL) of AX register, and so on. As yet we do not know how to place different values in high and low bytes of a two byte variable. This can be achieved by making use of a derived data type called 'union'. This in fact is the topic of the next section.

Unions

Unions are derived data types, the way structures are. But Unions have the same relationship to structures that you might have with a distant cousin who resembled you but turned out to be smuggling contraband in mexico. That is, unions and structures look alike, but are engaged in totally different enterprises.

Both structures and unions are used to group a number of different variables together. But while a structure enables us to to treat a number of different variables stored at different places in memory, a union enables us to treat the same space in memory as a number of different variables. That is, a union offers a way for a section of memory to be treated as a variable of one type on one occasion, and as a different variable of a different type on another occasion.

You might wonder why it would be necessary to do such a thing, but we will be seeing several very practical applications of unions soon. First, let us take a look at a simple example:

```
/* Demo of union at work */
main( )
{
    union a
    {
        int i ;
        char ch[2] ;
    } ;
    union a key ;

    key.i = 512 ;
    printf ( "\nkey.i = %d", key.i ) ;
    printf ( "\nkey.ch[0] = %d", key.ch[0] ) ;
    printf ( "\nkey.ch[1] = %d", key.ch[1] ) ;
}
```

And here is the output...

```
key.i = 512
key.ch[0] = 0
key.ch[1] = 2
```

As you can see, first we declared a data type of the type **union a**, and then a variable **key** to be of the type **union a**. This is similar to the way we declare first the structure type and then the structure variables. Also, the union elements are accessed exactly the same way in which the structure elements are accessed, using a '.' operator. However, the similarity ends here. To illustrate this let us compare the following data types:

```
struct a
{
    int i ;
```

```
        char ch[2] ;
    } ;
    struct a key ;
```

This data type would occupy 4 bytes in memory, 2 for **key.i** and one each for **key.ch[0]** and **key.ch[1]**, as shown below.

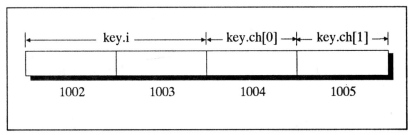

Figure 17.3

Now we declare a similar data type, but instead of using a structure we use a union.

```
    union a
    {
        int i ;
        char ch[2] ;
    } ;
    union a key ;
```

Representation of this data type in memory is shown below.

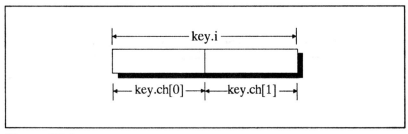

Figure 17.4

As shown in Figure 17.4, the union occupies only 2 bytes in memory. Note that the same memory locations which are used for **key.i** are also being used by **key.ch[0]** and **key.ch[1]**. It means that the memory locations used by **key.i** can also be accessed using **key.ch[0]** and **key.ch[1]**. What purpose does this serve? Well, now we can access the two bytes simultaneously (by using **key.i**) or the same two bytes individually (using **key.ch[0]** and **key.ch[1]**).

This is a frequent requirement while interacting with the hardware. i.e. sometimes we are required to access two bytes simultaneously and sometimes each byte individually. Faced with such a situation, using union is the answer, usually.

Perhaps you would be able to understand the union data type more thoroughly if we take a fresh look at the output of the above program. Here it is...

```
key.i = 512
key.ch[0] = 0
key.ch[1] = 2
```

Let us understand this output in detail. 512 is an integer, a 2 byte number. It's binary equivalent will be 0000 0010 0000 0000. We would expect that this binary number when stored in memory would look as shown below.

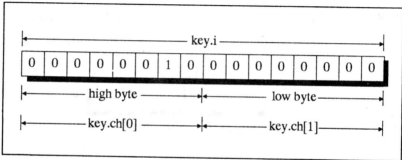

Figure 17.5

If the number is stored in this manner then, the output of key.ch[0] and key.ch[1] should have been 2 and 0. But, if you look at the output of the program written above, it is exactly the opposite. Why is it so? Because, when a two byte number is stored in memory, the low byte is stored before the high byte. It means, actually 512 would be stored in memory as shown in Figure 17.6.

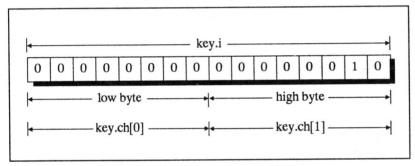

Figure 17.6

Now, we can see why value of **key.ch[0]** is printed as 0 and value of **key.ch[1]** is printed as 2.

One last thing. We can't assign different values to the different union elements at the same time. i.e. if we assign a value to **key.i**, it gets automatically assigned to **key.ch[0]** and **key.ch[1]**. Vice versa, if assign a value to **key.ch[0]** or **key.ch[1]**, it is bound to get assigned to **key.i**. Here is a program which illustrates this fact.

```
main( )
{
    union a
    {
        int i ;
        char ch[2] ;
    } ;
    union a key ;

    key.i = 512 ;
```

```
        printf ( "\nkey.i = %d", key.i ) ;
        printf ( "\nkey.ch[0] = %d", key.ch[0] ) ;
        printf ( "\nkey.ch[1] = %d", key.ch[1] ) ;

        key.ch[0] = 50 ;  /* assign a new value to key.ch[0] */
        printf ( "\nkey.i = %d", key.i ) ;
        printf ( "\nkey.ch[0] = %d", key.ch[0] ) ;
        printf ( "\nkey.ch[1] = %d", key.ch[1] ) ;
    }
```

And here is the output...

```
    key.i = 512
    key.ch[0] = 0
    key.ch[1] = 2
    key.i= 562
    key.ch[0] = 50
    key.ch[1] = 2
```

Before we move on to the next section, let us reiterate that a union provides a way to look at the same data in several different ways. For example, there can exist a union as shown below.

```
    union b
    {
        double d ;
        float f[2] ;
        int i[4] ;
        char ch[8] ;
    } ;
    union b data ;
```

In what different ways can the data be accessed from it? Sometimes as a complete set of eight bytes (**b.d**), sometimes as two sets of 4 bytes each (**b.f[0]** and **b.f[1]**), sometimes as four sets of 2 bytes each (**b.i[0]**, **b.i[1]**, **b.i[2]** and **b.[3]**) and sometimes as eight sets of 1 byte each (**b.ch[0]**, **b.ch[1]**... **b.ch[7]**).

Union of Structures

Just as one structure can be nested within another, a union too can be nested in another union. Not only that, there can be a union in a structure, or a structure in a union. Here is an example of stuctures nested in a union.

```
main( )
{
    struct a
    {
        int i ;
        char c[2] ;
    } ;
    struct b
    {
        int j ;
        char d[2] ;
    } ;
    union z
    {
        struct a key ;
        struct b data ;
    } ;
    union z strange ;

    strange.key.i = 512 ;
    strange.data.d[0] = 0 ;
    strange.data.d[1] = 32 ;

    printf ( "\n%d", strange.key.i ) ;
    printf ( "\n%d", strange.data.j ) ;
    printf ( "\n%d", strange.key.c[0] ) ;
    printf ( "\n%d", strange.data.d[0] ) ;
    printf ( "\n%d", strange.key.c[1] ) ;
    printf ( "\n%d", strange.data.d[1] ) ;
}
```

And here is the output...

```
512
512
0
0
32
32
```

Just as we do with nested structures, we access the elements of the union in this progam using the '.' operator twice. Thus,

strange.key.i

refers to the variable **i** in the structure **key** in the union **strange**. Analysis of the output of the above program is left to the reader.

The *int86( )* Function

The function used to make a software interrupt occur and thereby invoke a ROM-BIOS function is a standard library function called **int86( )**. The 'int' stands for 'interrupt' and the '86' refers to the 8086 family of microprocessors. This function needs three arguments:

- interrupt number corresponding to the ROM-BIOS function to be invoked.

- and two union variables

The first union variable represents values being sent to the ROM-BIOS routine, and the second represents the values being returned from the ROM-BIOS routines to the calling C program. The values are passed to and returned from ROM-BIOS routines through CPU registers.

Here is a sample call to the **int86( )** function...

```
int86 ( 16, &inregs, &outregs ) ;
```

where,

- 16 is the interrupt number

- **inregs** represents the register values being sent to ROM-BIOS function

- **outregs** represents the register values being returned by the ROM-BIOS function

Notice that the **int86( )** function requires the addresses of the unions, not the unions themselves (much in the same way **scanf( )** requires the addresses of variables).

Having obtained the knowledge of registers, interrupts, IVT and the steps involved in invoking the ROM-BIOS function, now we are finally ready to write a program that invokes a ROM-BIOS function.

Finding Memory Size

One of the functions in the ROM-BIOS returns the size of the memory (RAM) installed in the machine. This can be a useful utility if you don't happen to know how much memory the machine that you are using has. It can be even more useful to a program that uses large amounts of memory, runs on variety of computers that may have different memory sizes, and needs a way to find out just how much memory is available.

The arguments that should be passed to **int86( )** to invoke this ROM-BIOS function are mentioned below:

Interrupt number: 18
Input registers: none
Output registers : AX - Memory size in kilobytes

And here is the program...

```
/* Finding memory size using call to ROM-BIOS function */
main( )
{
    struct WORDREGS
    {
        unsigned int ax, bx, cx, dx, si, di, cflag, flags ;
    } ;
    struct BYTEREGS
    {
        unsigned char al, ah, bl, bh, cl, ch, dl, dh ;
    } ;

    union REGS
    {
        struct WORDREGS x ;
        struct BYTEREGS h ;
    } ;

    union REGS inregs, outregs ;
    int memsize ;

    int86 ( 18, &inregs, &outregs ) ;
    memsize = outregs.x.ax ;
    printf ( "\nTotal memory = %d", memsize ) ;
}
```

And here is the output...

```
Total memory = 640
```

On our reference computer (PC/XT) the memory size was 640 kb. On your computer the memory size may turn out to be different, say either 512 or 256 or any other standard figure. Let us now try to understand the program.

As you can see, the program uses two structures and a union. The first structure whose name is WORDREGS, consists of all the registers in their two byte interpretation. (In assembly language a two-byte data is called 'word', hence the name WORDREGS for 'word registers').

The WORDREGS structure contains variables **ax, bx, cx, dx, si, di, cflag** and **flags** which are look-alikes of actual CPU registers. All these variables are not needed for finding memory size, but might be needed for some other ROM-BIOS function and hence must always be passed to **int86( )**.

The second structure BYTEREGS, consist of AX, BX, CX and DX registers interpreted as eight one-byte variables.

These two structures are then combined to form a union called REGS. Thus, this union creates a set of variables that can be looked as either two-byte registers or one-byte registers. The variables **inregs** and **outregs** are defined to be of the type **union REGS**.

To access the registers we use the dot operator twice, as in,

```
outregs.x.ax
inregs.h.cl
```

These two forms would provide an access to ax and cl registers.

In our program, we don't need to send any values to the ROM-BIOS function, so nothing is placed in any of the registers before calling **int86( )**. ROM-BIOS function to find memory size is unusual in this respect; most other ROM-BIOS functions require appropriate values to be sent to them, as we will see.

On return from **int86( )**, the ROM-BIOS function places the memory size in the AX register, which we collect through the statement,

```
memsize = outregs.x.ax
```

Ultimately we print out the memory size.

Using the Declarations in *dos.h*

Actually the structures WORDREGS and BYTEREGS and the union REGS are already declared in a file called 'dos.h'. Thus, if we include this file in our program, we can dispense with the explicit declarations, as the following program shows:

```
/* Finding memory size using call to ROM-BIOS function */
#include "dos.h"
main( )
{
    union REGS inregs, outregs ;
    int memsize ;

    int86 ( 18, &inregs, &outregs ) ;
    memsize = outregs.x.ax ;
    printf ( "\nTotal memory = %d", memsize ) ;
}
```

This is certainly a more handy format, although it does not reveal as much about what is going on.

Positioning Cursor on the Screen

Let's look at an example that requires us to send values to the ROM-BIOS function. This program will call a ROM-BIOS function that positions the cursor in a desired row and column. The arguments that should be passed to **int86( )** to invoke this ROM-BIOS function are mentioned below:

Interrupt number: 16
Input registers:
    AH - 2, the service number
    DH - row number

DL - column number
Output registers: none

Note that there are number of services available under interrupt number 16, like positioning the cursor on the screen, changing the size of the cursor, writing a character on the screen, drawing a dot on the screen etc. A service number has been associated with each of these services. The service to position the cursor on screen has a number 2. The service number is always placed in the AH register.

```
/* Position cursor at appropriate posiion on screen */
#include "dos.h"
main( )
{
     union REGS inregs, outregs ;

     inregs.h.ah = 2 ;  /* service number */
     inregs.h.dh = 10 ;  /* row number    */
     inregs.h.dl = 2 ;  /* column number */
     int86 ( 16, &inregs, &outregs ) ;
     printf ( "Hello there!" ) ;
}
```

What does the **int86( )** function actually do? It makes the software interrupt to occur. Before calling **int86( )** we set the elements of the union REGS to the values desired by the ROM-BIOS function which gets called through **int86( )**. The **int86( )** function loads the actual CPU registers from the elements of the **union REGS**, before generating the software interrupt necessary to access the desired ROM-BIOS function. Upon return from the ROM-BIOS function, **int86( )** copies the latest register values into **outregs** variable (of type **union REGS**) whose address we pass to the **int86( )** function.

Interrupts to Access ROM-BIOS Services

So far we have used only two ROM-BIOS services. There are dozens of them more. These services are grouped together according to their similarities, under one interrupt. For example, a number of ROM-BIOS functions which allow interaction with the VDU are grouped together under the interrupt 16, all keyboard services under interrupt 22 and so on. Figure 17.7 shows these groups. A more detailed description of ROM-BIOS services under each interrupt is given in Appendix G.

Interrupt number		Purpose
Decimal	Hexadecimal	
Peripheral Device Services		
16	10	Video display services
19	13	Diskette services
20	14	Communications services
21	15	Cassette tape services
22	16	Keyboard services
23	17	Printer services
Equipmemt Status Services		
17	11	Equipment list service
18	12	Memory size service
Time/Date Services		
26	1A	Time and date services
Special Services		
5	5	Print screen service
24	18	Activate ROM BASIC
25	19	Activate bootstrap loader routine

Figure 17.7

DOS Function Requests

Most of the DOS services are grouped under interrupt number 33 (0x21). Appendix H lists the most frequently used DOS services. These services can be invoked using standard library functions **intdos( )** and **intdosx( )**, which are the DOS counterparts of the functions **int86( )** and **int86x( )**. The **int86x( )** and **intdosx( )** functions are used to invoke ROM- BIOS and DOS services respectively, if the service requires the use of DS and ES registers. If not, then the functions **int86( )** and **intdos( )** are used.

Summary

In this chapter we have explored how the hardware can be accessed through C, alongwith merits and demerits of different approaches involved. Through two examples we have explained how **int86( )** function can be used to call ROM-BIOS functions. We also learnt a new data type 'union' which offers way to look at same memory locations in different ways. We also saw how this data type could be used to simulate CPU registers.

For paucity of space we cannot discuss each and every ROM-BIOS and DOS functions available. They are far too many in number and variety. However, we have given a list of ROM-BIOS/DOS functions in Appendix G and H alongwith the input and output requirements of these functions. It would be interesting for you to explore them on your own. Also the exercise given at the end of this chapter when solved would certainly add clarity to your thought and concept.

Exercise

[A]   Pick up the correct alternative for each of the following:

(a)   To interact with the hardware which of the following is a
       reasonably reliable as well as a reasonably fast procedure
       (1) Using high level language functions
       (2) Using ROM-BIOS functions
       (3) Directly programming the hardware
       (4) None fo the above

(b)   Each address present in Interrupt Vector Table is
       (1) 4 bytes long
       (2) 2 bytes long
       (3) 1 bytes long
       (4) 8 bytes long

(c)   Pick the odd one out
       (1) Scratch-pad register
       (2) Segment registers
       (3) Flags register
       (4) Interrupt registers

(d)   Whether a particular operation is successfully carried out by
       DOS or not is indicated by the value stored in
       (1) Flags register
       (2) Ordinary variables
       (3) Segment register
       (4) Offset register

(e)   In a 8088 microprocessor each CPU register is
       (1) 12 bits long
       (2) 16 bits long
       (3) 8 bits long
       (4) 8 bytes long

(f)   The process of storing the contents of CPU register into the
       memory when an interrupt occurs, is called
       (1) Pushing values on the stack
       (2) Popping values off the stack
       (3) Setting up a stack pointer

(4) Setting up an instruction pointer

(g)   A ROM-BIOS routine makes use of the segment registers ES
      and DS. To call this routine which function would you use
      (1) int86( )
      (2) int86x( )
      (3) intdos( )
      (4) intdosx( )

(h)   While calling a ROM-BIOS/DOS routine, the service number
      should always be placed in
      (1) AH register
      (2) AL register
      (3) AX register
      (4) None of the above

[B]   What will be the output of the following programs:

(a)   main( )
      {
          union
          {
              int i[2] ;
              long l ;
          } u ;

          u.i[0] = 0x50 ;
          u.i[1] = 0x45 ;
          printf ("\n%lu", u.l) ;
      }

(b)   main( )
      {
          union a
          {
              int i1 ;
              int i2 ;

```
            char s[4] ;
      } ;
      union a m ;
      strcpy ( a.s, "AAA" ) ;
      printf ( "\n%s", a.s ) ;
      printf ( "\n%u %u", a.i1, a.i2 ) ;
}
```

[C] State whether the following statements are True or False:

(a) If ROM-BIOS functions are used in a program, they would increase the size of the executable file, the way standard library functions do.

(b) ROM-BIOS and DOS functions do not have names.

(c) The routine which gets executed when an interrupt occurs is called an Interrupt Service Routine.

(d) An interrupt can occur through hardware as well as software.

(e) All ROM-BIOS services return a value indicating success or failure in AX register.

(f) A union variable occupies as much data as what a corresponding structure variable would occupy, elements of both remaining same.

(g) Union provides us a way to look at the same memory locations in more than one way, which a structure cannot.

[D] Attempt the following:

NOTE: For most of the problems given below you would be required to invoke ROM-BIOS routines. The interrupt number, service number and other requirements of these routines are given in Appendix G and H.

(a)   Write a general purpose function **goto_rc( )** to place the cursor at any given position on the screen. Test this by displaying the message "Rat a tat tat" at 10th row, 20th column on the screen.

(b)   Write a general porpose function **size( )** which when called would change the size of the cursor in text mode. The function should be intelligent enough to hide the cursor when called upon to do so.

(c)   Write a program which would pick up all digits currently present on screen and replace them with smiling face.

(d)   Write a function **cls( )** which would wipe the contents of the screen and place the cursor on top left corner of the screen when called.

(e)   Implement the following procedure in a program:

Fill the entire screen with an alphabet 'A', then create a blank window of 16 rows by 30 columns on the screen. In this window display first 16 ascii values and their corresponding characters. As soon as the window is full, wipe out the window and fill it with the next 16 characters. Continue the process till you have displayed the entire ascii table.

(f)   While developing a package it is often required to display different messages with different attributes. Write a program to display the message "Tutu" in all possible attributes. Along-side each message, mention the attribute value which has been used to display the message.

(g)   Write a program to draw a line from coordinates (10, 10) to (150, 150). What is the limitation of your program?

(h)   Write a function **freehand( )** which when called allows you to draw freehand drawing. **freehand( )** must allow drawing interactively. Four arrow keys should allow drawing in four direction, whereas PgUp, Pgdn, Home and End keys should allow drawing diagonally.

(i)   Display a menu on the screen containing 4 items. Highlight the first item of the menu, and as the Up and Down arrow keys are hit the highlighted bar should move from one menu item to another. User must be able to select a menu item by hitting the enter key, when the highlighted bar is placed on that item.

18 *Operations On Bits*

o far we have dealt with characters, integers, floats and their
variations. The smallest element in memory on which we are
able to operate as yet is a byte; and we operated on it by making
use of the data type **char**. However, we haven't attempted to look
within these data types to see how they are constructed out of
individual bits, and how these bits can be manipulated. Being able to
operate on a bit level, can be very important in programming,
especially when a program must interact directly with the hardware.
This is because, the programming languages are byte oriented,
whereas hardware tends to be bit oriented. Let us now delve inside
the byte and see how it is contructed and how it can be manipulated
effectively. So let us take apart the byte... bit by bit.

Bitwise Operators

One of C's powerful features is a set of bit manipulation operators.
These permit the programmer to access and manipulate individual
bits within a piece of data. The various Bitwise Operators available
in C are shown in Figure 18.1.

Operator	Meaning
~	one's complement
>>	right shift
<<	left shift
&	Bitwise AND
|	Bitwise OR
^	Bitwise XOR (Exclusive OR)

Figure 18.1

These operators can operate upon **ints** and **chars** but not on **floats**
and **doubles**. Before moving on to the details of the operators, let us

first take a look at the bit numbering scheme in integers and characters. Bits are numbered from zero onwards, increasing from right to left as shown below:

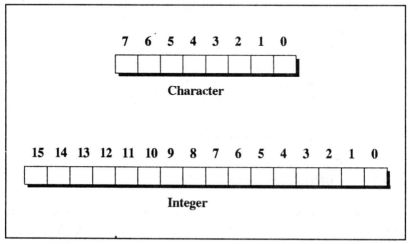

Figure 18.2

Throughout this discussion of bitwise operators we are going to use a function called **showbits( )**, but we are not going to show you the details of the function immediately. The task of **showbits( )** is to display the binary representation of any integer or character value.

We begin with a plain-jane example with **showbits( )** in action.

```
/* Print binary equivalent of integers using showbits( ) function */
main( )
{
    int j ;

    for ( j = 0 ; j <= 5 ; j++ )
    {
        printf ( "\nDecimal %d is same as binary ", j ) ;
        showbits ( j ) ;
    }
```

```
        }
```

And here is the output...

```
        Decimal 0 is same as binary 0000000000000000
        Decimal 1 is same as binary 0000000000000001
        Decimal 2 is same as binary 0000000000000010
        Decimal 3 is same as binary 0000000000000011
        Decimal 4 is same as binary 0000000000000100
        Decimal 5 is same as binary 0000000000000101
```

Let us now explore the various bitwise operators one by one.

One's Complement Operator

On taking one's complement of a number, all 1's present in the number are changed to 0's and all 0's are changed to 1's. For example one's complement of 1010 is 0101. Similarly one's complement of 1111 is 0000. Note that here when we talk of a number we are talking of binary equivalent of the number. Thus, one's complement of 65 means one's complement of 0000 0000 0100 0001, which is binary equivalent of 65. One's complement of 65 therefore would be, 1111 1111 1011 1110. One's complement operator is represented by the symbol ~. Following program shows one's complement operator in action.

```
        main( )
        {
            int j, k ;

            for ( j = 0 ; j <= 3 ; j++ )
            {
                printf ( "\nDecimal %d is same as binary ", j ) ;
                showbits ( j ) ;

                k = ~j ;
```

```
            printf ( "\nOne's complement of %d is ", j ) ;
            showbits ( k ) ;
        }
    }
```

And here is the output of the above program...

```
Decimal 0 is same as binary 0000000000000000
One's complement of 0 is 1111111111111111
Decimal 1 is same as binary 0000000000000001
One's complement of 1 is 1111111111111110
Decimal 2 is same as binary 0000000000000010
One's complement of 2 is 1111111111111101
Decimal 3 is same as binary 0000000000000011
One's complement of 3 is 1111111111111100
```

In real-world situations where could the one's complement operator be useful? Since it changes the original number beyond recognition, one potential place where it can be effectively used is in developement of a file encryption utility as shown below:

```
/* File encryption utility */
#include "stdio.h"
main( )
{
    encrypt( ) ;
}

encrypt( )
{
    FILE *fs, *ft ;
    char ch ;

    fs = fopen ( "SOURCE.C", "r" ) ; /* normal file */
    ft = fopen ( "TARGET.c", "w" ) ; /* encrypted file */

    if ( fs == NULL || ft == NULL )
```

```
    {
        printf ( "\nFile opening error!" ) ;
        exit ( 1 ) ;
    }

    while ( ( ch = getc ( fs ) ) != EOF )
        putc ( ~ch, ft ) ;

    fclose ( fs ) ;
    fclose ( ft ) ;
}
```

How would you write the corresponding decrypt function? Would there be any problem in tackling the end of file marker? It may be recalled here that the end of file is text files is indicated by a character whose ascii value is 26.

Right Shift Operator

Like one's complement operator 'right shift operator' too operates on a single variable. It is represented by >> and it shifts each bit in the operand to the right. The number of places the bits are shifted depends on the number following the operand.

Thus, **ch >> 3** would shift all bits in **ch** three places to the right. Similarly, **ch >> 5** would shift all bits 5 places to the right.

For example, if the variable **ch** contains the bit pattern 11010111, then, **ch >> 1** would give 01101011 and **ch >> 2** would give 00110101.

Note that as the bits are shifted to the right, blanks are created on the left. These blanks must be filled somehow. They are always filled with zeros. The following program demonstrates the effect of right shift operator.

```
main( )
{
    int i = 5225, j, k ;

    printf ( "\nDecimal %d is same as binary ", i ) ;
    showbits ( i ) ;

    for ( j = 0 ; j <= 5 ; j++ )
    {
        k = i >> j ;
        printf ( "\n%d right shift %d gives ", i, j ) ;
        showbits ( k ) ;
    }
}
```

The output of the above program would be...

```
Decimal 5225 is same as binary 0001010001101001
5225 right shift 0 gives 0001010001101001
5225 right shift 1 gives 0000101000110100
5225 right shift 2 gives 0000010100011010
5225 right shift 3 gives 0000001010001101
5225 right shift 4 gives 0000000101000110
5225 right shift 5 gives 0000000010100011
```

Note that if the operand is a multiple of 2 then shifting the operand one bit to right is same as dividing it by 2. Thus,

```
64 >> 1 gives 32
64 >> 2 gives 16
128 >> 2 gives 32
```

but,

```
27 >> 1 is 13
49 >> 1 is 24 .
```

Left Shift Operator

This is similar to the right shift operator, the only difference being that the bits are shifted to the left, and for each bit shifted, a 0 is added to the right of the number. The following program should clarify my point.

```
main( )
{
    int i = 5225, j, k ;

    printf ( "\nDecimal %d is same as ", i ) ;
    showbits ( i ) ;

    for ( j = 0 ; j <= 4 ; j++ )
    {
        k = i << j ;
        printf ( "\n%d left shift %d gives ", i, j ) ;
        showbits ( k ) ;
    }
}
```

The output of the above program would be...

```
Decimal 5225 is same as binary 0001010001101001
5225 left shift 0 gives 0001010001101001
5225 left shift 1 gives 0010100011010010
5225 left shift 2 gives 0101000110100100
5225 left shift 3 gives 1010001101001000
5225 left shift 4 gives 0100011010010000
```

Having acquainted ourselves with the left shift and right shift operators, let us now find out the practical utility of these operators.

As we learnt in Chapter 14 on 'Disk Basics' the date on which a file is created (or modified) is stored as a 2-byte entry in the 32 byte directory entry of that file. Similarly, a 2-byte entry is made of the time of creation or modification of the file. Remember that DOS doesn't store the date (day, month, and year) of file creation as a 8 byte string, but as a codified 2 byte entry, thereby saving 6 bytes for each file entry in the directory. The bitwise distribution of year, month and date in the 2-byte entry is shown in Figure 18.3.

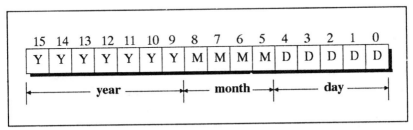

Figure 18.3

DOS converts the actual date into a 2 byte value using the following formula:

date = 512 * (year - 80) + 32 * month + day

Suppose 09/03/90 is the date, then on conversion the date will be,

date = 512 * (90 - 80) + 32 * 3 + 9 = 5225

The binary equivalent of 5225 is 0001 0100 0110 1001. This binary value is placed in the date field in the directory entry of the file as shown below.

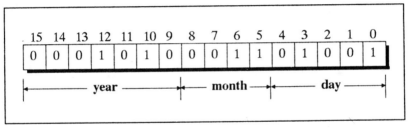

Figure 18.4

Just to verify this bit distribution, let us take the bits representing the month,

```
month = 0011
      = 1 * 2 + 1 * 1
      = 3
```

Similarly, the year and the day can also be verified.

When we issue the command DIR, the file's date is again presented on the screen in the usual date format of mm/dd/yy. How does this integer to date conversion takes place? Obviously, using left shift and right shift operators.

When we take a look at Figure 18.4 depicting the bit pattern of the 2- byte date field, we see that the year, month and day exist as a bunch of bits in contiguous locations. Separating each of them is a matter of applying the bitwise operators.

For example, to get year as a separate entity from the two byte entry we right shift the entry by 9 to get the year. Just see, how...

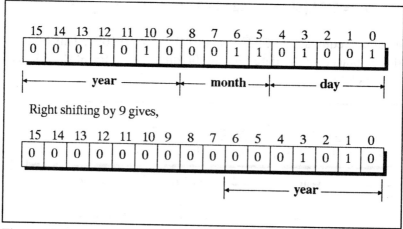

Figure 18.5

On similar lines, left shifting by 7, followed by right shifting by 12 yields month.

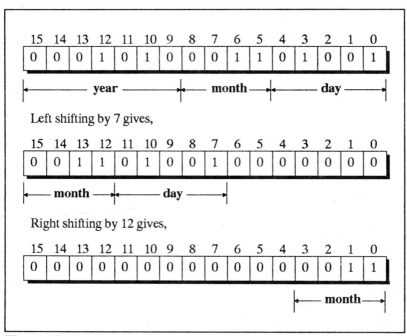

Figure 18.6

Finally, for obtaining the day, left shift by 11 and then right shift by 11. Left shifting by 11 gives 0100100000000000. Right shifting by 11 gives 0000000000001001.

This entire logic can be put into a program as shown below:

```
/* Decoding date field in directory
entry using bitwise operators */
main( )
{
        unsigned int d = 9, m = 3, y = 1990, year, month, day, date ;

        date = ( y - 1980 ) * 512 + m * 32 + d ;
```

```
        printf ( "\nDate = %u", date ) ;

        year = 1980 + ( date > 9 ) ;
        month = ( (date < 7 ) > 12 ) ;
        day = ( (date < 11 ) > 11 ) ;
        printf ( "\nYear = %u ", year ) ;
        printf ( "Month = %u ", month ) ;
        printf ( "Day = %u", day ) ;
}
```

And here is the output...

```
Date = 5225
Year = 1990  Month = 3  Day = 9
```

Bitwise AND Operator

This operator is represented as **&**. Remember it is different than the **&&**, the logical AND operator. The **&** operator operates on two operands. While operating upon these two operands they are compared on a bit-by-bit basis. Hence both the operands must be of the same type (either **char** or **int**). The second operand is often called an AND mask. The **&** operator operates on a pair of bits to yield a resultant bit. The rules that decide the value of the resultant bit are shown below:

first bit	second bit	first bit & second bit
0	0	0
0	1	0
1	0	0
1	1	1

Figure 18.7

This can be represented in a more understandable form as a 'Truth Table' as shown below.

&	0	1
0	0	0
1	0	1

Figure 18.8

The example given below shows more clearly what happens while ANDing one operand with another. The rules given in the above applied are applied to each pair of bits one by one.

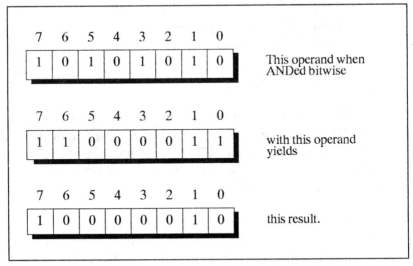

Figure 18.9

Work through the Truth Table and confirm that the result obtained is really correct.

Thus, it must be clear that the operation is being performed on individual bits, and the operation performed on one pair of bits is completely independent of the operation performed on the other pairs.

Probably, the best use of the AND operator is to check whether a particular bit of an operand is ON or OFF. This is explained in the following example.

Suppose, from the bit pattern 10101101 of an operand, we want to check whether bit number 3 is ON (1) or OFF (0). Since we want to check the bit number 3, the second operand for the AND operation we choose is, $1 * 2^3$, which is equal to 8. This operand can be represented bitwise as 00001000.

Then the ANDing operation would be,

```
10101101      original bit pattern
00001000      AND mask
--------------
00001000      resulting bit pattern
```

The resulting value we get in this case is 8, i.e the value of the second operand. The result turned out to be 8 since the third bit of the first operand was ON. Had it been OFF, the bit number 3 in the resulting bit pattern would have evaluated to 0 and the complete bit pattern would have been 00000000.

Thus, depending upon the bit number to be checked in the first operand we decide the second operand, and on ANDing these two operands the result decides whether the bit was ON or OFF. If the bit is ON (1), the resulting value turns out to be a non-zero value which is equal to the value of second operand, and if the bit is OFF (0) the result is zero as seen above. The following program puts this logic into action.

```
/* To test whether a bit in a number is ON or OFF */
main( )
{
    int i = 65, j ;

    printf ( "\nvalue of i = %d", i ) ;
    j = i & 32 ;

    if ( j == 0 )
        printf ( "\nand its fifth bit is off" ) ;
    else
        printf ( "\nand its fifth bit is on" ) ;

    j = i & 64 ;

    if ( j == 0 )
        printf ( "\nwhereas its sixth bit is off" ) ;
    else
        printf ( "\nwhereas its sixth bit is on" ) ;
}
```

And here is the output...

```
Value of i = 65
and its fifth bit is off
whereas its sixth bit is on
```

In every 32-byte file entry present in the directory, there is an attribute byte. The status of a file is governed by the value of individual bits in this attribute byte. The AND operator can be used to check the status of the bits of this attribute byte. The meaning of each bit in the attribute byte is shown in Figure 18.10.

Bit numbers								Meaning
7	6	5	4	3	2	1	0	
.	.	.	.	.	.	.	1	Read only
.	.	.	.	.	.	1	.	Hidden
.	.	.	.	.	1	.	.	System
.	.	.	.	1	.	.	.	Volume label entry
.	.	.	1	.	.	.	.	Sub-directory entry
.	.	1	.	.	.	.	.	Archive bit
.	1	.	.	.	.	.	.	Unused
1	.	.	.	.	.	.	.	Unused

Figure 18.10

Now, suppose we want to check whether a file is a hidden file or not. A hidden file is one which is never shown in the directory, even though it exists on the disk. From the above bit classification of attribute byte, we only need to check whether bit number 1 is ON or OFF.

So, our first operand in this case becomes the attribute byte of the file in question, whereas the second operand is the $1 * 2^1 = 2$, as discussed earlier. Similarly, it can be checked whether the file is a system file or not, whether the file is read-only file or not, and so on.

The second, and equally important use of the AND operator is in changing the status of the bit, or more precisely to switch OFF a particular bit.

If the first operand happens to be 00000111, then to switch OFF bit number 1, our AND mask bit pattern should be 11111101. On applying this mask, we get,

```
00000111    original bit pattern
11111101    AND mask
------------
00000101    resulting bit pattern
```

Here in the AND mask we keep the value of all other bits as 1 except the one which is to be switched OFF (which is purposefully kept as 0). Therefore, irrespective of whether the first bit is ON or OFF previously, it is switched OFF. At the same time the value 1 provided in all the other bits of the AND mask (second operand) keeps the bit values of the other bits in the first operand unaltered.

Let's summarise the uses of bitwise AND operator:

(a)   It is used to check whether a particular bit in a number is ON or OFF.
(b)   It is used to turn OFF a particular bit in a number.

Bitwise OR operator

Another important Bitwise operator is the OR operator which is represented as |. The rules that govern the value of the resulting bit obtained after ORing of two bits is shown in the following truth table.

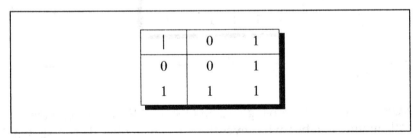

|	0	1
0	0	1
1	1	1

Figure 18.11

Using the Truth table confirm the result obtained on ORing the two operands as shown below.

```
11010000    original bit pattern
00000111    OR mask
------------
11010111    resulting bit pattern
```

Bitwise OR operator is usually used to put ON a particular bit in a number.

Let us consider the bit pattern 11000011. If we want to put ON bit number 3, then the OR mask to be used would be 00001000. Note that all the other bits in the mask are set to 0 and only the bit which we want to set ON in the resulting value is set to 1.

Bitwise XOR operator

The XOR operator is represented as ^ and is also called an Exclusive OR Operator. The OR operator returns 1, when any one of the two bits or both the bits are 1, whereas XOR returns 1 only if one of the two bits is 1. The truth table for the XOR operator is given below.

^	0	1
0	0	1
1	1	0

Figure 18.12

XOR operator is used to toggle a bit ON or OFF. A number XORed with another number twice gives the original number. This is shown in the following program.

```
main( )
{
    int b = 50 ;
```

```
        b = b ^ 12 ;
        printf ( "\n%d", b ) ; /* this will print 62 */

        b = b ^ 12 ;
        printf ( "\n%d", b ) ; /* this will print 50 */
}
```

The *showbits( )* Function

We have used this function quite often in this chapter. Now we have
sufficient knowledge of bitwise operators and hence are in a position
to understand it. The function is given below followed by a brief
explanation.

```
showbits ( int n )
{
    int i, k, andmask ;

    for ( i = 15 ; i >= 0 ; i-- )
    {
        andmask = 1 < i ;
        k = n & andmask ;

        k == 0 ? printf ( "0" ) : printf ( "1" ) ;
    }
}
```

All that is being done in this function is using an AND operator and
a variable **andmask** we are checking the status of individual bits. If
the bit is OFF we print a 0 otherwise we print a 1.

First time through the loop, the variable **andmask** will contain the
value 1000000000000000, which is obtained by left-shifting 1, fifteen places. If the variable **n**'s most significant bit is 0, then **k** would

contain a value 0, otherwise it would contain a non-zero value. If **k** contains 0 then **printf( )** will print out 0 otherwise it will print out 1.

On the second go-around of the loop, the value of **i** is decremented and hence the value of **andmask** changes, which will now be 0100000000000000. This checks whether the next most significant bit is 1 or 0, and prints it out accordingly. The same operation is repeated for all bits in the number.

Summary

To help manipulate hardware oriented data, individual bits rather than bytes, we learnt C's powerful set of bitwise operators. We covered operators like one's complement, right-shift, left-shift, bitwise AND, OR, and XOR, along with their utility in real-world programming.

Exercise

[A]   Answer the following:

(a)   Using DOS service number 67 (refer Appendix H for details of this service) write a program to hide a given file from a given directory.

(b)   Using DOS service number 67 write a program to display the current attributes of any file in a given directory.

(c)   The list of equipment attached to your computer is stored in BIOS Data Area as a two-byte sequence. Using ROM-BIOS interrupt number 17 (refer Appendix H for the details of the service) write a program to display this equipment list on the screen. The bitwise distribution of the two-byte sequence is given below:

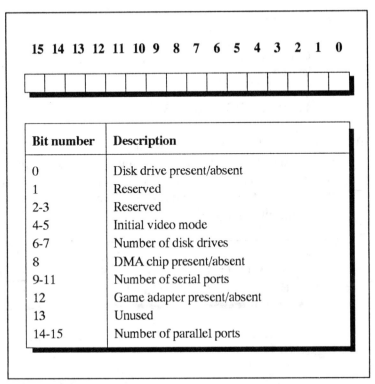

Figure 18.13

(d) An animal could be either a canine (dog, wolf, fox etc.), a feline (cat, hynx, jaguar etc.), a catacean (whale, narwhal etc.) or a marsupial (koala, wombat etc.). The information whether a particular animal is canine, feline, catacean, or marsupial is stored in bit number 0, 1, 2 and 3 respectively of a integer variable called **type**. Bit number 4 of the variable **type** stores the information about whether the animal is Carnivore or Herbivore.

For the following animal, complete the program to determine whether the animal is a herbivore or a carnivore. Also determine whether the animal is a canine, feline, catacean or a marsupial.

```
struct animal
{
    char name[30] ;
    int type ;
}
struct animal a = { "OCELOT", 18 } ;
```

(e)   The time field in the directory entry is 2 bytes long. Distribution of different bits which account for hours, minutes and seconds is given below. Write a function which would receive the two-byte time entry and return to the calling function, the hours, minutes and seconds.

15	14	13	12	11	10	9	8	7	6	5	4	3	2	1	0
H	H	H	H	H	M	M	M	M	M	M	S	S	S	S	S

Figure 18.14

(f)   Using the bit distribution of bytes 0x417 and 0x418 in BIOS Data Area, write a program to display the current status of various shift and toggle keys. Refer Chapter 16, Figure 16.1 for bitdistribution of 0x417 and 0x418.

(g)   What will be the output of the following program:

```
main( )
{
    int i = 32, j = 65, k, l, m, n, o, p ;
    k = i | 35 ;  l = ~k ;  m = i & j ;
    n = j ^ 32 ;  o = j < 2 ;  p = i > 5 ;
    printf ( "\nk = %d l = %d m = %d", k, l, m ) ;
    printf ( "\nn = %d o = %d p = %d", n, o, p ) ;
}
```

19 *The Leftovers*

T he topics discussed in this chapter were either too large or far too removed from the mainstream C programming for inclusion in the earlier chapters. These topics provide certain useful programming features, and could prove to be of immense help in certain programming strategies. In this chapter we would examine enumerated data types, the typedef keyword, type-casting, bit fields and pointers to functions.

Enumerated Data Type

The enumerated data type gives you an opportunity to invent your own data type and define what values the variable of this data type can take. This can help in making the program listings more readable, which can be an advantage when a program gets complicated or when more than one programmer would be working on it. Using enumerated data type can also help you reduce programming errors.

As an example, one could invent a data type called **mar_status** which can have four possible values - single, married, divorced or widowed. Don't confuse these values with variable names; married for instance has the same relationship to the variable **mar_status** as the number 15 has with an integer variable.

The format of the **enum** definition is similar to that of a structure. Here's how the example stated above can be implemented:

```
enum mar_status
{
    single, married, divorced, widowed
};
enum mar_status person1, person2 ;
```

Like structures this declaration has two parts:

(a)   The first part declares the data type and specifies its possible values. These values are called 'enumerators'.

(b) The second part declares variables of this data type.

Now we can give values to these variables:

```
person1 = married ;
person2 = divorced ;
```

Remember we can't use values that aren't in the original declaration. Thus, the following expression would cause an error:

```
person1 = unknown ;
```

Internally, the compiler treats the enumerators as integers. Each value on the list of permissible values corresponds to an integer, starting with 0. Thus, in our example, single, is stored as 0, married is stored as 1, divorced as 2 and widowed as 3.

This way of assigning numbers can be overridden by the programmer by initialising the enumerators to different integer values as shown below.

```
enum mar_status
{
    single = 100, married = 200, divorced = 300, widowed = 400
} ;
enum mar_status person1, person2 ;
```

Uses of Enumerated Data Type

Enumerated variables are usually used to clarify the operation of a program. For example, if we need to use employee departments in a payroll program, it makes the listing easier to read if we use values like Assembly, Manufacturing, Accounts rather than the integer values 0, 1, 2, etc. The following program illustrates the point I am trying to make.

```
main( )
{
    enum emp_dept
    {
        assembly, manufacturing, accounts, stores
    } ;
    struct employee
    {
        char name[30] ;
        int age ;
        float bs ;
        enum emp_dept department ;
    } ;
    struct employee e ;

    strcpy ( e.name, "Lothar Mattheus" ) ;
    e.age = 28 ;
    e.bs = 5575.50 ;
    e.department = manufacturing ;

    printf ( "\nName = %s", e.name ) ;
    printf ( "\nAge = %d", e.age ) ;
    printf ( "\nBasic salary = %f", e.bs ) ;
    printf ( "\nDept = %d", e.department ) ;

    if ( e.department == accounts )
        printf ( "\n%s is an accounant", e.name ) ;
    else
        printf ( "\n%s is not an accounant", e.name ) ;
}
```

And here is the output of the program...

```
Name = Lothar Mattheus
Age = 28
Basic salary = 5575.50
Dept = 1
```

Lothar Mattheus is not an accountant

Let us now dissect the program. We first defined the data type **enum emp_dept** and specified the four possible values, namely, assembly, manufacturing, accounts and stores. Then we defined a variable **department** of the type **enum emp_dept** in a structure. The structure **employee** has three other elements containing employee information.

The program first assigns values to the variables in the structure. The statement,

     e.department = manufacturing ;

assigns the value manufacturing to **e.department** variable. This is much more informative to anyone reading the program than a statement like,

     e.department = 1 ;

The next part of the program shows an important weakness of using **enum** variables... there is no way to use the enumerated values directly in input/output functions like **printf( )** and **scanf( )**.

The **printf( )** function is not smart enough to perform the translation; the department is printed out as 1 and not manufacturing. Of course we can write a function to print the correct enumerated values, using a **switch** statement, but that would reduce the clarity of the program. Even with this limitation, however, there are many situations in which enumerated variables are god sent!

Renaming Data types with *typedef*

There is one more technique which in some situations can help to clarify the source code of a C program. This techinque is to make use of the **typedef** declaration. Its purpose is to redefine the name of an existing variable type.

For example, consider the following statement in which the type **unsigned long int** is redefined to be of the type **TWOWORDS**:

```
typedef unsigned long int TWOWORDS ;
```

Now we can declare variables of the type **unsigned long int** by writing,

```
TWOWORDS var1, var2 ;
```

instead of

```
unsigned long int var1, var2 ;
```

Thus, **typedef** provides a short and meaningful way to call a data type. Usually, uppercase letters are used to make it clear that we are dealing with a renamed data type.

While the increase in readability is probably not great in this example, it can be significant when the name of a particular data type is long and unwieldy, as it often is with structure declarations. For example, consider the following structure declaration:

```
struct employee
{
    char name[30] ;
    int age ;
    float bs ;
} ;
struct employee e ;
```

This structure declaration can be made more handy to use when renamed using **typedef** as shown below:

```
struct employee
{
    char name[30] ;
```

```
        int age ;
        float bs ;
} ;
typedef struct employee EMP ;
EMP e1, e2 ;
```

Thus, by reducing the length and apparent complexity of data types, **typedef** can help to clarify source listing and save time and energy spent in understanding a program.

Type Casting

Sometimes we are needed to force the compiler to explicitly convert the value of an expression to a particular data type. This would be clear from the following example:

```
main( )
{
    float a ;
    int x = 6, y = 4 ;

    a = x / y ;
    printf ( "\nValue of a = %f", a ) ;
}
```

And here is the output...

```
Value of a = 1.000000
```

The answer turns out to be 1.000000 and not 1.5. This is because, 6 and 4 are both integers and hence **6 / 4** yields an integer, 1. This 1 when stored in **a** is converted to 1.000000 . But what if we don't want the quotient to be truncated. One solution is to make either **x** or **y** as **float**. Let us say that other requirements of the program does not permit us to do this. In such a case what do we do? Use type casting. The following program illustrates this.

```
main( )
{
    float a ;
    int x = 6, y = 4 ;

    a = ( float ) x / y ;
    printf ( "\nValue of a = %f", a ) ;
}
```

And here is the output...

```
Value of a = 1.500000
```

This program uses type casting. This consists of putting a pair of parentheses around the name of the data type. In this program we said,

```
a = ( float ) x / y ;
```

The expression (**float**) causes the variable **x** to be converted from type **int** to type **float** before being used in the division operation.

Here is another example of type casting:

```
main( )
{
    float a = 6.35 ;

    printf ( "\nValue of a on type casting = %d", ( int ) a ) ;
    printf ( "\nValue of a = %f", a ) ;
}
```

And here is the output...

```
Value of a on type casting = 6
Value of a = 6.350000
```

Note that the value of **a** doesn't get permanently changed as a result of type casting. Rather it is the value of the expression that undergoes type conversion whenever the cast appears.

Bit Fields

If in a program a variable is to take only two values 1 and 0, we really need only a single bit to store it. Similarly, if a variable is to take values from 0 to 3, then two bits are sufficient to store these values. And if a variable is to take values from 0 through 7, then three bits will be enough, and so on.

Why waste an entire integer when one or two or three bits will do? Well, for one thing, there aren't any one bit or two bit or three bit data types available in C. However, when there are several variables whose maximum values are small enough to pack into a single memory location, we can use 'bit fields' to store several values in a single integer. To demonstrate how bit fields work, let us consider an example. Suppose we want to store the following data about an employee. Each person can:

(a)   be male or female
(b)   be single, married, divorced or widowed
(c)   have one of the eight different hobbies
(d)   can choose from any of the fifteen different schemes proposed by the company to pursue his/her hobby.

This means we need one bit to store gender, two to store marital status, three for hobby, and four for scheme (with one value used for those who are not desirous of availing any of the schemes). We need ten bits altogether, which means we can pack all this information into a single integer, since an integer is 16 bits long.

To do this using bit fields, we declare the following structure:

```
struct employee
```

```
    {
        unsigned gender  : 1 ;
        unsigned mar_stat : 2 ;
        unsigned hobby : 3 ;
        unsigned scheme : 4 ;
    } ;
```

The colon in the above declaration tells the compiler that we are talking about bit fields and the number after it tells how many bits to allot for the field.

Once we have established a bit field, we can reference it just like any other structure element, as shown in the program given below:

```
#define MALE 0 ;
#define FEMALE 1 ;
#define SINGLE 0 ;
#define MARRIED 1 ;
#define DIVORCED 2 ;
#define WIDOWED 3 ;

main( )
{
    struct employee
    {
        unsigned gender  : 1 ;
        unsigned mar_stat : 2 ;
        unsigned hobby : 3 ;
        unsigned scheme : 4 ;
    } ;
    struct employee e ;

    e.gender = MALE ;
    e.mar_status = DIVORCED ;
    e.hobby = 5 ;
    e.scheme = 9 ;
```

```
        printf ( "\nGender = %d", e.gender ) ;
        printf ( "\nMarital status = %d", e.mar_status ) ;
}
```

And here is the output...

```
Gender = 0
Marital status = 2
```

Pointers to Functions

Every type of variable that we have discussed so far, with the exception of register, has an address. We have seen how we can reference variables of the type **char, int, float** etc... through their addresses - that is by using pointers. Pointers can also point to C functions. And why not? C functions have addresses. If we know the function's address we can point to it, which provides another way to invoke it. Let us see how this can be done.

```
main( )
{
    int display( ) ;

    printf ( "\nAddress of function display is %u", display ) ;
    display( ) ; /* usual way of invoking a function */
}

display( )
{
    puts ( "\nLong live viruses!!" ) ;
}
```

The output of the program would be:

```
Address of function display is 1125
Long live viruses!!
```

Note that to obtain the address of a function all that we have to do is mention the name of the function, as has been done in the **printf( )** statement above. This is similar to mentioning the name of the array to get its base address.

Now let us see how using the address of a function we can manage to invoke it. This is shown in the program given below:

```
/* Invoking a function using a pointer to a function */
main( )
{
    int display( ) ;
    int ( *func_ptr )( ) ;

    func_ptr = display ;  /* assign address of function */
    printf ( "\nAddress of function display is %u", func_ptr ) ;
    ( *func_ptr )( ) ;  /* invokes the function display( ) */
}

int display( )
{
    puts ( "\nLong live viruses!!" ) ;
}
```

The output of the program would be:

```
Address of function display is 1125
Long live viruses!!
```

In **main( )** we declare the function **display( )** as a function returning an **int**. But what are we to make of the declaration,

```
int ( *func_ptr )( ) ;
```

that comes in the next line? We are obviously declaring something that, like **display( )**, will return an **int**, but what is it? And why is ***func_ptr** enclosed in parentheses?

If we glance down a few lines in our program, we see the statement,

```
func_ptr = display ;
```

so we know that **func_ptr** is being assigned the address of **display( )**. Therefore, **func_ptr** must be a pointer to the function **display( )**. Thus, all that the declaration

```
int ( *func_ptr )( ) ;
```

means is, that **func_ptr** is a pointer to a function, which returns an **int**. And to invoke the function we are just required to write the statement,

```
( *func_ptr )( ) ;
```

Pointers to functions are certainly awkward and offputting. And why use them at all when we can invoke a function in a much simpler manner? What is the possible gain of using this esoteric feature of C? There are two possible uses:

(a)   in writing memory resident programs
(b)   in writing viruses, or vaccines to remove the viruses

Both these topics form interesting and powerful C applications and would call for separate book on each if full justice is to be given to them. Much as I would have liked to, for want of space I would have to exclude these topics.

Functions Returning Pointers

The way functions return an **int**, a **float**, a **double** or any other data type, it can even return a pointer. However, to make a function return a pointer it has to be explicitly mentioned in the calling function as well as in the function definition. The following program illustrates this.

```
main( )
{
    int *p ;
    int *fun( ) ;

    p = fun ( ) ;
}

int *fun( )
{
    int i = 20 ;
    return ( &i ) ;
}
```

This program just indicates how an integer pointer can be returned from a function. Beyond that it doesn't serve any useful purpose. This concept can be put to use while handling strings. For example look at the following program which copies one string into another and returns the pointer to the target string.

```
main( )
{
    char *str ;
    char *copy( ) ;
    char source[ ] = "Jaded" ;
    char target[10] ;

    str = copy ( target, source ) ;
    printf ( "\n%s", str ) ;
}

char *copy ( char *t, char *s )
{
    char *r ;

    r = t ;
```

```
while ( *s != '\0' )
{
    *t = *s ;
    t++ ;
    s++ ;
}

*t = '\0' ;
return ( r ) ;
}
```

Here, we send the base addresses of **source** and **target** strings to **copy( )**. In the **copy( )** function the **while** loop copies the characters in the source string into the target string. Since during copying **t** is continuously incremented, before entering into the loop the initial value of **t** is safely stored in the character pointer **r**. Once copying is over this character pointer **r** is returned to **main( )**.

Functions with Variable Number of Arguments

We have used **printf( )** so often without realising how it works properly irrespective of how many arguments we pass to it. How do we go about writing such routines which can take variable number of arguments? And what have pointers got to do with it? There are three macros available in the file "stdarg.h" called **va_start, va_arg** and **va_list** which allow us to handle this situation. These macros provide a method for accessing the arguments of the function when a function takes a fixed number of arguments followed by a variable number of arguments. The fixed number of arguments are accessed in the normal way, whereas the optional arguments are accessed using the macros **va_start** and **va_arg**. Out of these macros **va_start** is used to initialise a pointer to the beginning of the list of optional arguments. On the other hand the macro **va_arg** is used to advance the pointer to the next argument. Let us put these concepts into action using a program. Suppose we wish to write a function **findmax( )**

which would find out the maximum value from a set of values, irrespective of the number of values passed to it.

```
# include "stdarg.h"
main( )
{
    int max ;

    max = findmax ( 5, 23, 15, 1, 92, 50 ) ;
    printf ( "\nmaximum = %d", max ) ;

    max = findmax ( 3, 100, 300, 29 ) ;
    printf ( "\nmaximum = %d", max ) ;
}

findmax ( int tot_num )
{
    int max, count, num ;

    va_list ptr ;

    va_start ( ptr, tot_num ) ;
    max = va_arg ( ptr, int ) ;

    for ( count = 1 ; count < tot_num ; count++ )
    {
        num = va_arg ( ptr, int ) ;
        if ( num > max )
            max = num ;
    }

    return ( max ) ;
}
```

Here we are making two calls to **findmax( )** first time to find maximum out of 5 values and second time to find maximum out of 3 values. Note that for each call the first argument is the count of arguments that follow the first argument. The value of the first argument passed to **findmax( )** is collected in the variable **tot_num**. **findmax( )** begins with a declaration of a pointer **ptr** of the type **va_list**. Observe the next statement carefully:

```
va_start ( ptr, tot_num ) ;
```

This statement sets up **ptr** such that it points to the first variable argument in the list. If we are considering the first call to **finndmax( )** **ptr** would now point to 23. The next statement **max = va_arg (ptr, int)** would assign the integer being pointed to by **ptr** to **max**. Thus 23 would be assigned to **max**, and **ptr** would now start pointing to the next argument i.e., 15. The rest of the program is fairly straight forward. We just keep picking up successive numbers in the list and keep comparing them with the latest value in **max**, till all the arguments in the list have been scanned. The final value in **max** is then returned to **main( )**.

How about another program to fix your ideas? This one calls a function **display( )** which is capable of printing any number of arguments of any type.

```
#include "stdarg.h"
main( )
{
    display ( 1, 2, 5, 6 ) ;
    display ( 2, 4, 'A', 'a', 'b', 'c' ) ;
    display ( 3, 3, 2.5, 299.3, -1.0 ) ;
}

display ( int type, int num )
{
    int i, j ;
    char c ;
    float f ;
    va_list ptr ;
```

```
va_start ( ptr, num ) ;
printf ( "\n" ) ;

switch ( type )
{
    case 1 :
        for ( j = 1 ; j <= num ; j++ )
        {
            i = va_arg ( ptr, int ) ;
            printf ( "%d ", i ) ;
        }
        break ;

    case 2 :
        for ( j = 1 ; j <= num ; j++ )
        {
            c = va_arg ( ptr, char ) ;
            printf ( "%c ", c ) ;
        }
        break ;

    case 3 :
        for ( j = 1 ; j <= num ; j++ )
        {
            f = ( float ) va_arg ( ptr, double ) ;
            printf ( "%f ", f) ;
        }
}
}
```

Here we pass two fixed arguments to the function **display( )**. The first one indicates the data type of the arguments to be printed and the second indicates the number of such arguments to be printed. Once again through the statement **va_start (ptr, num)** we set up **ptr** such that it points to the first argument in the variable list of arguments. Then depending upon whether the value of **type** is 1, 2 or 3 we print out the arguments as **ints**, **chars** or **floats**.

Summary

In this chapter you learnt features which are not so commonly used. However in a professional software developed through C, some of these features may come in handy. The enumerated data type and the **typedef** declaration add to the clarity of the program. Type casting makes the data type conversions for specific operations. Bit fields help to make the program brief and compact. Pointers to functions provide one more way to call functions. We also learnt how to return a pointer from a function and how to pass a variable number of arguments to a function.

Exercise

[A] What will be the output of the following programs:

(a)
```
main( )
{
    enum status { pass, fail, atkt } ;
    enum status stud1, stud2, stud3 ;
    stud1 = pass ;
    stud2 = fail ;
    stud3 = atkt ;
    printf ( "\n%d %d %d", stud1, stud2, stud3 ) ;
}
```

(b)
```
main( )
{
    printf ( "%f", ( float ) ( ( int ) 3.5 / 2 ) ) ;
}
```

(c)
```
main( )
{
    float i, j ;
    i = ( float ) 3 / 2 ;
```

```
            j = i * 3 ;
            printf ( "\n%d", ( int ) j ) ;
    }
```

[B] Point out the error, if any, in the following programs:

(a)   main( )
```
        {
            typedef struct patient
            {
                char name[20] ;
                int age ;
                int systolic_bp ;
                int diastolic_bp ;
            } ptt ;
            ptt p1 = { "anil", 23, 110, 220 } ;
            printf ( "\n%s %d", p1.name, p1.age ) ;
            printf ( "\n%d %d", p1.systolic_bp, p1.diastolic_bp ) ;
        }
```

(b)   main( )
```
        {
            void show( ) ;
            void ( *s )( ) ;
            s = show ;
            ( *s )( ) ;
        }
        void show( )
        {
            printf ( "\ndon't show off. It won't pay in the long run" ) ;
        }
```

(c)   main( )
```
        {
            int show( ) ;
            int ( *s )( ) ;
```

```
            s = show( );
            ( *s )( ) ;
    }
    float show( )
    {
            printf ( "\nControl did reach here" ) ;
            return ( 3.33 ) ;
    }
```

(d)   ```
       main( )
       {
               void show(int, float) ;
               void (*s)(int, float) ;
               s = show ;
               (*s)(10, 3.14) ;
       }
       show (int i, float f)
       {
               printf ("\n %d %f", i, f) ;
       }
       ```

[C]    Attempt the following:

(a)    The list of equipment attached to your computer is stored as a two-byte sequence in BIOS Data Area. Using ROM-BIOS interrupt number 17 write a program to display this equipment list on the screen. Refer Chapter 18, Figure 18.13 for the bitwise distribution of the two-byte sequence.

       Hint: Use bit-fields

(b)    Write programs which can simulate the following possible virus activities, using the concept of pointer to a function:

       (1) Dancing dolls: Every character present on the screen should keep changing from small case to capital irrespec-
       ```

tive of whether you are working in dbase or wordstar or any other software.

(2) Rain Rain here again: The characters present on the screen should keep falling down to the bottom of the screen. The character which should start falling should get chosen randomly.

(3) The background colour of the screen should keep changing after every 10 seconds.

(4) Every character sent to the printer is incremented by 1 before it goes to the printer. Thus, if the user tries to print 'Hello' on the printer, your program should see to it that what is sent to printer is "Ifmmp".

20 *Graphics Programming*

Computer graphics is one of the most powerful and interesting facet of computers. There is a lot that you can do in graphics apart from drawing figures of various shapes. All video games, animation, multimedia predominantly works using computer graphics. The intention of this chapter is to give you a feel of how some of these things are achieved in C. The aim is to make you comfortable with the basic concepts in graphics, introduce you to the standard library graphics functions and then let you explore on your own. Instead of discussing each standard library graphics function in detail I thought it worthwhile to put them to use in a program. Here is the first program...

```c
# include "graphics.h"
main( )
{
    int gd = DETECT, gm, x, y ;
    int array[ ] = { 540, 220, 590, 270, 570, 320, 510, 320, 490, 270,
                    540, 220 } ;

    initgraph ( &gd, &gm, "c:\\tc\\bgi" ) ;

    x = getmaxx( ) ;
    y = getmaxy( ) ;

    setcolor ( WHITE ) ;
    rectangle ( x / 30, y / 20, x / 5, y / 4 ) ;
    outtextxy ( x / 30 + 15, y / 8 + 5, "Rectangle" ) ;

    circle ( x / 2, y / 6, 75 ) ;
    putpixel ( x / 2, y / 6, WHITE ) ;
    outtextxy ( x / 2 - textwidth ( "Circle" ) / 2, y / 6 + 10, "Circle" ) ;

    arc ( x / 1.2, y / 6, 300, 90, 80 ) ;
    outtextxy ( x / 1.2, y / 6, "Arc" ) ;
```

```
line ( x / 30, 10 * y / 15, x / 6, 10 * y / 15 ) ;
outtextxy ( x / 30 + 10, 10 * y / 15 + 10, "Line" ) ;

ellipse ( x / 2, 10 * y / 17, 0, 360, 100, 50 ) ;
putpixel ( x / 2, 10 * y / 17, WHITE ) ;
outtextxy ( x / 2 - textwidth ( "Ellipse" ) / 2,
                10 * y / 17 + 10, "Ellipse" ) ;

drawpoly ( 6, array ) ;
outtextxy ( 515, 270, "Polygon" ) ;

getch( ) ;
closegraph( ) ;
restorecrtmode( ) ;
}
```

When we start drawing any graphics on the screen we need a header file called GRAPHICS.H and a library file called GRAPHICS.LIB. The header file contains definitions and explanations of all the functions and constants we'll need, whereas the graphics functions are kept in the graphics library file. Both these files are provided as part of TURBO C.

First thing that we need to do before we can carry out any drawing activity is, switch over to the graphics mode. This is not simple, since depending on the adapter and monitor that is installed on your computer, only some of the several graphics modes may be available to you. These modes have been given numbers. Out of all the modes available, we would like to switch over to the one which offers the best possible resolution.

Did we say resolution? Well, the number of dots or picture elements (pixels) available to us on the screen in the graphics mode, is known as the resolution. The greater the number of dots, the higher the resolution. Simply put, this means that more the dots available, clearer would be our picture.

To switch over to the graphics mode that offers the best resolution we need to call the function **initgraph( )**. It figures out the best resolution and puts the number corresponding to that mode in the variable **gm**. The **gm** number tells us which monitor we are using, and its resolution, the number of video pages it supports and the colors that are available.

Note that I've written the programs in this chapter on a color monitor driven by a VGA adapter, the maximum resolution of which is 640 x 480 (i.e. 640 pixels from left to right and 480 pixels from top to bottom). For other adapters I expect you to make the necessary changes in the programs.

To understand **gd**, we have to understand the concept of device drivers. Device drivers are small programs which talk directly to the hardware. Since we can't be machine-dependent at any time, we need programs we can communicate with in a standardized way. These programs in turn communicate with the machine. These intermediary programs are known as device drivers.

Graphics drivers are a subset of device drivers and are applicable only in the graphics mode. They work in the above fashion to execute whatever task we have assigned them. Turbo C offers certain graphics drivers. These are the files with a BGI extension. Depending on what adapter is used, one of these drivers gets selected. Our programs have been developed on the VGA adapter. Thus we need the EGAVGA.BGI file as our graphics driver. In our program, **gd** has been assigned the value DETECT, thereby asking **initgraph( )** to figure out which BGI file is needed. This file is then loaded into memory. If we do not initiate **gd** with DETECT then it is our responsibility to set up **gd** and **gm** with appropriate values.

Since most of the times we don't want to be bothered with this responsibility we use the DETECT macro.

So much about the graphics modes and changing over to the appropriate graphics mode. Two things happen the moment we change over to the graphics mode. Firstly, the cursor disappears since the graphics modes do not support the conventional cursor. Secondly, a coordinate system is established whereby the top left corner of the screen is treated as origin **(0, 0)**. As usual, the x-axis goes horizontally across, and the y-axis goes vertically downward.

The basic tools we'll need for drawing shapes are functions like **putpixel( )**, **line( )**, **circle( )**, **ellipse( )**, **arc( )** and **drawpoly( )**. All these functions have been used in our program. Their general form is shown in Figure 20.1. Before drawing the rectangle we have used two functions **getmaxx( )** and **getmaxy( )**. These fetch the maximum x and y coordinates for the chosen graphics mode.

Function	Meaning
putpixel (x1, y1) ;	Lits the pixel at (**x1, y1**).
line (x1, y1, x2, y2) ;	Draws a line from (**x1, y1**) to (**x2, y2**).
circle (xc, yc, rad) ;	Draws a circle with center (**xc, yc**) and radius **rad.**
rectangle (x1, y1, x2, y2) ;	Draws a rectangle with (**x1, y1**) and (**x2, y2**) as corners.
ellipse (xc, yc, start, end, rad, yrad) ;	Draws an ellipse with (**xc, yc**) as center with **xrad** and **yrad** as x and y radius. If **start** is 0 and **end** is 180 only the upper half of the ellipse is drawn.
arc (xc, yc, start, end, rad) ;	Draws an arc with (**xc,yc**) as center, **rad** as radius and **start** and **end** as the starting and ending angles.

Figure 20.1

All Lines Are Not Same

In the previous program we drew a line using the **line( )** function. The coordinates passed to this functions were with respect to the origin **(0, 0)**, represented by the pixel at the top-left corner of the screen. Another way to draw a line is to use a combination of two functions **moveto( )** and **lineto( )**. The **moveto( )** function moves the C.P. to the specified coordinates. What is this C.P.? It stands for Current Position. When we initialise the graphics system C.P. is at the origin. On executing some drawing functions C.P. changes, whereas in others it doesn't. For example, after drawing a line using the **line( )** function C.P. doesn't change, whereas, on drawing a line using the function **lineto( )** the C.P. changes to the end point of the line drawn.

It is also possible to draw a line relative to a particular point on the screen using the **linerel( )** function. The coordinates passed to **linerel( )** specify where we want the line to end using the said point as our origin. To reach the starting point we can use either the function **moveto( )** or **moverel( )**. The first function moves the C.P. to the given coordinates with **(0, 0)** as the origin, whereas, the second moves the C.P. by a relative distance from its current position. The following program uses the three methods mentioned above to draw lines on the screen.

```
#include <graphics.h>
#include <stdlib.h>
#include <stdio.h>
#include <conio.h>
main( )
{
    int gd = DETECT, gm ;
    char msg[80] ;

    initgraph ( &gd, &gm, "c:\\tc\\bgi" ) ;

    outtextxy ( 100, 0, "Demonstration of Moveto, Lineto, Moverel,
            Linerel" ) ;
    rectangle ( 0, 10, 639, 479 ) ;

    line ( 100, 50, 100, 350 ) ; /* draws a line */

    moveto ( 300, 50 ) ; /* moves the C.P. */
    lineto ( 300, 350 ) ; /* draws a line up to the point */

    moverel ( 200, -300 ) ; /* moves the C.P. by relative
                        distance from its current position */
```

```
linerel ( 0, 300 ) ;  /* draws a line from the C.P. to a point a relative
                          distance away from the current value of C.P. */

outtextxy ( 104, 50, "( 100, 50 )" ) ;
outtextxy ( 104, 350, "( 100, 350 )" ) ;
outtextxy ( 90, 375, "Line" ) ;

outtextxy ( 304, 50, "( 300, 50 )" ) ;
outtextxy ( 304, 350, "( 300, 350 )" ) ;
outtextxy ( 280, 375, "Moveto, Lineto" ) ;

outtextxy ( 504, 50, "( 500, 50 )" ) ;
outtextxy ( 504, 350, "( 500, 350 )" ) ;
outtextxy ( 480, 375, "Moverel, Linerel" ) ;

getch( ) ;
closegraph( ) ;
restorecrtmode( ) ;
}
```

This program draws three lines. The first line has been drawn using the usual **line( )** function. The second one has been drawn using the **moveto( )**, **lineto( )** functions. Note that for drawing this line we have reached our starting point **(300, 50)** by calling the **moveto( )** function and then drawn a line up to **(300, 350)** using the **lineto( )** function. This shifts the C.P. to **(300, 350)**. The third line is drawn by first shifting the C.P. from its current position by a relative distance of 200 pixels to the right and 300 pixels up using the **moverel( )** function. Next the line is drawn using the function **linerel( )**, once again using the relative distances.

Stylish Lines

So far we have drawn only solid lines. However, situations may demand to draw lines with other line styles. For example, we may use dashed lines to indicate hidden edges of an object, or center lines to indicate center lines of a circle, and so on. Turbo C provides four different line styles to draw solid, dotted, center and dashed lines. These styles can be used to draw either normal or thick lines. It also permits us to use a line style created by us to draw the lines.

To be able to draw lines of different styles we must use the function **setlinestyle( )**. Its prototype looks like this:

setlinestyle (type, pattern, thickness) ;

The first parameter specifies the type of line (solid, dashed, etc.). The second parameter is applicable only if the line style is user-defined. The third parameter specifies the line thickness. The various line styles have been enumerated in 'graphics.h' as under:

0	Solid Line
1	Dotted Line
2	Center Line (alternating dashes and dots)
3	Dashed Line
4	User-defined Line

The thickness parameter can take the value 1 or 3. The former corresponds to a line thickness of one pixel (normal), the latter to a thickness of three pixels (thick). Let us now use this information to draw lines of different styles.

```
# include "graphics.h"
main( )
{
    int gd = DETECT, gm, maxy, x, style ;
    char str[40] ;
    struct linesettingstype ls ;
```

```
initgraph ( &gd, &gm, "c:\\tc\\bgi" ) ;

maxy = getmaxy( ) ;

setcolor ( WHITE ) ;
outtextxy ( 10, 20, "Normal width" ) ;

x = 20 ;
for ( style = 0 ; style <= 4 ; style++ )
{
    setlinestyle ( style, 0, 1 ) ;

    if ( style == 0 )
        getlinesettings ( &ls ) ;  /* save line setting */

    if ( style == 4 )
    {
        setlinestyle ( 4, 15, 1 ) ;
        line ( x, 50, x, maxy - 50 ) ;
    }
    else
        line ( x, 50, x, maxy - 50 ) ;

    itoa ( style, str, 10 ) ;
    outtextxy ( x, maxy - 20, str ) ;
    x = x + 50 ;
}

outtextxy ( 375, 20, "Thick width" ) ;

x = 375 ;
for ( style = 0 ; style <= 4 ; style++ )
{
    setlinestyle ( style, 0, 3 ) ;
```

```
        if ( style == 4 )
        {
            setlinestyle ( 4, 15, 3 ) ;
            line ( x, 50, x, maxy - 50 ) ;
        }
        else
            line ( x, 50, x, maxy - 50 ) ;

        itoa ( style, str, 10 ) ;
        outtextxy ( x, maxy - 20, str ) ;
        x = x + 50 ;
    }

    /* restore line settings */
    setlinestyle ( ls.linestyle, ls.upattern, ls.thickness ) ;

    getch( ) ;
    closegraph( ) ;
    restorecrtmode( ) ;
}
```

Here we have drawn ten lines, five of these have a thickness of 1 pixel, whereas, the other five have a thickness of 3 pixels. In each set, four lines are of available line styles and one is of user-defined style. To define our own style for drawing a line we have to build a 16-bit pattern. In this pattern whenever a bit is 1, the corresponding pixel in the line is drawn in the current drawing color. For example, a solid line corresponds to a pattern of FFFFh (all pixels drawn), while a dashed line can correspond to a pattern of 3333h or 0F0Fh. In our program we have used the pattern with a value 0005h.

After setting the style to **solid** and thickness to 1 we have saved the current line settings in a **linesettingstype** structure by calling the function **getlinesettings( )**. This function stores the style, pattern and thickness in the **linesettingstype** structure which is defined in 'graphics.h' as follows:

```
struct linesettingstype
{
    int linestyle ;
    unsigned upattern ;
    int thickness ;
} ;
```

The settings saved using **getlinesettings( )** have been restored once all lines have been drawn, by calling the **setlinestyle( )** function.

Drawing and Filling Images

With the basics over, let us now get into more complicated stuff. Stuff which would permit us to draw bars and then fill them up with different patterns. Here is a program which shows how this can be achieved...

```
# include "graphics.h"
main( )
{
    int gd = DETECT, gm, maxx, maxy, x = 40, y = 40, fst ;
    char str[40] ;
    char *pattern[ ] = {
                        "EMPTY_FILL", "SOLID_FILL", "LINE_FILL",
                        "LTSLASH_FILL", "SLASH_FILL",
                        "BKSLASH_FILL", "LTBKSLASH_FILL",
                        "HATCH_FILL", "XHATCH_FILL",
                        "INTERLEAVE_FILL", "WIDE_DOT_FILL",
                        "CLOSE_DOT_FILL", "USER_FILL"
                    } ;

    initgraph ( &gd, &gm, "c:\\tc\\bgi" ) ;
```

```
maxx = getmaxx( ) ;
maxy = getmaxy( ) ;
rectangle ( 0, 10, maxx, maxy ) ;

setcolor ( WHITE ) ;
outtextxy ( 175, 0, "Pre-defined Fill styles" ) ;

/* display different predefined fill styles */
for ( fst = 0 ; fst < 12 ; fst++ )
{
    setfillstyle ( fst, MAGENTA ) ;
    bar ( x, y, x + 80, y + 80 ) ;
    rectangle ( x, y, x + 80, y + 80 ) ;

    itoa ( fst, str, 10 ) ;
    outtextxy ( x, y + 100, str ) ;
    outtextxy ( x, y + 110, pattern[fst] ) ;

    x = x + 150 ;
    if ( x > 490 )
    {
        y = y + 150 ;
        x = 40 ;
    }
}

getch( ) ;
closegraph( ) ;
restorecrtmode( ) ;
}
```

In this program we have drawn 12 rectangles and filled them with the available fill patterns. To achieve this we have first used the **bar( )** function to fill a rectangular area with a pattern and then enclosed it by calling the **rectangle( )** function. Note that the **bar( )** function doesn't draw the boundary but fills the interior with the current fill pattern and current fill color, whereas the **rectangle( )** function draws the rectangle in current color but doesn't fill the insides of it.

The following figure shows the fill patterns defined in 'graphics.h' along with their enumerated integer values:

Name	Value	Description
EMPTY_FILL	0	Fill with background color
SOLID_FILL	1	Solid fill
LINE_FILL	2	Fill with -------
LTSLASH_FILL	3	Fill with /////
SLASH_FILL	4	Fill with /////, thick lines
BKSLASH_FILL	5	Fill with \\\\\, thick lines
LTBKSLASH_FILL	6	Fill with \\\\\
HATCH_FILL	7	Light hatch fill
XHATCH_FILL	8	Heavy cross-hatch fill
INTERLEAVE_FILL	9	Interleaving line fill
WIDE_DOT_FILL	10	Widely spaced dot fill
CLOSE_DOT_FILL	11	Closely spaced dot fill
USER_FILL	12	User-defined fill pattern

Figure 20.2

If we want we can save the current fill pattern and current fill color through statements given below:

```
struct fillsettingstype old ;
getfillsettings ( &old ) ;
```

The **fillsettingstype** structure has been defined in 'graphics.h' as follows:

```
struct fillsettingstype
{
    int pattern ;
    int color ;
} ;
```

If saved earlier, the fill pattern and the fill color can be restored through a call to **setfillstyle( )**:

```
setfillstyle ( old.pattern, old.color ) ;
```

Patterns with A Difference

In the previous program we have used the standard fill patterns to fill the rectangles. Let us now see how to make use of user-defined fill patterns. To use the predefined fill patterns we had used the function **setfillstyle( )**. Likewise, to use the user-defined fill patterns we need to use the function **setfillpattern( )**. Its prototype looks like this...

```
setfillpattern ( char *pattern, int color ) ;
```

The first parameter is a pointer to a sequence of 8 bytes, with each byte corresponding to 8 pixels in the pattern. Whenever a bit in a pattern byte is set to 1, the corresponding pixel will be plotted. The second parameter specifies the color in which the pattern would be drawn.

In the following program we have stored 12 patterns in an array and then drawn rectangles and filled them with these patterns in magenta color.

```
# include "graphics.h"
main( )
{
```

```
int gd = DETECT, gm, maxx, maxy, x = 40, y = 40, fst ;
char str[40] ;
char patterns[ ][8] =
{
    { 0xAA, 0x55, 0xAA, 0x55, 0xAA, 0x55, 0xAA, 0x55 },
    { 0x33, 0x33, 0xCC, 0xCC, 0x33, 0x33, 0xCC, 0xCC },
    { 0xF0, 0xF0, 0xF0, 0xF0, 0x0F, 0x0F, 0x0F, 0x0F },
    { 0x00, 0x10, 0x28, 0x44, 0x28, 0x10, 0x00, 0x00 },
    { 0x00, 0x70, 0x20, 0x27, 0x24, 0x24, 0x07, 0x00 },
    { 0x00, 0x00, 0x00, 0x18, 0x18, 0x00, 0x00, 0x00 },
    { 0x00, 0x00, 0x3C, 0x3C, 0x3C, 0x3C, 0x00, 0x00 },
    { 0x00, 0x7E, 0x7E, 0x7E, 0x7E, 0x7E, 0x7E, 0x00 },
    { 0x00, 0x00, 0x22, 0x08, 0x00, 0x22, 0x1C, 0x00 },
    { 0xFF, 0x7E, 0x3C, 0x18, 0x18, 0x3C, 0x7E, 0xFF },
    { 0x00, 0x10, 0x10, 0x7C, 0x10, 0x10, 0x00, 0x00 },
    { 0x00, 0x42, 0x24, 0x18, 0x18, 0x24, 0x42, 0x00 }
} ;

initgraph ( &gd, &gm, "c:\\tc\\bgi" ) ;

maxx = getmaxx( ) ;
maxy = getmaxy( ) ;
rectangle ( 0, 10, maxx, maxy ) ;

setcolor ( WHITE ) ;
outtextxy ( 175, 0, "User-defined Fill styles" ) ;

/* display different user-defined fill styles */
for ( fst = 0 ; fst < 12 ; fst++ )
{
    setfillpattern ( &patterns[fst][0], MAGENTA ) ;
    bar ( x, y, x + 80, y + 80 ) ;
    rectangle ( x, y, x + 80, y + 80 ) ;

    itoa ( fst, str, 10 ) ;
```

```
        outtextxy ( x, y + 100, str ) ;

        x = x + 150 ;
        if ( x > 490 )
        {
            y = y + 150 ;
            x = 40 ;
        }
    }

    getch( ) ;
    closegraph( ) ;
    restorecrtmode( ) ;
}
```

Why Use A *bar( )*?

In the last program we first filled a pattern in a rectangular area by calling the **bar( )** function and then enclosed it in a rectangle by calling the **rectangle( )** function. Is this really necessary? Can we not combine the operations? We can, by using the **floodfill( )** function. This function needs three parameters: the x and y coordinates of a point and color. The function starts to fill the screen from the specified point till it encounters a closed boundary of the specified color.

In the following program we have drawn three rectangles and filled the first two with a standard pattern and the last with a user-defined pattern. While building the first rectangle we have drawn the rectangle through the **rectangle( )** function (instead of **bar( )**).

Next we have set the fill pattern and fill color by calling the function **setfillstyle( )**. Then using this fill style and color we have filled the rectangle using the **floodfill( )** function. The other two rectangles and their patterns have been constructed as in the last program.

```
# include "graphics.h"
main( )
{
    int gd = DETECT, gm, maxx, maxy ;
    char pattern[ ] = { 0x00, 0x70, 0x20, 0x27, 0x24, 0x24,
                        0x07, 0x00 } ;

    initgraph ( &gd, &gm, "c:\\tc\\bgi" ) ;

    maxx = getmaxx( ) ;
    maxy = getmaxy( ) ;
    rectangle ( 0, 10, maxx, maxy ) ;

    setcolor ( WHITE ) ;
    outtextxy ( 175, 0, "color shapes and patterns" ) ;

    setcolor ( WHITE ) ;
    rectangle ( 80, 150, 180, 250 ) ;

    setfillstyle ( SOLID_FILL, RED ) ;
    floodfill ( 81, 151, WHITE ) ;
    outtextxy ( 100, 300, "floodfill" ) ;

    setfillstyle ( BKSLASH_FILL, RED ) ;
    bar ( 250, 150, 350, 250 ) ;
    rectangle ( 250, 150, 350, 250 ) ;
    outtextxy ( 250, 300, "setfillstyle" ) ;
    outtextxy ( 230, 320, "(using std. pattern)" ) ;

    setfillpattern ( pattern, RED ) ;
    bar ( 420, 150, 520, 250 ) ;
    rectangle ( 420, 150, 520, 250 ) ;
    outtextxy ( 420, 300, "setfillpattern" ) ;
    outtextxy ( 420, 320, "(using user-defined)" ) ;
```

```
        getch( ) ;
        closegraph( ) ;
        restorecrtmode( ) ;
}
```

Note that while using the **floodfill( )** function one must make sure that the right color is specified or else the function will seek a boundary you don't want.

Filling Regular and Non-Regular Shapes

To fill regular shapes like polygons and ellipses there exist standard library functions like **fillpoly( )** and **fillellipse( )**. These functions fill the polygon (or ellipse) with the current fill style and current fill color that may have been set up by calling **setfillstyle( )** or **setfillpattern( )**. However, if we are to fill non-regular shapes like the intersecting area between an overlapping triangle and circle, we have to once again take recourse to the **floodfill( )** function.

The following program draws an ellipse and a triangle and fills them by calling the **fillellipse( )** and **fillpoly( )** functions. Next it draws an overlapping triangle and circle and fills the intersecting and non-intersecting areas by repeatedly calling the **floodfill( )** function. The parameters passed to **fillellipse( )** include coordinates of the center, x-radius and y-radius. The parameters passed to **drawpoly( )** and **fillpoly( )** are same: the number of points used to build the polygon and the base address of the array containing the coordinates of these points.

```
# include "graphics.h"
main( )
{
        int gd = DETECT, gm, maxx, maxy, x = 600, y = 450 ;
```

```
int array[ ] = { 350, 180, 400, 80, 450, 180, 350, 180 } ;

initgraph ( &gd, &gm, "c:\\tc\\bgi" ) ;

maxx = getmaxx( ) ;
maxy = getmaxy( ) ;
rectangle ( 0, 20, maxx, maxy ) ;
setcolor ( WHITE ) ;
outtextxy ( 150, 10, "Fill Figures using different functions" ) ;
ellipse ( x / 4, 10 * y / 35, 0, 360, 100, 50 ) ;

outtextxy ( x / 4 - textwidth ( "Ellipse" ) / 2, 10 *
                    y / 24 + 10, "Ellipse" ) ;
setfillstyle ( SOLID_FILL, RED ) ;
fillellipse ( x / 4, 10 * y / 35, 100, 50 ) ;

drawpoly ( 4, array ) ;
fillpoly ( 4, array ) ;
outtextxy ( 370, 200, "Polygon" ) ;

circle ( 280, 320, 70 ) ;
line ( 190, 350, 370, 350 ) ;
moveto ( 190, 350 ) ;
linerel ( 100, -120 ) ;
linerel ( 80, 120 ) ;
outtextxy ( 210, 410, "User-defined figure" ) ;

floodfill ( 280, 320, WHITE ) ;

setfillstyle ( SOLID_FILL, BLUE ) ;
floodfill ( 192, 349, WHITE ) ;
floodfill ( 368, 349, WHITE ) ;
floodfill ( 290, 231, WHITE ) ;

setfillstyle ( SOLID_FILL, DARKGRAY ) ;
```

```
        floodfill ( 240, 289, WHITE ) ;
        floodfill ( 330, 289, WHITE ) ;
        floodfill ( 280, 351, WHITE ) ;

        getch( ) ;
        closegraph( ) ;
        restorecrtmode( ) ;
}
```

Of Palettes and Colors

In Chapter 1 we saw how VGA generates colors. Let us now put
that theory into practice. Here is a program which does this...

```
# include "graphics.h"
# include "stdlib.h"
main( )
{
    int gd = DETECT, gm, i, j, x, y, color, startcolor, height, width ;
    struct palettetype palette ;
    struct viewporttype vp ;

    initgraph ( &gd, &gm, "c:\\tc\\bgi" ) ;

    getpalette ( &palette ) ;

    rectangle ( 0, 20, 639, 479 ) ;
    outtextxy ( 200, 10, "Palette demonstration" ) ;

    getviewsettings ( &vp ) ;
    width  = ( vp.right - vp.left ) / 16 ;
    height = ( vp.bottom - vp.top - 20 ) / 16 ;
    x = 0 ;
    y = 20 ;
    startcolor = 0 ;
```

```
for ( j = 0 ; j <= 15 ; j++ )
{
    color = startcolor ;
    for ( i = 0 ; i <= 15 ; i++ )
    {
        setfillstyle ( SOLID_FILL, color++ ) ;
        bar ( x, y, x + width, y + height ) ;
        x = x + width + 1 ;
    }
    startcolor++ ;
    x = 0 ;
    y += height + 1 ;
}
getch( ) ;

while ( !kbhit( ) )
    setpalette ( random ( 16 ), random ( 65 ) ) ;

setallpalette ( &palette ) ;

getch( ) ;
closegraph( ) ;
restorecrtmode( ) ;
}
```

To begin with, we have determined the drawing area available to us
by calling the function **getviewsettings( )**. This function fills the
elements of the structure **viewporttype** with the coordinates of the
current viewport (drawing area). Using these coordinates we have
calculated the height and width of the rectangles that we propose to
draw on the screen. Next, we have drawn 16 rows and 16 columns
of rectangles using a pair of **for** loops. The rectangles have been
drawn using the **bar( )** function which uses the fill pattern and fill
color as set by a call to the function **setfillstyle( )**. To ensure that the

first rectangle in each row has a different color we have used the variables **color** and **startcolor**. Once the screen is filled with 256 rectangles, using the **setpalette( )** function we have changed the color values. Which color number gets changed to what color value is decided at random since we have generated both the numbers using the **random( )** function. The colors keep getting changed in a **while** loop till we do not interrupt the process by pressing a key. Once we hit a key the control goes outside the **while** loop, whereupon we change all the colors to their original values (which we have earlier saved in the **palettetype** structure by calling **getpalette( )** function) through the function **setallpalette( )**.

Note that we have not redrawn any of the rectangles. We have only changed the color values in the palette. By doing so, all rectangles on the screen which had the earlier color values are changed to reflect the new color values in the palette.

Outputting Text

So far we have outputted text using the function **outtextxy( )**. However, there is more to outputting text than what we have covered. The following program would put the whole issue in the right perspective.

```
# include "graphics.h"
main( )
{
    int gd = DETECT, gm, x = 10, y, i, j ;
    char str[ ] = "Fonts" ;
    char *demo[ ] = {
                "Default Font Demonstration" ,
                "Triplex Font Demonstration",
                "Small Font Demonstration",
                "Sansserif Font Demonstration",
```

```
                    "Gothic Font Demonstration",
                    "Script Font Demonstration",
                    "Simplex Font Demonstration",
                    "Triplex Script Font Demonstration",
                    "Complex Font Demonstration",
                    "European Font Demonstration",
                    "Bold Font Demonstration"
            } ;

    initgraph ( &gd, &gm, "c:\\tc\\bgi" ) ;

    setcolor ( WHITE ) ;

    for ( i = 0 ; i <= 10 ; i++ )
    {
        rectangle ( 0, 20, 639, 479 ) ;
        settextstyle ( 0, 0, 1 ) ;
        outtextxy ( 150, 10, demo[i] ) ;

        y = 30 ;
        for ( j = 1 ; j <= 4 ; j++ )
        {
            settextstyle ( i, HORIZ_DIR, j ) ;
            outtextxy ( 10, y, str ) ;
            y += ( textheight ( str ) + 10 ) ;
        }

        settextstyle ( i, VERT_DIR, 0 ),
        setusercharsize ( 2, 1, 3, 2 ) ;
        outtextxy ( 10, y, str ) ;

        getch( ) ;
        clearviewport( ) ;
    }
```

```
        closegraph( ) ;
        restorecrtmode( ) ;
}
```

In the earlier programs when we used the **outtextxy( )** function the text got printed using a default font, direction and point size. The function **settextstyle( )** enables us to change the font, direction and character size. Turbo C provides us with ten fonts in addition to the default font. These are Triplex, Small, Sans serif, Gothic, Script, Simplex, Triplex Script, Complex, European and Bold. We can output the text either horizontally (default) or vertically. And we can choose any one of the 10 point sizes of characters. For point size 1 each character is displayed in a 8 x 8 pixel rectangle. If the point size is 2 then the character is displayed using 16 x 16 pixel rectangle and so on.

The general form of **settextstyle( )** function is given below,

settextstyle (font, direction, point size) ;

In our program we have kept the direction of output horizontal and changed the font and the point size through a pair of loops. To determine the position at which the text is to be outputted each time through the loop, we have used the function **textheight( )** which determines the height of a string as per the current font. Instead of using all the 10 point sizes we have run the inner loop only four times do demonstrate four point sizes.

Once outside the inner **for** loop we have used the **setusercharsize()** function to use a user-defined point size. This function gives you finer control over the size of the text. Its prototype looks like this...

setusercharsize (int multx, int divx, int multy, int divy) ;

The parameters passed to this function help us to specify factors by which the width and height are scaled. The default width is scaled by **multx : divx**, and the default height is scaled by **multy : divy**.

For example, to make the text twice as wide and 50% taller than the default, we have set,

```
multx = 2 ;  divx = 1 ;
multy = 3 ;  divy = 2 ;
```

Justifying Text

Not only can we control the font, direction and point size of the text that is drawn on the screen in the graphics mode, we can also exercise control over its orientation (justification) with respect to C.P. Justification of text simply means positioning it with reference to C.P. Remember that each character occupies a block of pixels. Using the **settextjustify( )** function we can align this block horizontally or vertically such that C.P. is at the top, center or bottom of this block (for vertical justification) and to the left, center or right of this block (for horizontal justification). The default justification settings are LEFT_TEXT (for horizontal) and TOP_TEXT (for vertical). This means the block of character(s) would be to the left of C.P. and below it. The other settings and their values as enumerated in the file 'graphics.h' are shown in Figure 20.3.

Name	Value	Description
LEFT_TEXT	0	Horizontal
CENTRE_TEXT	1	Horizontal and Vertical
RIGHT_TEXT	2	Horizontal
BOTTOM_TEXT	0	Vertical
TOP_TEXT	2	Vertical

Figure 20.3

The following program shows all possible combinations of vertical and horizontal justification for displaying a string of text.

```
#include <graphics.h>
#include <stdlib.h>
#include <stdio.h>
#include <conio.h>
void cross ( int x, int y ) ;

/* horizontal text justification settings */
char *horizontal[ ] = {
                "LEFT_TEXT",
                "CENTER_TEXT",
                "RIGHT_TEXT"
                } ;

/* vertical text justification settings */
char *vertical[ ] = {
                "BOTTOM_TEXT",
                "CENTER_TEXT",
                "TOP_TEXT"
                } ;

main( )
{
     int gd = DETECT, gm ;
     int midx, midy, i, j ;
     char msg[80] = "Hello, Good Morning" ;
     char msg1[80], msg2[80] ;

     initgraph ( &gd, &gm, "c:\\tc\\bgi" ) ;

     midx = getmaxx( ) / 2 ;
     midy = getmaxy( ) / 2 ;
```

```
/* loop through text justifications */
for ( i = LEFT_TEXT ; i <= RIGHT_TEXT ; i++ )
{
    for ( j = BOTTOM_TEXT ; j <= TOP_TEXT ; j++ )
    {
        cleardevice( ) ;
        cross ( midx, midy ) ;  /* create cross hairs on the screen */
        settextjustify ( i, j ) ;  /* set the text justification */
        outtextxy ( midx, midy, msg ) ;  /* output the message */
        settextjustify ( LEFT_TEXT, TOP_TEXT ) ;
        outtextxy ( 100, 350, "HORIZONTAL JUSTIFICATION = " ) ;
        sprintf ( msg1, "%s", horizontal[i] ) ;
        outtextxy ( 320, 350, msg1 ) ;
        outtextxy ( 100, 400, "VERTICAL JUSTIFICATION = " ) ;
        sprintf ( msg2, "%s", vertical[j] ) ;
        outtextxy ( 320, 400, msg2 ) ;

        getch( ) ;
    }
}

closegraph( ) ;
restorecrtmode( ) ;
}

/* draw a "+" at (x, y) */
void cross ( int x, int y )
{
    line ( x - 20, y, x + 20, y ) ;
    line ( x, y - 20, x, y + 20 ) ;
}
```

A Bit of Animation

Drawing images is all right, what if we want to move them on the screen? This can be achieved through two functions **getimage( )** and **putimage( )**. The former reads any specified image from the screen, and the latter places it at a predetermined subsequent location, giving the illusion of movement. The following program shows how these functions can be used in tandem to move a ball on the screen.

```
# include "graphics.h"
# include "alloc.h"
main( )
{
    int gd = DETECT, gm, area, x = 25, y = 25, ch, xdirn = 1, ydirn = 1 ;
    int maxx, maxy ;
    char *buff ;

    initgraph ( &gd, &gm, "c:\\tc\\bgi" ) ;

    setcolor ( WHITE ) ;
    setfillstyle ( SOLID_FILL, RED ) ;
    circle ( 50, 50, 25 ) ;
    floodfill ( 50, 50, WHITE ) ;

    area = imagesize ( 25, 25, 75, 75 ) ;
    buff = malloc ( area ) ;
    getimage ( 25, 25, 75, 75, buff ) ;

    maxx = getmaxx( ) ;
    maxy = getmaxy( ) ;
    rectangle ( 0, 20, maxx, maxy ) ;
    outtextxy ( 250, 10, "Animation" ) ;
```

```
while ( 1 )
{
    if ( kbhit( ) )
    {
        ch = getch( ) ;

        /* if ENTER is hit reverse the direction of movement */
        if ( ch =='\r' )
        {
            xdirn *= -1 ;
            ydirn *= -1 ;
        }
        else
        {
            if ( ch == 27 )
                break ;
        }
    }

    putimage ( x, y, buff, XOR_PUT ) ;
    delay ( 0 ) ;
    x = x + ( xdirn * 5 ) ;
    y = y + ( ydirn * 2 ) ;
    putimage ( x, y, buff, XOR_PUT ) ;

    /* check if ball touches horizontal boundaries */
    if ( x > maxx - 50 || x < 0 )
    {
        sound ( 50 ) ;
        delay ( 10 ) ;
        nosound( ) ;
        xdirn *= -1 ;
    }

    /* check if ball touches vertical boundaries */
```

```
    if ( y > maxy - 50 || y < 20 )
    {
        sound ( 50 );
        delay ( 10 );
        nosound( );
        ydirn *= -1 ;
    }
}

getch( );
closegraph( );
restorecrtmode( );
}
```

To begin with, we have drawn a circle and filled it with a SOLID_FILL pattern in RED color. After this we wish to capture the image of this filled circle in memory. For this we need to know how many bytes would be required to store the image in memory. We get this by calling **imagesize( )**, which returns the bytes required to store an image in memory. The parameters passed to **imagesize( )** are the top and bottom corners of the rectangle enclosing the circle (or the image to be stored).

The next step is to allocate memory, which is done by calling the function **malloc( )**. The pointer returned by **malloc( )** is stored in the variable **buff**.

Then the function **getimage( )** is called which requires five parameters, the first four being the coordinates of the top left and bottom right of the block, and the last being the address of the memory location from where **getimage( )** will start storing the image.

The function **putimage( )** is the other side of the coin. It requires four parameters: the first two are the coordinates of the top left corner of the block, the third is the address in memory from where the image is to be retrieved, and the fourth specifies how the image should be displayed.

Having picked up the image in memory we should now erase the image from its original place and place it at a new location. This cycle should be repeated several times so that we get the impression of a ball moving on the screen. To implement this cycle of erasing-drawing-erasing we have employed a **while** loop. Every time through the loop, the first call to **putimage( )** erases the ball and the second call draws it at a new position.

How come the same **putimage( )** can sometimes draw the image and at other times erase it? The value of the fourth argument supplied to **putimage( )** decides whether it would draw or erase. The value of this argument and its significance is given in the following figure.

Argument passed	Status of image		Resultant image on screen
	Memory	Screen	
XOR_PUT	Present	Present	Erased
XOR_PUT	Present	Absent	Drawn
OR_PUT	Present	Present	Superimposed
OR_PUT	Present	Absent	Superimposed
COPY_PUT	Present	Present	Replaced
COPY_PUT	Present	Absent	Replaced

Figure 20.4

The variables **xdirn** and **ydirn** are used to change the trajectory of movement of ball. Anytime enter key is hit the direction in which the ball is traversing is reversed. Anytime the ball hits the boundary, the

sound( ) function is used to activate the speaker followed by **nosound( )** to stop the sound. **delay( )** serves the purpose of letting the speaker beep for sometime before it is shut out by **nosound( )**.

System Metrics

If we draw a line, by default it is drawn as a solid line in white color. If we display text then by default it is drawn in DEFAULT_FONT, horizontally with each character built out of a matrix of 8 x 8 pixels. The text displayed, by default, is justified to the left horizontally and to the top vertically. Likewise, if we draw a rectangle using a **bar( )** function, it is filled with a default pattern in default color. The point that I am trying to make is there are a lot of default values that the graphics library functions assume. Can we not find all these default settings through a program? We can, and that too in as simple a manner as shown below:

```
#include <dos.h>
#include <math.h>
#include <conio.h>
#include <stdio.h>
#include <stdlib.h>
#include <stdarg.h>
#include "graphics.h"

char *fonts[ ] = {
            "DefaultFont",  "TriplexFont", "SmallFont",
            "SansSerifFont", "GothicFont", "ScriptFont",
            "SimplexFont",  "TriplexScriptFont",
            "ComplexFont",  "EuropeanFont", "BoldFont"
        };

char *linestyles[ ] = {
            "SolidLn",  "DottedLn",  "CenterLn",
```

```
                              "DashedLn", "UserBitLn"
                    } ;

char *fillstyles[ ] = {

                    "EmptyFill",    "SolidFill",  "LineFill",
                    "LtSlashFill",   "SlashFill",  "BkSlashFill",
                    "LtBkSlashFill", "HatchFill",  "XHatchFill",
                    "InterleaveFill", "WideDotFill", "CloseDotFill"
                    } ;

char *textdirect[ ] = {
                    "HorizDir", "VertDir"
                    } ;

char *horizontal[ ] = {
                    "LeftText", "CenterText", "RightText"
                    } ;

char *vertical[ ] = {
                    "BottomText", "CenterText", "TopText"
                    } ;

struct pts
{
    int x, y ;
} ;

int gprintf ( int *xloc, int *yloc, char *fmt, ... ) ;

main( )
{
    struct viewporttype  viewinfo ;
    struct linesettingstype lineinfo ;
    struct fillsettingstype fillinfo ;
    struct textsettingstype textinfo ;
```

```
struct palettetype palette, far *pal ;

float aspectratio ;
int maxx, maxy, maxcolors, errorcode, xasp, yasp, low,
high ;

char *driver, *mode ;
int x, y, gd = DETECT, gm, i ;

initgraph ( &gd, &gm, "c:\\tc\\bgi" ) ;

rectangle ( 0, 20, 639, 479 ) ;
outtextxy ( 200, 10, "system metrics" ) ;

getviewsettings ( &viewinfo ) ;
getlinesettings ( &lineinfo ) ;
getfillsettings ( &fillinfo ) ;
gettextsettings ( &textinfo ) ;
getpalette ( &palette ) ;
getaspectratio ( &xasp, &yasp ) ;
aspectratio = xasp / yasp ;
driver = getdrivername( ) ;
mode = getmodename ( gm ) ;
getmoderange ( gd, &low, &high ) ;
gm = getgraphmode( ) ;
maxcolors = getmaxcolor( ) + 1 ;
pal = getdefaultpalette( ) ;

x = 20 ;
y = 30 ;

settextjustify ( LEFT_TEXT, TOP_TEXT ) ;

gprintf ( &x, &y, "Graphics device   : %-20s (%d)", driver, gd ) ;
gprintf ( &x, &y, "Graphics mode    : %-20s (%d)", mode, gm ) ;
```

```
gprintf ( &x, &y, "Max Mode Number    : %d", getmaxmode( ) ) ;
gprintf ( &x, &y, "Mode Range is      : %d to %d", low, high ) ;
gprintf ( &x, &y, "Screen resolution  : ( 0, 0, %d, %d )", getmaxx( ),
         getmaxy( ) ) ;
gprintf ( &x, &y, "Current view port  : ( %d, %d, %d, %d )",
viewinfo.left, viewinfo.top, viewinfo.right, viewinfo.bottom ) ;
gprintf ( &x, &y, "Clipping           : %s",
         viewinfo.clip ? "ON" : "OFF" ) ;
gprintf ( &x, &y, "Aspect Ratio       : %f", aspectratio ) ;
gprintf ( &x, &y, "Current position   : ( %d, %d )", get( ), gety( ) ) ;
gprintf ( &x, &y, "Colors available   : %d", maxcolors ) ;
gprintf ( &x, &y, "Current color      : %d", getcolor( ) ) ;
gprintf( &x, &y, "Current BkColor     : %d", getbkcolor( ) );
gprintf ( &x, &y, "Line style         : %s",
         linestyles[ lineinfo.linestyle ] ) ;
gprintf ( &x, &y, "Line thickness     : %d", lineinfo.thickness ) ;
gprintf ( &x, &y, "Current fill style : %s", fillstyles[ fillinfo.pattern ] ) ;
gprintf ( &x, &y, "Current fill color : %d", fillinfo.color ) ;
gprintf ( &x, &y, "Current font       : %s", fonts[ textinfo.font ] ) ;
gprintf ( &x, &y, "Text direction     : %s",
         textdirect[ textinfo.direction ] ) ;
gprintf ( &x, &y, "Character size     : %d", textinfo.charsize ) ;
gprintf ( &x, &y, "Horizontal justify : %s",
         horizontal[ textinfo.horiz ] ) ;
gprintf ( &x, &y, "Vertical justify   : %s", vertical[ textinfo.vert ] ) ;
gprintf ( &x, &y, "Palette size       : %d", getpalettesize( ) ) ;

for ( i = 0 ; i <= 15 ; i++ )
    gprintf ( &x, &y, "value of color[%d] = %d ", i, pal -> colors[i] ) ;

getch( ) ;
closegraph( ) ;
restorecrtmode( ) ;
}
```

```
int gprintf ( int *x, int *y, char *fmt, ... )
{
    va_list  ptr ;
    char str[140] ;

    va_start ( ptr, fmt ) ;
    vsprintf ( str, fmt, ptr ) ;
    outtextxy ( *x, *y, str ) ;
    *y = *y + textheight ( "H" ) + 2 ;
    va_end ( ptr ) ;
}
```

The purpose of each standard library graphics function used in this program to extract the default values of various parameters is as follows:

Function	Description
getviewsettings( )	Gets information about the current viewport.
getlinesettings( )	Gets the current line style, pattern and thickness.
getfillsettings( )	Gets information about current fill pattern and color.
gettextsettings( )	Gets information about the current graphic text font.
getpalette( )	Gets information about the current palette's size and colors.
getaspectratio( )	Gets the aspect-ratio values in x and y aspect factors.

getdrivername( )	Returns a pointer to the name of the current graphics driver.
getmodename( )	Returns the name of the specified graphics mode.
getmoderange( )	Gets the range of modes for a given graphics driver.
getgraphmode( )	Returns the current graphics mode.
getmaxcolor( )	Returns maximum color value.
getdefaultpalette( )	Gets information about the palette initialised by the driver during **initgraph( )**.
getmaxmode( )	Returns maximum graphics mode number for the current driver.
getmaxx( )	Returns maximum x screen coordinate.
getmaxy( )	Returns maximum y screen coordinate.
getx( )	Returns the x coordinate of the current graphics position.
gety( )	Returns the y coordinate of the current graphics position.
getcolor( )	Returns the current drawing color.
getbkcolor( )	Returns the current background color.
getpalettesize( )	Returns the size of the palette.

In this program the text has been outputted on the screen using the function **gprintf( )**. This function works similar to **printf( )** except that it is capable of displaying output in graphics mode. The advantage of this function is that it can collect a variable number of arguments. Each time it is called we have passed to it the position where the text is to be outputted on the screen, the format string and a list of variables whose values are to be printed. The macros **va_start, va_list, va_end** are defined in the file 'stdarg.h'. Out of these, the **va_start** macro is used to set up a pointer to the format string. Next, the string to be outputted is written to the string **str[ ]** by calling the **vsprintf( )** function. The contents of the string are then displayed on the screen using the usual **outtextxy( )** function.

21 *Mouse Programming*

Graphical User Interfaces (GUIs) and mouse go hand in hand. Though some GUIs do exist which manage the show without a mouse, the mouse has more or less become a standard input device with any GUI worth its name. A mouse is used to point at the icons which form the menu in a GUI - much like the way a child points to something he wants.

These point-and-shoot menus of GUI bring along ease and convenience along with all the added agility of the real-life look alike of the mouse. As a result, more and more packages today are not only menu driven, but also mouse driven. The use of a mouse requires a program to sense its presence. Just attaching the mouse to the computer is not enough. What we also need to do is load a device driver program that understands the mouse. A device driver is a program which senses the signals coming from the port to which the mouse is attached. On sensing the signals, the driver translates these into the related action on the screen. This device driver is usually available as a program called MOUSE.COM or WITTYMS.COM, which work with different variety of mice.

The mouse has a separate cursor (often called a mouse 'pointer') which looks like an arrow and functions in the same way as the normal cursor. As we move the mouse, the mouse pointer moves correspondingly. It is just like using arrow keys. The only difference being, the speed at which the mouse cursor moves is much faster than that of an ordinary cursor. If desired, we can change the speed of the mouse pointer, and even its shape. Once the mouse driver is loaded, the various mouse functions can be accessed by setting up the AX register with different values (service numbers) and issuing interrupt number 33h. Some of these functions are used in the following program.

```
#include "dos.h"
#include "graphics.h"
```

```
union REGS i, o ;
main( )
{
    int gd = DETECT, gm, maxx, maxy, x, y, button ;

    initgraph ( &gd, &gm, "c:\\tc\\bgi" ) ;
    maxx = getmaxx( ) ;
    maxy = getmaxy( ) ;

    rectangle ( 0, 56, maxx, maxy ) ;
    setviewport ( 1, 57, maxx - 1, maxy - 1, 1 ) ;

    gotoxy ( 26, 1 ) ;
    printf ( "Mouse Demonstration Program" ) ;

    if ( initmouse( ) == 0 )
    {
        closegraph( ) ;
        restorecrtmode( ) ;
        printf ( "\nMouse driver not loaded" ) ;
        exit ( 1 ) ;
    }

    restrictmouseptr ( 1, 57, maxx - 1, maxy - 1 ) ;
    showmouseptr( ) ;
    gotoxy ( 1, 2 ) ;
    printf ( "Left Button" ) ;
    gotoxy ( 15, 2 ) ;
    printf ( "Right Button" ) ;
    gotoxy ( 55, 3 ) ;
    printf ( "Press any key to exit..." ) ;

    while ( !kbhit( ) )
    {
```

```
        getmousepos ( &button, &x, &y ) ;

        gotoxy ( 5, 3 ) ;
        ( button & 1 ) == 1 ? printf ( "DOWN" ) : printf ( "UP" ) ;

        gotoxy ( 20, 3 ) ;
        ( button & 2 ) == 2 ? printf ( "DOWN" ) : printf ( "UP" ) ;

        gotoxy ( 65, 2 ) ;
        printf ( "X = %03d  y = %03d", x, y ) ;
    }
}

/* initialises mouse */
initmouse( )
{
    i.x.ax = 0 ;
    int86 ( 0x33, &i, &o ) ;
    return ( o.x.ax ) ;
}

/* displays mouse pointer */
showmouseptr( )
{
    i.x.ax = 1 ;
    int86 ( 0x33, &i, &o ) ;
}

/* restricts mouse movement */
restrictmouseptr ( int x1, int y1, int x2, int y2 )
{
    i.x.ax = 7 ;
    i.x.cx = x1 ;
    i.x.dx = x2 ;
    int86 ( 0x33, &i, &o ) ;
```

```
        i.x.ax = 8 ;
        i.x.cx = y1 ;
        i.x.dx = y2 ;
        int86 ( 0x33, &i, &o ) ;
}

/* gets mouse coordinates and button status */
getmousepos ( int *button, int *x, int *y )
{
        i.x.ax = 3 ;
        int86 ( 0x33, &i, &o ) ;
        *button = o.x.bx ;
        *x = o.x.cx ;
        *y = o.x.dx ;
}
```

Mouse can be used in text mode as well as in graphics mode. Usually it is used in graphics mode. Hence we must first change over to graphics mode. In our program the function **initgraph( )** is responsible for switching the mode from text to graphics. DETECT is a macro defined in 'graphics.h'. It requests **initgraph( )** to automatically determine which graphics driver to load in order to switch to the highest resolution graphics mode. The **initgraph( )** function takes three parameters, the graphics driver, the graphics mode and the path to the driver file.

Once the driver has been loaded, **initgraph( )** sets up the numeric values of the graphics driver and the graphics mode chosen in the variables **gd** and **gm** respectively. Here we are assuming that the driver files are in the directory 'c:\tc\bgi'. Hence the path passed to **initgraph( )** is 'c:\\tc\\bgi'.

Once we are into the graphics mode we have called the functions **getmaxx( )** and **getmaxy( )** to obtain the maximum x and y coordinates in the current graphics mode. Then we have drawn a rectangle using the function **rectangle( )** and set the viewport area which restricts any drawing activity within the viewport.

Next we have called the function **initmouse( )** to initialise the mouse. It checks if the mouse driver has been loaded or not (by issuing interrupt 33h, service number 0) and then reports the status to **main( )**. If mouse is not initialised successfully then the **closegraph( )** function unloads the graphics driver and **restorecrtmode( )** takes the screen back to the mode that existed prior to the calling of **initgraph( )**, which in our case is the text mode. If you have loaded the mouse driver successfully then in all probability the mouse would be successfully initialised.

Most softwares today provide windowing feature. Not just windows on the screen as boxes, but windows that restrict cursor movement. Like a screen within a screen. If we define the size of the window then we can make sure that the cursor only moves within the window. This is what programs like Windows and even DBMSs like Foxpro and dBase give us. There is nothing too difficult about it. It's just a matter of putting the right values in the right registers. In our program this has been achieved by the function **restrictmouseptr( )**. Next, another function called **showmouseptr( )** has been called. It actually displays the mouse pointer on the screen.

Both the tasks of restricting the mouse pointer movement and displaying the mouse pointer are achieved by invoking appropriate services available under interrupt number 33h. In fact once the mouse driver has been loaded, anything to be done with the mouse is always done by some service or the other available under interrupt 33h.

Then the control enters a **while** loop where we check to see which button has been pressed and accordingly display either 'UP' or

'DOWN'. Additionally, the current coordinates of the mouse pointer are also displayed. If a key is hit from the keyboard we exit the loop. Details of some of the more commonly used mouse services are given on the following page.

Drawing With Mouse

Now that we know how to initialise the mouse, display the mouse pointer, hide it if required, get the current position of the mouse cursor and status of the mouse buttons we can put all this to use to do something worthwhile. Drawing rectangles using mouse, for example. I have written the following program for a VGA color monitor in 640 x 480 resolution graphics mode. But it works even on other monitors with lower resolutions without making any changes.

```c
#include "graphics.h"
#include "dos.h"
#include "alloc.h"

union REGS i, o ;
int midx, midy ;
char far *p1, far *p2, far *p3, far *p4 ;

main( )
{
    int gd = DETECT, gm, button, x, y, sx, sy, tx, ty, x1, y1, x2, y2 ;

    if ( initmouse( ) == 0 )
    {
        printf ( "\nMouse driver not loaded..." ) ;
        exit ( 1 ) ;
    }
```

Interrupt	Service	Purpose
33h	0	Reset mouse and get status Call with: AX = 0 Returns: AX = FFFFh If mouse support is available AX = 0 If mouse support is not available
33h	1	Show mouse pointer Call with: AX = 1 Returns: Nothing
33h	2	Hide mouse pointer Call with: AX = 2 Returns: Nothing
33h	3	Get mouse position and button status Call with: AX = 3 Returns: BX = mouse button status Bit Significance 0 left button is down 1 right button is down 2 center button is down CX = x coordinate DX = y coordinate
33h	4	Set mouse pointer position Call with: AX = 4 CX = x coordinate DX = y coordinate Returns: Nothing
33h	7	Set horizontal limits for pointer Call with: AX = 7 CX = minimum x coordinate DX = maximum x coordinate Returns: Nothing
33h	8	Set vertical limits for pointer Call with: AX = 8 CX = minimum y coordinate DX = maximum y coordinate

Figure 21.1

```
initgraph ( &gd, &gm, "c:\\tc\\bgi" ) ;
gotoxy ( 1, 1 ) ;
printf ( "Draw box....." ) ;
gotoxy ( 60, 1 ) ;
printf ( "Right button to exit" ) ;

do
{
    showmouseptr( ) ;
    getmousepos ( &button, &tx, &ty ) ;

    if ( button & 1 == 1 )
    {
        hidemouseptr( ) ;
        sx = x = x1 = x2 = tx ;
        sy = y = y1 = y2 = ty ;
        setcolor ( WHITE ) ;
        save ( x1, y1, x2, y2 ) ;
        rectangle ( x1, y1, x2, y2 ) ;
        getmousepos ( &button, &tx, &ty ) ;

        while ( ( button & 1 ) == 1 )
        {
            if ( x != tx || y != ty )
            {
                setcolor ( BLACK ) ;
                rectangle ( x1, y1, x2, y2 ) ;
                restore ( x1, y1 ) ;
                x = tx ;
                y = ty ;

                if ( x < sx )
                {
                    x1 = x ;
                    x2 = sx ;
```

```
                    }
                    else
                    {
                        x1 = sx ;
                        x2 = x ;
                    }

                    if ( y < sy )
                    {
                        y1 = y ;
                        y2 = sy ;
                    }
                    else
                    {
                        y1 = sy ;
                        y2 = y ;
                    }

                    setcolor ( WHITE ) ;
                    save ( x1, y1, x2, y2 ) ;
                    rectangle ( x1, y1, x2, y2 ) ;
                }

                getmousepos ( &button, &tx, &ty ) ;
            }

        restore ( x1, y1 ) ;
        showmouseptr( ) ;
    }
} while ( ( button & 2 ) != 2 ) ;

gotoxy ( 1, 1 ) ;
printf ( "Press any key to exit" ) ;
gotoxy ( 60, 1 ) ;
printf ( " " ) ;
```

```
        getch( ) ;
        closegraph( ) ;
}

save ( int x1, int y1, int x2, int y2 )
{
    unsigned area1, area2, area3, area4 ;

    midx = x1 + (x2 - x1) / 2 ;
    midy = y1 + (y2 - y1) / 2 ;

    area1 = imagesize ( x1, y1, midx, midy ) ;
    p1 = farmalloc ( area1 ) ;
    area2 = imagesize ( midx + 1, y1, x2, midy ) ;
    p2 = farmalloc ( area2 ) ;
    area3 = imagesize ( x1, midy + 1, midx, y2 ) ;
    p3 = farmalloc ( area3 ) ;
    area4 = imagesize ( midx + 1, midy + 1, x2, y2 ) ;
    p4 = farmalloc ( area4 ) ;

    if ( p1 == NULL || p2 == NULL || p3 == NULL || p4 == NULL )
    {
        closegraph( ) ;
        printf ( "Memory allocation error!" ) ;
        exit ( 2 ) ;
    }

    getimage ( x1, y1, midx, midy, p1 ) ;
    getimage ( midx + 1, y1, x2, midy, p2 ) ;
    getimage ( x1, midy + 1, midx, y2, p3 ) ;
    getimage ( midx + 1, midy + 1, x2, y2, p4 ) ;
}

restore ( int x1, int y1 )
{
```

```
    putimage ( x1, y1, p1, OR_PUT ) ;
    putimage ( midx + 1, y1, p2, OR_PUT ) ;
    putimage ( x1, midy + 1, p3, OR_PUT ) ;
    putimage ( midx + 1, midy + 1, p4, OR_PUT ) ;

    farfree ( p1 ) ;
    farfree ( p2 ) ;
    farfree ( p3 ) ;
    farfree ( p4 ) ;
}

initmouse( )
{
    i.x.ax = 0 ;
    int86 ( 0x33, &i, &o ) ;
    return ( o.x.ax ) ;
}

showmouseptr( )
{
    i.x.ax = 1 ;
    int86 ( 0x33, &i, &o ) ;
}

hidemouseptr( )
{
    i.x.ax = 2 ;
    int86 ( 0x33, &i, &o ) ;
}

restrictmouseptr ( int x1, int y1, int x2, int y2 )
{
    i.x.ax = 7 ;
    i.x.cx = x1 ;
    i.x.dx = x2 ;
```

```
        int86 ( 0x33, &i, &o ) ;
        i.x.ax = 8 ;
        i.x.cx = y1 ;
        i.x.dx = y2 ;
        int86 ( 0x33, &i, &o ) ;
}

getmousepos ( int *button, int *x, int *y )
{
        i.x.ax = 3 ;
        int86 ( 0x33, &i, &o ) ;
        *button = o.x.bx ;
        *x = o.x.cx ;
        *y = o.x.dx ;
}
```

Building Mouse Cursors

In text mode the mouse cursor appears as a block, whereas in graphics mode it appears as an arrow. If we wish, we can change the graphics cursor to any other shape the way Windows or Ventura does. The mouse cursor in graphics mode occupies a 16 by 16 pixel box. By highlighting or de-highlighting some of the pixels in this box we can get a mouse cursor of the desired shape. For example, the bit-pattern shown in figure .2 can be used to generate the cursor which looks like an hour-glass.

The 1's in the mouse pointer bitmap indicate that the pixel would be drawn, whereas the zeros indicate that the pixel would stand erased. It is important to note that though the mouse pointer bit pattern is 32 bytes long, while actually writing a program to change the pointer shape we need a 64 byte bitmap. This is done to ensure that when the cursor reaches a position on the screen where something is already written or drawn, only that portion gets overwritten which is going to be occupied by the mouse cursor. Of the 64 bytes, the first

32 bytes contain a bit mask which is first ANDed with the screen image, and then the second 32 bytes bit mask is XORed with the screen image. The following program changes the mouse cursor in graphics mode to resemble an hour glass.

1 1 1 1 1 1 1 1 1 1 1 1 1 1 1 1	0 0 0 0 0 0 0 0 0 0 0 0 0 0 0 0
1 0 0 0 0 0 0 0 0 0 0 0 0 0 0 1	0 0 0 0 0 0 0 0 0 0 0 0 0 0 0 0
1 1 1 1 1 1 1 1 1 1 1 1 1 1 1 1	0 0 0 0 0 0 0 0 0 0 0 0 0 0 0 0
1 0 0 0 0 0 0 0 0 0 0 0 0 0 0 1	0 0 0 0 0 0 0 0 0 0 0 0 0 0 0 0
0 1 0 0 0 0 0 0 0 0 0 0 0 0 1 0	1 0 0 0 0 0 0 0 0 0 0 0 0 0 0 1
0 0 1 0 0 0 0 0 0 0 0 0 0 1 0 0	1 1 0 0 0 0 0 0 0 0 0 0 0 0 1 1
0 0 0 0 1 0 0 0 0 0 0 1 0 0 0 0	1 1 1 1 0 0 0 0 0 0 0 0 1 1 1 1
0 0 0 0 0 0 1 0 0 1 0 0 0 0 0 0	1 1 1 1 1 1 0 0 0 0 1 1 1 1 1 1
0 0 0 0 0 0 1 0 0 1 0 0 0 0 0 0	1 1 1 1 1 1 0 0 0 0 1 1 1 1 1 1
0 0 0 0 1 0 0 0 0 0 0 1 0 0 0 0	1 1 1 1 0 0 0 0 0 0 0 0 1 1 1 1
0 0 1 0 0 0 0 0 0 0 0 0 0 1 0 0	1 1 0 0 0 0 0 0 0 0 0 0 0 0 1 1
0 1 0 0 0 0 0 0 0 0 0 0 0 0 1 0	1 0 0 0 0 0 0 0 0 0 0 0 0 0 0 1
1 0 0 0 0 0 0 0 0 0 0 0 0 0 0 1	0 0 0 0 0 0 0 0 0 0 0 0 0 0 0 0
1 1 1 1 1 1 1 1 1 1 1 1 1 1 1 1	0 0 0 0 0 0 0 0 0 0 0 0 0 0 0 0
1 0 0 0 0 0 0 0 0 0 0 0 0 0 0 1	0 0 0 0 0 0 0 0 0 0 0 0 0 0 0 0
1 1 1 1 1 1 1 1 1 1 1 1 1 1 1 1	0 0 0 0 0 0 0 0 0 0 0 0 0 0 0 0
Mouse pointer bitmap	Screen Mask

Figure 21.2

```
#include "graphics.h"
#include "dos.h"
```

```
union REGS i, o ;
struct SREGS s ;

int cursor[32] = {
                /* hour-glass screen mask */
                0x0000, 0x0000, 0x0000, 0x0000,
                0x8001, 0xc003, 0xf00f, 0xfc3f,
                0xfc3f, 0xf00f, 0xc003, 0x8001,
                0x0000, 0x0000, 0x0000, 0x0000,

                /* the mouse pointer bitmap */
                0xffff, 0x8001, 0xffff, 0x8001,
                0x4002, 0x2004, 0x1008, 0x0240,
                0x0240, 0x0810, 0x2004, 0x4002,
                0x8001, 0xffff, 0x8001, 0xffff,
            } ;

main( )
{
    int gd = DETECT, gm ;

    initgraph ( &gd, &gm, "c:\\tc\\bgi" ) ;

    if ( initmouse( ) == 0 )
    {
        closegraph( ) ;
        printf ( "\n Mouse not installed!" ) ;
        exit ( 1 ) ;
    }

    gotoxy ( 10, 1 ) ;
    printf ( "Press any key to exit..." ) ;
    changecursor ( cursor ) ;
    showmouseptr( ) ;
    getch( ) ;
```

```
}

initmouse( )
{
    i.x.ax = 0 ;
    int86 ( 0x33, &i, &o ) ;
    return ( o.x.ax ) ;
}

showmouseptr( )
{
    i.x.ax = 1 ;
    int86 ( 0x33, &i, &o ) ;
}

changecursor ( int *shape )
{
    i.x.ax = 9 ;  /* service number */
    i.x.bx = 0 ;  /* actual cursor position from left */
    i.x.cx = 0 ;  /* actual cursor position from top */
    i.x.dx = ( unsigned ) shape ;  /* offset address of pointer image */
    segread ( &s ) ;
    s.es = s.ds ;  /* segment address of pointer */
    int86x ( 0x33, &i, &i, &s ) ;
}
```

More Mouse Cursors

In the last program we saw how to change the default mouse cursor. Once we know this we can think of building different shapes of mouse cursors, each to signify a different operation or mode. This is what is done by Ventura to show in which mode are we working currently. The following program shows how this can be managed. The functions **initmouse( )**, **changecursor( )**, **showmouseptr( )**,

getmousepos( ), **hidemouseptr( )** which have been discussed in the last three programs have not been reproduced here.

```
# include "graphics.h"
# include "dos.h"
#include "alloc.h"

union REGS i, o ;
struct SREGS s ;

int c[ ][32] = {
                /* Cursor 1. Hand-screen mask + pointer bit map*/
                0xe1ff, 0xe1ff, 0xe1ff, 0xe1ff, 0xe1ff, 0x0000,
                0x0000, 0x0000, 0x0000, 0x0000, 0x0000, 0x0000,
                0x0000, 0x0000, 0x0000, 0x0000, 0x1e00, 0x1200,
                0x1200, 0x1200, 0x13ff, 0x1249, 0x1249, 0xf249,
                0x9001, 0x9001, 0x9001, 0x8001, 0x8001, 0x8001,
                0xffff, 0x0000,

                /* Cursor 2. Arrow-screen mask + pointer bit map*/
                0xffff, 0xffff, 0xe003, 0xf003, 0xf803, 0xfc03,
                0xfe03, 0xfc03, 0xf803, 0xf043, 0xe0e3, 0xc1f3,
                0x83fb, 0x07ff, 0x8fff, 0xdfff, 0x0000, 0x0000,
                0x1ffc, 0x0804, 0x0404, 0x0204, 0x0104, 0x0204,
                0x0444, 0x08a4, 0x1114, 0x220c, 0x4404, 0x8800,
                0x5000, 0x2000,

                /* Cursor 3. Hour glass mask + bit map*/
                0x0000, 0x0000, 0x0000, 0x0000, 0x8001, 0xc003,
                0xf00f, 0xfc3f, 0xfc3f, 0xf00f, 0xc003, 0x8001,
                0x0000, 0x0000, 0x0000, 0x0000, 0xffff, 0x8001,
                0xffff, 0x8001, 0x4002, 0x2004, 0x1008, 0x0240,
                0x0240, 0x0810, 0x2004, 0x4002, 0x8001, 0xffff,
                0x8001, 0xffff,
```

```
                    /* Cursor 4. Para-screen mask + pointer bit map*/
                    0x0000, 0x0000, 0x0000, 0x0000, 0x0000, 0x0000,
                    0x0000, 0x0000, 0x0000, 0x0000, 0x0000, 0x0000,
                    0x0000, 0x0000, 0x0000, 0x0000, 0xffff, 0xffff,
                    0xffff, 0x0007, 0x0007, 0xeee7, 0x0007, 0x0007,
                    0xeee7, 0x0007, 0x0007, 0xeee7, 0x0007, 0x0007,
                    0xeee7, 0xeee7
                } ;

main( )
{
    int gd = DETECT, gm, button, x, y, area, i, choice ;
    char *p ;

    initgraph ( &gd, &gm, "c:\\tc\\bgi" ) ;

    if ( initmouse( ) == 0 )
    {
        closegraph( ) ;
        puts ( "Mouse not installed!" ) ;
        exit ( 1 ) ;
    }

    for ( i = 0 ; i < 4 ; i++ )
    {
        changecursor ( c[i] ) ;
        showmouseptr( ) ;
        getmousepos ( &button, &x, &y ) ;
        area = imagesize ( x - 15, y - 7, x + 32, y + 24 ) ;
        p = malloc ( area ) ;
        getimage ( x - 15, y - 7, x + 32, y + 24, p ) ;
        putimage ( i * 48 + 1, 1, p, COPY_PUT ) ;
        rectangle ( i * 48, 0, ( i + 1 ) * 48, 33 ) ;
    }
```

```
gotoxy ( 10, 25 ) ;
printf ( "Press any key to exit..." ) ;
choice = 1 ;
disp ( choice, p ) ;
changecursor ( c[choice - 1] ) ;

while ( !kbhit( ) )
{
    getmousepos ( &button, &x, &y ) ;

    if ( ( button & 1 ) == 1 )
    {
        for ( i = 0 ; i < 4 ; i++ )
        {
            if ( choice - 1 == i )
                continue ;

            if ( y > 0 && y < 33 )
            {
                if ( x > i * 48 && x < ( i + 1 ) * 48 )
                {
                    hidemouseptr( ) ;
                    disp ( choice, p ) ;
                    choice = i + 1 ;
                    disp ( choice, p ) ;
                    changecursor ( c[choice - 1] ) ;
                    showmouseptr( ) ;
                }
            }
        }
    }

    getch( ) ;
}
```

```
disp ( int choice, char *p )
{
    getimage ( ( choice - 1 ) * 48 + 1, 1, choice * 48, 32, p ) ;
    putimage ( ( choice - 1 ) * 48 + 1, 1, p, NOT_PUT ) ;
}
```

Freehand Drawing Using Mouse

Let us now try to gather all that we know about the mouse and its
functions to develop a utility for drawing freehand... the way it is
done in softwares like Paintbrush, Corel Draw etc. Here is the
program...

```
#include "dos.h"
#include "graphics.h"

union REGS i, o ;

main( )
{
    int gd = DETECT, gm, maxx, maxy, x, y, button, prevx, prevy ;

    initgraph ( &gd, &gm, "c:\\tc\\bgi" ) ;

    maxx = getmaxx( ) ;
    maxy = getmaxy( ) ;
    rectangle ( 0, 0, maxx, maxy ) ;
    setviewport ( 1, 1, maxx - 1, maxy - 1, 1 ) ;

    if ( initmouse( ) == 0 )
    {
        closegraph( ) ;
        restorecrtmode( ) ;
```

```
            printf ( "Mouse driver not loaded" ) ;
            exit ( 1 ) ;
    }

    restrictmouseptr ( 1, 1, maxx - 1, maxy - 1 ) ;
    showmouseptr( ) ;

    while ( !kbhit( ) )
    {
        getmousepos ( &button, &x, &y ) ;
        if ( ( button & 1 ) == 1 )
        {
            hidemouseptr( ) ;
            prevx = x ;
            prevy = y ;

            while ( ( button & 1 ) == 1 )
            {
                line ( prevx, prevy, x, y ) ;
                prevx = x ;
                prevy = y ;
                getmousepos ( &button, &x, &y ) ;
            }

            showmouseptr( ) ;
        }
    }
}

initmouse( )
{
    i.x.ax = 0 ;
    int86 ( 0x33, &i, &o ) ;
    return ( o.x.ax )
}
```

```
showmouseptr( )
{
    i.x.ax = 1 ;
    int86 ( 0x33, &i, &o ) ;
}

hidemouseptr( )
{
    i.x.ax = 2 ;
    int86 ( 0x33, &i, &o ) ;
}

restrictmouseptr ( int x1, int y1, int x2, int y2 )
{
    i.x.ax = 7 ;
    i.x.cx = x1 ;
    i.x.dx = x2 ;
    int86 ( 0x33, &i, &o ) ;

    i.x.ax = 8 ;
    i.x.cx = y1 ;
    i.x.dx = y2 ;
    int86 ( 0x33, &i, &o ) ;
}

getmousepos ( int *button, int *x, int *y )
{
    i.x.ax = 3 ;
    int86 ( 0x33, &i, &o ) ;
    *button = o.x.bx ;
    *x = o.x.cx ;
    *y = o.x.dx ;
}
```

In **main( )** the loop **while (!kbhit( ))** allows the drawing of as many freehand drawings as the user desires, the process stopping when the user hits a key from the keyboard. The freehand drawing begins on hitting the left mouse button, and grows as the mouse is dragged with the left button depressed. On releasing the left button that freehand drawing is terminated. When the actual drawing is in progress the mouse pointer is hidden, and it reappears when the mouse button is released.

Menus Using Mouse

Quite often we navigate within menus of best-selling softwares using mouse without thinking for a moment how these menus are developed. The following program shows how such programs can be written. Care has been taken to ensure that the menu would work for all memory models and for different types of adapters like CGA, EGA, VGA etc.

```
#include "dos.h"
#include "graphics.h"
#include "alloc.h"

char *menu[ ] = { "Samosa", "Sambarwada", "Dahiwada", "Exit" } ;
union REGS i, o ;

main( )
{
    int gd = DETECT, gm, choice = 1, bill = 0, width = 0, i, count ;
    char **buffer ;

    initgraph ( &gd, &gm, "c:\\tc\\bgi" ) ;

    if ( initmouse( ) == 0 )
    {
```

```
            printf ( "\nUnable to initialise Mouse..." ) ;
            exit( ) ;
      }

      count = sizeof ( menu ) / sizeof ( char * ) ;
      settextstyle ( TRIPLEX_FONT, 0, 3 ) ;
      displaymenu ( menu, count, 100, 100 ) ;

      for ( i = 0 ; i < count ; i++ )
      {
            if ( textwidth ( menu[i] ) > width )
                  width = textwidth ( menu[i] ) ;
      }

      buffer = malloc ( sizeof ( menu ) ) ;
      savemenu ( menu, buffer, width, count, 100, 100 ) ;

      while ( choice != 4 )
      {
            choice = getresponse ( menu, buffer, width, count, 100, 100 ) ;
            gotoxy ( 50, 15 ) ;
            printf ( "You selected %s ", menu[choice - 1] ) ;
      }
}

displaymenu ( char **menu, int count, int x1, int y1 )
{
      int i, h ;

      h = textheight ( menu[0] ) ;

      for ( i = 0 ; i < count ; i++ )
            outtextxy ( x1, y1 + i * ( h + 5 ), menu[i] ) ;
}
```

```
savemenu ( char **menu, char **buffer, int width, int count, int x1, int y1 )
{
    int i, x2, yy1, yy2, area, h ;

    h = textheight ( menu[0] ) ;

    for ( i = 0 ; i < count ; i++ )
    {
        x2 = x1 + width ;
        yy1 = y1 + i * ( h + 5 ) ;
        yy2 = y1 + ( i + 1 ) * ( h + 5 ) ;

        area = imagesize ( x1, yy1, x2, yy2 ) ;
        buffer[i] = malloc ( area ) ;
        getimage ( x1, yy1, x2, yy2, buffer[i] ) ;
    }
}

getresponse ( char **menu, char **buffer, int width, int count, int x1,
                int y1 )
{
    int choice = 1, prevchoice = 0, x, y, x2, y2, button ;
    int in, i, h ;

    h = textheight ( menu[0] ) ;
    y2 = y1 + count * ( h + 5 ) ;
    x2 = x1 + width ;
    rectangle ( x1 - 5, y1 - 5, x2 + 5, y2 + 5 ) ;

    while ( 1 )
    {
        getmousepos ( &button, &x, &y ) ;

        if ( x >= x1 && x <= x2 && y >= y1 && y <= y2 )
        {
```

```
in = 1 ;

for ( i = 1 ; i <= count ; i++ )
{
    if ( y <= y1 + i * ( h + 5 ) )
    {
        choice = i ;
        break ;
    }
}

if ( prevchoice != choice )
{
    hidemouseptr( ) ;
    highlight ( buffer, choice, h, x1, y1 ) ;

    if ( prevchoice )
        dehighlight ( buffer, prevchoice, h, x1, y1 ) ;

    prevchoice = choice ;
    showmouseptr( ) ;
}

if ( ( button & 1 ) == 1 )
{
    while ( ( button & 1 ) == 1 )
        getmousepos ( &button, &x, &y ) ;

    if ( x >= x1 && x <= x2 && y >= y1 && y <= y2 )
        return ( choice ) ;
}
}
else
{
    if ( in == 1 )
```

```
                {
                    in = 0 ;
                    prevchoice = 0 ;
                    hidemouseptr( ) ;
                    dehighlight ( buffer, choice, h, x1, y1 ) ;
                    showmouseptr( ) ;
                }
            }
        }
}

highlight ( char **buffer, int ch, int h, int x1, int y1 )
{
    putimage( x1, y1 + ( ch - 1 ) * ( h + 5 ), buffer[ch - 1], NOT_PUT ) ;
}

dehighlight ( char **buffer, int ch, int h, int x1, int y1 )
{
    putimage( x1, y1 + ( ch - 1 ) * ( h + 5 ), buffer[ch - 1], COPY_PUT ) ;
}

initmouse( )
{
    i.x.ax = 0 ;
    int86 ( 0x33, &i, &o ) ;
    return ( o.x.ax )
}

showmouseptr( )
{
    i.x.ax = 1 ;
    int86 ( 0x33, &i, &o ) ;
}

hidemouseptr( )
```

```
{
    i.x.ax = 2 ;
    int86 ( 0x33, &i, &o ) ;
}

getmousepos ( int *button, int *x, int *y )
{
    i.x.ax = 3 ;
    int86 ( 0x33, &i, &o ) ;
    *button = o.x.bx ;
    *x = o.x.cx ;
    *y = o.x.dx ;
}
```

Note that the menu items are stored in an array of pointers to strings **menu[ ]**. Once the graphics system and the mouse has been initialised, the number of items in the menu are determined, text style is set and the menu is displayed on the screen using the function **displaymenu( )**. To highlight or de-highlight the menu items, rather than building the items from scratch their existing images are stored in a buffer.

The space for this buffer is allocated using **malloc( )** and the actual saving of images is done through the function **savemenu( )**. The base addresses of these images are stored in an array of pointers, pointed to by the variable **buffer**. Using these addresses let us now see how do we go about moving the highlighted bar using mouse and then make a selection from the menu by clicking on the left mouse button. All this is achieved by the function **getresponse( )**.

To begin with, the **getresponse( )** function checks the position of the mouse pointer. If the mouse pointer is inside the area occupied by the menu then it checks on which menu item is it placed and highlights that item. If the user attempts to move the mouse pointer outside this menu item then it is de-highlighted. If an item is highlighted and the left mouse button is clicked then it is assumed that the menu item has been selected and an appropriate value is returned. Observe that, to highlight an item, the **putimage( )** function has been used in such a manner that the existing image of the item is just reversed.

22 *Additional Prob-lems*

651

Constants, Variables and Expressions

[1] Write C expressions corresponding to the following assuming all quantities to be of type **float**.

(a) $x^5 + 10x^4 + 8x^3 + 4x + 2$

(b) $((ax + b)/c) + ((dy + e)/2f) - (a/bd)$

(c)
$$A = B_0 \left(\frac{P_2}{\pi}\right)^{\frac{(g+1)}{k}}$$

(d)
$$B = 2\pi \, \log(\sqrt{l/g}) \left(\frac{1}{4} \sin^3 A/2 + e^{1.32}\right)$$

(e)
$$\lambda = \sqrt{4D^2 - (\beta - \omega)^2} + \tan^{-1}\frac{(\delta + \mu)}{2C}$$

(f)
$$V = 2\nabla \mu r \left[e\, A + \frac{R}{l} \log A \sec A + \frac{1}{\varphi}\left(\frac{r}{\gamma^3}\right) \sin^4 A \cos \theta\right]$$

[2] Evaluate the following expressions:

float a = 2.5, b = 2.5 ;
(a) a + 2.5 / b + 4.5
(b) (a + 2.5) / b + 4.5
(c) (a + 2.5) / (b + 4.5)
(d) a / 2.5 / b
(e) b++ / a + b--

[3] Evaluate each of the following expressions (The expressions are to be evaluated independent of one another):

int i = 3, j = 4, k = 2;
(a) i * = k = ++ j + i
(b) i = j/= k + 4

[4]   Classify the following constants as decimal, octal or hexadecimal:

     (a) 01234
     (b) -02456
     (c) 0x1111
     (d) -128734689
     (e) -0xaAbB
     (f) 122

[5]   The ideal compressor outlet temperature and efficiency for a gas turbine are given by

$$T = T_0 \left(\frac{P_2}{P_1} \right)^{\frac{(g-1)}{g}}$$

and

$$e = 1 - \left(\frac{P_1}{P_2} \right)^{\frac{(g-1)}{g}}$$

where T_0 is the inlet temperature, P_1 the inlet pressure, P_2 the outlet pressure, and g the ratio of specific heats. Write a program to compute and output T and e for $T_0 = 450$, $P_1 = 10$, $P_2 = 55$ and $g = 1.5$.

Control Instructions

[1]   Given a quadratic equation $ax^2 + bx + c = 0$. Write a program to find the roots of it.

[2]   Given fifty pairs of length and breadth of rectangles, write a program to find all the rectangles whose area is greater than

their perimeters. For example, the area of the rectangle with length = 5 and breadth = 4 is greater than its perimeter.

[3] Given three points (**x1**, **y1**), (**x2**, **y2**) and (**x3**, **y3**), write a program to check if they are collinear.

[4] Given the coordinates (**x**, **y**) of a point and radius of a circle, write a program which will determine whether the point lies inside the circle, on the circle or outside the circle.

[5] A machine is purchased which will produce earnings of Rs. 1000 per year while it lasts. The machine costs Rs. 6000 and will have a salvage value of Rs. 2000 when it is condemned. If 12 percent per annum can be earned on alternative investments what would be the minimum life of the machine to make it a more attractive investment compared to alternative investments?

[6] Given a point (**x**, **y**), write a program to find out if it lies on the x-axis, y-axis or at the origin, viz. (0, 0).

[7] Extend the above program to find whether it lies in the first, second, third or fourth quadrant in x-y plane.

[8] A university has the following rules for a student to qualify for a degree with A as the main subject and B as the subsidiary subject:

(a) He should get 55 percent or more in A and 45 percent or more in B.
(b) If he gets less than 55 percent in A he should get 55 percent or more in B. However, he should get atleast 45 percent in A.
(c) If he gets less than 45 percent in B and 65 percent or more in A he is allowed to reappear in an examination in B to qualify.
(d) In all other cases he is declared to have failed.

Write a program to receive marks in A and B and output whether the student has passed, failed or is allowed to reappear in B.

[9] The policy followed by a company to process customer orders is given by the following rules:

   (a) If a customer order is less than or equal to that in stock and his credit is OK, supply his requirement.
   (b) If his credit is not OK do not supply. Send him an intimation.
   (c) If his credit is Ok but the item in stock is less than his order, supply what is in stock. Intimate to him the date the balance will be shipped.

Write a C program to implement the company policy.

[10] When interest, compounds **q** times per year at an annual rate of **r** % for **n** years, the principal **p** compounds to an amount **a** as per the following formula

$$a = p(1 + r/q)^{nq}$$

Write a program to read 10 sets of **p, r, n** & **q** and calculate the corresponding **a**s.

[11] A projectile fired at an angle θ has a horizontal range **R** given by

$$R = \frac{V^2 \sin \theta \, \cos \theta}{g}$$

Where V = initial velocity and g = 32.2 ft/sec^2. Write a program to compute **R** for the following set of values.

V	θ
200	20
200	70
200	45
175	60
179	75
210	20

[12] The period **P** of a pendulum is given by the following formula.

$$p = 2\pi \ \sqrt{l/g} \ \left(\frac{1}{4} \sin^2 \alpha/2 + 1\right)$$

where g = 980 cm/sec^2, l = pendulum length, α = angle of displacement.

Write a program to read pendulum number, **l** and α for 10 different pendulums and compute the period of each pendulum. Also print the pendulum number whose period is smallest.

[13] A tank having the shape of an inverted right circular cone of radius **R** and height **h** is initially filled with water. At the bottom of the tank is a hole of radius **r** through which water drains under the influence of gravity. The equation for the time **t** it takes to empty is

$$t = \frac{R^2}{5 r^2} \frac{\sqrt{2h}}{\sqrt{g}}$$

Where **g** is the gravitational constant 32.17 ft/sec^2. Compute the time to empty tanks of the following dimensions.

Tank height	Tank radius	Hole radius
6.5	4.0	0.2
10.35	5.5	1.0
15.65	6.0	4.0

17.0	4.9	2.5
14.55	7.5	2.0
16.65	5.75	0.5

Also determine which tank would be emptied earliest.

[14] The length **L** of a belt needed to wrap around two pulleys of diameters **D** and **d** and whose centres are separated by a distance **C** is given by,

$$L = \sqrt{4\,C^2 - (D - d)^2} + \pi\frac{(D+d)}{2} + (D-d)\sin^{-1}\frac{(D-d)}{2C}$$

Write a program to compute belt lengths for each of the following sets of data:

D	d	C
22	8	60
20	10	18
21	11	15
19	10	14
18	12	16

[15] A piston is connected to a crankshaft of radius **r** by a connecting rod of length **l**. The velocity **v** of the piston as a function of the crankshaft angle **A** and revolutions per minute **N** of the shaft is given by,

$$V = 2\pi\,N r \left[\sin A + \frac{r}{l}\sin A \cos A + \frac{1}{2}\left(\frac{r}{l^3}\right) \sin^3 A \cos A \right]$$

Write a program to compute the velocity in meters/sec for each of the following.

N   A   l   r

3000	68	0.75	0.25
4000	95	0.75	0.2
3300	180	0.95	0.1
4500	90	0.6	0.15
800	270	0.5	0.15
990	75	0.7	0.25

[16] The natural logarithm can be approximated by the following series.

$$\frac{x-1}{x} + \frac{1}{2}\left(\frac{x-1}{x}\right)^2 + \frac{1}{2}\left(\frac{x-1}{x}\right)^3 + \frac{1}{2}\left(\frac{x-1}{x}\right)^4 + \ldots$$

If **x** is input through the keyboard, write a program to calculate the sum of first seven terms of this series.

[17] The following formulae describe properties of portions of circle, with radius **r**, and central angle θ in degrees.

$$Area = \pi r^2$$

$$Length\ of\ arc = \pi r \frac{\theta}{180}$$

$$length\ of\ chord = 2\,r \sin(\theta/2)$$

$$area\ of\ segment = \frac{\pi r^2 \theta}{360} - \frac{r^2 \sin \theta}{2}$$

If values of **r** and θ are entered through the keyboard, write a program to calculate the above properties of the circle. Note that your program must work till the user keeps on supplying the values of **r** and θ.

[18] A projectile fired at an angle θ with an initial velocity V_0 will travel a distance **r** according to the following formula:

$$r = \frac{V_o^2 \sin 2\theta}{g}$$

Where **g** is the acceleration = 9.81 m/sec^2.

It will be in motion for a time **t** given by

$$t = \frac{V_o \sin \theta}{g}$$

and reach a maximum height **h** given by,

$$h = \frac{V_o^2 \sin \theta}{g}$$

For all angles from 20 to 70 degrees in 10-degree increments and initial velocity of 50 m/sec write a program to prepare the following table.

Projectile Characteristics

Angle	Range	Time	Height
20	-	-	-
30	-	-	-
40	-	-	-
50	-	-	-
60	-	-	-
70	-	-	-

[19] The heat flow **Q** from an insulated pipe is given by the following formula:

$$Q = \frac{2\pi K L (T_i - T_o)}{\log_e (D_2/D_1)}$$

where **L** = pipe length, T_i = Temperature inside, T_o = Temperature outside, **D₂** = Outer diameter of pipe (with insulation), **D₁** = Inner diameter of pipe (without insulation) and **K** = Thermal conductivity factor of the insulation.

Assume a pipe 50 feet long with a diameter of 8 inches and a thermal conductivity factor of 0.035. The outer temperature should be 150 degrees and the inner temperature should be 850 degrees.

Write a program to construct a table of heat flow versus thickness of insulation in half inch increments from 1 to 4 inches.

[20] For a cylindrical tube of outside diameter **D₀** and an inside diameter **Dᵢ**, the moment of inertia is,

$$\frac{\pi (D_o^{\,4} - D_i^{\,4})}{64}$$

and the radius of gyration is,

$$\frac{\sqrt{D_o^{\,2} - D_i^{\,2}}}{4}$$

The external tube diameter and initial thickness are input through the keyboard. Prepare a table for moment of inertia and radius of gyration, incrementing the thickness by a step given by the programs user. Terminate the program when the tube becomes a solid.

[21] In a crankshaft, connecting rod and piston arrangement, the displacement **D** of the piston is given by

$$D = r \left[1 - \cos A + \frac{r}{2l} \sin^2 A + \left(\frac{r}{2l} \right)^3 \sin^4 A \right]$$

Prepare a table of displacement versus the crankshaft angle from 0 to 360 degrees in uniform increments of 10 degrees. The program should read the values of **r** and **l**.

Functions

[1]   Write functions to add, subtract, multiply and divide two complex numbers $(x + iy)$ and $(a + ib)$.

[2]   Write a C function to evaluate the series

$$\sin(x) = x - (x^3/3!) + (x^5/5!) - (x^7/7!) + \dots$$

to five significant digits.

[3]   Given three variables **x, y, z** write a function to circularly shift their values to right. In other words if $x = 5, y = 8, z = 10$ after circular shift $y = 5, z = 8$ and $x = 10$. Call the function with variables **a, b, c** to circularly shift their values.

[4]   Write a function to find the binary equivalent of a given decimal integer and display it.

[5]   Given **N** and **K**. Write a function to compute the binomial coefficient

$$\frac{N!}{K!(N-K)!}$$

[6]   If the lengths of the sides of a triangle are denoted by **a, b**, and **c**, then area of triangle is given by

$$area = \sqrt{S(S-a)(S-b)(S-c)}$$

where, $S = (a + b + c)/2$

[7]   Write a function to compute the distance between two points
        and use it to develop another function that will compute the
        area of the triangle whose vertices are **A(x1, y1)**, **B(x2, y2)**,
        and **C(x3, y3)**. Use these functions to develop a function which
        returns a value 1 if the point **(x, y)** lies inside the triangle ABC,
        otherwise a value 0.

[8]   Using the formulae

        $$r = \sqrt{x^2 + y^2 + z^2}$$
        $$\theta = \tan^{-1}(\sqrt{x^2 + y^2}/Z)$$
        $$\varphi = \tan^{-1}(y/x)$$

        write a function that will transform cartesian coordinates into
        spherical coordinates.

[9]   Write a function to calculate **N!** which is defined as
        1.2.3.4......N, and 0! is defined to be 1.

        Write another function to calculate the Binomial Coefficient
        given by,

        $$\frac{N!}{K!(N-K)!}$$

        Then write a **main( )** that makes use of the aforesaid functions
        to evaluate:

        (a) $$p = \frac{(i + j + k)!}{i!\, j!\, k!}$$

        where **p** is the number of permutations on a set of **m** objects
        of which **i** are of one type, **j** are of a second type, and **k** are
        of a third type, it being assumed that objects of any of the
        three given types are indistinguishable from one another.

(b) $$PROB = \frac{N!}{K!(N-K)!}\, p^k\, q^{n-k}$$

where in a sequence of independent trials of an experiment each trial has a probability of success **p** and a probability of failure **q**, and PROB is the probability of exactly **k** successes in **n** trials of the experiment.

[10] Write a function to compute the greatest common divisor given by Euclid's algorithm, exemplified for J = 1980, K = 1617 as follows:

```
1980/1617 = 1     1980 - 1 x 1617 = 363
1617/363 = 4      1617 - 4 x 363 = 165
363/165 = 2       363 - 2 x 165 = 33
5/33 = 5          165 - 5 x 33 = 0
```

Thus, the greatest common divisor is 33.

Pointers

[1] Given the following information answer the questions which follow:

Variable name	Address	Contents
P	2568	425
q	4284	2568
r	6242	4284
a[0]	8468	232
a[10]	8478	2568

(a) &p = ?
(b) *q = ?
(c) **r = ?
(d) &q = ?
(e) *(&q) = ?
(f) &(*r) = ?

(g) &a[0] = ?
(h) a = ?
(i) a[0] = ?
(j) &a[5] = ?
(k) a[10] = ?
(l) *a[10] = ?

[2]   Match the following with reference to the following program segment:

```
int i, j = 25 ;
int *pi, *pj = &j ;
......
......  /* more lines of program */
......
*pj = j + 5 ;
i = *pj + 5 ;
pi = pj ;
*pi = i + j ;
```

Each integer quantity occupies 2 bytes of memory. The value assigned to **i** begins at (hexadecimal) address F9C and the value assigned to **j** begins at address F9E. Match the value represented by Left Hand Side quantities with the Right.

1.	&i	a.	30
2.	&j	b.	F9E
3.	pj	c.	35
4.	*pj	d.	FA2
5.	i	e.	F9C
6.	pi	f.	67
7.	*pi	g.	unspecified
8.	(pi + 2)	h.	65
9.	(*pi + 2)	i.	F9E
10.	* (pi + 2)	j.	F9E
		k.	FA0
		l.	F9D

[3]   Match the following with reference to the following program segment:

```
int x[3][5] = {
                { 1, 2, 3, 4, 5 },
                { 6, 7, 8, 9, 10 },
                { 11, 12, 13, 14, 15 }
            }, *n = &x ;
```

1.	*(*(x + 2) + 1)	a.	9
2.	*(*x + 2) + 5	b.	13
3.	*(*(x + 1))	c.	4
4.	*(*(x) + 2) + 1	d.	3
5.	*(*(x + 1) + 3)	e.	2
6.	*n	f.	12
7.	*(n + 2)	g.	14
8.	(*(n + 3) + 1)	h.	7
9.	*(n + 5) + 1	i.	1
10.	++*n	j.	8
		k.	5
		l.	10
		m.	6

[4]   Match the following with reference to the following program segment:

```
struct
{
    int x, y ;
} s[] = { 10, 20, 15, 25, 8, 75, 6, 2 } ;
int *i ;
i = s ;
```

1.	*(i + 3)	a	85
2.	s[i[7]].x	b.	2
3.	s[(s + 2)->y / 3[i]].y	c.	6
4.	i[i[1]-i[2]]	d.	7

5.	i[s[3].y]	e.	16
6.	(s + 1)->x + 5	f.	15
7.	*(1 + i)**(i + 4) / *i	g.	25
8.	s[i[0] - i[4]].y + 10	h.	8
9.	(*(s + *(i + 1) / *i)).x + 2	i.	75
10.	++i[i[6]]	j.	100
		k.	10
		l.	20

[5]   Match the following with reference to the following program segment: segment

```
unsigned int arr[3][3] = {
                    2,4,6,
                    9,1,10,
                    16,64,5
          };
```

1.	**arr	a.	64
2.	**arr < *(*arr + 2)	b.	18
3.	*(*arr + 2) / (*(*arr + 1) > **arr)	c.	6
4.	*(arr[1] + 1)	arr[1][2]	d.	3
5.	*(arr[0])	*(arr[2])	e.	0
6.	arr[1][1] < arr[0][1]	f.	16
7.	arr[2][1] & arr[2][0]	g.	128
8.	arr[2][2]	arr[0][1]	h.	11
9.	arr[0][1] ^ arr[0][2]	i.	20
10.	++**arr + --arr[1][1]	j.	2
		k.	5
		l.	4

Arrays and Strings

[1]   Write a program to find the equation of a straight line passing through **n** pairs of x and y coordinates.

[2] Write a program which interchanges the odd and even components of an array.

[3] Write a program to find if a square matrix is symmetric.

[4] A factory has 3 divisions and stocks 4 categories of products. An inventory table is updated for each division and for each product as they are received. There are three independent suppliers of products to the factory:

(a) Design a data format to represent each transaction.
(b) Write a program to take a transaction and update the inventory.
(c) If the cost per item is also given write a program to calculate the total inventory value.

[5] Write a function to find the norm of a matrix. The norm is defined as the square root of the sum of squares of all elements in the matrix.

[6] A dequeue is an ordered set of elements in which elements may be inserted or retrieved from either end. Using an array simulate a dequeue of characters and the operations retrieve left, retrieve right, insert left, insert right. Exceptional conditions such as dequeue full or empty should be indicated. Two pointers (namely, left and right) are needed in this simulation.

[7] Write a program which concatenates a string to the left of a given string.

[8] Write a program to delete all vowels from a sentence. Assume that the sentence is not more than 80 characters long.

[9] Write a program which will read a line and delete from it all occurrences of the word 'the'.

[10] Write a program which takes a set of names of individuals and abbreviates the first, middle and other names except the last name by their first letter.

[11] Write a program to count the number of occurrences of any two vowels in succession in a line of text. For example, in the following sentence:

"Please read this application and give me gratuity"

Such occurrences are ea, ea, ui.

[12] A queue is a data structure in which a new element is inserted at the back of the queue and an element is retrieved from the front (the other end) of the queue. For example, given a queue,

A B C D E F X Y Z
front   back

a retrieval operation will retrieve **A**. An insert operation will insert an element behind **Z**. Write functions to add an element to a queue and to retrieve an element from the queue. The functions must have parameters to indicate queue full, queue empty conditions and set point for adding and retrieving elements.

[13] Given an array **p[5]**, write a function to shift it circularly left by two positions. Thus, if p[0] = 15, p[1]= 30, p[2] = 28, p[3] = 19, p[4] = 61 then after the shift p[0] = 28, p[1] = 19, p[2] = 61, p[3] = 15 and p[4] = 30. Call this function with a (4 x 5) matrix and get its rows left shifted.

[14] A 6 x 6 matrix is entered through the keyboard and stored in a a 2-dimensional array **mat[7][7]**. Write a program to obtain the Determinant value of this matrix.

[15] For the following set of sample data, compute the standard deviation and the mean.

-6, -12, 8, 13, 11, 6, 7, 2, -6, -9, -10, 11, 10, 9, 2.

The formula for standard deviation is

$$\frac{\sqrt{(x_i - \bar{x})^2}}{n}$$

Where x_i are the data items and $\bar{x}$ is the mean.

[16] The area of a triangle can be computed by the sine law when 2 sides of the triangle and the angle between them are known.

Area = (1/2) ab sin (angle)

Given the following 6 triangular pieces of land, write a program to find their area and determine which is largest.

Plot No.	a	b	angle
1	137.4	80.9	0.78
2	155.2	92.62	0.89
3	149.3	97.93	1.35
4	160.0	100.25	9.00
5	155.6	68.95	1.25
6	149.7	120.0	1.75

[17] For the following set of **n** data points (**x, y**), compute the corelation coefficient **r**, given by

$$r = \frac{\sum xy - \sum x \sum y}{\sqrt{[n \sum x^2 - (\sum x)^2][n \sum y^2 - (\sum y)^2]}}$$

x	y
34.22	102.43
39.87	100.93
41.85	97.43
43.23	97.81
40.06	98.32
53.29	98.32
53.29	100.07
54.14	97.08
49.12	91.59
40.71	94.85
55.15	94.65

[18] For the following set of points given by **(x, y)** fit a straight line given by

y = a + bx

where,

$a = \bar{y} - b\bar{x}$ and

$$b = \frac{n \sum xy - \sum x \sum y}{[n \sum x^2 - (\sum x)^2]}$$

x	y
3.0	1.5
4.5	2.0
5.5	3.5
6.5	5.0
7.5	6.0
8.5	7.5
8.0	9.0
9.0	10.5
9.5	12.0

10.0   14.0

[19]   Fit an exponential curve of the form $y = ax^b$ for the above data points.

[20]   The X and Y coordinates of 10 different points are entered through the keyboard. Write a program to find the distance of last point from the first point. (Sum of distance between consecutive Points).

Structures

[1]   Create a structure to specify data on students given below:

Roll number, Name, Department, Course, Year of joining

Assume that there are not more than 450 students in the college.

    (a) Write a function to print names of all students who joined in a particular year.
    (b) Write a function to print the data on a student whose roll number is given.

[2]   Create a structure to specify data of customers in a bank. The data to be stored is: Account number, Name, Balance in account. Assume maximum of 200 customers in the bank.

    (a) Write a function to print the Account number and name of each customer with balance below Rs. 100.
    If a customer requests for withdrawal or deposit, it is given in the form:
    Acct. no, amount, (1 for deposit, 0 for withdrawal)
    (b) Write a program to give a message, "the balance is insufficient for the specified withdrawal".

[3]   An automobile company has serial numbers for engine parts
       starting from AA0 to FF9. The other characteristics of parts to
       be specified in a structure are: Year of manufacture, material
       and quantity manufactured.

       (a) Specify a structure to store information corresponding to
           a part.
       (b) Write a program to retrieve information on parts with serial
           numbers between BB1 and CC6.

[4]   Linked list is a very common data structure often used to store
       similar data in memory. While the elements of an array occupy
       contiguous memory locations, those of a linked list are not
       constrained to be stored in adjacent locations. The individual
       elements are stored "somewhere" in memory, rather like a
       family dispersed, but still bound together. The order of the
       elements is maintained by explicit links between them. Thus,
       a linked list is a collection of elements called nodes, each of
       which stores two items of information: one, an element of the
       list, and two, a link, i.e. a pointer or an address that indicates
       explicitly the location of the node containing the successor of
       this list element.

       Write a program to build a linked list by adding new nodes at
       the beginning, at the end or in the middle of the linked list. Also
       write a function **display( )** which displays all the nodes present
       in the linked list.

[5]   Add a function **delete( )** to program [5] above, which can delete
       any node in the linked list.

[6]   Write a program to maintain a linked list such that that every
       element added to the linked list gets inserted at such a place
       that the linked list is always maintained in ascending order.

[7] Write a program to reverse the links in the existing linked list such that the last node becomes the first node and the first becomes the last.

[8] A stack is a data structure in which addition of new element or deletion of existing element always takes place at the same end. This end is often known as 'top' of stack. This situation can be compared to a stack of plates in a cafeteria where every new plate added to the stack is added at the 'top'. Similarly every new plate taken off the stack is also from the 'top' of the stack. There are several applications where stack can be put to use. For example, recursion, keeping track of function calls, evaluation of expressions etc. Write a program to implement a stack using a linked list.

[9] Unlike a stack, in a queue the addition of new element takes place at the end (called 'rear' of queue) whereas deletion takes place at the other end (called 'front' of queue). Write a program to implement a queue using a linked list.

[10] A record contains name of cricketer, his age, number of test matches that he has played and the average runs that he has scored in each test match. Create an array of structures to hold records of 20 such cricketers and then write a program to read these records and arrange them in ascending order by average runs. Use the **qsort**() standard library function.

Files

[1] A hospital keeps a file of blood donors in which each record has the format:

Name: 20 Columns
Address: 40 Columns
Age: 2 Columns
Blood Type: 1 Column (Type 1,2,3 or 4)

Write a program to read the file and print a list of all blood donors whose age is below 25 and blood is type 2.

[2] Given a list of names of students in a class. Write a program to store the names in a file on disk, display the **n**[th] name in the list (**n** is data to be read), display all names starting with S.

[3] Assume that a Master file contains two fields, Roll no. and name of the student. At the end of the year, a set of students join the class and another set leaves. A Transaction file contains the roll numbers and an appropriate code to add or delete a student.

Write a program to create another file which contains the updated list of names and roll numbers. Assume that the Master file and the Transaction file are arranged in ascending order by roll numbers. The updated file should also be in ascending order by roll numbers.

[4] In a small firm employee numbers are given in serial numerical order, that is 1, 2, 3 etc.

(a) Create a file of employee data with following information: employee no, name, sex, gross salary
(b) If more employees join, append their data to the file.
(c) If an employee with serial number 25 (say) leaves, delete the record by making gross salary 0.
(d) If some employee's gross salary increases, write a program to retrieve the record and update the salary.

[5] Given a text file, create another text file deleting the words "a", "the", "an" and replacing each one of them with a blank space.

[6] You are given a data file EMPLOYEE.DAT with the following record structure:

```
struct employee {
```

```
int empno ;
char name[30] ;
int basic, grade ;
};
```

Every employee has a unique **empno** and there are no gaps. Records are entered into the data file in ascending order of employee number, **empno**. It is intended to check whether there are missing employee numbers. Write a program segment to read the data file records sequentially and display the list of missing employee numbers.

[7] Write a program to carry out the following:

(a) to read a text file "TRIAL.TXT" consisting of a maximum of 50 lines of text, each line with a maximum of 80 characters.
(b) Count and display the number of words contained in the file.
(c) Display the total number of four letter words in the text file.

(Assume that the end of a word may be a space, a comma or a fullstop followed by one or more spaces or a a newline character)

[8] Write a program to read a list of words, sort the words in alphabetical order and display them one word per line. Also give the total number of words in the list. Output format should be:

Total Number of words in the list is ------------
Alphabetical listing of words

Assume the end of the list is indicated by ZZZZZZ and there are maximum of 25 words in the Text file.

[9]   Write a program to carry out the following:

(a) To read a text file 'INPUT.TXT'.
(b) Print each word in reverse order.

Note: Assume that each word length is maximum of 10 characters and each word is separated by newline/blank character.

For example,

 Input: INDIA IS MY COUNTRY
 Output: AIDNI SI MY YRTNUOC

[10]   Write a C program to read a large text file 'NOTES.TXT' and print it on the printer in cut-sheets, introducing page breaks at the end of every 50 lines and a pause message on the screen at the end of every page for the user to change the paper.

[11]   A file contains a C program, but by mistake a novice has typed it out in capitals. It's a long program, therefore you cannot afford to have it retyped. Write a utility which reads this program and converts it to an appropriate small-case program and writes it to a target file. Use functions **fgets( )** and **fputs( )**.

Miscellaneous

[1]   A company pays normal wage for work during week days from Monday to Friday and 1.5 times wage for work on Saturday and Sunday. Given data in the following form:

Employee Number, Wage/hour, hours worked on Monday, hours on Tuesday, ..., hours on Sunday.

Write a program to write out the Employee number and weekly wages. Use enumerated data type in your program.

[2] With respect to the following program segment, say whether the subsequent remarks are true or false.

```
typedef struct {
                int month ;
                int day ;
                int year ;
            } date ;
struct {
        int acct_no ;
        char acct_type ;
        char name [80] ;
        float balance ;
        date lastpayment ;
    } customer, *pc = &customer ;
```

(a) **customer.balance** and (***pc**).**balance** refers to the same value

(b) **pc->lastpayment.month** is syntactically valid

(c) ***(pc.lastpayment.month)** is syntactically invalid

(d) ***(customer.name + 2)** and **customer.name[2]** both refer to **pc->(name + 2)**

(e) ***((*pc).name + 2)** refers to the second character of customer's name

[3] Unless typecasting is used the following programs would give an error/warning. Indicate where and how you would use typecasting to avoid the error/warnings.

```
(a)     main( )
        {
            int i = 32 ;
            float *p ;
            p = &i ;  /* error */
```

```
            }

    (b)     main( )
            {
                char far *scr ;
                scr = 0xB8000000 ;  /* error */
                *scr = 'A' ;
            }

    (c)     main( )
            {
                struct a
                {
                    int i ;
                    char c ;
                } ;
                struct a var1 = { 10, 'A' } , var2, *ptr ;
                char ch ;

                ptr = &var1 ;
                var2 = *ptr ;  /* typecasting not required */

                /* one way accessing 'A' */
                ch = ptr -> c ;
                printf ( "\n%c", ch ) ;

                /* another way of accessing 'A' */
                ch = * ( ptr + 2 ) ;  /* error */
                printf ( "\n%c", ch ) ;
            }

    (d)     main( )
            {
                struct a
                {
                    int i ;
```

```
        char ch ;
    } ;
    struct a var1 = { 10, 'A' } , var2 ;
    char *ptr ;

    ptr = ( char * ) &var1 ;
    var2 = * ( ptr ) ; /* error */
    printf ( "\n%d %c", var2.i, var2.ch ) ;
}
```

[4]   Point out the error if any in the following program. If there is no error, what would be the output of the program.

```
main( )
{
    struct a
    {
        int i ;
        char ch ;
    } ;
    struct a var1 = { 10, 'A' }, *ptr1, *ptr2 ;
    void **pp ;

    ptr1 = &var1 ;
    pp = ( void ** ) &ptr1 ;
    ptr2 = * ( ( struct a ** ) pp ) ;
    printf ( "\n%d %c", ptr2->i, ptr2->ch ) ;
}
```

A   *Precedence Table*

Description	Operator	Associativity
Function expression	( )	Left to right
Array expression	[ ]	Left to right
Structure operator	->	Left to right
Structure operator	.	Left to right
Unary minus	-	Right to left
Increment/Decrement	++ --	Right to left
One's complement	~	Right to left
Negation	!	Right to left
Address of	&	Right to left
Value at address	*	Right to left
Type cast	(type)	Right to left
Size in bytes	sizeof	Right to left
Multiplication	*	Left to right
Division	/	Left to right
Modulus	%	Left to right
Addition	+	Left to right
Subtraction	-	Left to right
Left shift	<<	Left to right
Right shift	>>	Left to right
Less than	<	Left to right
Less than or equal to	<=	Left to right
Greater than	>	Left to right
Greater than or equal to	>=	Left to right
Equal to	==	Le fFft to right
Not equal to	!=	Left to right
Bitwise AND	&	Left to right
Bitwise exclusive OR	^	Left to right

Figure A1.1 (continued on next page)

Description	Operator	Associativity
Bitwise inclusive OR	|	Left to right
Logical AND	&&	Left to right
Logical OR	||	Left to right
Conditional	? :	Right to left
Assignment	=	Right to left
	*= /= %=	Right to left
	+= -= &=	Right to left
	^= |=	Right to left
	<<= >>==	Right to left
Comma	,	Right to left

Figure A1.1 (continued)

B Standard Library Functions

Arithmetic Functions
Data Conversion Functions
Character Classification Functions
String Manipulation Functions
Searching and Sorting Functions
I/O Functions
File Handling Functions
Directory Control Functions
Buffer Manipulation Functions
Disk I/O Functions
Memory Allocation Functions
Process Control Functions
Graphics Functions
Time Related Functions
Miscellaneous Functions
DOS Interface Functions

Let alone discussing each standard library function in detail, even a complete list of these functions would occupy scores of pages. However, the book would be left incomplete if it has nothing to say about standard library functions. I have tried to reach a compromise and have given a list of standard library functions which are more popularly used so that you know what to search for in the manual. An excellent book dedicated totally to standard library functions is Waite group's, Turbo C Bible, written by Nabjyoti Barkakti.

Following is the list of selected standard library functions. The functions have been classified into broad categories.

Arithmetic Functions

Function	Use
abs	Returns the absolute value of an integer
cos	Calculates cosine
cosh	Calculates hyperbolic cosine
exp	Raises the exponential e to the xth power
fabs	Finds absolute value
floor	Finds largest integer less than or equal to argument
fmod	Finds floating-point remainder
hypot	Calculates hypotenuse of right triangle
log	Calculates natural logarithm
log10	Calcultes base 10 logarithm
modf	Breaks down argument into integer and fractional parts
pow	Calculates a value raised to a power
sin	Calculates sine
sinh	Calculates hyperbolic sine
sqrt	Finds square root
tan	Calculates tangent
tanh	Calculates hyperbolic tangent

Data Conversion Functions

Function	Use
atof	Converts string to float
atoi	Converts string to int
atol	Converts string to long
ecvt	Converts double to string
fcvt	Converts double to string
gcvt	Converts double to string
itoa	Converts int to string
ltoa	Converts long to string
strtod	Converts string to double
strtol	Converts string to long integer
strtoul	Converts string to an unsigned long integer
ultoa	Converts unsigned long to string

Character Classification Functions

Function	Use
isalnum	Tests for alphanumeric character
isalpha	Tests for alphabetic character
isdigit	Tests for decimal digit
islower	Tests for lowercase character
isspace	Tests for white space character
isupper	Tests for uppercase character
isxdigit	Tests for hexadecimal digit
tolower	Tests character and converts to lowercase if uppercase
toupper	Tests character and convers to uppercase if lowercase

String Manipulation Functions

Function	Use
strcat	appends one string to another
strchr	Finds first occurrence of a given character in a string
strcmp	Compares two strings
strcmpi	Compares two strings without regard to case
strcpy	Copies one string to another
strdup	Duplicates a string
stricmp	Compares two strings without regard to case (identical to strcmpi)
strlen	Finds length of a string
strlwr	Converts a string to lowercase
strncat	Appends a portion of one string to another
strncmp	Compares a portion of one string with portion of another string
strncpy	Copies a given number of characters of one string to another
strnicmp	Compares a portion of one string with a portion of another without regard to case
strrchr	Finds last occurrence of a given character in a string
strrev	Reverses a string
strset	Sets all characters in a string to a given character
strstr	Finds first occurrence of a given string in another string
strupr	Converts a string to uppercase

Searching and Sorting Functions

Function	Use
bsearch	Performs binary search
lfind	Performs linear search for a given value
qsort	Performs quick sort

I/O Functions

Function	Use
close	Closes a file
fclose	Closes a file
feof	Detects end-of-file
fgetc	Reads a character from a file
fgetchar	Reads a character from keyboard (function version)
fgets	Reads a string from a file
fopen	Opens a file
fprintf	Writes formatted data to a file
fputc	Writes a character to a file
fputchar	Writes a character to screen (function version)
fputs	Writes a string to a file
fscanf	Reads formatted data from a file
fseek	Repositions file pointer to given location
ftell	Gets current file pointer position
getc	Reads a character from a file (macro version)
getch	Reads a character from the keyboard
getche	Reads a character from keyboard and echoes it
getchar	Reads a character from keyboard (macro version)
gets	Reads a line from keyboard
inport	Reads a two-byte word from the specified I/O port
inportb	Reads one byte from the specified I/O port
kbhit	checks for a keystroke at the keyboard
lseek	Repositions file pointer to a given location
open	Opens a file
outport	Writes a two-byte word to the specified I/O port
outportb	Writes one byte to the specified I/O port
printf	Writes formatted data to scren
putc	Writes a character to a file (macro version)
putch	Writes a character to the screen
putchar	Writes a character to screen (macro version)
puts	Writes a line to file
read	Reads data from a file
rewind	Repositions file pointer to beginning of a file

scanf   Reads formatted data from keyboard
sscanf   Reads formatted input from a string
sprintf   Writes formatted output to a string
tell   Gets current file pointer position
write   Writes data to a file

File Handling Functions

Function	Use
remove	Deletes file
rename	Renames file
unlink	Deletes file

Directory Control Functions

Function	Use
chdir	Changes current working directory
getcwd	Gets current working directory
fnsplit	Splits a full path name into its components
findfirst	Searches a disk directory
findnext	Continues findfirst search
mkdir	Makes a new directory
rmdir	Removes a directory

Buffer Manipulation Functions

Function	Use
memchr	Returns a pointer to the first occurrence, within a specified number of characters, of a given character in the buffer

memcmp	Compares a specified number of characters from two buffers
memcpy	Copies a specified number of characters from one buffer to another
memicmp	Compares a specified number of characters from two buffers without regard to the case of the letters
memmove	Copies a specified number of characters from one buffer to another
memset	Uses a given character to initialise a specified number of bytes in the buffer

Disk I/O Functions

Function	Use
absread	Reads absolute disk sectors
abswrite	Writes absolute disk sectors
biosdisk	BIOS disk services
getdisk	Gets current drive number
setdisk	Sets current disk drive

Memory Allocation Functions

Function	Use
calloc	Allocates a block of memory
farmalloc	Allocates memory from far heap
farfree	frees a block from far heap
free	Frees a block allocated with malloc
malloc	Allocates a block of memory
realloc	Reallocates a block of memory

Process Control Functions

Function	Use
abort	Aborts a process
atexit	Executes function at program termination
execl	Executes child process with argument list
exit	Terminates the process
spawnl	Executes child process with argument list
spawnlp	Executes child process using PATH variable and argument list
system	Executes an MS-DOS command

Graphics Functions

Function	Use
arc	Draws an arc
ellipse	Draws an ellipse
floodfill	Fills an area of the screen with the current color
getimage	Stores a screen image in memory
getlinestyle	Obtains the current line style
getpixel	Obtains the pixel's value
lineto	Draws a line from the current graphic output position to the specified point
moveto	Moves the current graphic output position to a specified point
pieslice	Draws a pie-slice-shaped figure
putimage	Retrieves an image from memory and displays it
rectangle	Draws a rectangle
setcolor	Sets the current color
setlinestyle	Sets the current line style
putpixel	Sets a pixel's value
setviewport	Limits graphic output and positions the logical origin within the limited area

Time Related Functions

Function	Use
clock	Returns the elapsed CPU time for a process
difftime	Computes the difference between two times
ftime	Gets current system time as structure
strdate	Returns the current system date as a string
strtime	Returns the current system time as a string
time	Gets current system time as long integer
setdate	Sets DOS date
getdate	Gets system date

Miscellaneous Functions

Function	Use
delay	Suspends execution for an interval (milliseconds)
getenv	Gets value of environment variable
getpsp	Gets the Program Segment Prefix
perror	Prints error message
putenv	Adds or modifies value of environment variable
random	Generates random numbers
randomize	Initialises random number generation with a random value based on time
sound	Turns PC speaker on at specified frequency
nosound	Turns PC speaker off

DOS Interface Functions

Function	Use
FP_OFF	Returns offset portion of a far pointer
FP_SEG	Returns segment portion of a far pointer
getvect	Gets the current value of the specified interrupt vector

keep	Installs terminate-and-stay-resident (TSR) programs
int86	Invokes MS-DOS interrupts
int86x	Invokes MS-DOS interrupt with segment register values
intdos	Invokes MS-DOS service using registers other than DX and AL
intdosx	Invokes MS-DOS service with segment register values
MK_FP	Makes a far pointer
segread	Returns current values of segment registers
setvect	Sets the current value of the specified interrupt vector

C   *Chasing The Bugs*

C programmers are great innovators of our times. Unhappily, among their most enduring accomplishments are several new techniques for wasting time. There is no shortage of horror stories about programs that took twenty times to 'debug' as they did to 'write'. And one hears again and again about programs that had to be rewritten all over again because the bugs present in it could not be located.

A typical C programmer's 'morning after' is red eyes, blue face and a pile of crumpled printouts and dozens of reference books all over the floor. Bugs are C programmer's birth right. But how do we chase them away. No sure-shot way for that. I thought if I make a list of more common programming mistakes it might be of help. They are not arranged in any particular order. But as you would realise surely a great help!

[1] Omitting the ampersand before the variables used in **scanf( )**.

     For example,

```
int choice ;
scanf ( "%d", choice ) ;
```

     Here, the **&** before the variable **choice** is missing. Another common mistake with **scanf( )** is to give blanks either just before the format string or immediately after the format string as in,

```
int choice ;
scanf ( " %d ", choice ) ;
```

     Note that this is not a mistake, but till you don't understand **scanf( )** thoroughly, this is going to cause trouble. Safety is in eliminating the blanks. Thus, the correct form would be,

```
int choice ;
scanf ( "%d", &choice ) ;
```

[2]   Using the operator = instead of the operator ==.

What do you think will be the output of the following program:

```
main( )
{
    int i = 10 ;

    while ( i = 10 )
    {
        printf ( "got to get out" ) ;
        i++ ;
    }
}
```

At first glance it appears the message will be printed once and the control will come out of the loop since **i** becomes 11. But, actually we have fallen in an indefinite loop. This is because the = used in the condition always assigns the value 10 to **i**, and since **i** is non-zero the condition is satisfied and the body of the loop is executed over and over again.

[3]   Ending a loop with a semicolon.

Observe the following program.

```
main( )
{
    int j = 1 ;

    while ( j <= 100 ) ;
    {
        printf ( "\nCompguard" ) ;
        j++ ;
    }
}
```

Inadverently, we have fallen in an indefinite loop. Cause is the semicolon after **while**. This in effect makes the compiler feel that you wanted the loop to work in the following manner:

```
while ( j <= 100 )
    ;
```

By all means an indefinite loop since **j** never gets incremented and hence eternally remains less that 100.

[4]   Omitting the **break** statement at the end of a **case** in a **switch** statement.

Remember that if a **break** is not included at the end of a **case**, then execution will continue into the next **case**.

```
main( )
{
    int ch = 1 ;

    switch ( ch )
    {
        case 1 :
            printf ( "\nGoodbye" ) ;
        case 2 :
            printf ( "\nLieutenant" ) ;
    }
}
```

Here, since the **break** has not been given after the **printf( )** in **case 1,** the control runs into **case 2** and executes the second **printf( )** as well.

However, this sometimes turns out to be a blessing in disguise. Especially, in cases when we are checking whether the value of a variable equals a capital letter or a small case letter. This example has been succinctly explained in Chapter 4.

[5]   Using **continue** in a **switch**.

It is a common error to believe that the **way the** keyword **break** is used with **while, for, do-while** and a **switch**; similarly the keyword **continue** can also be used with them. Remember, **continue** works only in loops, never with a **switch**.

[6]   A mismatch in the number, type and order of actual and formal arguments.

```
yr = romanise ( year, 1000, 'm' ) ;
```

Here, three arguments in the order **int, int** and **char** are being passed to **romanise( )**. When **romanise( )** receives these arguments they must be received in the same order by the formal arguments. A careless mismatch might give strange results.

[7]   Omitting provisions for returning non-integer value from a function.

If we make the following function call,

```
area = area_circle ( 1.5 ) ;
```

then while defining **area_circle( )** function later in the program, care should be taken to make it capable of returning a floating point value. Note that unless otherwise mentioned then the compiler will assume that this function returns a value of the type **int**.

[8]   Inserting a semicolon at the end of a macro definition.

How do you recognise a C programmer? Ask him to write a paragraph in English and watch whether he ends each sentence with a semicolon. This usually happens because a C programmer becomes habitual to ending all statements with a semicolon. However, a semicolon at the end of a macro definition might create a problem. For example,

```
#define UPPER 25 ;
```

would lead to a syntax error if used in an expression such as

```
if ( counter == UPPER )
```

This is because on preprocessing, the **if** statement would take the form

```
if ( counter == UPPER; )
```

[9]   Omitting parentheses around a macro expansion.

```
#define SQR(x) x * x
main( )
{
    int a ;

    a = 25 / SQR( 5 ) ;
    printf ( "\n%d", a ) ;
}
```

In this example we expect the value of **a** to be 1, whereas it turns out to be 25. This so happens because on preprocessing the arithmetic statement takes the following form:

```
a = 25 / 5 * 5 ;
```

[10] Leaving a blank space between the macro template and the macro expansion.

```
#define ABS (a)  ( a = 0 ? a : -a)
```

Here, the space between **ABS** and **(a)** makes the preprocessor believe that you want to expand **ABS** into **(a)**, which is certainly not what you want.

[11] Using an expression that has side effects in a macro call.

```
#define SUM(a)  ( a + a )
main( )
{
    int w, b = 5 ;

    w = SUM( b++ ) ;
    printf ( "\n%d", w ) ;
}
```

On preprocessing, the macro would be expanded to,

```
w = ( b++ ) + ( b++ ) ;
```

If you are wanting to first get sum of 5 and 5 and then increment **b** to 6, that would not happen using the above macro definition.

[12] Confusing a character constant and a character string.

In the statement

```
ch = 'z' ;
```

a single character is assigned to **ch**. In the statement

```
ch = "z" ;
```

a pointer to the character string "a" is assigned to **ch**.

Note that in the first case, the declaration of **ch** would be,

```
char ch ;
```

whereas in the second case it would be,

char *ch ;

[13] Forgetting the bounds of an array.

```
main( )
{
    int num[50], i ;

    for ( i = 1 ; i <= 50 ; i++ )
        num[i] = i * i ;
}
```

Here, in the array **num** there is no such element as **num[50]**, since array counting begins with 0 and not 1. Compiler would give no warning if our program exceeds the bounds. If not taken care of, in extreme cases the computer might even hang.

[14] Forgetting to reserve an extra location in a character array for the null terminator.

Remember each character array ends with a '\0', therefore its dimension should be declared big enough to hold the normal characters as well as the '\0'.

For example, the dimension of the array **word[ ]** should be 9 if a string "Jamboree" is to be stored in it.

[15] Confusing the precedences of the various operators.

```
main( )
{
    char ch ;
    FILE *fp ;

    fp = fopen ( "text.c", "r" ) ;
```

```
        while ( ch = getc ( fp ) != EOF )
            putch ( ch ) ;

        fclose ( fp ) ;
}
```

Here, the value returned by **getc( )** will be first compared with EOF, since **!=** has a higher priority than **=**. As a result the value that is assigned to **ch** will be the true/false result of the test: 1 if the value returned by **getc( )** is not equal to EOF, and 0 otherwise. The correct form of the above **while** would be,

```
        while ( ( ch = getc ( fp ) ) != EOF )
            putch ( ch ) ;
```

[16] Confusing the operator **->** with the operator **.** while referring to a structure element.

Remember, on the left of the operator **.** only a structure variable can occur, whereas on the left of the operator **->** only a pointer to a structure can occur.

```
main( )
{
    struct emp
    {
        char name[35] ;
        int age ;
    } ;
    struct emp e = { "Dubhashi", 40 } ;
    struct emp *ee ;

    printf ( "\n%d", e.age ) ;
    ee = &e ;
    printf ( "\n%d", ee->age ) ;
}
```

[17] Forgetting to use the **far** keyword for referring memory locations beyond the data segment.

```
main( )
{
    unsigned int *s ;

    s = 0x413 ;
    printf ( "\n%d", *s ) ;
}
```

Here, it is necessary to use the keyword **far** in the declaration of variable **s**, since the address that we are storing in **s** (0x413) is a address of location present in BIOS Data Area, which is far away from the data segment. Thus, the correct declaration would look like,

```
unsigned int far *s ;
```

[18] Exceeding the range of integers and chars.

```
main( )
{
    char ch ;

    for ( ch = 0 ; ch <= 255 ; ch++ )
        printf ( "\n%c %d", ch, ch ) ;
}
```

Can you believe that this is an indefinite loop? Probably, a closer look would confirm it. Reason is, **ch** has been declared as a **char** and the valid range of **char** constant is -128 to +127. Hence, the moment **ch** tries to become 128 (through **ch++**), the value of character range is exceeded, therefore the first number from the negative side of the range, -128, gets assigned to **ch**. Naturally the condition is satisfied and the control remains withing the loop eternally.

D Hexadecimal Numbering

Numbering Systems
Relation Between Binary and Hex

W hile working with computers we are very often required to use hexadecimal numbers. The reason for this is: everything a computer does is based on binary numbers, and hexadecimal notation is a convenient way of expressing binary numbers. Before justifying this statement let us first discuss what numbering systems are, why computers use binary numbering system, how binary and hexadecimal numbering systems are related and how to use hexadecimal numbering system in everyday life.

Numbering Systems

When we talk about different numbering systems we are really talking about the base of the numbering system. For example, binary numbering system has base 2 and hexdecimal numbering system has base 16, just the way decimal numbering system has base 10. What in fact is the 'base' of the numbering system? Base represents number of digits you can use before you run out of digits. For example, in decimal numbering system, when we have used digits from 0 to 9, we run out of digits. That's the time we put a 1 in the column to the left - the ten's column - and start again in the one's column with 0, as shown below:

```
 0
 1
 2
 3
 4
 5
 6
 7
 8
 9   last available digit
10   start using a new column
11
12
13
```

14

...

...

Since decimal numbering system is a base 10 numbering system any number in it is constructed using some combination of digits 0 to 9. This seems perfectly natural. However, the choice of 10 as a base is quite arbitrary, having its origin possibly in the fact that man has 10 fingers. It is very easy to use other bases as well. For example, if we wanted to use base 8 or octal numbering system, which uses only eight digits (0 to 7), here's how the counting would look like:

0
1
2
3
4
5
6
7   last available digit
10   start using a new column
11
12

...

...

Similarly, a hexadecimal numbering system has a base 16. In hex notation, the ten digits 0 through 9 are used to represent the values zero through nine, and the remaining six values, ten through fifteen, are represented by symbols A to F. The hex digits A to F are usually written in capitals, but lowercase letters are also perfectly acceptable. Here is how the counting in hex would look like:

0
1
2
3

```
4
5
6
7
8
9
A
B
C
D
E
F    last available digit
10   start using a new column
11
...
...
```

Many other numbering systems can also be imagined. For example, we use a base 60 numbering system, for measuring minutes and seconds. From the base 12 system we retain our 12 hour system for time, the number of inches in a foot and so on. The moral is that any base can be used in a numbering system, although some bases are convenient than others.

The hex numbers are built out of hex digits in much the same way the decimal numbers are built out of decimal digits. For example, when we write the decimal number 342, we mean,

```
    3 times 100 (square of 10)
  + 4 times 10
  + 2 times 1
```

Similarly, if we use number 342 as a hex number, we mean,

```
    3 times 256 (square of 16)
  + 4 times 16
  + 2 times 1
```

Relation Between Binary and Hex

As it turns out, computers are more comfortable with binary numbering system. In a binary system, there are only two digits 0 and 1. This means you can't count very far before you need to start using the next column:

```
0
1   last available digit
10  start using a new column
11
...
...
```

Binary numbering system is a natural system for computers because each of the thousands of electronic circuits in the computer can be in one of the two states: on or off. Thus, binary numbering system corresponds nicely with the circuits in the computer: 0 means off, and 1 means on. 0 and 1 are called bits, a short-form of binary digits.

Hex numbers are used primarily as a shorthand for binary numbers that the computers work with. Every hex digit represents four bits of binary information (Refer Figure D.1). In binary numbering system 4 bits taken at a time can give rise to sixteen different numbers, so the only way to represent each of these sixteen 4 bit binary numbers in a simple and short way is to use a base sixteen numbering system.

Suppose we want to represent a binary number 11000101 in a short way. One way is to find it deimal equivalent is to multiply each binary digit with an appropriate power of 2 as shown below:

$$1 * 2^7 + 1 * 2^6 + 0 * 2^5 + 0 * 2^4 + 0 * 2^3 + 1 * 2^2 + 0 * 2^1 + 1 * 2^0$$

which is equal to 197.

Hex	Binary	Hex	Binary
0	0000	8	1000
1	0001	9	1001
2	0010	A	1010
3	0011	B	1011
4	0100	C	1100
5	0101	D	1101
6	0110	E	1110
7	0111	F	1111

Figure D.1

Another method is much simpler. Just look at Figure D.1. From it find out the hex digits for the two four-bit sets (1100 and 0101). These happen to be C and 5. Therefore, the binary number's hex equivalent is C5. You would agree this is a easier way to represent the binary number than to find its decimal equivalent. In this method neither multiplication nor addition is needed. In fact, since there are only 16 hex digits, it's fairly easy to memorise the binary equivalent of each one. Quick now, what's binary 1100 in hex? That's right C. You are already getting the feel of it. With a little practice it is easy to translate even long numbers into hex. Thus, 1100 0101 0011 1010 binary is C53A hex.

As it happens with many unfamiliar subjects, learning hexadecimal requires a little practice. Try your hand at converting some binary numbers and vice versa. Soon you will be talking hexadecimal as if you had known it all your life.

E   *ASCII Chart*

There are 256 distinct characters used by IBM compatible family of microcomputers. Their values range from 0 to 255. These can be grouped as under:

Character Type	No. Of Characters
Capital Letters	26
Small-case Letters	26
Digits	10
Special Symbols	32
Control Characters	34
Graphic Characters	128
Total	256

Figure E.1

Out of the 256 character set, the first 128 are often called Ascii characters and the next 128 as Extended Ascii characters. Each Ascii character has a unique appearence. The following simple program can generate the Ascii chart :

```
main( )
{
    int ch ;

    for ( ch = 0 ; ch <= 255 ; ch++ )
        printf ( "%d %c\n", ch, ch ) ;
}
```

This chart is shown on the following page. Out of the 128 graphic characters (Extended Ascii characters), there are characters which are used for drawing single line and double line boxes in text mode. For convenience these characters are shown below:

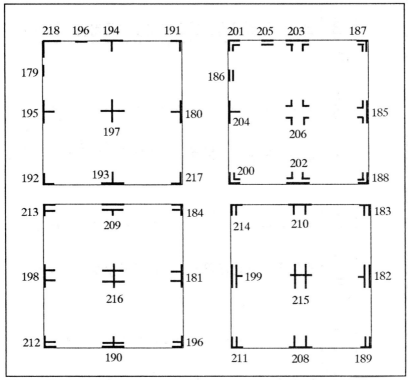

Figure E.2

Value	Char	Value	Char	Value	Char	Value	Char	Value	Char	Value	Char
0		22	▬	44	,	66	B	88	X	110	n
1	☺	23	↨	45	-	67	C	89	Y	111	o
2	☻	24	↑	46	.	68	D	90	Z	112	p
3	♥	25	→	47	/	69	E	91	[	113	q
4	♦	26	↑	48	0	70	F	92	\	114	r
5	♣	27	↓	49	1	71	G	93	]	115	s
6	♠	28	⌐	50	2	72	H	94	^	116	t
7	•	29	↕	51	3	73	I	95	_	117	u
8	◘	30	◄	52	4	74	J	96	`	118	v
9	○	31	►	53	5	75	K	97	a	119	w
10	◙	32		54	6	76	L	98	b	120	x
11	♂	33	—	55	7	77	M	99	c	121	y
12	♀	34	:	56	8	78	N	100	d	122	z
13	♪	35	#	57	9	79	O	101	e	123	{
14	♫	36	$	58	:	80	P	102	f	124	|
15	☼	37	%	59	;	81	Q	103	g	125	}
16	►	38	&	60	<	82	R	104	h	126	~
17	◄	39	'	61	=	83	S	105	i	127	⌂
18	↕	40	(	62	>	84	T	106	j	128	Ç
19	‼	41	)	63	?	85	U	107	k	129	ü
20	¶	42	*	64	@	86	V	108	l	130	é
21	§	43	+	65	A	87	W	109	m	131	â

Value	Char	Value	Char	Value	Char	Value	Char	Value	Char	Value	Char
132	ä	154	Ü	176	░	198	╞	220	▄	242	≥
133	à	155	¢	177	▒	199	╟	221	▌	243	≤
134	å	156	£	178	▓	200	╚	222	▐	244	⌠
135	ç	157	¥	179	│	201	╔	223	▀	245	⌡
136	ê	158	₧	180	┤	202	╩	224	α	246	÷
137	ë	159	ƒ	181	╡	203	╦	225	ß	247	≈
138	è	160	á	182	╢	204	╠	226	Γ	248	°
139	ï	161	í	183	╖	205	═	227	π	249	∙
140	î	162	ó	184	╕	206	╬	228	Σ	250	·
141	ì	163	ú	185	╣	207	╧	229	σ	251	√
142	Ä	164	ñ	186	║	208	╨	230	µ	252	ⁿ
143	Å	165	Ñ	187	╗	209	╤	231	τ	253	²
144	É	166	ª	188	╝	210	╥	232	Φ	254	■
145	æ	167	º	189	╜	211	╙	233	Θ	255	
146	Æ	168	¿	190	╛	212	╘	234	Ω		
147	ô	169	⌐	191	┐	213	╒	235	δ		
148	ö	170	¬	192	└	214	╓	236	∞		
149	ò	171	½	193	┴	215	╫	237	φ		
150	û	172	¼	194	┬	216	╪	238	ε		
151	ù	173	¡	195	├	217	┘	239	∩		
152	ÿ	174	«	196	─	218	┌	240	≡		
153	Ö	175	»	197	┼	219	█	241	±		

F Addressing Scheme Of 8086

How C Tackles Segment:Offset Scheme

The way the 8086 family of microcomputers access memory is little odd. This appendix explains the procedure in detail, along with how this addressing procedure is tackled in C. Throughout this appendix whereever the word 8086 appears it means the 8086 family of microprocessors.

There are two facts which need to be reconciled:

(a)   The 8086 family of microprocessors working under a real mode operating system like MS-DOS use a 20-bit address bus to access any memory location.

(b)   The addresses are placed in CPU registers which under real mode can be only 16-bits long.

Since under real mode the registers are 16 bits long the largest address that can be stored in them is 65535 (2^{16} or 64 kb). This in effect means that the 8086 family of microprocessors should be able to access only 64 kb memory addresses.

The 8086 finds a solution to this problem by using a segment:offset addressing scheme. According to this scheme, 8086 divides the addressable memory (1 mb) space into a number of segments each containing maximum of 64 kb. To access individual bytes in this scheme it uses an additional address called offset address which points to an exact location within a 64 kb segment. Thus location of any byte in memory is specified using the segment:offset address; the segment addrress indicating the 64 kb segment in which the byte is lying and the offset address indicating the exact location number of the byte within the segment.

Since the maximum size of a segment can be 64 kb the offset address would always be less than or equal to 65535. This offset address can easily be stored in a 16-bit CPU register. However, storing a segment address would pose a problem. Let us see, what is this problem.

Each segment begins at a location that is completely divisible by 16. For example, the conventional VDU memory (B-block) begins at location 0xB0000 (20-bit address), which is exactly divisible by 16. The segment address is stored in a CPU register called segment register. But the segment regiser is a 16-bit register; how can it hold a 20-bit or a 5 digit hex number? What it does is, it stores only the first 4 hex digits. It can afford to do this since segment address is always a multiple of 16 and hence always contains 0 as the last digit (as in 0xB0000).

To obtain an absolute 20-bit address, from the segment:offset pair the following method is used.

(a)   The segment address is shifted 4 bits to the left.

(b)   Offset address is added to this left-shifted segment address.

For example, suppose we want to convert the segment:offset address 0xB000:0xB800 to an absolute address, the segment address is shifted 4 bits to the left which yields the address 0xB0000. To this left-shifted segment address the offset address is added to obtain 0xB8000. This process is shown below:

```
      0xB0000    left-shifted segment address
 +    0x8000     offset address
      -------------
      0xB8000    20-bit absolute address
```

Ths 20-bit absolute address can easily be placed in the 20-bit address bus. Note that each hex digit converted to binary gives a 4-bit binary number. So shifting a hex number 1 digit to the left is as good as shifting its binary equivalent by 4 bits.

How C Tackles Segment:Offset Scheme

In C the segment:offset address pair is treated a little differently. If a pointer is going to address a location within the program's normal data segment then a two-byte address is used. In fact this is what is done when we use ordinary pointers to **chars**, **ints** or **floats**.

As against this if a pointer is going to address a location which is outside the normal data segment then the segment:offset scheme should be used. For example, when a pointer is to point at a location in VDU memory, the segment:offset scheme which gives a 20-byte absolute address should be used.

However, instead of using an absolute 20-bit address, C uses a 32-bit representation consisting of a 16-bit segment, followed by a 16-bit offset address. Thus, the segment:offset pair of 0xB000:0x8000 is converted to 0xB0008000. But now the problem is a normal pointer can't hold 32-bit addresses. Therefore, what is done is a **far** keyword is used which tells the compiler to treat the pointer as a 32-bit pointer. Thus, a **far** pointer is the one that holds a 32 bit address, rather than the usual 2-byte address. The following example shows the usage of a **far** pointer.

```
main( )
{
    char far *s ;

    s = 0xB0008000 ;
    *s = 'Z' ;
}
```

The **far** keyword is used extensively while directly writing characters to VDU memory, for referring values in IVT etc. You can find **far** in action in Chapter 15.

Can you now figure out whether the two **far** addresses 0xB8000000 and 0xB0008000 refer the same locations in memory or not?

G *ROM-BIOS Services*

T his appendix is divided into two parts: first part gives a short summary of various ROM-BIOS services available under different interrupts. Out of various ROM-BIOS srevices available, those which are pertaining to the same subject are grouped under one interrupt. Thus, all VDU services are grouped under interrupt number 16, all keyboard services are grouped under interrupt number 22 and so on. The second part contains a long summary of each of the ROM-BIOS services.

Short Summary of ROM-BIOS Services

Subject	Interrupt		Service	Description
	Dec	**Hex**	**(hex)**	
Print screen	5	5	n/a	Send screen contents to printer
Video	16	10	0	Set video mode
Video	16	10	1	Set cursor size
Video	16	10	2	Set cursor postion
Video	16	10	3	Read cursor postion
Video	16	10	5	Set active display page
Video	16	10	6	Scroll window up
Video	16	10	7	Scroll window down
Video	16	10	B	Set colour palette
Video	16	10	C	Write pixel dot
Video	16	10	D	Read pixel dot
Video	16	10	F	Get current video mode
Equipment	17	11	n/a	Get list of peripheral equipment
Memory	18	12	n/a	Get memory size
Disk	19	13	0	Reset disk controller
Disk	19	13	1	Get disk status
Disk	19	13	2	Read disk sectors
Disk	19	13	3	Write disk sectors
Disk	19	13	4	Verify disk sectors

Subject	Interrupt		Service	Description
	Dec	**Hex**	**(hex)**	
Disk	19	13	5	Format disk track
Disk	19	13	8	Get current drive parameters
Disk	19	13	9	Initialise two hard disk base tables
Disk	19	13	A	Read long
Disk	19	13	B	Write long
Disk	19	13	C	Seek to cylinder
Disk	19	13	D	Reset fixed disk system
Disk	19	13	10	Test for drive ready
Disk	19	13	11	Recalibrate drive
Disk	19	13	14	Controller diagnostics
Disk	19	13	15	Get disk type
Disk	19	13	16	Get disk change status
Disk	19	13	17	Set disk type
Disk	19	13	18	Set media type for format
Devices	21	15	86	Suspend execution for an interval
Memory	21	15	88	Get extended memory size
Keyboard	22	16	0	Read next keyboard character
Keyboard	22	16	1	Report whether character ready
Keyboard	22	16	2	Get shift status
Printer	23	17	0	Send one byte to printer
Printer	23	17	1	Initialise printer
Printer	23	17	2	Get printer status
Bootstrap	25	19	n/a	Reboot computer
Time	26	1A	0	Read contents of clock tick counter
Time	26	1A	1	Set value in clock tick counter
Time	26	1A	2	Get time from CMOS time/date chip
Time	26	1A	3	Set time in CMOS time/date chip
Time	26	1A	4	Get date from CMOS time/date chip
Time	26	1A	5	Set date in CMOS time/date chip

Subject	Interrupt		Service	Description
	Dec	Hex	(hex)	
Time	26	1A	6	Set alarm in CMOS time/date chip

Long Summary of ROM-BIOS Services

Following is the long summary of various ROM-BIOS srvices. For each service, the interrupt number to invoke it, the input registers to be set up, the values returned by the ROM-BIOS service, and comments about the service (wherever necessary) have been mentioned.

Screen Printing Service

Print screen

Interrupt   0x5

Returns   Nothing

Notes   Sends screen contents to printer. Works in text mode.

Video Services

Set video mode

Interrupt   0x10

Input   AH = 0x00
             AL = video mode

Returns   Nothing

Notes   Video modes in AL are:
             0x0 : 40 x 25 text, 16 grey
             0x1 : 40 x 25 text, 16/8 colour
             0x2 : 80 x 25 text, 16 grey
             0x3 : 80 x 25 text, 16/8 colour
             0x4 : 320 x 200 graphics, 4 colour
             0x5 : 320 x 200 graphics, 4 grey
             0x6 : 640 x 200 graphics, mono
             0x7 : 80 x 25 text, mono
             0x8 : 160 x 200 graphics, 16 colour
             0x9 : 320 x 200 graphics, 16 colour
             0xA : 640 x 200 graphics, 4 colour
             0xD : 320 x 200, 16 colour EGA, VGA
             0xE : 640 x 200, 16 colour EGA, VGA
             0xF : 640 x 350, mono on EGA, VGA
             0x10 : 640 x 350, 4 or 16 colour EGA, VGA
             0x11 : 640 x 480, graphics, 2 colours
             0x12 : 640 x 480, graphics, 16 colours, VGA
             0x13 : 320 x 200, graphics, 256 colours, VGA

Set cursor size

Interrupt   0x10
             Input
             AH = 0x01
             CH = starting scan line
             CL = ending scan line

Returns   Nothing

Notes   Cursor blinking is under hardware control.

Set cursor position

Interrupt   0x10

Input	AH = 0x02
	BH = display page number
	DH = row
	DL = column

Returns	Nothing

Notes	0,0 is upper left. To turn off the cursor, set to (0,25)

Read current cursor position

Interrupt	0x10

Input	AH = 0x03
	BH = display page number

Returns	CH = starting scan line
	CL = ending scan line
	DH = row
	DL = column

Set active display page

Interrupt	0x10

Input	AH = 0x05
	AL = page number

Returns	Nothing

Scroll window up

Interrupt	0x10

Input   AH = 0x06
                 AL = lines to scroll up
                 BH = filler attribute
                 CH = upper row
                 CL = left column
                 DH = lower row
                 DL = right column

Returns   Nothing

Scroll window down

Interrupt   0x10

Input   AH = 0x07
                 AL = lines to scroll down
                 BH = filler attribute
                 CH = upper row
                 CL = left column
                 DH = lower row
                 DL = right column

Returns   Nothing

Set colour palette

Interrupt   0x10

Input   AH = 0x0B
                 BH = palette colour ID
                 BL = colour to be used with palette
Notes   This works for CGA/EGA/VGA only.

Write pixel dot

Interrupt   0x10

Input   AH = 0x0C
AL = pixel value
CX = pixel column
DX = pixel row
BH = page

Returns   Nothing

Read pixel dot

Interrupt   0x10

Input   AH = 0x0D
CX = pixel column
DX = pixel row
BH = page

Returns   AL = pixel value

Get current video mode

Interrupt   0x10

Input   AH = 0x0F

Returns   AH = number of character columns on screen
AL = video mode
BH = page number

Equipment List Service

Get peripheral equipment list

Interrupt   0x11

Input   Nothing

Returns   AX = equipment list

Notes   Bit setting for AX are as follows
           00 = disk drive present/absent (0:absent, 1:present)
           01 = math co-processor (0:absent, 1:present)
           02-03 = RAM in 16 kb blocks
           04-05 = initial video mode
           00 = (unused)
           01 = 40 x 25 colour
           10 = 80 x 25 colour
           11 = 80 x 25 mono
           06-07 = number of disk drives
           08 = DMA present (0:present, 1:absent)
           09-11 = number of serial ports
           12 = game port (0:absent, 1:present)
           13 = serial printer
           14-15 = number of printers

Memory Service

Get Memory Size In kb

Interrupt   0x12

Input   Nothing

Returns   AX = memory size (in kb)

Disk Services

Reset disk controller

Interrupt   0x13

Input   AH = 0x0
             DL = drive
                 0x00-0x7F floppy disk
                 0x80-0xFF fixed disk

Returns   Nothing

Get disk status

Interrupt   0x13

Input   AH = 0x01
             DL = drive
                 0x00-0x7F floppy disk
                 0x80-0xFF fixed disk

Returns   AL = status code

Notes   Status code values in AL are
             AL = 0 : no error
             AL = 1 : bad command
             AL = 2 : address mark not found
             AL = 3 : write attempt to write-protected disk (F)
             AL = 4 : sector not found
             AL = 5 : reset failed (H)
             AL = 6 : floppy disk removed (F)
             AL = 7 : bad parameter table (H)
             AL = 8 : DMA overrun (F)
             AL = 9 : DMA across 64 kb boundary

AL = A : bad sector flag (H)
AL = B : bad track flag (H)
AL = C : media type not found (F)
AL = D : invalid number of sectors on format (H)
AL = E : control data address mark detected (H)
AL = F : DMA arbitration level out of range (H)
AL = 10 : bad CRC
AL = 11 : ECC corrected data error (H)
AL = 20 : NEC controlor failure
AL = 40 : seek failed
AL = 80 : time out (failed to respond)
AL = AA : drive not ready (H)
AL = BB : undefined error (H)
AL = CC : write fault (H)
AL = E0 : status register error (H)
AL = FF : sense operation failed (H)
H = fixed disk only, F = floppy disk only

Read disk sectors

Interrupt	0x13
Input	AH = 0x02
	AL = number of sectors
	CH = track number
	CL = sector number
	DH = head number
	DL = drive number
	0x00-0x7F floppy disk
	0x80-0xFF fixed disk
	ES:BX = pointer to buffer
Returns	If function successful
	Carry flag = clear
	AH = 0x00
	AL = number of sectors read

If function unsuccessful
Carry flag = set
AH = status code (refer interrupt 0x13, function 0x01)

Write disk sectors

Interrupt   0x13

Input   AH = 0x03
             AL = number of sectors
             CH = track number
             CL = sector number
             DH = head number
             DL = drive number
                 0x00-0x7F floppy disk
                 0x80-0xFF fixed disk
             ES:BX = pointer to buffer

Returns   If function successful
             Carry flag = clear
             AH = 0x00
             AL = number of sectors written
             If function unsuccessful
             Carry flag = set
             AH = status code
             CF = succes/failure flag
             AH = status code (refer interrupt 0x13, function 0x01)

Verify disk sectors

Interrupt   0x13

Input   AH = 0x04
             AL = number of sectors
             CH = track number

CL = sector number
DH = head number
DL = drive number
   0x00-0x7F floppy disk
   0x80-0xFF fixed disk
ES:BX = pointer to buffer

Returns   If function successful
Carry flag = clear
AH = 0x00
AL = number of sectors verified
If function unsuccessful
Carry flag = set
AH = status code (refer interrupt 0x13, function 0x01)

Format disk track

Interrupt   0x13

Input   AH = 0x05
AL = number of sectors
CH = track number
CL = sector number
DH = head number
DL = drive number
ES:BX = pointer to 4-byte address fields consisting of
   byte 0 = track
   byte 1 = head
   byte 2 = sector
   byte 3 = bytes/sector
      0 if 128 bytes per sector
      1 if 256 bytes per sector
      2 if 512 bytes per sector (standard)
      3 if 1024 bytes per sector

Returns   If function successful

Carry flag = clear
AH = 0x00
If function unsuccessful
Carry flag = set
AH = status code (refer interrupt 0x13, function 0x01)

Get current drive parameters

Interrupt   0x13

Input   AH = 0x08
          DL = drive
             0x00-0x7F   floppy disk
             0x80-0xFF   fixed disk

Returns   If function successful
          Carry flag = clear
          BL = drive type (PC/AT floppy disks)
             0x01   if 360 kb, 40 track, 5.25"
             0x02   if 1.2 mb, 80 track, 5.25"
             0x03   if 720 kb, 80 track, 3.5"
             0x04   if 1.44 mb, 80 track, 3.5"
          CH = low 8 bits of maximum cylinder number
          CL = bits 6-7   high-order 2 bits of maximum cylinder number
            bits 0-5   maximum sector number
          DH = maximum head number
          DL = number of drives
          ES:DI = segment:offset of disk drive parameter table
          If function unsuccessful
          Carry flag = set
          AH = status code (refer interrupt 0x13, function 0x01)
          On PC/XT this service is supported on fixed disk only.

Initialise two fixed disk base tables

Interrupt   0x13

Input   AH = 0x09
            DL = drive
                0x80-0xFF   fixed disk

Returns   If function successful
            Carry flag = clear
            AH = 0x00
            If function unsuccessful
            Carry flag = set
            AH = status code (refer interrupt 0x13, function 0x01)

Notes   On PC/XT vector for interrupt 0x41 must point to disk
            parameter table. On PC/AT and above vector for inter-
            rupt 0x41 must point to table for drive 0; and the one for
            interrupt 46 must point to table for drive 1.

Read long

Interrupt   0x13

Input   AH = 0x0A
            AL = number of sectors
            DL = drive
               0x80-0xFF   fixed disk
            DH = head number
            CH = cylinder number
            CL = sector number (see notes)
            ES:BX = pointer to buffer

Returns   If function successful
            Carry flag = clear
            AH = 0x00

AL = number of sectors read
If function unsuccessful
Carry flag = set
AH = status code (refer interrupt 0x13, function 0x01)

Notes   This service is supported on fixed disks only. The upper 2 bits of the 10-bit cylinder number are placed in the upper 2 bits of register CL.

Write long

Interrupt   0x13

Input   AH = 0x0B
               AL = number of sectors
               DL = drive ID
                   0x80-0xFF   fixed disk
               DH = head number
               CH = cylinder number
               CL = sector number (see notes)
               ES:BX = pointer to buffer

Returns   If function successful
               Carry flag = clear
               AH = 0x00
               AL = number of sectors written
               If function unsuccessful
               Carry flag = set
               AH = status code (refer interrupt 0x13, function 0x01)

Notes   This service is supported on fixed disks only. The upper 2 bits of the 10-bit cylinder number are placed in the upper 2 bits of register CL.

Seek to cylinder

Interrupt   0x13

Input   AH = 0x0C
                 CH = lower 8 bits of cylinder
                 CL = upper 2 bits of cylinder in bits 6-7
                 DH = head
                 DL = drive
                     0x80-0xFF fixed disk

Returns   If function successful
                 Carry flag = clear
                 AH = 0x00
                 If function unsuccessful
                 Carry flag = set
                 AH = status code (refer interrupt 0x13, function 0x01)

Notes   This service is supported on fixed disks only.

Reset fixed disk system

Interrupt   0x13

Input   AH = 0x0D
                 DL = drive
                     0x80-0xFF   fixed disk

Returns   If function successful
                 Carry flag = clear
                 AH = 0x00
                 If function unsuccessful
                 Carry flag = set
                 AH = status code (refer interrupt 0x13, function 0x01)

Notes   This service is supported on fixed disks only.

Test for drive ready

Interrupt   0x13

Input   AH = 0x10
             DL = drive ID
                0x80-0xFF   fixed disk

Returns   If function successful
             Carry flag = clear
             AH = 0x00
             If function unsuccessful
             Carry flag = set
             AH = status code (refer interrupt 0x13, function 0x01)

Notes   This service is supported on fixed disks only.

Recalibrate drive

Inturrupt   0x13

Input   AH = 0x11
             DL = drive ID
                0x80-0xFF   fixed disk

Returns   If function successful
             Carry flag = clear
             AH = 0x00
             If function unsuccessful
             Carry flag = set
             AH = status code (refer interrupt 0x13, function 0x01)
Notes   This service is supported on fixed disks only.

Controller diagnostics

Interrupt   0x13

Input   AH = 0x14

Returns   If function successful
Carry flag = clear
AH = 0x00
If function unsuccessful
Carry flag = set
AH = status code (refer interrupt 0x13, function 0x01)

Notes   This service is supported on fixed disks only.

Get disk type

Interrupt   0x13

Input   AH = 0x15
DL = drive ID
      0x00-0x7F   floppy disk
      0x80-0xFF   fixed disk

Returns   If function successful
Carry flag = clear
AH = disk type code
CX:DX = number of 512-byte sectors, when AH = 3
If function unsuccessful
Carry flag = set
AH = status code (refer interrupt 0x13, function 0x01)

Notes   This function is not supported on the PC or PC/XT. Disk
type codes are:
AH = 0 : disk non-existent
AH = 1 : disk, no change detection present

AH = 2 : disk change detection present
AH = 3 : fixed disk

Get disk change status

Inturrupt   0x13

Input   AH = 0x16

Returns   DL = drive that had disk change
                    0x00-0x7F   floppy disk
                AH = disk change status

Notes   This function is not supported on the PC or PC/XT.
                Status codes in AH are:
                    00 = no disk change
                    01 = disk changed

Set disk type

Interrupt   0x13

Input   AH = 0x17

                AL = floppy disk type code
                    0x00   not used
                    0x01   320/360 kb floppy disk in 360 kb drive
                    0x02   320/360 kb floppy disk in 1.2 mb drive
                    0x03   1.2 mb floppy disk in 1.2 mb drive
                    0x04   720 kb floppy disk in 720 kb drive
                DL = drive
                    0x00-0x7F   floppy disk

Returns   If function successful
                Carry flag = clear

AH = 0x00
If function unsuccessful
Carry flag = set
AH = status code (refer interrupt 0x13, function 0x01)

Notes   This function is not supported for floppy disks on the PC
            or PC/XT. Disk type codes for AL are:
            AL = 00 : no disk
            AL = 01 : regular disk, regular drives
            AL = 03 : high-capacity disk in high-capacity drives

Set media type for format

Interrupt   0x13

Input   AH = 0x18
            CH = number of cylinders
            CL = sectors per track
            DL = drive
                0x00-0x7F floppy disk

Returns   If function successful
            Carry flag = clear
            AH = 0x00
            ES:DI = segment:offset of disk parameter table for
            media type
            If function unsuccessful
            Carry flag = set
            AH = status code (refer interrupt 0x13, function 0x01)

Keyboard Services

Read next keyboard character

Interrupt   0x16

Input   AH = 0x00

Returns   AH = scan code
             AL = ascii code

Report whether character ready

Interrupt   0x16

Input   0x01

Returns   zero flag = 0 - character available to be received, 1 - no
             character in keyboard buffer
             AH = scan code
             AL = ascii code

Get shift status

Interrupt   0x16

Input   AH = 0x02

Returns   AL shift status bits

Notes   Shift status bits are
                 Bit 0 = 1 : Right shift depressed
                 Bit 1 = 1 : Left shift depressed
                 Bit 2 = 1 : Ctrl depressed
                 Bit 3 = 1 : Alt depressed
                 Bit 4 = 1 : Scroll Lock on
                 Bit 5 = 1 : Num Lock on
                 Bit 6 = 1 : Caps Lock on
                 Bit 7 = 1 : Insert on

Printer Services

Send one byte to printer

Interrupt   0x17

Input   AH = 0x00
             AL = character
             DX = printer number (0 = LPT1, 1 = LPT2, 2 = LPT3)

Returns   AH = success/failure code

Notes   Status code values are
               Bit 0 = 1 : time out
               Bit 3 = 1 : I/O error
               Bit 4 = 1 : printer selected
               Bit 5 = 1 : out of paper
               Bit 6 = 1 : printer acknowledge
               Bit 7 = 1 : printer not busy

Initialise printer

Interrupt   0x17

Input   AH = 0x01
             DX = printer number (0 = LPT1, 1 = LPT2, 2 = LPT3)

Returns   AH = status code (refer interrupt 0x13, function 0x01)

Notes   Status code is the same as for service 0x01.

Get printer status

Interrupt   0x17

Input   AH = 0x02
             DX = printer number (0 = LPT1, 1 = LPT2, 2 = LPT3)

Returns   AH = status code (refer interrupt 0x13, function 0x01)

Notes   Status code is the same as for service 0x01.

Miscellaneous Services

Delay

Interrupt   0x15

Input   AH = 0x86
             CX, DX = number of microseconds to wait.

Returns   Nothing.

Get extended memory size

Interrupt   0x15

Input   AH = 0x88

Returns   Nothing

Notes   Applies to AT and later only.

Reboot computer

Interrupt   0x19

Input   Nothing

Time of Day Services

Read contents of the clock tick counter

Interrupt   0x1A

Input   AH = 0x00

Returns   AL = midnight signal, 0x00 if midnight passed since last
read, non-zero otherwise
CX = tick count, high portion
DX = click count, low portion

Set value in clock tick counter

Interrupt   0x1A

Input   AH = 0x01
CX = tick count, high portion
DX = click count, low portion

Returns   Nothing

Get current time from CMOS time/date chip

Interrupt   0x1A

Input   AH = 0x02

Returns   CH = hours in Binary Coded Decimal (BCD)
CL = minutes in BCD
DH = seconds in BCD
DL = 1 if daylight saving time, 0 if standard time

Notes   Applies to AT and later only.

Set time in CMOS time/date chip

Interrupt   0x1A

Input   AH = 0x03
             CH = hours in Binary Coded Decimal (BCD)
             CL = minutes in BCD
             DH = seconds in BCD
             DL = 1 if daylight saving time, 0 if standard time

Returns   Nothing

Read date from CMOS time/date chip

Interrupt   0x1A

Input   AH = 0x04

Returns   CL = day in Binary Coded Decimal (BCD)
             DH = month in BCD
             CL = year in BCD
             CH = century in BCD

Set date in CMOS time/date chip

Interrupt   0x1A

Input   AH = 0x05
             CL = day in Binary Coded Decimal (BCD)
             DH = month in BCD
             CL = year in BCD
             CH = century in BCD

Returns   Nothing

Set alarm in CMOS date/time chip

Interrupt   0x1A

Input   AH = 0x06
             CH = hours in Binary Coded Decimal (BCD)
             CL = minutes in BCD
             DH = seconds in BCD

Returns   If function successful
             Carry flag = clear
             If function unsuccessful
             Carry flag = set

Notes   The program using this routine must place the address
             of its interrupt handler for the alarm in the vector for
             interrupt 0x4A.

Reset Alarm

Interrupt   0x1A

Input   AH = 0x07

Returns   Nothing

H   *Selected DOS Services*

Long Summary of DOS services

This appendix is divided into two parts. First part gives a table of various DOS srevices available. All these services are grouped under interrupt number 0x21. The second part gives a long summary of selected DOS services. We had to avoid the temptation of discussing all the DOS services here, because they are far too many to be given full justice in a dedicated C language book.

Long Summary of DOS Services

Following is the long summary of various DOS services. For each service, the input registers to be set up, the values returned by the DOS service, and comments about the service (wherever necessary) have been mentioned.

The interrupt number for all services is 0x21. These services can be invoked by using the functions **intdos( )** and **intdosx( )**. These functions assume the interrupt number to be 0x21.

Set disk transfer address

Input   AH = 0x1A
           DS:DX = address of disk transfer area

Returns   Nothing

Notes   Useful if you want to write your own DIR command.

Get FAT information for any drive

Input   AH = 0x1C
           DL = Drive number (0 = default, 1 = A, 2 = B, etc.)

Returns   If function successful
           DS:BX = Segment offset of Media descriptor

0xF8 - Hard disk
0xFC - 5.25 inch single sided, 9 sector
0xFD - 5.25 inch double sided, 9 sectors
0xFE - 5.25 inch single sided, 8 sectors
0xFF - 5.25 inch double sided, 8 sectors
DX = number of clusters
AL = number of sectors/cluster
CX = bytes/sector
If function unsuccessful (invalid drive or critical error)
AL = 0xFF

Get disk free space

Input	AH = 0x36
	DL = Drive number (0 = default, 1 = A, 2 = B, etc.)
Returns	If function successful
	AX = number of sectors/cluster
	BX = number of available clusters on disk
	CX = number of bytes/sector
	DX = Total number of clusters on drive
	If function unsuccessful (drive invalid)
	AX = 0xFFFF
Notes	Useful if you want to check whether a file can be accomodated on a disk or not.

Make directory

Input	AH = 0x39
	DS:DX = segment:offset address of directory name
Returns	If function successful
	Carry flag = clear
	If function unsuccessful

Carry flag = set
AX = error code

Remove directory

Input   AH = 0x3A
               DS:DX = segment:offset address of directory name

Returns   If function successful
               Carry flag = clear
               If function unsuccessful
               Carry flag = set
               AX = error code

Change directory

Input   AH = 0x3B
               DS:DX = segment:offset address of directory name

Returns   If function successful
               Carry flag = clear
               If function unsuccessful
               Carry flag = set
               AX = error code

Delete file

Input   AH = 0x41
               DS:DX = segment:offset address of file name

Returns   If function successful
               Carry flag = clear
               If function unsuccessful
               Carry flag = set
               AX = error code

Notes   Wild card characters not allowed in file name.

Get file attributes

Input   AH = 0x43
              AL = 0
              DS:DX = segment:offset address of file name

Returns   If function successful
              Carry flag = clear
              CX = Current file attributes
              If function unsuccessful
              Carry flag = set
              AX = error code

Notes   File attributes are bit encoded. Refer Chapter 14, Figure 14.5 for specifications of these bits.

Set file attributes

Input   AH = 0x43
              AL = 1
              CX = file attributes
              DS:DX = segment:offset address of file name

Returns   If function successful
              Carry flag = clear
              CX = Current file attributes
              If function unsuccessful
              Carry flag = set
              AX = error code

Notes   File attributes are bit encoded. Refer Chapter 14,5 Figure 14. for specifications of these bits.

Get current directory

Input   AH = 0x47
            DL = Drive number (0 = default, 1 = A, 2 = B, etc.)
            DS:DI= segment:offset address of buffer where DOS
            places the current directory name.

Returns   If function successful
            Carry flag = clear
            and buffer is filled with full pathname from root of
            current directory.
            If function unsuccessful
            Carry flag = set
            AX = error code

Find first matching file

Input   AH = 0x4E
            DS:DX = segment:offset address of file name. Filename
            can contain wild card characters
            CX = file attributes used while searching

Returns   If function successful (matching file found)
            Carry flag = clear
            Disk transfer area is set up with the file information. The
            file information is 43 bytes long and contains following
            details:
                 0 - 20   reserved bytes
                 21 file attribute
                 22 - 23 time of creation/modification
                 24 - 25 date of creation/modification
                 26 - 30 file size
                 31 - 42 file name
            If function unsuccessful (no matching files)
            Carry flag = set
            AX = error code

Notes   This service is useful if you want to write your own DIR
             command

Find next matching file

Input   AH = 0x4F
             Assumes that DTA points to buffer used by previous
             successful interrpt 0x21, function 0x4E or 0x4E.

Returns   If function successful (matching file found)
             Carry flag = clear
             Disk transfer area is set up with the file information. The
             file information is 43 bytes long and contains detail
             given in service 0x4E.
             If function unsuccessful (no more matching files)
             Carry flag = set
             AX = error code

Notes   This service is useful if you want to write your own DIR
             command

Rename file

Input   AH = 0x56
             DS:DX = segment:offset address of file to be renamed.
             Wild card characters are not allowed.
             ES:DI = segment:offset address of new name of file.
             Wild card characters are not allowed.

Returns   If function successful
             Carry flag = clear
             If function unsuccessful
             Carry flag = set
             AX = error code

Notes   The path and new file name can be different than origi-
              nal. However, the drive must be same. In MS-DOS
              version 3.0 and later, this function can also be used to
              rename directories.

Index

K

Techmedia-COMPUTER BOOKS

TITLE	PRICE

2

TITLE	PRICE
◆CORBA	
CORBA PROGRAMMING UNLEASHED ..... JAN.'99	
◆COBOL	
COBOL UNLEASHED	450/-
Teach Yourself COBOL in 21 Days	
(with YEAR 2000 problems solutions)	300/-
◆COM / DCOM	
TEACH YOURSELF COM/DCOM IN 14 DAYS JAN.'99	
COM/DCOM PRIMER PLUS-WAITE GROUP . JAN.'99	
◆CORELDRAW 8	
Teach Yourself CORELDRAW 8 in 24 Hours ...	135/-
◆DIGITAL PHOTOGRAPHY	
Teach Yourself DIGITAL PHOTOGRAPHY	
in 14 Days	180/-
◆DATA COMMUNICATION	
Understanding DATA COMMUNICATION - Fifth	
Edition (Covers PDA's, ISDN, SNMP, TCP/IP) .	150/-
◆DELPHI	
DELPHI 4 DEVELOPER'S GUIDE .... JAN.'99	
◆DOS	
Peter Norton's COMPLETE GUIDE	
TO DOS 6.22	399/-
◆DB2	
DB2 Developer's Guide (Also cover V4 and V5)	
(W/CD) - 3RD ED.	495/-
TEACH YOURSELF DB2 UNIVERSAL	
DATABASE IN 21 DAYS (W/CD)	240/-
◆DIRECTOR - MACROMEDIA	
Inside MACROMEDIA DIRECTOR 6	
with Lingo (W/CD)	450/-
MACROMEDIA WEB PUBLISHING	
Unleashed (W/CD)	450/-
◆EXCHANGE SERVER	
MS EXCHANGE SERVER 5 Unleashed (W/CD)	450/-
◆EXCEL 97	
Teach Yourself MS EXCEL 97 in 24 Hours	135/-
◆FRONTPAGE 98	
Teach Yourself MS Front Page 98 in a week	180/-
◆GENERAL COMPUTING	
HOW COMPUTERS WORKS -	
5TH EDITON (W/CD) .... JAN.'99	
◆HOMEPAGE	
Teach Yourself to create HOMEPAGE	
in 24 Hours (W/CD)	180/-
◆HTML	
HTML 4 Unleashed (W/CD)	450/-
HTML 4 HOW TO (W/CD) - WAITE GROUP	399/-
Teach Yourself DYNAMIC HTML in a week	195/-
Teach Yourself WEB PUBLISHING with	
HTML in 14 Days (W/CD)	570/-
Teach Yourself HTML 4 in 24 Hours	150/-
Dynamic HTML Unleashed...............................	300/-
◆ILLUSTRATOR 7	
Teach Yourself ILLUSTRATOR 7 in 24 Hours	135/-
TEACH YOURSELF ILLUSTRATOR 8	
IN 24 HOURS .... JAN.'99	

TITLE	PRICE
◆INFORMIX	
INFORMIX Unleashed (W/CD)	499/-
◆INTERNET SECURITY	
INTERNET SECURITY Professional Reference	
(W/CD)	499/-
Maximum Security - A Hacker's Guide to Protecting	
Your Internet Site and Network (W/CD)	499/-
◆INTRANETS	
INTRANETS Unleashed (W/CD)	499/-
◆INTERNET	
Teach Yourself THE INTERNET STARTER	
KIT in 24 Hours (W/CD)	180/-
Teach Yourself INTERNET in 24 Hours	150/-
HOW INTERNET WORKS (FIFTH EDN.) ... JAN.'99	
◆INTERNET EXPLORER 4	
Teach Yourself INTERNET EXPLORER 4	
in 24 Hours	120/-
◆JAVA	
DATA STRUCTURES & ALGORITHMS IN JAVA	
(W/CD)-Mitch Waite Signature Series	270/-
Java 1.1 Unleashed - third Revised Edition	
(W/CD)	499/-
PETER NORTON's Guide to JAVA	
Programming (W/CD)	450/-
Teach Yourself JAVA 1.1 in 21 Days -	
Second Edition (W/CD)	225/-
JAVA Industrial Strength (W/CD)	450/-
OBJECT-ORIENTED PROGRAMMING	
IN JAVA (W/CD) - MITCHELL WAITE	450/-
OBJECT-ORIENTED DESIGN IN JAVA	
(W/CD) - MITCHELL WAITE	270/-
DATA STRUCTURES & ALGORITHMS	
IN JAVA (W/CD)	270/-
◆JAVA 1.1	
Teach Yourself JAVA 1.1 Programming	
in 24 Hours (W/CD)	165/-
JAVA 1.1 Interactive Course	
(W/CD) - Waite Group	495/-
JAVA 1.1 Developer's Guide (W/CD)...............	499/-
JAVA 1.1 Certification Training Guide (W/CD) ...	399/-
Maximum JAVA 1.1-(W/CD)	450/-
Teach Yourself More JAVA 1.1 in 21 Days	165/-
◆JAVA 1.2	
JAVA 1.2 UNLEASHED (W/CD)	499/-
TEACH YOURSELF JAVA 1.2 IN 24 HOURS .	150/-
◆JAVA SCRIPT	
JAVA SCRIPT Interactive Course	
(W/CD) - Waite Group	450/-
◆JDBC	
Teach Yourself DATABASE Programming	
with JDBC in 21 Days (W/CD)	275/-
◆LINUX	
LINUX Unleashed (W/CD)...............................	499/-
RED HAT LINUX Unleashed	
(Revised 2nd Edition) (W/CD)	399/-
Teach Yourself LINUX in 24 Hours (W/CD)	195/-
◆LOTUS NOTES	
LOTUS NOTES & DOMINO SERVER 4.5	
Unleashed (W/CD)	450/-
Teach Yourself LOTUS NOTES 4.5 in 14 Days ..	195/-

TITLE	PRICE

◆**LOTUS SMARTSUITE - MILLENNIUM**
TEACH YOURSELF LOTUS SMARTSUITE
MILLENNIUM IN 24 HOURS 150/-
◆**LDAP**
LDAP PROGRAMMING PROGRAMMING
DIRECTORY-ENABLED APPLICATIONS WITH
LIGHTWEIGHT DIRECTORY ACCESS
PROTOCOL 499/-
◆**MFC**
Microsoft FOUNDATION CLASS 4 BIBLE
(W/CD) 499/-
◆**MCPS : MICROSOFT CERTIFIED**
PRODUCT SPECIALIST
NETWORKING WITH MS TCP/IP -
STUDY GUIDE (W/CD) 450/-
◆**MCSD : MICROSOFT CERTIFIED**
SOLUTION DEVELOPER
Visual Basic 5 - Training Guide (W/CD) 495/-
◆**MCSE : MICROSOFT CERTIFIED**
SOFTWARE ENGINEERS
NETWORKING ESSENTIALS -
TRAINING GUIDE (W/CD) 425/-
SQL SERVER 6.5 ADMINISTRATION -
TRAINING GUIDE (W/CD) 425/-
SQL SERVER 6.5 DESIGN & IMPLEMENTATION -
TRAINING GUIDE (W/CD) 425/-
WINDOWS NT SERVER 4 -
TRAINING GUIDE (W/CD) 425/-
WINDOWS NT SERVER 4 ENTERPRISE -
TRAINING GUIDE (W/CD) 425/-
WINDOWS 95 - TRAINING GUIDE (W/CD) 425/-
WINDOWS NT WORKSTATION 4 - TRAINING
GUIDE (W/CD) 425/-
MCSE CORE REQUIREMENTS
(4 BOOKS SET)
WINDOWS NT SERVER 4 (W/CD) +
WINDOWS NT SERVER 4 ENTERPRISE (W/CD) +
NETWORKING ESSENTIALS (W/CD) +
WINDOWS NT WORKSTAIONS 4 (W/CD)..1650/-
◆**MCSE: TEACH YOURSELF SERIES**
Teach Yourself MCSE TCP/IP in 14 Days 195/-
Teach Yourself MCSE WINDOWS NT Server 4.0
in 14 Days 195/-
Teach Yourself MCSE WINDOWS NT
WORKSTATION in 14 Days 195/-
TEACH YOURSELF MCSE WINDOWS 98
IN 14 DAYS .... JAN.'99
◆**MCSE STUDY GUIDE SERIES**
MCSE: STUDY GUIDE WINDOWS 95 &
NETWORKING ESSENTIALS (W/CD) 425/-
MCSE: STUDY GUIDE TCP/IP SYSTEM
MANAGEMENT SERVER (W/CD) 425/-
MCSE: STUDY GUIDE WINDOWS NT SERVER &
WORKSTATION 4 (W/CD) 425/-
◆**MCSE FAST TRACK SERIES**
Windows NT Server 4 .... 120/-
Windows NT Workstation 4 .... 120/-

TITLE	PRICE

◆**MCSE FAST TRACK SERIES**
Networking Essentails 120/-
Internet Informaion Server 4 .... 120/-
Windows NT Serer 4 Enterprise 120/-
TCP/IP 120/-
◆**MS-OFFICE 4.3 / WIN**
Inside MS-OFFICE 4.3 Professional for
WINDOWS (W/DISK) 450/-
◆**MS-OFFICE 97 / WIN 95**
MS OFFICE 97 Interactive Course -
Waite Group 399/-
MS OFFICE 97 Unleashed (W/CD) 399/-
Teach Yourself MS OFFICE 97 in 24 Hours 135/-
TEACH YOURSELF MS OFFICE 97
IN 24 HOURS - 2ND EDITION 150/-
◆**NETSCAPE COMMUNICATOR 4**
Teach Yourself NETSCAPE COMMUNICATOR 4
in 24 Hours 150/-
◆**NETWORKING**
Teach Yourself NETWORKING in 24 Hours 150/-
Networking Essentials Unleashed 399/-
HOW NETWORK WORKS (4TH EDITION) . JAN.'99
◆**NETWORK COMPUTING**
NC Guide Development Strategies for
Network Computer - Waite Group 499/-
◆**ODBC**
Teach Yourself ODBC Programming in 21 Days 225/-
◆**OLE DB & ADO**
Teach Yourself OLE DB AND ADO
in 21 Days (W/CD) 275/-
◆**ORACLE**
Developing CLIENT/SERVER Applications
with ORACLE DEVELOPER/2000 (W/CD) 423/-
TEACH YOURSEFL ORACLE
DEVELOPER/2000 IN 21 DAYS .... JAN.'99
Teach Yourself ORACLE 8 in 21 Days 195/-
ORACLE CERTIFIED PROGRAMMING
TRAINING GUIDE - ORACLE DBA .... JAN.'99
OCP TRAINING GUIDE :
ORACLE DBA (W/CD) 399/-
Teach Yourself ORACLE 8 DATABASE
Development in 21 Days (W/CD) 270/-
Teach Yourself PL/SQL in 21 Days (W/CD) 275/-
ORACLE 8 SERVER Unleashed 450/-
ORACLE 8 HOW TO - WAITE GROUP 300/-
Developing Personal ORACLE 7 for
WINDOWS 95 Applicaitons (W/CD) 360/-
ORACLE 7.3 Developer's Guide (W/CD) 399/-
ORACLE DBA SURVIVAL GUIDE (W/CD) 399/-
ORACLE 8 DATA WAREHOUSING Unleashed . 450/-
Oracle 8 Server Unleashed 450/-
ORACLE Performance Tuning &
Optimization (W/CD) 450/-
ORACLE HOW - TO (W/CD) - Waite Group 375/-
ORACLE Electronic Resource Kit (W/3 CDs) ... 799/-
ORACLE UNLEASHED (W/CD)-(Second
Revised Edition also Cover Oracle 8) 599/-

TITLE	PRICE

◆PREMIERE - ADOBE
ADOBE PREMIERE 5.0 — CLASS ROOM
IN A BOOK (W/CD) 270/-

◆PROGRAMMING LANGUAGE
The Handbook of Programming Language -
HPL VOL. I - OBJECT-ORIENTED
PROGRAMMING LANGUAGE 399/-
VOL. II - IMPERATIVE PROGRAMMING
LANGUAGES 240/-
VOL. III - LITTLE LANGUAGES & TOOLS . 300/-
VOL. IV - FUNCTIONAL, AND LOGIC PROG.
LANGUAGES 210/-

◆PAGEMAKER
PAGEMAKER 6.5 Complete 360/-

◆PC
Peter Norton's Inside The PC, 7th Edition 240/-
Teach Yourself PCs in 24 Hours 150/-

◆PC - SERVICING / HARDWARE
Peter Norton's Guide to UPGRADING &
REPAIRING PCs 225/-
TEACH YOURSELF UPGRADEING AND
FIXING PC'S IN 24 HOURS 135/-
Winn Rosch HARDWARE BIBLE (W/CD) 450/-

◆PERL
PERL 5 HOW - TO (W/CD) - Waite Group 399/-
PERL 5 Interactive Course (W/CD) - Waite Group .. 495/-
Teach Yourself PERL 5 in 21 Days (W/CD) 300/-

◆PHOTOSHOP-ADOBE
ADOBE PHOTOSHOP 4 Interactive Course
(W/CD) - Waite Group 495/-
Inside ADOBE PHOTOSHOP (W/CD) 399/-
PHOTOSHOP 4 Complete (W/CD) 450/-
PHOTOSHOP 4 Studio Skills (W/CD) 195/-
Teach Yourself PHOTOSHOP 4 in 24 Hours 120/-
Teach Yourself PHOTOSHOP 4 in 14 Days (W/CD) 180/-

◆PHOTOSHOP 5
INSIDE ADOBE PHOTOSHOP 5 (W/CD) 399/-
Adobe Photoshop 5 - Classroom in a
Book (W/CD) 275/-

◆POWER BUILDER 5.0
POWER BUILDER 5 Unleashed (W/CD) 450/-
POWER BUILDER 5 HOW - TO
(W/CD) - Waite Group 399/-

◆POWER BUILDER 6.0
POWER BUILDER 6.0 UNLEASHED (W/CD) 450/-

◆POWER POINT 97
Teach Yourself MS POWER POINT 97
in 24 Hours 135/-

◆PL / SQL
Teach Yourself PL/SQL in 21 Days (W/CD) 275/-

◆MS-PROJECT
TEACH YOURSELF MS - PROJECT 98
IN 24 HOURS 150/-

◆QUARK XPRESS
TeacH Yourself QUARK XPRESS 4
in 14 Days (W/CD) 180/-

◆SAP R/3
SAP R/3 Planning & Implementation 360/-

◆SYBASE
SYBASE SQL SERVER 11 Unleashed (W/CD)..499/-
SQL Unleashed (W/CD) 499/-
Teach Yourself SQL in 21 Days 180/-
Teach Yourself SQL in 24 Hours 150/-

◆SQL - MICROSOFT
MS SQL SERVER 6.5 Unleashed (W/CD) 450/-
TEACH YOURSELF MS-SQL SERVER 6.5
IN 21 DAYS 195/-
TECH YOURSELF MS SQL SERVER 7
IN 21 DAYS .... JAN.'99
MS SQL SERVER 7 PROGRAMMING
UNLEASHED .... JAN.'99

◆TRANSACT - SQL
Teach Yourself TRANSACT - SQL in 21 Days ... 225/-

◆TCP/IP
Teach Yourself Inside TCP/IP - 3rd Edition 300/-
Networking with Microsoft TCP/IP (W/CD) 450/-
Teach Yourself TCP/IP in 14 Days (2nd Edition) 150/-
Teach Yourself TCP/IP in 24 Hours 135/0
TCP/IP BLUEPRINTS (W/CD) 360/-

◆TURBO C++
Teach Yourself TURBO C++ 4.5 for WINDOWS
in 21 Days 270/-

◆UNIX
Exploring The UNIX System - 3rd Revised Edition .. 150/-
Teach Yourself UNIX in 24 Hours 180/-
Teach Yourself UNIX SHELL Programming
in 14 Days 165/-
UNIX SYSTEM V Primer - Waite Group 150/-
UNIX SYSTEM ADMINISTRATOR'S
Unleashed (W/CD) 599/-
UNIX Unleashed, INTERNET Edition (W/CD) ... 450/-

◆VISUAL BASIC 5
Developing ACTIVE X Components with
VISUAL BASIC 5-(W/CD) 450/-
Doing Objects in MS VISUAL BASIC 5-(W/CD) 360/-
MCSD Training Guide : Visual Basic 5 (W/CD) . 495/-
Teach Yourself VISUAL BASIC 5 in 24 Hours
(W/CD) 180/-
VISUAL BASIC Unleashed (W/CD) 375/-
Teach Yourself VISUAL BASIC 5 in 21 Days 270/-
Teach Yourself VISUAL BASIC 5 in 21 Days
(W/CD) Vol. II 210/-
Teach Yourself VISUAL BASIC 5
in 21 Days 2-Vols + CD 435/-
Teach Yourself DATABASE Programming with
VISUAL BASIC 5 in 21 Days (W/CD) 330/-
Teach Yourself MORE VISUAL BASIC 5
in 21 Days 195/-
VISUAL BASIC for Applications Unleashed
(W/CD) (Covers Office 97, Internet, Active X) .. 399/-
VISUAL BASIC 5 Interactive Course
(W/CD) - Waite Group 495/-
VISUAL BASIC 5 SUPER BIBLE -
Set - 2 Vols. (W/CD) - Waite Group 795/-
VISUAL BASIC 5 CLIENT/SERVER HOW-TO
(W/CD) - Waite Group 450/-
VISUAL BASIC 5 Developer's GUIDE (W/CD) .. 399/-

TITLE	PRICE

TITLE	PRICE	TITLE	PRICE

◆WINDOWS NT - SERVER
Inside Windwos NT Server 4 (W/CD) 450/-
Peter Norton's Maximizing
   WINDOWS NT SERVER 4 .... 399/-
Teach Yourself NT Server 4 in 14 Days 225/-
◆WINDOWS NT - WORKSTATION
Peter Norton's Complete Guide to
   WINDOWS NT 4 WORKSTATION 450/-
Teach YourselF NT WorkStation 4 in 24 Hour ... 165/-
◆WIRELESS NETWORKING
Wireless Networking Handbook 499/-
◆WEB
Teach Yourself HOW TO BECOME A
   WEBMASTER in 14 Days (W/CD) 210/-
Teach Yourself ACTIVE WEB DATABASE
   Programming in 21 Days (W/CD) 399/-
Creating COMMERCIAL WEB PAGES (W/CD) . 450/-
Adobe WEB Design & Publishing
   Unleashed (W/CD) 450/-

◆WEB
Most Popular WEB SITES (W/CD) 480/-
DESIGNING INTERACTIVE WEBSITES (W/CD) ... 270/-
WEB Site Construction Kit for WIN 95 (W/CD) . 270/-
   (HTML 4, DYNAMIC HTML, STYLE SHEETS,
   JAVASCRIPT, VBSCRIPT,- JSCRIPT,
   NETSCAPE NAVIGATOR 4 TAGS, INTERNET
   EXPLORER 4 TAGS)
Dynamic Web Publishing Unleashed,
   (HTML, JAVASCRIPT, JAVA, CGI, STYLE
   SHEETS) Second Edition 300/-
World Wide WEB Directory (W/CD) 450/-
World Wide WEB Yellow Pages (W/CD) 450/-
(COMPUTERS, COOKING, EDUCATION,
   ENTERTAINMENT, FINANCE,- HEALTH
   & FITNESS, MYTHOLOGY, SPORTS, TRAVEL,
   WOMEN'S ISSUES)
◆WEB AUTHORING
WEB AUTHORING DESK Reference 450/-

7

BPB-COMPUTER BOOKS

TITLE	PRICE
➤80386/80486 & HARDWARE	
Microprocessor Data Handbook	180/-
MODERN - All About Hard Disk drive.	150/-
MODERN - All About Floppy Disk & Drives	120/-
MODERN - All About Mother Board	150/-
MODERN - All About Keyboard & Mouse	120/-
Programming the 80386	180/-
The 386/486 PC : A Power User's Guide	99/-
The PC DATA Handbook	99/-
PC Magazine Programmer's Technical Ref.	180/-

> A+ Certification Programme : *This program is offered for individuals who wish to demonstrate their knowledge of computer hardware and computer operating systems. This certifications is becoming in demand and a number of large employers are beginning to ask for it when hiring new MIS employees.*

➤A+ CERTIFICATION PROGRAMME	
A+ STUDY GUIDE : CORE MODULE	299/-
A+ STUDY GUIDE : DOS / WINDOWS	299/-
A+ EXAM NOTES : CORE MODULE	99/-
A+ EXAM NOTES : DOS / WINDOWS	99/-
➤ACCESS	
ABCs of MS ACCESS	99/-
Learn MS ACCESS for Windows in a day	45/-
PCLL Teaches MS ACCESS (W/D)	180/-
➤ACCESS 2	
PCLL-Teaches ACCESS 2.0 (W/D)	150/-
➤ACCESS 7.0 / WIN 95	
Teach Yourself ACCESS for Windows 95	165/-
Learn MS ACCESS 7.0 for Windows 95 in a day	45/-
➤ACCESS 97	
ACCESS 97 Developers Hand Book (W/CD-ROM)	499/-
ACCESS 97 - No Experience Required	150/-
ACCESS 97 - TRAINING GUIDE	60/-
Mastering ACCESS 97 for Win 95 / NT (W/CD-ROM)	450/-
Teach Yourself Access 97 For Windows 95	180/-
➤ACTIVE X	
Active X - No Experience Required	180/-
MASTERING ACTIVE X AND COM (W/CD).JAN'99	
➤AMIPRO	
Learn AMIPRO 3.0 in a day	45/-

TITLE	PRICE
➤ANIMATION	
Graphics Programming & ANIMATION	180/-
➤ARTIFICIAL INTELLIGENCE	
Knowledge Engineering & EXPERT Systems	90/-
NEURO-INTELLIGENT Systems	150/-
Understanding ARTIFICIAL INTELLIGENCE	120/-
➤ACCOUNTING	
Computerised ACCOUNTING	135/-
Financial Management and Accounting System (W/D)	300/-
➤MAIN – AS/400	
AS/400 Disk Saving Tips & Techniques	120/-
AS/400 Companion	90/-
Navigating the AS/400 A Hands on Guide	180/-
➤ASSEMBLER	
Learn MS-ASSEMBLER in a day	45/-
Teach Yourself ASSEMBLER (W/D)	180/-
➤ASSEMBLY LANGUAGE	
ASSEMBLY LANGUAGE Techniques IBM for PC	150/-
Developing Utilities in ASSEMBLY LANGUAGE (W/D)	99/-
➤ASTROLOGY	
Computer ASTROLOGY (W/D)	345/-
➤AUTOCAD	
Inside AUTOCAD	180/-
Encyclopedia AUTOCAD	450/-
Learn AUTOCAD in a Day	45/-
Mastering AUTOCAD	240/-
➤AUTOCAD 11	
AUTOCAD 11 Instant Reference	54/-
Illustrated AUTOCAD (Release 11)	195/-
Mastering AUTOCAD (Release 11)	300/-
➤AUTOCAD 12	
ABCs of AUTOCAD (Release 12)	150/-
Advanced AUTOCAD (Release 12)	195/-
Mastering AUTOCAD Release 12 (W/D)	350/-
AUTOCAD 12 Instant Reference	60/-
Learn AUTOCAD 12 in a Day	45/-
Mastering AUTOCAD Release 12 for Windows	775/-
➤AUTOCAD 13	
AUTOCAD 13 for DOS & WINDOWS Inst. Ref.	66/-
Teach Yourself AUTOCAD 13 (W/D)	150/-
Mastering AUTOCAD 13 /WIN /WIN 95 /NT (W/CD-ROM)	450/-
➤AUTOCAD 14	
AUTOCAD 14 instant reference	54/-

TITLE	PRICE

➢AUTOCAD 14
Mastering AUTOCAD 14 (W/CD) 450/-
Mastering AUTOCAD 14 for Mechanical
   Engineers (W/CD) 499/-
AUTOCAD 14 - No Experience Required 180/-
Mastering AUTOCAD 3D (W/CD) 720/-

➢AUTOCAD – CAD/CAM
Understanding CAD/CAM 150/-

➢AUTOLISP
ABCs of AUTOLISP 120/-
AUTOLISP & Customisation Made Simple 150/-
Illustrated AUTOLISP 120/-

➢BAR CODES
Understanding BAR CODES 120/-

➢BASIC
BASIC : Step by Step Programming 45/-
BASIC : Work Book 36/-
BASIC For Beginners 30/-
BASIC for Schools 54/-
BASIC Programming Lab Workbook 75/-
Computer Programming in BASIC –
   The Easy Way 75/-
Electrical Engineering Computation By Computer
   Graphics Aided Basic Programming 150/-
Programming Expertise in BASIC 90/-
Your First BASIC Program 60/-
Learning IBM BASIC 120/-

➢BORLAND C/C++
BORLAND C++ 3.0 for Windows 3.1 .... 195/-
BORLAND C++ Techniques & Utilities (W/D) 240/-
BORLAND C++ 4.0 Upgrade Book 99/-
Clean Coding in BORLAND C++ 150/-
Illustrated BORLAND C++ 3.0 .... 150/-
Programming Output Drivers Using
   BORLAND C++ 54/-
Windows Programming with BORLAND C++ . 300/-

➢C
AL Stevens Teaches C (W/D) 195/-
Advanced Fractal Programming in C 225/-
C - DATA BASE Development 120/-
C Language for Programmers 120/-
C Pearls 150/-
C Projects (W/D) 300/-
C Under DOS Test 54/-
C with Assembly Language 150/-
Database Management Using C (W/D) 195/-
Data Structure Using C Lab Workbook (W/D) 150/-
ENCYCLOPEDIA C 495/-
EXPLORING C 150/-
GO THROUGH C 120/-
GRAPHICS UNDER C 195/-
GRAPHIC USER INTERFACE Programming
   With C 180/-

➢C
GRAPHICS Programming in C 300/-
Illustrated C 120/-
Illustrated C Programming 120/-
Image Processing in C (W/D) 350/-
Learn C in Three Days 45/-
LET US C - 3RD REVISED EDITION 150/-
Programming with ANSI C 120/-
Mastering C 120/-
Numerical Techniques in C 75/-
Question Bank unix C Programming 66/-
Teach Yourself - C 99/-
The Hidden Treasures of C 75/-
Test your C Skils 150/-
Understanding C 90/-
Understanding Pointers in C (2nd Revised ed.) . 150/-
Undocumented DOS Through C 195/-
Working With C (For DOE – 'A' & 'B' Level) ... 150/-
Writing TSR's through C 225/-
WRITING UTILITIES IN C .... JAN'99
The C Odyssey - Vol. I DOS 250/-
The C Odyssey - Vol. II Advanced DOS 250/-
The C Odyssey - Vol III UNIX 250/-
The C Odyssey - Vol. IV Networks RDBMS .. 250/-
The C Odyssey - Vol. V C++ & Graphics 250/-
The C Odyssey - Vol. VI Windows 250/-
The C Odyssey - Vol. VII OS/2 .... 250/-
The Complete ANSI C 252/-

➢C++
A Comprehensive Guide to C++ 99/-
Advanced GRAPHICS Programming
   In C & C++ 350/-
Applying C++ (W/D) 225/-
Black Belt C++ : Master Collection for
   Programmers 150/-
C - Elements of Style for C & C++ 90/-
C++ - No Experience Required 165/-
C/C++ Programmer's Guide (W/D) 240/-
C/C++ Programming Lab Workbook 120/-
C++ COMMUNICATIONS UTILITIES (W/D) ... 300/-
C++ An Intro. of Experienced C Programmers 75/-
C++ COMPONENTS & ALGORITHMS (W/D) 300/-
C++ Database Development (W/D) 225/-
C++ Neural Networks & Fuzzy Logic (W/D) ... 300/-
C++ PROGRAMMING .... JAN'99
Convert To C & C++ 120/-
Learn MFC C++ Classes (W/2 Disks) 180/-
LET US C++ .... JAN'99
Mastering C++ (From C to C++ in 2 Weeks)
   (W/D) 295/-
MASTER TEMPLATES IN C++ - .... JAN'99
Object Oriented Programming with C++ 120/-
OBJECT ORIENTED PROGRAMMING
   WITH C++ .... JAN'99
OBJECT ORIENTED PROGRAMMING
   DEVELOPMENT – A REALISTIC
   APPROACH IN C++ .... JAN'99

TITLE	PRICE

➢C++
Programming On-Line Help Using C++ 180/-
Teach Yourself C++ (W/D) (Revised Edition). 150/-
Write Your Own Programming Language
Using C++ 54/-
Your First C/C++ Program (W/D) 180/-

➢CISCO
CCNP : ADVANCED CISCO ROUTER
CONFIGURATION STUDY GUIDE (W/CD) . FEB'99
CCNP : CISCO LAN SWITCHING
CONFIGURATION STUDY GUIDE (W/CD) . APR'99
CISCO - CCNA STUDY GUIDE (W/CD) 499/-

➢COMPUSERVE
Learn COMPUSERVE for Windows in a day ... 54/-

➢CARTOONS
Laughing Bytes (Hilarious Cartoons) 36/-

➢CASE TOOLS
CASE TOOLS : Concepts & Applications 180/-

➢CLIENT/SERVER
CLIENT/SERVER Computing SYBASE SQL
SERVER 225/-
CLIENT/SERVER Computing with ORACLE... 225/-
Developing CLIENT/SERVER Applications 275/-
Guide to CLIENT/SERVER Databases
(2nd Ed.) 180/-
Mastering ORACLE 7 & CLIENT/SERVER
Computing (W/D) 345/-
NOVELL's CLIENT-SERVER Applications &
Architecture 350/-

➢CLIPPER
111 CLIPPER Functions (W/D) 150/-
CLIPPER - 5 & 5.01 Programming Guide 195/-
CLIPPER 5 & 5.01: A Developers Guide 450/-
CLIPPER 5.01/87 Test 45/-
CLIPPER 5.2 Power Programming
Guide (W/D) 250/-
CLIPPER Applications 75/-
CLIPPER Programming Guide (Summer 87) . 180/-
Illustrated CLIPPER 5.0 & 5.01 .... 135/-
Learn CLIPPER..... Fast 45/-
Writing Applications with CLIPPER (W/D) 225/-

➢CNA
CNA Study Guide (W/2D) 1399/-
CNA Study Guide (Revi. Edn.) W/CD 1925/-

➢CNE
CNE -4 Study Guide for Netware 4.1
Certification (W/CD) 495/-

➢COBOL
COBOL : Language of Business 75/-
COBOL Programming Lab Workbook 99/-
Structured Programming in COBOL 99/-
MASTERING COBOL .... FEB'99

TITLE	PRICE

➢COMPUTER - TEXTBOOKS
A First Course in Computer SCIENCE
(ICSE class IX TO XII) 120/-
Computers Don't Byte: A Beginners Guide to
Understanding Computers 45/-
Computer Basics 30/-
COMPUTER Concepts & Facts 36/-
COMPUTER Fundamentals 99/-
COMPUTER Programming 54/-
Basic Computing - Book A 33/-
Basic Computing - Book B 33/-
Basic Computing - Book C 33/-
Basic Computing - Book D 33/-
Basic Computing - Book E 33/-
Basic Computing - Book F 33/-
Basic Computing Principles 54/-
COMPUTER Fundamentals and C++
Programming VOL.I (CBSE-XI) 81/-
COMPUTER FUNDAMENTALS AND
C++ PROGRAMMING VOL.II (CBSE-XII) ... 150/-
COMPUTER TUTOR 24/-
Fun with Computers Vol. I 36/-
Fun with Computers Vol. II 36/-
Fun with Computers Vol. III 36/-
Fun with Computers Vol. IV 36/-
Fun with Computers Vol. V 36/-
Fun with Computers Vol. VI 36/-
INFORMATICS PRACTICES VOL. I 150/-
Introducing COMPUTERS - Part - I Revised ... 39/-
Introducing COMPUTERS - Part - II Revised .. 39/-
Introducing COMPUTERS - Part - III Revised . 39/-
Introduction to COMPUTER SCIENCE Vol.-I ... 99/-
Introduction to COMPUTER SCIENCE Vol.-II ... 99/-
Let us Learn COMPUTERS (Revised Edition) . 45/-
Programming in PASCAL -Volume I 75/-
Programming in PASCAL -Volume II 60/-
Questions & Answers on Computer 120/-
We can use the COMPUTERS - A 33/-
We can use the COMPUTERS - B 33/-
We can use the COMPUTERS - C 33/-
We can use the COMPUTERS - D 33/-
We can use the COMPUTERS - E 33/-
We can use the COMPUTERS - F 33/-
Your First Computer 120/-

➢COREL DRAW - 4 - 5 - 6 - 7 - 8
Learn COREL DRAW In a Day 45/-
Looking Good with COREL DRAW (4&5) 150/-
Teach Yourself - COREL DRAW 4.0 .... 120/-
Teach Yourself - COREL DRAW 5.0 .... 120/-
Teach Yourself - COREL DRAW 6.0 .... 135/-
Mastering COREL DRAW 6 (W/CD-ROM) 450/-
Mastering COREL DRAW 7 (W/CD-ROM) 450/-
Mastering COREL DRAW 8 (W/CD-ROM) 450/-

➢CD RECORDABLE
CD Recordable Hand Book (W/CD-ROM) 399/-
Complete Recordable CD Guide (W/CD-ROM) ..390/-

TITLE	PRICE	TITLE	PRICE

CROSSTALK
Mastering CROSSTALK XVI 120/-

DATABASE
Relational DATABASE — Theory & Practice ... 99/-
The Database Dictionary 150/-

DBASE III PLUS
ABCs of dBASE III PLUS 81/-
Advanced Techniques in dBASE III PLUS 180/-
dBASE III Plus/dBASE IV Test 39/-
dBASE Workbook 36/-
dBASE III PLUS: A Comprehensive
  Users Manual 90/-
dBASE Programmers Utilities (W/D) 150/-
dBASE III PLUS Instant Reference 60/-
dBASE III PLUS Programmers Reference Guide ... 275/-
dBASE III PLUS Programming Tips &
  Techniques 180/-
dBASE III PLUS Students & Instructor
  Work Book 99/-
dBASE III PLUS Tips & Tricks 99/-
Illustrated dBASE III PLUS Book 99/-
Learn dBASE Programming in a Day 45/-
Mailing List Using dBASE 45/-
Mastering dBASE III PLUS 99/-
Quick Guide to dBASE 90/-
Understanding dBASE III PLUS 99/-

DBASE IV
Illustrated dBASE IV 1.1 .... 120/-
Teach Yourself dBASE V for Windows 120/-
Understanding dBASE IV 1.5 .... 275/-

DBASE V
Understanding dBASE V for Windows 640/-

DATA COMPRESSION
DATA COMPRESSION Book 2nd Edition (W/D) ... 225/-

DATA PROCESSING
DATA PROCESSING AND INFORMATION
  TECHNOLOGY 135/-

DELPHI - 2 / 3
From DELPHI 2 you (W/D) 180/-
Mastering DELPHI 2 for Win 95 & NT
  (W/CD-ROM) 399/-
Mastering DELPHI 3 (W/CD) 495/-
Teach Yourself DELPHI (W/D) 150/-

DICTIONARY
Computer DICTIONARY 36/-
The PC User's Pocket DICTIONARY 66/-
DICTIONARY of Networking 75/-

DTP
DeskTop Publishing on PC 99/-
DeskTop Publishing on PC - Hindi 60/-

ELECTRONIC MAIL
CC : MAIL Plain & Simple 150/-

EXCEL
Murphy's Laws of EXCEL 225/-
Mastering EXCEL - 4 for Windows 195/-

EXCEL 5 / WIN
EXCEL 5 for Windows Instant Reference 45/-
Learn EXCEL 5.0 For Windows In a Day 45/-
MS EXCEL 5.0 For Windows at a Glance 60/-
Mastering EXCEL - 5 for Windows 225/-
PCLL-Teaches EXCEL 5.0 for Windows (W/D) 150/-

EXCEL 7 / WIN 95
Learn MS EXCEL 7.0 for Windows 95 in a day . 45/-
PCLL-Teaches EXCEL 7.0 for Windows 95
  (W/D) 165/-
Teach Yourself EXCEL 7.0 for Windows 95
  (W/D) 150/-

EXCEL 97
Abcs of EXCEL 97 .... 120/-
Mastering EXCEL 97 .... 399/-
Excel 97 - Training Guide 60/-

EXCHANGE SERVER
Mastering MS Exchange Server 5 .... 450/-

FLOPPY DISK
FLOPPY DISK : INTERNALS 54/-
Modern All About FLOPPY DISK & DRIVES . 120/-

FORTRAN-77
Programming in MS FORTRAN 77 for IBM PC
  & Compatibles (2nd Edn.) 99/-
Programming Through FORTRAN 77 -
  A Practical Approach 75/-

FOXBASE+
Illustrated FOXBASE+ 2.1 .... 99/-
FOXBASE+ 2.1:Programming & AppLications.. 60/-

FOXPRO — 2
FOXPRO 2 - A Developers Guide 120/-
FOXPRO 2 - The Art of Visual Programming .. 99/-
FOXPRO 2 - C & MULTIUSER - Programming 150/-
Illustrated FOXPRO 2 .... 120/-
Mastering FOXPRO 2 .... 150/-
Learn FOXPRO 2.0 in A Day 45/-

FOXPRO — 2.5
FOXPRO 2.5 Made Simple 165/-
FOXPRO 2.5 for DOS at a Glance 60/-
FOXPRO 2.5 for WINDOWS at a Glance 75/-
Learn FOXPRO 2.5 for WINDOWS in a day ... 45/-
Complete FOXPRO 2.5 Language Reference .. 99/-
PCLL-Teaches FOXPRO 2.5 for Windows (W/D) .. 150/-

FOXPRO — 2.6
Developing & Distributing
  FOXPRO 2.5/2.6 / Win Appl. (W/D) 99/-
Mastering FOXPRO 2.5 & 2.6 (Special Edition) . 345/-
Programming FOXPRO 2.5 & 2.6 (W/D) 480/-
Programmers Guide to FOXPRO 2.5/2.6 (W/D) 375/-
FOXPRO 2.6 Code Book 180/-

TITLE	PRICE	TITLE	PRICE

➤VISUAL – FOXPRO—3
Mastering Visual FOXPRO 3 Special Edition . 345/-
PCLL Teaches Visual FOXPRO 3.0 (W/D) 180/-
Teach Yourself VISUAL FOXPRO 3
   for Windows (W/D) 180/-

➤VISUAL – FOXPRO— 5
Teach Yourself Visual FoxPro 5.0 /for win (W/D) ... 195/-

➤FRACTALS
Advanced FRACTAL Programming in C 225/-
Fun With FRACTALS (W/D) 375/-

➤FRONT PAGE 97
ABCs of FRONT PAGE 97 .... 150/-
Learn MS FRONT PAGE 97 (W/Disk) 99/-
Mastering FRONT PAGE 97 (W/CD) 450/-

➤FRONT PAGE 98
FRONT PAGE 98 - No Experience Required
   Weisskopt 150/-
Mastering MS-FRONT PAGE 98 (W/CD) 450/-

➤GENERAL BOOKS
ALMOST PERFECT : How a Bunch of Regular
   Guys Built WORDPERFECT Corporation
   (Hard Bound) 150/-
SILICON SAMURAI : How Japan Conquered
   the World's I.T. Industry (Hard Bound) 225/-
कम्प्यूटर – एक पूर्ण परिचय (द्वितीय संस्करण). .. 45/-
Little Book On Computer 45/-
Learn Computers in a Day 54/-

➤GRAPHICS
Computer GRAPHICS Secrets & Solutions 120/-
Designing GUI Applications for Windows (W/D) 225/-

➤GW BASIC
MODERN All About GW-BASIC for Schools
   & Colleges 180/-
Programming in GW-BASIC (2nd Edn.) 54/-

➤HARD DISK
HARD DISK Management - PC & PS/2 .... 90/-
Modern All About of HARD DISK Drive 150/-
HARD DISK Survival Guide (W/D) 225/-
HARD DISK Technical Guide (W/CD) 450/-

➤HARVARD GRAPHICS
Learn HARVARD GRAPHICS 3.0 in a Day 54/-
Presentation with HARVARD GRAPHICS 60/-

➤HEALTH & FITNESS
Your Personal FITNESS Trainer with Interactive
   (W/CD-ROM) 450/-

➤HUMAN COMMUNICATION
HUMAN Communication 99/-

➤HTML
Mastering HTML 4.0 (W/CD-ROM) 450/-
HTML 4.0 - No Experience Required 180/-
HTML Example Book 150/-
Dynamic HTML: Master the Essentials 240/-

➤IBM PC-AT
Mastering XENIX on the IBM PC AT 150/-

➤IBM PS/2
IBM PS/2 Handbook 99/-

➤IBM PC-XT
IBM XT Clone Handbook 99/-

➤IBM-PC/XT/AT
ABCs of IBM PC's & Compatibles 60/-
IBM PC & PS/2 GRAPHICS Handbook 135/-
New PETER NORTON Programmer's Guide to
   the IBM PC & PS/2 .... 345/-
PC Buyer's Survival Guide 195/-
PC Companion 120/-
PC Power - Boosting Your PC's Performance ... 150/-
Programmers' Guide To PC & PS/2
   VIDEO System 300/-

➤IBM-PC/XT/AT — SERVICING
Build Your Own Computer (2nd Edition) 54/-
Exploring and Upgrading your PC 399/-
How Computer Works with Interactive CD-ROM 480/-
How Computer Works (Without CD) 300/-
Inside The Grey Box-Choosing, Building &
   Upgrading PC 120/-
PC Upgrade Guide for Everybody 90/-
PC Upgrade & Maintenance : No Experience
   Required 150/-
Complete PC Upgrade & Maintenance
   Guide 8th Edition (W/2CD-ROM'S) 599/-
UPGRADING, MAINTAINING & SERVICING
   IBM PC's & Compatibles (W/D) 275/-

➤INGRES-RDBMS
INGRES and Relational Databases 150/-
Introduction to INGRES 225/-
Mastering INGRES 225/-

➤GENERAL – INTERNET
ABCs of the INTERNET (2nd Rev. Edn.) 99/-
INTERNET Basic Reference from A to Z 180/-
INTERNET Dictionary 99/-
INTERNET Instant Reference (3rd Edn.) 90/-
INTERNET Roadmap 90/-
INTERNET Toolkit 120/-
INTERNET For Kids 54/-
INTERNET - No Experience Required 150/-
Learn INTERNET Relay Chat 60/-
Learning to use the INTERNET 120/-
Learning Guide to the INTERNET (WITH CD)
   Johnson 225/-
Mastering the INTERNET (W/CD-ROM) 450/-
Mastering WEB DESIGN (W/CD-ROM) 450/-
MASTERING NETSCAPE FAST TRACK
   SERVER 225/-
Surfing the INTERNET with NETSCAPE
   NAVIGATOR 2 (W/D) 150/-
Surfing the INTERNET with NETSCAPE
   NAVIGATOR 3 (W/CD-ROM) 240/-
INTERNET COMPLETE 180/-

TITLE	PRICE

➤**INTERNET EXPLORER**
ABC of MS Internet Explorer 3 .... 99/-
ABC of MS Internet Explorer 4
(With Free MS-Internet Explorer 4.0 CD) ... 150/-
MASTERING INTERNET EXPLORER 4
(WITH FREE MS-INTERNET
EXPLORER 4.0 CD).................................. **450/-**

➤**IIS**
Mastering MS INTERNET INFORMATION
SERVER.. 399/-
MCSE: Internet Info Server 3 Study Guide
(W/CD) 450/-
MCSE: INTERNET INFO SERVER 4
STUDY GUIDE (W/2CDs) **450/-**

➤**INTRANETS**
ABCs Of INTRANETS 120/-
Building INTRANETS on NT, Netware
and Solaris 399/-
INTRANETS: The Surf Within (W/CD) 270/-
Mastering INTRANETS FOR WIN 95 /NT
(W/CD-ROM) 450/-
Practical Guide to INTRANET Client Server
Applications Using the Web (W/CD) 225/-

➤**ISDN**
Mastering ISDN 300/-

➤**ISO 9000**
Getting ISO 9000 for a Software Organisation ... 225/-

➤**JAVA**
JAVA 1.1 Certification Study Guide (W/CD) ... 450/-
JAVA 1.1 DEVELOPERS Handbook
(W/CD-ROM) 450/-
JAVA 1.1 : No Experience Required
(W/CD-ROM) 225/-
Java Workshop Programming (W/D) 150/-
Mastering JAVA 1.1 (W/CD-ROM) 450/-
Mastering Java (W/CD-ROM) 399/-
Abcs of JAVA Script 150/-
Mastering JAVA Beans (W/CD-ROM) 399/-
Mastering JAVA Scripts (w/CD-ROM) 450/-
Learn Advance JAVA script Programming
(W/CD) 399/-

➤**JAVA 1.2**
JAVA 1.2 - IN RECORD TIME (W/CD) **180/-**

➤**PRINTERS – LASERJET**
LASERJET Unlimited 180/-

➤**LiNUX**
Complete LINUX Kit (W/CD-ROM) 450/-
LINUX Configuration & Installation
(Including Slackware) (W/2CD's) 300/-
MASTERING LINUX - INTERNET EDITION
(W/CD) .... **JAN'99**

➤**LOGO**
LOGO Work Book 36/-
The School LOGO Book 45/-
Working with LOGO 36/-

➤**LOTUS 1-2-3**
ABCs of 1-2-3 (Release 2.2) 90/-
ABCs of 1-2-3 (Release 3) 90/-
Illustrated LOTUS 1-2-3 (Release 2.2) 99/-
Illustrated LOTUS 1-2-3 (Release 3) 135/-
Illustrated LOTUS 1-2-3 Book 120/-
Learn LOTUS 1-2-3 in a Day (Revised Edition).. 45/-
Learn LOTUS 1-2-3 Rel. 4 for Windows In a Day ... 45/-
Learn LOTUS 1-2-3 Rel. 5 for Windows in a day 54/-
LOTUS 1-2-3 (Students & Instructor Work Book) 99/-
LOTUS 1-2-3 Instant Reference 2.3 & 2.4....... 45/-
LOTUS 1-2-3 Release 5 Quick & Easy 360/-
LOTUS 1-2-3 Release 5 For WINDOWS
Instant Reference 54/-
LOTUS 1-2-3 For Windows at a Glance 75/-
Mastering 1-2-3 .... 150/-
Mastering 1-2-3 (Release 3) 180/-
Manual LOTUS 1-2-3 .... 54/-
Teach Yourself LOTUS 1-2-3 .... 120/-
Up & Running with LOTUS 1-2-3 (Release 2.3) 180/-
Understanding 1-2-3 Release 4.0 for Windows .. 540/-
Understanding LOTUS 1-2-3 Release 5 /
WINDOWS 640/-

➤**LOTUS SMARTSUITE**
Compact Guide to LOTUS SMARTSUITE 180/-
Mastering LOTUS SMARTSUITE 97 / WIN 95 ..... 450/-
MASTERING LOTUS SMARTSUITE
MILLENNIUM EDN. PREMIUM EDN. .... JAN'99

➤**LOTUS-NOTES 4.5 & DOMINO**
ABCs OF LOTUS NOTES 4.5 .... 120/-
Learn LOTUS DOMINO (W/D) 99/-
LOTUS NOTES 4.5 Administrator Guide 300/-
LOTUS NOTES Developer's Guide for
Users Rel 4.0-4.5 (W/CD-ROM) 275/-
LOTUS NOTES Plain & Simple 180/-
Mastering LOTUS NOTES 4 (W/CD-ROM) 399/-
Mastering LOTUS NOTES 4.5 & DOMINO
(W/CD-ROM) 450/-
Teach Yourself LOTUS NOTES 4.5 (W/D) 225/-

➤**MIS**
MANAGEMENT INFORMATION SYSTEM
(8TH EDITION)... 99/-

➤**MACROMEDIA**
Mastering MACROMEDIA DIRECTOR 5
(W/CD-ROM) 450/-
MASTERING MACROMEDIA DIRECTOR 6
(W/CD-ROM) **450/-**

➤**MAPI**
Inside MAPI (W/CD ROM) 1078/-

TITLE	PRICE

MCPS INTERNET SYSTEMS SPECIALIST

Suggested Retail Price 1350/-
Save Rs. 150/-
You Pay Only 1200/-

The most efficient and affordable way to prepare for the Microsoft Certified Product Specialist: Internet Systems Specialist Certification.

3 Books & 3CDs
- NT Server 4.0 Study Guide
- TCP/IP for NT Server 4 Study Guide
- Internet Information Server 3 Study Guide

EVERYTHING YOU NEED TO PREPARE FOR THE INTERNET SYSTEMS SPECIALIST EXAMS.

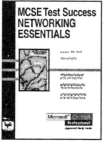

16

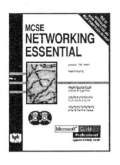

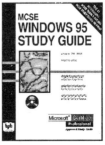

TITLE	PRICE	TITLE	PRICE

➢**HARDWARE – KEYBOARD AND MOUSE**
Modern All About Keyboard and Mouse 120/-

➢**HARDWARE – MODEM**
Learn to use your MODEM in a Day 60/-
The MODEM Technical Guide (W/CD) 450/-
Your first MODEM 150/-

➢**HARDWARE – MONITORS**
MODERN-All About MONITORS 60/-
MODERN-MONITOR Circuits &
FAULT-FINDING VOl. I 45/-
MODERN-MONITOR Circuits &
FAULT-FINDING VOl. II 45/-
MODERN-MONITOR Circuits &
FAULT-FINDING VOl. III 54/-
मॉडर्न कम्प्यूटर मानीटर सर्विसिंग मेन्युल
(M-Tek & Vintron) 45/-
MODERN-Colour VGA MONITOR
Servicing Manual 45/-
मॉडर्न कम्प्यूटर मानीटर सर्विसिंग मेन्युल
(TRL - DUAL) 45/-
मॉडर्न कम्प्यूटर मानीटर सर्विसिंग मेन्युल
(M-Tek - DUAL) 45/-
Programmer's Guide to the EGA/VGA 275/-

➢**HARDWARE – SMPS**
A Complete Guide to SMPS for PC
(HardWare & Software) 45/-
Modern - Computer SMPS Servicing Manual
Pioneer, Power, TVSE (हिन्दी) 45/-
Modern - Computer SMPS Servicing
Manual Vintron, Microtek, Bull Power (हिन्दी) . 45/-
Modern - Computer SMPS Circuits & Faults
Finding Vol. I 45/-

➢**MS-DOS**
ABCs of DOS 5 .... 90/-
Advanced MS DOS Programming 275/-
Amazing DOS Games 99/-
DOS (3.3 & 5) Instant Reference 45/-
DOS 3.3 & 5.0 Test 45/-
DOS 6 Running Start 75/-
DOS 6.0 & 6.22 Companion 99/-
DOS 6.0 & 6.2 Instant Reference 54/-
DOS Quick Reference Manual -Volume I
(upto ver.-5) 45/-
DOS Quick Reference Manual -Volume II
(upto ver.-6.2) 45/-
Illustrated MS-DOS 5 (Upto Version - 5) 99/-
Illustrated MS DOS 6.22 .... 99/-
DOS A Developers Guide (upto ver:-5) 225/-
Learn DOS in a Day (Upto 6.2) 45/-
MS-DOS 5 Power User's Guide 60/-
PCLL Teaches DOS 6 & 6.2 .... 150/-
MS-DOS System Programming (W/D) 225/-
Mastering DOS 6 & 6.2 - Special Edition 325/-
Murphy's Laws of DOS-6 .... 99/-
Teach Yourself - DOS 90/-
MS-DOS Handbook 99/-

➢**MULTIMEDIA/ SOUND BLASTER / CD-ROM**
Choosing & Using Your First CD-ROM
Drive -(W/CD-ROM) 350/-
Multimedia on the PC (W/D) 120/-
Multimedia Magic (W/CD) 270/-
SOUND BLASTER Book 300/-
The Magic PC Stereo Gram Book (W/CD) 450/-

➢**NORTON UTILITIES**
Learn NORTON UTILITIES in a Day 45/-
NORTON Desktop for Windows Instant Reference. 240/-
Understanding NORTON UTILITIES 6 .... 299/-

➢**NETWORKING**
ABCs of LOCAL AREA NETWORKS 99/-
Complete Encyclopedia Of Networking
(W/CD-ROM) 495/-
Dictionary of NETWORKING 75/-
Fix Your own LAN 270/-
Introduction to LOCAL AREA NETWORKS
(Revised Edition) 150/-
MASTERING LOCAL AREA NETWORKS .. FEB'99
LAN Security Handbook (W/D) 225/-
LAN Troubleshooting Handbook (W/D) 240/-
LOCAL AREA NETWORKS 99/-
Multiprotocol Network Design & Troublshooting . 450/-
NT NETWORK SECURITY 450/-
NETWORK Concepts & Architectures 150/-
PC Magazine - Guide to CONNECTIVITY 225/-
The NETWORK Technical Guide (W/CD) 450/-
Welcome to NETWORKING - A Guide to LAN's 99/-

➢**NOVELL NETWARE**
Learn NOVELL NETWARE in A Day 45/-
NETWARE 2.2 & 3.11 Users Guide 240/-
NETWARE 3.12 Administrator's Handbook 180/-
NETWARE Programmer's Guide for 286/386. 180/-
NOVELL's Guide to Netware 3.12 Networks .. 270/-
NOVELL NETWARE - Tips, Tricks &
Techniques 225/-
NOVELL NETWARE 386-3.11 User's
Perspective 195/-
NOVELL's Applications Notes for
NETWARE 4.01 .... 350/-
NOVELL's CLIENT/SERVER Applications &
Architecture 350/-
NOVELL's Guide to NETWARE 4.01
NETWORKS 225/-
NOVELL's Guide to Personal NETWARE 360/-
NOVELL's Problem Solving Guide for
NETWARE Systems (For Version 3.X/4.X) . 180/-
PCLL-Teaches NETWARE (W/D) 150/-
The Official NOVELL NETWARE Little Hand Book..180/-
Troubleshooting NETWARE For The 286 .... 275/-
NOVELL's Quick Access Guide to
NETWARE 3.11 Networks 60/-
Troubleshooting NETWARE For The 386 .... 350/-
Troubleshooting Netware Systems
(W/2 CD ROMs) 499/-
**THE COMPLETE NETWORK UPGRADE &
MAINTEINANCE GUIDE (W/CD) .... JAN'99**

———————————— 19 ————————————

QUAN BOOK *NOW AVAILABLE*
Published by BPB PUBLICATIONS WITH DOEACC **Rs. 123/-**
FOR PAPER A7 - A10 **'A' Level VOL.II**

TITLE	PRICE	TITLE	PRICE

➤ORACLE
Client Server Computing with ORACLE 225/-
Mastering ORACLE 6.0.... .... 180/-
ORACLE : Building High Performance On-line
Systems 150/-
SQL, PL/SQL - THE PROGRAMMING
LANGUAGE OF ORACLE......................... **240/-**
ORACLE 6.0: The Basics 150/-
ORACLE 7 : The Complete Reference 180/-
ORACLE 6/7 - SQL Report Writer 180/-
The ORACLE Cook Book (W/D) 225/-
Commercial Application Development
Using ORACLE DEVELOPER 2000 .... 240/-
Understanding ORACLE 250/-
Mastering ORACLE 7 & Client/Server
Computing (W/D) 2nd Edition 345/-
The First Step to ORACLE 75/-
LEARN PERSONAL ORACLE 8.0 WITH
POWER OBJECTS 2.0 .... **195/-**
ORACLE PROGRAMMING WITH
VISUAL BASIC **297/-**
MASTERING ORACLE 8 (W/CD) .... **APR'99**

➤OLE-2
OLE-2 Programmer's Reference Vol. I 805/-
OLE-2 Programmer's Reference Vol. II 670/-
Mastering OLE 2 (W/D) 180/-

➤OUTLOOK 97
ABCs of OUTLOOK 97 .... 120/-

➤PAGEMAKER
Learn PAGEMAKER 5.0 for Windows in a Day.. 54/-
Mastering PAGEMAKER 4 on IBM PC 150/-
Mastering PAGEMAKER 5.0 for Windows (W/D)... 300/-
PAGEMAKER 5.0 by Example (W/D) 345/-
Mastering PAGEMAKER 6 for Win 95
(W/CD-ROM) 399/-
Teach Yourself PAGEMAKER 6.5 for WIN & MAC
(W/CD) 240/-

➤PEOPLESOFT
PEOPLESOFT ADMINISTRATOR'S GUIDE .. **MAR'99**

➤PERL
MASTERING PERL 5 .... **MAR'99**

➤PARADOX
Mastering PARADOX 4.5 for Windows 396/-

➤PASCAL
Data Structure Using PASCAL LAB Workbook
(W/D) 120/-
Introductory PASCAL 60/-
Learn PASCAL in three days 45/-
PASCAL : An Introduction 45/-
PASCAL Programming — 2nd Edition 150/-
PASCAL Programming Lab Workbook............. 99/-
Programming in Borland PASCAL (W/D)........ 525/-
Programming in PASCAL - Volume I
(CBSE- XI) 75/-
Programming in PASCAL - Volume II
(CBSE - XII) 60/-

➤PC TOOLS
Learn PC TOOLS in a Day 45/-
PC TOOLS 7.1... 99/-
Up & Running with PC TOOLS Deluxe 6 .... 45/-
PC TOOLS 7.1 Instant Reference 45/-

➤PERL / CGI
PERL/CGI : No Experience Required 150/-

➤PFS : FIRST CHOICE
Understanding PFS: FIRST CHOICE 150/-

➤PHOTOSHOP
Adobe PHOTOSHOP Handbook...................... 300/-
Teach Yourself PHOTOSHOP 4
for WIN/MAC (W/CD) 240/-

➤POWER BUILDER
Commercial Applications in POWER BUILDER .. 225/-
POWER BUILDER : Concepts & Applications ... 225/-
POWER BUILDER 4 : A Developer's Guide
(W/D) 350/-
POWER BUILDER 4.0 (W/D) 325/-

➤POWER BUILDER 5 & 6
DEVELOPING ENTERPRISE APPLICATIONS
WITH POWERBUILDER 6.0 (W/CD) **270/-**
Teach Yourself POWER BUILDER 5.0 (W/D) 225/-
POWER BUILDER 5.0: A Developer's Guide
(W/CD) 450/-
POWERBUILDER VEDAS (W/CD)
(Covers version 6) **450/-**

➤POWER POINT
Learn MS POWER POINT 7.0 for Win 95
in a day 45/-
Mastering POWERPOINT 4 for Windows 150/-
Mastering POWER POINT 97 .... 195/-
Teach Yourself POWER POINT for WIN95.... 180/-

➤PRINTSHOP
The Official PRINTSHOP Deluxe H/B 180/-

➤PRINTER
Getting the Most FROM your HP Laserjet (W/D) .. 150/-
Laser PRINTER Unlimited 150/-
Modern all about PRINTER 99/-
Winn L. Rosch's PRINTER Bible (W/CD-ROM) . 450/-

➤PROCOMM PLUS
Learn PROCOMM PLUS 2.0 for Windows
in a day 54/-
Mastering PROCOMM PLUS 150/-

➤PROGRAMMING
Foundations of PROGRAMMING 60/-
Mixed Language PROGRAMMING (W/D) 225/-
PROGRAMMING Techniques for PC's 66/-
Plug & Play PROGRAMMING (W/D) 180/-
Structured Programming: go to Controversy
to OBJECT ORIENTED PROGRAMMING .. 120/-
Welcome to PROGRAMMING (W/D) 180/-

➤PROJECT
PCLL-Teaches MS PROJECT 4.0
for Windows (W/D) 150/-
Teach Yourself MS PROJECT
for Windows 95 (W/D) 180/-

➤QUATTRO PRO
Learn QUATTRO PRO 5.0 in a Day 45/-
Mastering QUATTRO PRO 5 for Windows..... 295/-
Mastering QUATTRO PRO for Windows 396/-

➤RS-232
The RS-232 Solution.................................... 150/-

TITLE	PRICE

➤SAP's
Developing SAP's R/3 Applications with
ABAP/4 (W/CD-ROM)................................. 499/-
SAP R/3 SYSTEM ADMINISTRATION: THE
OFFICIAL SAP GUIDE (W/CD) 399/-
SAP R/3 IMPLEMENTATION WITH ASAP (W/CD)
THE OFFICIAL SAP GUIDE .... JAN'99

➤SERIAL COMMUNICATION
Mastering SERIAL COMMUNICATIONS 180/-
SERIAL COMMUNICATIONS:A C++ Development
Guide (W/D) 275/-

➤SGML FILTERS
PRACTICAL GUIDE TO SGML FILTERS
(W/2 DISKS) 180/-

➤SOFTWARE
ALMOST PERFECT : How a Bunch of Regular
Guys Built WORDPERFECT CORPORATION .. 150/-
Getting ISO 9000 for SOFTWARE Organizations
(2nd Rev. Ed.) 225/-
How Computer Works (W/CD-ROM) 480/-
SOFTWARE FACTORY : Managing
SOFTWARE Development & Maintenance . 150/-

➤SOFTWARE ENGINEERING
Object Oriented SOFTWARE ENGINEERING 150/-

➤SQL
Optimizing SQL (W/D) 180/-
SQL Spoken Here 120/-
Understanding SQL 225/-

➤SQL 7
MASTERING SQL SERVER 7 .... JAN'99
SQL SERVER 7 - IN RECORD TIME .... JAN'99

➤SYBASE
CLIENT/SERVER Computing SYBASE
SQL Server 225/-

➤SYSTEM ANALYSIS & DESIGN
Introducing SYSTEMS ANALYSIS - NCC 90/-
Introducing SYSTEMS DESIGN - NCC 90/-

➤TCP/IP & SNA
Demystifying TCP/IP 90/-
Integrating TCP/IP into SNA 225/-
Troubleshooting TCP/IP 399/-

➤TSR
Write TSR's Now 99/-
Writing TSR's Through C 225/-

➤TURBO C
Mastering TURBO C 180/-
TURBO C Programming Techniques 99/-
Programming Guide to TURBO C2 .... 180/-

➤TURBO C++
Illustrated TURBO C++ 150/-
Object Oriented Programming Using TURBO C++ .. 45/-
TURBO C ++ Techniques & Applications 180/-

➤TURBO PASCAL
Advanced Techniques in TURBO PASCAL 90/-
Mastering TURBO PASCAL 150/-
Mastering TURBO PASCAL - 6 .... 150/-
TURBO PASCAL 6.0 .... 75/-
TURBO PASCAL Companion 75/-

TITLE	PRICE

➤TURBO PROLOG
Illustrated TURBO PROLOG......................... 120/-
Introduction to TURBO PROLOG 120/-

➤UNIX/XENIX
Advanced UNIX : A Programmer's Guide 180/-
Illustrated UNIX System V 195/-
Inside XENIX 96/-
Peter Norton Guide to UNIX 180/-
Question Bank UNIX C Programming.............. 66/-
Teach Yourself...UNIX 99/-
Test Your UNIX Skills 81/-
ABCs of SCO UNIX 90/-
Running UNIX 180/-
UNIX ... Power ... UNLEASHED 120/-
UNIX C SHELL Desk REFERENCE 120/-
UNIX Power UTILITIES 150/-
UNIX Desk Reference – Guide to Commands,
Concepts of Latest Release of UNIX Linux BSD. 135/-
UNIX Quick ! 99/-
Understanding UNIX....................................... 270/-
UNIX Programming On the 80286/80386 .... 150/-
UNIX Power Tools (W/CD-ROM) 395/-
UNIX Shells Bourne-Korn-C 150/-
UNIX Shell Programming 175/-
Working With UNIX 150/-

➤VENTURA
Learn VENTURA 4.0 in A Day......................... 45/-
Mastering VENTURA 3.0 .... 150/-
VENTURA Publisher Test 54/-

➤VIRUS
Computer VIRUS Protection HandBook (W/D) 180/-
Science of Viruses & Vaccubes (W/2 DISKS) 300/-

➤VISUAL BASIC
VISUAL BASIC Utilities (W/D) 240/-
Programming in VISUAL BASIC....................... 75/-
Teach Yourself ... VISUAL BASIC 3.0 (W/D). 195/-

➤VBA
VBA Developer's Handbook (W/CD-ROM) 495/-

➤VISUAL BASIC 4
Developing Utilities in VISUAL BASIC 4.0 (W/D) 99/-
Learn VISUAL BASIC 4.0 in three days........... 45/-
PCLL - Teaches MS VISUAL BASIC 4 (W/D) ... 165/-
The VISUAL BASIC 4.0 Example Book (W/D) ... 120/-
Teach Yourself VISUAL BASIC 4.0 for WIndows
95 (W/D) 195/-
The Fast Track to VISUAL BASIC 4 .... 120/-

➤VISUAL BASIC 5 - 6
Mastering VISUAL BASIC 5 (W/CD).............. 450/-
VISUAL BASIC 5 : No Experience Required ... 450/-
VISUAL BASIC 5 Developer's Handbook (W/CD) .. 450/-
learn VISUAL BASIC 5.0 In Three Days (W/D) .. 66/-
VISUAL BASIC 6 COMPLETE .... APR'99
MASTERING VISUAL BASIC 6 (W/CD) 399/-
VISUAL BASIC 6 IN RECORD TIME 275/-
EXPERT GUIDE TO VISUAL BASIC 6 (W/CD) .. 399/-
VISUAL BASIC 6 DEVELOPER'S
HANDBOOK (W/CD) .... JAN'99

➤C – VISUAL C++
MS VISUAL C++ 5 No Experience Required . 180/-
VISUAL C++ Programming 240/-
ADVANCED VISUAL C++ .... JAN'99

TITLE	PRICE	TITLE	PRICE

➤C – VISUAL C++

VISUAL C++ PROJECTS .... JAN'99
Mastering MS VISUAL C++ 4 (W/CD-ROM) .. 450/-
Teach Yourself VISUAL C++ 4 .... 180/-
Visual C++ A Developer's Guide (W/D) 225/-
Writing Visual Basic Controls Using VISUAL C++ .. 180/-
MASTERING VISUAL C++ 6 (W/CD) 399/-
VISUAL C++ 6 IN RECORD TIME 225/-

➤VISUAL J++

Mastering VISUAL J++ (W/CD-ROM) 450/-
VISUAL J++ 1.1 No Experience Required 135/-

➤CLIPPER – VISUAL OBJECTS

Rick Spence'S Guide to CA-VISUAL OBJECTS 225/-

➤INTERNET – WORLD WIDE WEB

Learning to Use the WORLDWIDE WEB 150/-
Mastering OFFICE 97 WEB PUBLISHING 360/-

➤WORLD WIDE WEB DESIGN

World Wide Web Bible (W/CD ROM) 399/-
Mastering WEB Design (W/CD-ROM) 450/-
THE WEB PAGE WORKBOOK (W/D) 150/-
Building Business Web Sites (W/CD-ROM) 450/-
THE COMPLETE WEBSITE UPGRADE &
   MAINTENANCE GUIDE (W/CD) .... JAN'99

➤WIN FAX

Just the Fax All about WIN FAX 150/-

➤WINDOWS

ABCs of WINDOWS 3.1 .... 99/-
Compact Guide To WINDOWS, WORD & EXCEL..180/-
Advanced Tools for WINDOWS Developers (W/D) 540/-
Creating Help for WINDOWS Applications (W/D) 99/-
Designing GUI Applications for WINDOWS (W/D)
   Leavens 225/-
Illustrated WINDOWS 3.1 .... 150/-
PC Computing Customizing Windows 3.1 (W/D) ... 180/-
Learn WINDOWS in a Day 45/-
Programming WINDOWS 3.1 (W/D) 345/-
Making WINDOWS Application Work Together
   (W/D) 240/-
Mastering WINDOWS 3.1 (Special Edition) 250/-
MS WINDOWS At A Glance 60/-
PCLL-Teaches WINDOWS 3.1 (W/D) 150/-
Programming for WINDOWS 45/-
Teach Your Self WINDOWS 3.1 .... 120/-
The WINDOWS PROBLEM Solver 150/-
Up & Running with WINDOWS 3.1 .... 225/-
WINDOWS 3.1 Instant Reference 54/-
WINDOWS 3.0/3.1 Test 54/-
WINDOWS 3.1 A Developer's Guide (W/D) ... 345/-
WINDOWS 3.1 GRAPHICS Programming (W/D) .. 225/-
WINDOWS Programming with Borland C++ (W/D) 300/-
WINDOWS Rapid Application Development (W/D) 275/-
WINDOWS Custom Controls 225/-
Writing WINDOWS Application from
   Start to Finish (W/2D) 350/-
HANDS ON PROGRAMMING WINDOWS
   SERIES (7 VOLS.)
Book I - Introduction to WINDOWS
   Programming (W/D) 99/-
Book II - CHILD WINDOWS (W/D) 99/-
Book III - Painting the Screen (W/D) 99/-

➤WINDOWS

Book IV - Transferring Data to & from
   WINDOWS (W/D) 99/-
Book V - Mouse, Timer & Keyboard Inputs (W/D) ... 99/-
Book VI - Text & Special Fonts, Menus &
   Printing (W/D) 99/-
Book VII - App studio graphics editor (W/D) ... 99/-
Mastering WINDOWS Utilities Programming
   with C++ (W/D) 525/-

➤WINDOWS 3.11 INTERNET EDITION

Mastering WINDOWS 3.11 Internet Edition
   (W/CD) 399/-

➤WINDOWS FOR WORKGROUPS 3.11

Guide to WINDOWS for WORKGROUPS 120/-

➤WINDOWS 95

Alan Simpson's Easy Guide to WINDOWS 95 99/-
Getting Ready for WINDOWS 95 .... 99/-
LEARN WINDOWS 95 IN A DAY 45/-
Mastering WINDOWS 95 .... 350/-
MASTERING WINDOWS 95 INTERNET
   EDITION (W/2 CD'S) 570/-
PCLL - Teaches WINDOWS 95 (W/D) 150/-
Programming WINDOWS 95 (W/CD) 799/-
Teach yourself WINDOWS 95 .... 135/-
The Learning Guide to WINDOWS 95............ 120/-
Upgrading to WINDOWS 95 Special Edition .. 180/-
WINDOWS 95 Instant Reference 60/-
WINDOWS 95 - NO EXPERIENCE REQUIRED . 150/-

➤WINDOWS 98

ABCs OF WINDOWS 98 .... 165/-
EXPERT GUIDE TO WINDOWS 98 (W/CD).. 399/-
LEARNING GUIDE TO WINDOWS 98 .... JAN'99
LEARN ACTIVE DESKTOP PROGRAMMING
   WINDOWS 98 .... 225/-
MASTERING WINDOWS 98 PREMIUM
   EDITION (W/2CD) 630/-
UPGRADING TO WINDOWS 98 .... 180/-
WINDOWS 98 ADMINISTRATOR'S GUIDE . JAN'99
WINDOWS 98 COMPLETE 249/-
WINDOWS 98 DEVELOPER'S
   HANDBOOK (W/CD) 450/-
WINDOWS 98 INSTANT REFERENCE 54/-
WINDOWS 98 -NO EXPERIENCE REQUIRED ... 150/-
WINDOWS 98 - TRAINING GUIDE 60/-

➤WINDOWS NT

Learn WINDOWS NT in A Day 54/-
Mastering WINDOWS NT Server 3.51 .... 399/-
NT NETWORK SECURITY (W/CD) 450/-
EXPERT GUIDE TO WINDOWS NT REGISTRY
   (W/CD) 399/-

➤WINDOWS NT 4.0 SERVER

Fast Track to NT 4.0 Server 150/-
NT 4.0 / Windows 95 Developers Handbook
   (W/CD) 499/-
Mastering WINDOWS NT Server 4.0 .... 499/-
WINDOWS NT Server 4 : No Experience
   Required 150/-